LOANWORDS
INDEX

Educational Linguistics/TESOL/ICC
Graduate School of Education
University of Pennsylvania
3700 Walnut Street/Cl
Philadelphia, PA 19104

LOANWORDS
INDEX

A Compilation of More Than 14,000
Foreign Words and Phrases That Are
Not Fully Assimilated into English and
Retain a Measure of Their Foreign
Orthography, Pronunciation, or Flavor,
the Collection Based on More Than
20,000 Citations from Major English-Language
Reference Sources and the Whole Arranged
with the Sources Identified, Supplemented by
a Descriptive Bibliography and an Index
in Which the Loanwords Are
Listed by Language

FIRST EDITION

Laurence Urdang
Editor in Chief

Frank R. Abate
Managing Editor

GALE RESEARCH COMPANY
BOOK TOWER • DETROIT, MICHIGAN 48226

Editorial Staff:

Laurence Urdang, *Editor in Chief*

Frank R. Abate, *Managing Editor*

Janet T. Cohen, *Editor*

Peter M. Gross, *Editor*

Charles F. Ruhe, *Editor*

Sue H. Grossman, *Editorial Assistant*

Copyright © 1983 by Gale Research Company

ISBN 0-8103-1545-9

Contents

Contents

6

Index of Words and Phrases—by Language (continued)

Index of Words and Phrases—by Language (continued)

Foreword

Considerable publicity has been accorded Franglais ('the use of English words in French') in recent years. The apparent consternation with which the French view the "corruption" of their language is not matched by speakers of English—at least, not today, when English, having become perhaps the most acquisitive language on earth, has developed a lexicon that is greater than that of any other known tongue. It is important to note, however, that having many words does not, necessarily, mean that a language with a smaller list of individual lexical items fails in offering to its speakers a facility for expression: languages accomplish that facility by the compounding of familiar native roots and by loading a given word with a great number of meanings.

The former system is exemplified by German, whose speakers have little trouble with compounds like *Sprachwissenschaft*, literally *Sprach* 'speech' + *Wissenschaft* 'science' = 'linguistics,' or *Sprachschatz*, literally *Sprach* 'speech' + *Schatz* 'treasure' = 'vocabulary,' akin to our loanword *thesaurus*, from the Greek word meaning 'treasure.' On the other hand, English has trouble with ambiguities like *linguist*, which to a philologist means 'an expert in linguistics' and to the people at large means 'one who can speak many languages.' Among language professionals, 'one who can speak many languages' is called a *polyglot* to avoid confusion with *linguist*.

The latter system, called *polysemy* 'many meanings (for the same word),' is at work in English as much as it is in other languages. One need only look up a word like *run* or *take* or *set* in a large dictionary to see how many hundreds of meanings such common words can acquire. It is worth noting that despite the propensity of English to borrow words from other languages, the process of polysemy is still very much at work. For instance, *acid* has acquired the meaning of *lysergic acid diethylamide*, even though the alternate (albeit technical) designation *LSD* is in the language. *DNA* (desoxyribonucleic acid) and *RNA* (ribonucleic acid) have not, as far as available evidence shows, been referred to as "acid," the opportunity for humor in the genetics laboratory notwithstanding.

Not all borrowings from other languages are successful. In the 1960s oceanographers, exasperated by the misnomer *tidal wave* (since such waves are

9

not caused by tides but by undersea disturbances, usually of a volcanic nature), adopted the Japanese *tsunami* in order to dissociate the technical term from the notion of 'tide.' It was later discovered that *tsunami* means nothing more than *'tidal wave'* in Japanese.

Other loanwords have fared differently in the history of English. After the Norman Conquest, many French words were borrowed by English, especially in areas of government, law, and economy. These continued to exist side by side with their native English (Germanic) equivalents and today are regarded as native English words:

Germanic	Romance
motherly	*maternal*
fatherly	*paternal*
brotherhood	*fraternity*
home	*residence*
friendly	*amicable*
hate	*detest, despise*
king	*sovereign*

In some instances, English elements have been compounded with French, as in the following, in which the first element is English, the second French:

> *a-round, be-cause, fore-front, out-cry, over-power, un-able, black-guard, salt-cellar.*

. . . and in these, in which the order is reversed:

> *aim-less, duke-dom, false-hood, court-ship, plenti-ful, dainti-ness, trouble-some, genial-ly, heir-loom, hobby-horse, scape-goat.*

There are other instances of borrowings in English, like *shirt* and *skirt*, both Scandinavian in origin, which arrived at different periods. The meaning of the base form in the source language had changed sufficiently to allow both words to survive in English, each with its distinct sense.

Therein lies the essential reason for English borrowing: no word with the *precise* meaning of the term borrowed yet exists in the language. The emphasis on "precise" is deliberate, for, although the denotative sense of the word may exist in English, its connotations may not; and that helps to explain why we have many apparent synonyms. For example, *motherly* and *maternal* may denote the same things, but the former is warm and friendly while the latter carries the connotation of detached, almost scientific coolness: its formality is quite forbidding and not at all "motherly." But examine other "synonyms": *cliché*, originally French, means the same as *stereotype*, a coinage in English from Greek elements, originally applied as a printing term, later used as a metaphor for 'anything hackneyed.' The difference between the words is, in this case, not one of warmth but of familiarity: *cliché* is used more frequently than *stereotype*. The interesting thing to note about *cliché* is that it means 'stereotype plate' in French. There are many such examples—*tsunami/tidal wave* was one.

One of the more difficult aspects of the study of loanwords is merely deciding if, in contemporary English, a certain word is a loanword or not. We have seen that *skirt* and *shirt* were both loanwords; but, surely, no one would today consider them such, as they are felt to have been completely assimilated. Similarly, *suave*. But what of *blasé, soirée,* and *soignée?* Those words that have retained their accents seem somehow to have retained enough of their foreign appearance to make them "feel" foreign. And what of phrases like *table d'hôte*, which has all but lost its circumflex accent and is as common as *maître d'hôtel*, which sports two circumflexes (and has become *maitre d'*), and *a la mode*, which does not mean 'with ice cream on the side' in French? Umlauts also give a word a foreign look: *gemütlich* certainly looks foreign, *gemuetlich* only slightly less so; *smörgåsbord*, which looks formidable in its native garb, seems much more at home to us as *smorgasbord*, which is the way we see it today more often than not; and who spells *cabaña* with the tilde any longer in English advertising copy for tropical resort hotels—let alone pronounce it "kaba'nya"? Some words are easier to adopt than others: *samovar, cabochon, amoretto, cherub, seraph,* and *llama* seem to present no difficulty.

Many French words are borrowed into English to give the language a little tone (or *ton?*); thus we have *friseur* for "hairdresser,' alongside the older *coiffeur* (or, less common, *coiffeuse*)—and a *friseur* may be expected to charge more, as well. To be sure, *à la Normande* commands a higher price for a dish on a menu than "served with brown gravy," and *farci* gains more profits than "stuffed." French is the source language for nearly all terms in ballet, itself of French origin but scarcely felt to be a loanword: *pirouette, entrechat, plié,* and other terms relating to ballet retain the flavor of foreignisms even though they have been used in English for a long time. Not so, on the other hand, for *checkmate*, a well-documented borrowing from Persian, or *succotash* (from Algonquian), or *juggernaut* (from Hindi), or *bungalow* (also from Hindi), or *soy* (from Japanese) or *boor* (from Dutch)—and so on.

Not all such words have been borrowed for the sake of subtle nuance: as *succotash, épergne, chipmunk, igloo, kimono,* and thousands of other words exemplify, many terms are readily assimilated from other languages because their cultures embrace not only ideas but objects unfamiliar to speakers of English. Many such words are not long regarded as loanwords, though their acceptance depends to some extent on the frequency with which the objects need to be referred to. For instance, *kilt* and *sporran* and *plaid* (from Celtic) are quite common, while *skean dhu*, the dagger worn as part of the Highland Scots ceremonial dress, is probably relatively rare in (American) English reference; through British colonialism, we have not only *bungalow* and *juggernaut* but *tiffin, purdah,* and *pariah*. Weapons like *boomerang* (Australian) and *scimitar* (Italian), items of clothing like *caftan* (Persian) and *cummerbund* (Urdu), food terms like *taco* (Spanish), *pizza* (Italian), and *yam* (West African via Spanish) and thousands of other words for objects are so thoroughly assimilated into English as to deny their classification as loanwords, even though, in many cases, the borrowings are recent.

Foreword 12

In *Going Native: The Regeneration of Saxon English* [Publication of the American Dialect Society Number 69, University of Alabama Press, 1982], Dennis Baron, the author, opens with the following words:

> About 450 years after the Norman conquest of Britain, users of the English language began feeling uncomfortable about its extensive borrowings from French and the classical languages, Latin and Greek. From the sixteenth to the twentieth centuries, some writers have seen English as a primitive and impoverished tongue that was forced to swell its vocabulary with foreign imports from more cultured climes in order to express effectively the innovations and complexities of modern life. Most commentators on the English language have accepted and even celebrated its ability to absorb new words and adapt to new linguistic influences, treating the huge English word-hoard as a treasure to be protected and nourished. But others, viewing all borrowing as a harmful dilution of the ancient Saxon purity of English, have sought at various times to rescue the language from the undue influence of the French, the Papists, the Greek and Latin scholars, the culture-famished middle classes, the mad scientists and technocrats, or the free-lance neologists, all of whom created new words on non-English models with alarming and irreverent abandon.

Baron's book, which is not only interesting but well-written and the evident product of much reflective scholarship, discusses the multifarious aspects of loanwords in English and describes in some detail the attitudes representative of the Renaissance, Neoclassical and Romantic, and the late nineteenth and early twentieth-century periods. In his Conclusion, the author comments:

> It is true that many printed works now begin with *forewords* rather than *prefaces* and books of instruction are likely to be *handbooks* (revived *ca.* 1814) as well as *manuals*, but generally speaking the attempts to nativize the English vocabulary through purging and replacement, like most of the other attempts at reforming the English language, have failed.

—and to *manuals* might be added *enchiridions* (or, if one insists on linguistic purity, *enchiridia*).

In *Loanwords Index*, we have attempted a compilation of words that could be considered loanwords today. As these have been selected from the works being indexed in preference to thousands of entries also listed, some rationale must have been established. Unfortunately, none that is entirely consistent is readily forthcoming. As in the case of dictionaries of "difficult" words which contain entries that seem uncommonly "easy" for some, the dictionaries of loanwords that have been consulted contain entries that have not been included either because they were felt to have been completely assimilated (and the source was old) or because such compilations often include foreign quotations, mottoes, and slogans (which are not properly loanwords) or other entries that are only very rarely encountered in English, hence too unusual to include. In the circumstances, the *Index* should not be regarded as an attempt to establish any standard for discriminating loanwords from other phenomena in the language.

The sources examined, which are listed in the Bibliography with brief descriptions, are in almost all cases books that are likely to be found in libraries of moderate size. Most of the sources are not especially new; some are older works that have been updated in recent years. The editors would be especially grateful for any suggestions for the improvement of the *Loanwords Index* by the addition of reference works that could be added to advantage, by the establishment of surer criteria by which loanwords may be classified—we have tended to err on the side of inclusion—or in any other way.

Laurence Urdang

Essex, Connecticut
March 1983

How To Use This Book

The main listing for each entry in *Loanwords Index* gives the word or phrase in alphabetical order followed by its source language; below this are one or more alphabetic symbols separated by semicolons. These symbols, in capital letters, represent the sources where the terms are listed. Both the symbols and their corresponding sources are given in the Bibliography, where each source is identified and briefly described. In an additional index, marked with border tabs, all entries are arranged alphabetically under their respective languages. For a complete list of the languages represented, see Contents, pages 5 ff..

Under the main listing a symbol for a source may be followed by a virgule (/), then a number or term in italics. The style is explained as follows:

1. A symbol given alone indicates that the entry can be found as a headword listed alphabetically in the indicated source, e.g.,

   agilement, *French*
   OCM.

   in which **agilement** is the headword and OCM the source in which it can be found.

2. A symbol followed by a number indicates that the entry can be found on that page number in the source, e.g.,

   agitprop, *Russian*
   MRWEW/*17*.

   in which **agitprop** is a term used on page *17* of MRWEW, the source in which it can be found.

3. A symbol followed by a word or phrase indicates that the entry can be found under that particular headword listed alphabetically in the source, e.g.,

   air, *French*
   ICMM/*theme*.

   in which **air** is a term used in the entry for *theme*, and ICMM the source in which it can be found.

In all cases the editors have endeavored to represent the individual terms as they are found in the sources. Thus, if a source has a term with accents, peculiarly spelled, or in any other form, that style is maintained in *Loanwords*

Index. As a result, some entries that might differ only in minor typographic respects are shown separately. Here are some examples:

auto da fé, *Portuguese*
DFWPN.
auto-da-fé, *Portuguese*
DFPA; DFT.
auto-da-fé, *pl.* **autos-da-fé,** *Portuguese*
DFWPB.
auto de fe, *Spanish*
DFPA; DFPCQ.

These are shown separately in the *Index* to reflect the differences in the way the headwords are presented in the individual sources. The exception to this policy is that standard rules of capitalization have been imposed throughout the *Index,* despite the fact that some sources may capitalize all headwords, or all letters in headwords.

Accompanying some entries in the *Index,* abbreviations are given to indicate the following:

pl.—plural form
fem.—feminine form
masc.—masculine form
adj.—adjective
interj.—interjection

Bibliography

Listed below are all sources from which terms were taken in the compilation of *Loanwords Index*. They are given in alphabetic order by their respective alphabetic symbols, at left; for each the bibliographic information is followed by a brief description. The description provides information about the content and organization of the source and indicates how material from the source was selected and presented in the *Index*.

Please note that the alphabetic symbols for the sources are acronymic representations of the titles of the sources and (where necessary) their authors.

ACD

Antique Collector's Dictionary, Donald Cowie and Keith Henshaw, 208pp., New York: Gramercy Publishing Co., 1962.

A small book containing about 1600 terms, this source concentrates on the terminology of antiques; it is intended for British and American readers. Entries are brief but are supplemented by numerous illustrations. Many foreign terms common in the field of antiques are presented with an explanation of how they are used. All such terms of foreign origin, both headwords and terms within entries, have been included in the *Index*. The arrangement is alphabetic.

DA

Dictionary of Architecture, Henry H. Saylor, xii + 221pp., New York: John Wiley & Sons, 1952.

This is a small paperback designed as a handy reference tool for looking up spellings, pronunciations, and definitions of architectural terms. It covers the specialties of hydraulics, acoustics, heating, ventilation, electricity, hygiene, economics, climatology — as well as painting, sculpture, and art in general — all as they relate to architecture. Entries are concise, and include phonetic spellings for words whose pronunciation could be a problem. Illustrations are also provided. Many terms from other languages, particularly French, are given, and these can be found in the *Index*. The arrangement is alphabetic.

DEP

A Dictionary of English Phrases with Illustrative Sentences, Kwong Ki Chiu, xx + 915pp., Detroit: Gale Research Co., 1971 (originally published 1881).

In a brief section of this book (pages 837 to 849) is a list of foreign terms that were selected by the author as an aid to learners of English. Words and phrases common to English at the time of publication are given with definitions and language identifications; most are from French and Latin. All of these except lengthy quotations and the like have been included in the *Index*. The arrangement is alphabetic.

DFPA

Dictionary of Foreign Phrases and Abbreviations, 3rd edition, Kevin Guinagh, xx + 261pp., New York: Wilson, 1983.

This standard collection of foreign words, phrases, proverbs, and quotations found in general use and in certain specialized fields (such as law and medicine) also includes many abbreviations of foreign expressions. Definitions and explanations are clear and concise, pronunciations are provided, and most terms are identified as to area of use. For the *Index* have been excerpted words and phrases likely to be encountered by educated speakers of English; proverbs, most quotations, and abbreviations have been excluded. The arrangement is alphabetic.

DFPCQ

A Dictionary of Foreign Phrases and Classical Quotations, 11th edition, R. D. Blackman, ed., xvi + 262pp., New York: G. P. Putnam's Sons, 1893.

This book, arranged by individual languages, contains listings of words, phrases, maxims, proverbs, and quotations from Latin, Greek, French, Italian, Spanish, Portuguese, and German. Each entry is given with an idiomatic translation. Entries commonly encountered in English have been selected for the *Index*, proverbs and quotations excepted. Terms can be found listed alphabetically under their respective language in this work.

DFT　*Dictionary of Foreign Terms*, 2nd edition, C. O. Sylvester Mawson, rev. by Charles Berlitz, x + 368pp., New York: Harper & Row, 1975.

This is perhaps the largest and most widely known collection of foreign terms readily available in handy format. It contains more than 15,000 words and phrases, each given with language identification, translation, and brief description. The *Index* includes terms that are regularly encountered in English: items deemed obscure or proverbial in nature have been excluded. The arrangement is alphabetic.

DFWPB　*A Dictionary of Foreign Words and Phrases in Current English*, A. J. Bliss, x + 389pp., London: Routledge & Kegan Paul, 1979.

This dictionary is unique in its approach, which is to document words of non-Anglo-Saxon origin that are used in English. As such it includes many terms that are well-established in the language and no longer perceived as foreign. Headwords are given with their source, an indication of their usual context, a definition, and the date when borrowed into English. A useful appendix lists all headwords by original language and century of entry into English. Headwords that are likely to be considered foreign to English speakers and are regularly encountered by them have been included in the *Index*. The arrangement is alphabetic.

DFWPN　*Dictionary of Foreign Words and Phrases*, Maxim Newmark, 245pp., Westport, Connecticut: Greenwood Press, 1969.

This is a collection of some 10,000 foreign words and

phrases gleaned from English language sources. The entries are briefly translated and defined, and the language identified. Headwords have been selected from this source for the *Index*; mottoes, proverbs, titles, and the like have not been included. The arrangement is alphabetic.

DSTE

A Dictionary of Spanish Terms in English, Harold W. Bentley, xii + 243pp., New York: Octagon Books, 1973.

This is a scholarly study of the borrowing of Spanish terms into English; it is particularly concerned with terms common in the American Southwest. A long introduction explores the social and cultural background of these borrowings. Entries are lengthy, with definitions, variant forms, pronunciations for both Spanish and English usages, and dated citations given in context. Appendices include sections on words of American Indian origin, Spanish-based place names in use in the United States, bullfighting terms, and examples of Spanish-English bilingualism. The majority of headwords have been selected for the *Index*. The arrangement is alphabetic.

GG

Glossary of Geology, 2nd edition, Robert L. Bates and Julia A. Jackson, eds., xii + 751pp., Falls Church, Virginia: American Geological Institute, 1980.

Containing about 36,000 terms used in geology and related sciences, this comprehensive collection provides concise definitions plus synonyms and extensive cross references. All foreign language headwords are included in the *Index*. The arrangement is alphabetic.

HFY

Hooray for Yiddish!, Leo Rosten, 363pp., New York: Simon & Schuster, 1982.

Intended as an expansion on the same author's earlier *The Joys of Yiddish* (see **JOY** below), this book presents, in a pleasant and amusing style, a collection of Yiddish and Hebrew words, phrases, affixes, and constructions used in contemporary American English. Variant forms, phonetic pronunciations, and (where appropriate) multiple meanings are given, along with explanations and anecdotes to elucidate the meaning and usage of the terms. Those head-words and elements (and their variants) that are truly foreign – i.e., not mixtures of English and another language – are included in the *Index*. The arrangement is alphabetic.

ICMM   *The International Cyclopedia of Music and Musicians*, 10th edition, Oscar Thompson and Bruce Bohle, eds., xvi + 2511pp., New York: Dodd Mead & Co., 1975.

A large, one-volume encyclopedia of music, this is a comprehensive reference work containing much biographical and historical information. Many foreign terms common in the field of music are given as entries, however, and these are identified by language and given a full explanation. For more important terms the French, German, and Italian equivalents are given together under the main entry. Foreign terms that are headwords are in the *Index*. The arrangement is alphabetic.

JLE   "Japanese Loanwords in English," Garland Cannon, *Verbatim*, vol. IX, no. 1 (Summer 1982), pp. 9-10.

This article provides a brief explanatory text and then a list of 640 Japanese loanwords and their English derivatives, based on the author's own research and on entries found in standard English dictionaries. No definitions are given, but parts of speech and homonyms are indicated. All terms except those not likely to be considered foreign are included in the *Index*. The arrangement is alphabetic.

JOY   *The Joys of Yiddish*, Leo Rosten, xl + 533pp., New York: McGraw-Hill, 1968.

Far more than a dictionary, this "relaxed lexicon" presents a large number of Yiddish and Hebrew expressions, affixes, and constructions used in contemporary American English. Variants, pronunciations, and (where appropriate) multiple definitions are provided. Entries give full explanations, colorfully supplemented by contextual information and anecdotes. Headwords and their variants that are truly foreign, i.e., not containing any English elements, have been selected for the *Index*. The arrangement is alphabetic.

LB

The Language of Ballet: An Informal Dictionary, Thalia Mara, viii + 120pp., New York: Dance Horizons, 1966.

Written with the intention of standardizing the terminology of the field, this small dictionary documents terms of ballet particularly and the dance in general. Most entries are of French origin, and they are given with pronunciations and brief definitions, often supplemented by illustrations. All headwords and subentries, aside from personal names, are included in the *Index*. The arrangement is alphabetic.

LP

The Language of Painting, John N. Barron, 207pp., Cleveland: The World Publishing Co., 1967.

This dictionary contains more than 1000 entries focusing on terms used in Western painting, particularly those for materials and techniques, history of painting, and art criticism. Definitions are concise and are supplemented by illustrations; phonetic pronunciations and language identification are provided for foreign terms. All headwords of foreign origin are included in the *Index*. The arrangement is alphabetic.

MRWEW

"Modern Russian Words in English Writing," *The Barnhart Dictionary Companion*, vol. 1, no. 2 (April 1982), pp. 17-23.

This article mentions a number of Russian loanwords in its text, then gives more detailed information about certain more recently borrowed Russian words that are found in four widely read books about the Soviet Union. Those terms given fuller treatment have definitions, pronunciations, and complete contextual citations. The *Index* gives page numbers for those terms from the text of the article; others are arranged alphabetically.

OCM
The Oxford Companion to Music, 10th edition, Percy A. Scholes and John Owen Ward, eds., lx + 1189pp., Oxford: Oxford University Press, 1972.

A one-volume encyclopedia of music, this work was compiled for the general reader and the professional musician. Historical and biographical information are emphasized. The overall presentation is comprehensive yet well organized. For the *Index*, headwords and subentries that represent musical terms of foreign origin are included. The arrangement is alphabetic.

SPICE
Slang, Phrase, and Idiom in Colloquial English and Their Use, Thomas R. G. Lyell, xxxii + 764pp., Tokyo: The Hokuseido Press, 1931.

The title of this dictionary indicates its focus, and its intention is to document certain expressions and colloquialisms that may be troublesome for students of English as a second language. An introduction, preface, and complete index are provided. A number of foreign expressions common in English are included, and these are found in the *Index*. The arrangement is alphabetic.

Index of Words and Phrases
Alphabetic, with Sources

N.B.: *The policy of the editors has been to list words and phrases as they were found in the sources; hence, pecularities in spelling, diacritical marking, syntax, capitalization (especially of German nouns), and language identification, as well as other typographic details have been reproduced exactly as they appeared originally.*

A

a, *French*
DFWPN.

a, *Hungarian*
DFWPN.

a, *Italian*
DFWPN; OCM.

a, *Latin*
DFWPN.

a, *Portuguese*
DFWPN.

a, *Spanish*
DFWPN.

à, *French*
DFWPN; LB; OCM.

aanhangsel, *Dutch*
DFWPN.

aanleidinge, *Dutch*
DFWPN.

aanmerking, *Dutch*
DFWPN.

aard, *Dutch*
DFWPN.

a aver et tener, *Old French*
DFWPN.

ab, *German*
DFWPN; ICMM; OCM.

ab, *Latin*
DFWPN.

ab absurdo, *Latin*
DFT.

ab actu ad posse valet illatio, *Latin*
DFWPN.

abaculus, *Latin*
DFWPN.

abacus, *Latin*
DFWPN.

abaissé, *French*
DFWPN.

abajo, *Spanish*
DFWPN.

abandonné, *French*
OCM.

abanico, *Spanish*
DFWPN.

à bas, *French*
DFPA; DFT; DFWPN.

ab asino lanam, *Latin*
DFT.

abatis, *French*
DFT; DFWPN.

abatis de dinde, *French*
DFT/*abatis.*

abat-jour, *French*
DA; DFT; DFWPB; DFWPN.

abat-sons, *French*
DA; DFT.

abattis, *French*
DFT/*abatis.*

abattoir, *French*
DFWPB; DFWPN.

a battuta, *Italian*
DFT; ICMM.

abat-vent, *French*
DA; DFT.

abat-voix, *French*
DA; DFT.

abbadare, *Italian*
ICMM.

abbadia, *Italian*
DA.

abbandonarsi, *Italian*
ICMM.

abbandonataménte, *Italian*
ICMM.

abbandone, abbandono, con, *Italian*
ICMM.

abbandonevolmente, *Italian*
ICMM.

abbandono, *Italian*
OCM.

abbassamento, *Italian*
ICMM.

abbassamento di mano, *Italian*
ICMM.

abbassamento di voce, *Italian*
ICMM.

abbassare, *Italian*
OCM.

abbazzo, *Italian*
DA.

abbellimenti, *Italian*
ICMM; OCM.

abbellimento, *Italian*
DFT.

A-B-C Dieren, *German*
ICMM.

abdämpfen, *German*
OCM.

Abend, *German*
OCM.

Abendlied, *German*
OCM.

Abendmusiken, *German*
OCM.

a bene placito, *Italian*
DFWPN.

a beneplacito, *Italian*
DFPA; DFT.

aber, *German*
OCM.

ab extra, *Latin*
DFPA/*ab ex.*; DFPCQ; DFT;
DFWPN.

abgestossen, *German*
OCM.

à bientôt, *French*
DFPA; DFWPB.

abies, *Latin*
DFWPN.

abi in malam crucem, *Latin*
DFPCQ.

abilità, aria d', *Italian*
OCM.

ab imo pectore, *Latin*
DFPCQ; DFWPN.

ab inconvenienti, *Latin*
DFT.

ab incunabulis, *Latin*
DFPA; DFWPN.

ab initio, *Latin*
DEP; DFPCQ; DFT; DFWPB;
DFWPN; OCM.

ab integro, *Latin*
DFPCQ.

ab intestato, *Latin*
DFPA.

ab intra, *Latin*
DFPA; DFPCQ; DFT.

Ablaut, *German*
DFWPB; DFWPN.

ablösenabnehmend, *German*
OCM.

ab officio et beneficio, *Latin*
DFPCQ.

à bon compte, *French*
DFPA.

à bon droit, *French*
DFPA.

à bon marché, *French*
DFPA; DFT; DFWPN.

à bonne raison, *French*
DFT.

ab origine, *Latin*
DEP; DFPA; DFPCQ; DFT;
DFWPB; DFWPN.

abortus, *Latin*
DFWPN.

ab ovo, *Latin*
DEP; DFPA; DFT; DFWPB;
DFWPN.

ab ovo usque ad mala, *Latin*
DFPA; DFPCQ; DFT; DFWPN.

à bras ouverts, *French*
DFPA.

abrégé, *French*
ICMM.

abreuvoir, *French*
DA.

abricot, *French*
DFT.

abricot-pêche, *French*
DFT.

abrolhos, *Portuguese*
GG.

abruptio, *Italian*
ICMM.

abruzzese, *Italian*
OCM.

Absatz, *German*
ICMM.

abschwellen, *German*
ICMM.

absence d'esprit, *French*
DFPA.

absente febre, *Latin*
DFPA/*abs. feb.*.

absente reo, *Latin*
DFPA; DFPCQ; DFT.

absetzen, *German*
OCM.

absit omen, *Latin*
DFPA.

absque hoc, *Latin*
DFT/*absque*.

abstossen, *German*
ICMM; OCM.

Abstufung, *German*
ICMM.

Abtragung, *German*
GG.

ab uno disce omnes, *Latin*
DEP; DEP; DFPCQ; DFWPN.

aburagiri, *Japanese*
JLE.

ab urbe condita, *Latin*
DFPA; DFPCQ; DFT; DFWPB;
DFWPN.

abwechseln, *German*
OCM.

abwechselnd, *German*
ICMM.

abzuwechseln, *German*
OCM/*abwechseln*.

acajou, *French*
DA.

a capella, *Italian*
DFT; OCM.

a cappella, *Italian*
DFPA; DFWPB; DFWPN;
ICMM; OCM/*a capella*.

a capriccio, *Italian*
DFT; ICMM.

acariâtre, *French*
DFT.

accademia, *Italian*
OCM.

accarezzevole, *Italian*
OCM.

accarezzevolmente, *Italian*
OCM/*accarezzevole*.

accedas ad curiam, *Latin*
DFT.

accelerando, *Italian*
DFPA; DFPCQ; DFT; DFWPB;
DFWPN; ICMM; OCM.

accelerato, *Italian*
OCM/*accelerando*.

accento, *Italian*
OCM.

accentuare, *Italian*
ICMM.

accentué, *French*
OCM.

accentus, *Latin*
ICMM; OCM.

accentus ecclesiasticus, *Latin*
ICMM.

acciaccato, *Italian*
ICMM; OCM.

acciaccatura, *Italian*
DFT; DFWPN; OCM.

acciaio, istrumento d', *Italian*
OCM.

accipe hoc, *Latin*
DFPCQ.

accolade, *French*
ICMM.

accompagnamento, *Italian*
DFT; ICMM.

accompagnato, *Italian*
ICMM; OCM.

accompagnatore, *Italian*
DFT.

accoppiare, *Italian*
OCM.

accoppiato, *Italian*
ICMM.

accord, *French*
OCM.

accord à l'ouvert, *French*
ICMM.

accordamento, *Italian*
ICMM.

accordando, *Italian*
ICMM.

accordanza, *Italian*
ICMM.

accordare, *Italian*
ICMM; OCM.

accordata, *Italian*
OCM/*accordato.*

accordate, *Italian*
OCM/*accordato.*

accordati, *Italian*
OCM/*accordato.*

accordato, *Italian*
OCM.

accordatura, *Italian*
ICMM; OCM.

accorder, *French*
ICMM/*accordare*; OCM.

accordo, *Italian*
DFT; OCM.

accouchement, *French*
DFWPN.

accouplement, *French*
DA.

accoupler, *French*
OCM.

accrescendo, *Italian*
ICMM.

accrescere, *Italian*
ICMM.

accusé, *French*
OCM.

accusée, *French*
OCM/*accusé.*

aceite, *Spanish*
DFT.

aceituna, *Spanish*
DFT.

a cembalo, *Italian*
DFT; ICMM.

acequia, *Spanish*
DFT; DSTE; GG.

acequia madre, *Spanish*
DFT/*acequia.*

acer, *Latin*
DFWPN.

acetum, *Latin*
DFWPN.

acetum Italum, *Latin*
DFPA.

à chacun son goût, *French*
DFPCQ.

achar, *Hindi*
DFT.

acht, *German*
OCM.

Achtel, *German*
ICMM; OCM.

Achtelnote, *German*
ICMM; ICMM/*quaver*; OCM/
Achtel.

Achtelpause, *German*
ICMM.

Achtung, *German*
DFT; DFWPN.

a chula, *Portuguese*
ICMM.

a cinque, *Italian*
ICMM.

à coeur ouvert, *French*
DFPA.

à compte, *French*
DFPA.

à contre coeur, *French*
DFPA; DFPCQ.

à contre cœur, *French*
DFT.

à couvert, *French*
DFPA.

âcre, *French*
DFT.

a cruce salus, *Latin*
DFWPN.

acta, *Latin*
DFWPN.

acta eruditorum, *Latin*
DFWPN.

actum est, *Latin*
DFPCQ.

actus, *Latin*
DFWPN.

actus curiae, *Latin*
DFWPN.

actus Dei, *Latin*
DFWPN.

actus purus, *Latin*
DFPA.

acus, *Latin*
DFWPN.

acuto, *Italian*
ICMM.

ad, *Italian*
DFWPN.

ad, *Latin*
DFWPN.

ad absurdum, *Latin*
DFT.

adage, *French*
LB; OCM.

adagietto, *Italian*
DFT; DFWPN; ICMM; OCM.

ad agio, *Italian*
LB/*adage*.

adagio, *Italian*
DFPCQ; DFT; DFWPB;
DFWPN; ICMM; OCM.

adagio assai, *Italian*
ICMM.

adagissimo, *Italian*
ICMM.

ad arbitrium, *Latin*
DFPA; DFPCQ.

ad astra, *Latin*
DFT.

ad astra per ardua, *Latin*
DFWPN.

ad astra per aspera, *Latin*
DFPA; DFT/*ad astra*; DFWPN.

ad baculum, *Latin*
DFT.

ad canones, *Latin*
OCM.

ad captandam benevolentiam, *Latin*
DFPA.

ad captandum, *Latin*
DFPCQ; DFT.

ad captandum vulgus, *Latin*
DFPA; DFPCQ; DFT/*ad
captandum*; DFWPN.

ad crumenam, *Latin*
DFT.

addendum, *Latin*
DFWPN.

addendum, *pl.* **addenda,** *Latin*
DFPCQ; DFWPB.

addio, *Italian*
DFT; DFWPN.

additum, *Latin*
DFPCQ.

addolcendo, *Italian*
OCM.

addolorato, *Italian*
OCM.

Adel, *German*
OCM.

à demi, *French*
DFPA; DFT.

a demi jeu, *French*
ICMM.

a demi voix, *French*
ICMM.

a Deo et rege, *Latin*
DFPCQ.

à dessein, *French*
DFPA.

adeste fideles, *Latin*
DFWPN.

ad eundem, *Latin*
DFWPN.

adeus, *Portuguese*
DFT.

a deux, *French*
ICMM.

à deux, *French*
DFPA; DFT; DFWPN.

à deux cordes, *French*
OCM.

a deux mains, *French*
ICMM.

à deux mains, *French*
DFT/*à deux.*

a deux temps, *French*
ICMM.

ad extra, *Latin*
DFT.

ad extremum, *Latin*
DFPA/*ad ex.*; DFPCQ; DFT.

ad fidem, *Latin*
DFWPN.

ad finem, *Latin*
DEP; DFPA/*ad fin.*; DFPCQ;
DFT; DFWPB; DFWPN.

ad fugam, *Latin*
OCM.

ad gustum, *Latin*
DFPA.

ad hanc vocem, *Latin*
DFT.

ad hoc, *Latin*
DFPA; DFT; DFWPB; DFWPN.

ad hominem, *Latin*
DEP; DFPA; DFPCQ; DFT;
DFWPB.

ad hunc locum, *Latin*
DFPA/*ad h. l.*; DFT.

ad idem, *Latin*
DFT.

a die datus, *Latin*
DFPA.

adieu, *French*
DFPCQ; DFWPN.

adieu, *pl.* **adieux,** *French*
DFWPB.

ad ignorantiam, *Latin*
DFT.

ad infinitum, *Latin*
DEP; DFPA/*ad inf.*; DFPCQ;
DFT; DFWPB; DFWPN.

ad initium, *Latin*
DFPA/*ad init.*; DFT.

ad instar, *Latin*
DFPCQ.

ad interim, *Latin*
DEP.

a dio, *Spanish*
DSTE.

adios, *Spanish*
DFT; DFWPB; DSTE.

adiós, *Spanish*
DFWPN.

a Diós gracias [*sic*], *Spanish*
DFT.

adiratamente, *Italian*
DFT; ICMM.

adirato, *Italian*
ICMM; OCM.

à discrétion, *French*
DFPA.

ad judicium, *Latin*
DFPA; DFT.

Adjuvant, *German*
ICMM.

adjuvante Deo, *Latin*
DFPCQ.

ad Kalendas Graecas, *Latin*
DFPCQ.

ad lib, *Latin*
OCM/*ad libitum*; SPICE.

ad lib(itum), *Latin*
DFWPN.

ad libitum, *Latin*
DEP; DFPA/*ad lib.*; DFPCQ;
DFT; ICMM; OCM.

ad litem, *Latin*
DFPA; DFT.

ad literam, *Latin*
DFPA; DFPCQ.

ad litteram, *Latin*
DFWPN.

ad locum, *Latin*
DFPA.

ad majorem Dei gloriam, *Latin*
DFWPN.

ad manum, *Latin*
DFPA.

ad misericordiam, *Latin*
DFT.

ad modum, *Latin*
DFPCQ.

ad nauseam, *Latin*
DEP; DFPA; DFPCQ; DFT;
DFWPB; DFWPN; SPICE.

adobe, *Spanish*
DFWPB; DFWPN; DSTE; GG.

ad oculos, *Latin*
DFPA.

Adonai, *Hebrew*
DFT; DFWPN.

Adonai, *Yiddish*
HFY; JOY.

adornamento, *Italian*
ICMM.

Adoshem, *Yiddish*
HFY; JOY.

adoucir, *French*
ICMM.

ad placitum, *Latin*
ICMM.

ad populum, *Latin*
DFT.

ad quem, *Latin*
DFT; DFWPN.

ad quod, *Latin*
DFWPN.

ad rem, *Latin*
DEP; DFPA; DFPCQ; DFT;
DFWPB; DFWPN.

adret, *French*
GG.

à droite, *French*
DFPA; DFT.

adsuki (bean), *Japanese*
JLE.

adsum, *Latin*
DFPCQ.

ad summam, *Latin*
DFPCQ; DFWPN.

ad summum, *Latin*
DFPA.

a due, *Italian*
ICMM.

a due corde, *Italian*
ICMM; OCM.

a due cori, *Italian*
ICMM.

a due strumenti, *Italian*
ICMM.

a due voci, *Italian*
ICMM.

adulatoriamente, *Italian*
ICMM.

ad unguem, *Latin*
DFPCQ.

ad unum omnes, *Latin*
DFPCQ.

A dur, *German*
ICMM.

ad usum, *Latin*
DFPA; DFT.

ad valorem, *Latin*
DEP; DFPCQ; DFT; DFWPB;
DFWPN.

adversaria, *Latin*
DFPCQ; DFWPN.

adversus, *Latin*
DFT.

ad vesperas, *Latin*
ICMM/*vespers.*

ad vitam, *Latin*
DFWPN.

ad vivum, *Latin*
DFPCQ.

advocatus diaboli, *Latin*
DFPA; DFWPN.

advocatus juventutis, *Latin*
DFPA.

adytum, *Greek*
DFWPN.

adzuki (bean), *Japanese*
JLE.

aehnlich, *German*
OCM; OCM/*ähnlich.*

aengstlich, *German*
OCM/*ängstlich;* OCM.

Aeolsharfe, *German*
OCM.

aequal, *German*
OCM/*äqual;* OCM.

aequisonae voces, *Latin*
ICMM.

aequo animo, *Latin*
DFPA; DFT.

æquo animo, *Latin*
DEP; DFPCQ.

aere perennius, *Latin*
DFPCQ; DFWPN.

aeroforo, *Italian*
OCM.

aes alienum, *Latin*
DFPCQ; DFWPN.

aetate, *Latin*
DFWPN.

aetatis, *Latin*
DFT.

aetatis suae, *Latin*
DFPA; DFPCQ; DFT/*aetatis.*

aeusserst, *German*
OCM.

affabile, *Italian*
DFT; ICMM; OCM.

affaiblissant, *French*
OCM.

affaire, *French*
DFT.

affaire d'amour, *French*
DFPA; DFPCQ; DFT/*affaire.*

affaire (de coeur), *French*
DFWPB.

affaire de coeur, *French*
DFPCQ; DFWPN.

affaire de cœur, *French*
DFT/*affaire.*

affaire d' honneur, *French*
DEP.

affaire d'honneur, *French*
DFPA; DFPCQ; DFT/*affaire;*
DFWPB.

affaire du coeur, *French*
DFPA.

affaire du cœur, *French*
DEP.

affaire flambée, *French*
DFT/*affaire.*

affaires, *French*
DFWPN.

affanato, *Italian*
DFT.

affannato, *Italian*
OCM.

affannosamente, *Italian*
OCM/*affannoso.*

affannoso, *Italian*
ICMM; OCM.

Affekt, *German*
OCM.

Affektenlehre, *German*
ICMM.

affettivo, *Italian*
DFT; DFWPN.

affetto, *Italian*
OCM.

affetto, con, *Italian*
ICMM/*affettuoso.*

affettuosa, *Italian*
OCM/*affettuoso.*

affettuoso, *Italian*
DFPCQ; DFWPN; ICMM;
OCM.

affetuoso [*sic*], *Italian*
DFT.

affezione, *Italian*
OCM.

afflatus, *Latin*
DFPCQ; DFT; DFWPN.

affleuré, *French*
DA.

afflitto, *Italian*
OCM.

affrettando, *Italian*
DFT; ICMM; OCM/*affrettare.*

affrettare, *Italian*
OCM.

affrettatamente, *Italian*
OCM/*affrettare.*

affrettato, *Italian*
OCM/*affrettare.*

affrettoso, *Italian*
OCM/*affrettare.*

affrettuoso, *Italian*
OCM/*affrettare.*

aficionado, *fem.* **aficionada,** *Spanish*
DFWPB.

à fond, *French*
DFPA; DFT.

a fortiori, *Latin*
DEP; DFPA; DFPCQ; DFT;
DFWPB; DFWPN.

Afrikaans, *Dutch*
DFWPN.

aga, *Turkish*
DFT; DFWPN.

Agada, *Yiddish*
JOY/*Haggadah.*

agape, *pl.* **agapaé,** *Greek*
DFWPB.

à gauche, *French*
DFPA; DFT.

agenda, *Latin*
DFPCQ; DFWPN.

agent provocateur, *French*
DFPA; DFT; DFWPB; DFWPN.

ager publicus, *Latin*
DFPA.

agevole, *Italian*
DFT; ICMM; OCM.

agevolezza, *Italian*
ICMM; OCM/*agevole.*

aggadah, *Hebrew*
DFWPN.

aggio, *Italian*
DFPCQ.

aggiornamento, *Italian*
DFWPB.

aggiunta, aria, *Italian*
OCM.

aggiustamente, *Italian*
OCM.

aggradevole, *Italian*
OCM.

agha, *Turkish*
DFT/*aga.*

agiatamente, *Italian*
OCM.

agilement, *French*
OCM.

agilita, *Italian*
ICMM.

agilità, *Italian*
OCM.

agilité, *French*
ICMM; OCM/*agilità.*

agilmente, *Italian*
ICMM; OCM.

agitamento, *Italian*
OCM/*agitazione.*

agitatamente, *Italian*
OCM/*agitato.*

agitato, *Italian*
DFPCQ; DFT; DFWPB;
DFWPN; ICMM; OCM.

agitato allegro, *Italian*
ICMM.

agitato con passione, *Italian*
ICMM.

agitazione, *Italian*
ICMM; OCM.

agité, *French*
OCM/*agitazione.*

agitiert, *German*
OCM/*agitirt.*

agitirt, *German*
OCM.

agitprop, *Russian*
MRWEW/*17.*

aglio, *Italian*
DFWPN.

agneau, *French*
DFT.

agneau du printemps, *French*
DFT/*agneau.*

agnellotti, *Italian*
DFT.

agnomen, *Latin*
DFPCQ; DFWPN.

Agnus Dei, *Latin*
DFPCQ; DFT; DFWPN; ICMM;
OCM.

agoge, *Greek*
ICMM.

à gogo, *French*
DFWPB.

agon, *Greek*
DFWPN; ICMM.

agora, *Greek*
DFT; DFWPN.

agostadero, *Spanish*
DFT.

agouni, *Berber*
GG.

agraffé, *French*
DA.

à grand choeur, *French*
ICMM.

à grand orchestre, *French*
ICMM.

agréable, *French*
DFT.

agréation, *French*
DFWPN.

agréé, *French*
DFWPN.

agrégation, *French*
DFWPN.

agrégé, *French*
DFWPN.

agrémens, *French*
OCM.

agrément, *French*
DFT; DFWPN.

agréments, *French*
DFWPN; ICMM/*ornaments;*
OCM/*agrémens.*

agreste, *French*
OCM.

agua, *Spanish*
DFT.

aguada, *Spanish*
GG.

aguardiente, *Spanish*
DFT.

ahí, *Spanish*
DFWPN.

à haute voix, *French*
DFPA.

ähnlich, *German*
OCM; OCM/*aehnlich.*

à huis clos, *French*
DFPA; DFWPB; DFWPN.

ai, *Italian*
OCM.

aide (de camp), *pl.* **aides (de camp),**
French
DFWPB.

aide de camp, *French*
DFWPN.

aide-de-camp, *French*
DFPA; DFPCQ; DFT.

aide mémoire, *French*
DFPA.

aide-mémoire, *French*
DFT.

aigis, *Greek*
DFWPN.

aigre-doux, *French*
DFT.

aigrette, *French*
DFWPN.

aigu, *French*
OCM.

aiguë, *French*
OCM/*aigu.*

aiguière, *French*
DFT.

aiguille, *French*
DFT; DFWPN; GG.

aiguillette, *French*
DFT; DFWPN.

aikido, *Japanese*
JLE.

aikuchi, *Japanese*
JLE.

ailes de pigeons, *French*
LB.

aimable, *French*
DFT.

aîné (*masc.*), **ainée** (*fem.*), *French*
DFPA.

Aino, *Japanese*
JLE.

Ainu, *Japanese*
JLE.

air, *French*
ICMM/*theme.*

air à boire, *French*
ICMM.

air de caractère, *French*
OCM.

air détaché, *French*
ICMM.

air écossais, *French*
ICMM.

air, en l', *French*
LB.

air irlandais, *French*
ICMM.

airs russes, *French*
ICMM.

air varié, *French*
ICMM.

Ais, *German*
ICMM; OCM.

aise, *French*
OCM.

Aisis, *German*
OCM.

aisthesis, *Greek*
DFWPN.

ajarcara, *Spanish*
DA.

à jour, *French*
DA; DFT.

ajouter, *French*
OCM.

ajutage, *French*
DA.

akamatsu, *Japanese*
JLE.

akamushi (mite), *Japanese*
JLE.

akebi, *Japanese*
JLE.

Akebia, *Japanese*
JLE.

akeki, *Japanese*
JLE.

Akita, *Japanese*
JLE.

Akkord, *German*
ICMM; OCM.

Aktiengesellschaft, *German*
DFT.

à l', *French*
OCM/*à la.*

al, *Italian*
ICMM; OCM.

à la, *French*
DFPA; DFT; DFWPB; DFWPN;
LB; OCM.

ala, *Latin*
DFWPN.

à la belle étoile, *French*
DFPA.

à la bonne heure, *French*
DFPA; DFT; DFWPN.

à la bordelaise, *French*
DFT.

à la bourgeoise, *French*
DFPA; DFWPN.

à l'abri, *French*
DFPA.

à la broche, *French*
DFT.

à la campagnarde, *French*
DFT/*campagnard.*

à la campagne, *French*
DFPA.

à la carte, *French*
DFPA; DFPCQ; DFT; DFWPB;
DFWPN.

à la chinoise, *French*
DFT.

à la compagne, *French*
DFT.

à la corde, *French*
OCM.

à la diable, *French*
DFPA; DFT.

aladzha, *Tatar*
GG.

à la fin, *French*
DFT.

à la française, *French*
DFPA; DFT.

à la Française, *French*
DEP; DFPCQ.

à la grecque, *French*
DFPA; DFT.

à la hollandaise, *French*
DFT.

à la jardinière, *French*
DFT/*jardinière*; DFT.

alalá, *Spanish*
ICMM; OCM.

à la main, *French*
DFT.

à la maison, *French*
DFT.

à la maître d'hôtel, *French*
DFT.

à la marengo, *French*
DFWPN.

alameda, *Spanish*
DA; DFT; DFWPN; DSTE.

à l'américaine, *French*
DFT; DEP.

à la militaire, *French*
DFT.

alamo, *Spanish*
DFT; DSTE.

a la mode, *French*
DEP.

à la mode, *French*
DFPA; DFPCQ; DFT; DFWPB;
DFWPN.

à la napolitaine, *French*
DFPA.

à l'ancienne, *French*
DFWPN.

à l'Anglaise, *French*
DEP; DFPCQ; DFT.

à la parisienne, *French*
DFT.

à la pointe d'archet, *French*
OCM.

à la provençale, *French*
DFT.

à la rigueur, *French*
DFWPN.

à la russe, *French*
DFT.

a la rústica [*sic*], *French*
DFPA.

à la sourdine, *French*
DFPA; DFT.

à la suédoise, *French*
DFT.

alav ha-sholem, *Yiddish*
HFY.

alav ha-sholom, *Yiddish*
JOY.

à la viennoise, *French*
DFT.

à la villageoise, *French*
DFT.

alberca, *Spanish*
DFT.

alborada, *Spanish*
ICMM; OCM.

Albumblatt, *German*
OCM.

alcalde, *Spanish*
DSTE.

alcazar, *Spanish*
DA.

alcázar, *Arabic*
DFWPN.

alcázar, *Spanish*
DFT.

alcun', *Italian*
OCM/*alcuno*.

alcuna, *Italian*
OCM/*alcuno*.

alcuno, *Italian*
OCM.

al dente, *Italian*
DFPA; DFWPB.

alea jacta est, *Latin*
DFPA; DFT.

aleha ha-shalom, *Yiddish*
JOY.

aleha ha-sholem, *Yiddish*
HFY/*alav ha-sholem*.

aleichem sholem, *Yiddish*
HFY; JOY/*sholem aleichem*; JOY.

à l'espagnole, *French*
DFT.

à l'estragon, *French*
DFT.

alevai, *Yiddish*
JOY/*halevai*.

alevay, *Yiddish*
HFY.

alexandrin, *French*
DFWPN.

à l'extérieur, *French*
DFPA; DFT.

à l'extrémité, *French*
DFT.

aleyhem ha-sholem, *Yiddish*
HFY/*alav ha-sholem*.

alfalfa, *Spanish*
DSTE.

al fine, *Italian*
DFPA; DFT; ICMM.

al fresco, *Italian*
DFPA; DFPCQ; DFT; DFWPB;
DFWPN.

al fresco, *Spanish*
DSTE.

alguacil, *Spanish*
DSTE/*236.*

Alhambra, *Spanish*
DFWPN.

alhauna, *Spanish*
DA.

à l'huile, *French*
DFPA.

alias, *Latin*
DEP; DFPCQ.

alibi, *Latin*
DEP; DFPCQ.

alieni juris, *Latin*
DFPA.

alimenta, *Latin*
DFWPN.

à l'impromptu, *French*
DFPA.

à l'improviste, *French*
DFPA.

à l'intérieur, *French*
DFT.

aliquando bonus dormitat Homerus,
Latin
DEP; DFWPN.

aliquot, *Latin*
DFWPN.

à l'irlandaise, *French*
DFT.

à l'italienne, *French*
DFT.

aliud et idem, *Latin*
DFPCQ.

aliunde, *Latin*
DFT.

aliyah, *Yiddish*
HFY.

all', *Italian*
OCM.

allí, *Spanish*
DFWPN.

alla, *Italian*
OCM/*all'.*

alla breve, *Italian*
DFT; DFWPB; DFWPN;
ICMM; OCM.

alla caccia, *Italian*
DFPCQ; DFT.

alla capella, *Italian*
DFT.

alla cappella, *Italian*
DFPA; ICMM/*a cappella.*

alla danza tedesca, *Italian*
OCM.

alla fine, *Italian*
ICMM/*al fine.*

Allah, *Arabic*
DFT; DFWPN.

Allah akbar, *Arabic*
DFT.

allahu akbar, *Arabic*
DFPA.

alla milanese, *Italian*
DFWPN.

allant, *French*
OCM.

alla prima, *Italian*
DFWPB; DFWPN; LP.

allargando, *Italian*
ICMM; OCM.

alla vostra salute, *Italian*
DFPA; DFWPN.

alle, *German*
OCM.

alle, *Italian*
OCM.

alléchant, *French*
DFT.

allée, *French*
DA.

allége, *French*
DA.

allegramente, *Italian*
OCM.

allégrement, *French*
OCM/*allegramente*.

allegrettino, *Italian*
ICMM.

allegretto, *Italian*
DFPCQ; DFT; DFWPB;
DFWPN; ICMM; OCM.

allegrezza, *Italian*
OCM.

allegro, *Italian*
DFPCQ; DFT; DFWPB;
DFWPN; ICMM; LB; OCM.

allegro di molto, *Italian*
DFT/*allegro*.

allegro furioso, *Italian*
DFT/*allegro*.

allegro moderato, *Italian*
DFPA.

allegro non tanto, *Italian*
DFT/*tanto*; DFT/*allegro*.

allein, *German*
OCM.

allemand, *French*
DFT; DFWPN; OCM.

allemande, *French*
OCM.

allentamento, *Italian*
OCM.

allentando, *Italian*
DFT; OCM/*allentamento*.

allez, *French*
DFWPN.

Allium, *Latin*
DFWPN.

allmählich, *German*
OCM.

allmählig, *German*
OCM/*allmählich*.

allmälig, *German*
OCM/*allmählich*.

al loco, *Italian*
ICMM.

allonge, *French*
DFT.

allongée, *French*
LB.

allonger, *French*
OCM.

allons, *French*
DEP; DFT; DFWPN.

allora, *Italian*
OCM.

all' ottava, *Italian*
DFPA; DFT; ICMM; OCM.

allure, *French*
OCM.

alluvio maris, *Latin*
DFWPN.

alluvium, *Latin*
DFPCQ.

alluvium, *pl.* alluvia, *Latin*
DFWPB.

almain, *French*
OCM.

alma mater, *Latin*
DEP; DFPA; DFPCQ; DFT;
DFWPB; DFWPN; SPICE.

alman, *French*
OCM/*almain*.

almand, *French*
OCM/*almain*.

almena, *Spanish*
DA.

aloha, *Hawaiian*
DFT; DFWPB.

aloha oe, *Hawaiian*
DFWPN.

à loisir, *French*
DFPA.

a l'ordinaire, *French*
DEP.

à l'ordinaire, *French*
DFT.

alouette, *French*
DFWPN.

aloyau, *French*
DFT.

alpaca, *Spanish*
DSTE.

Alpenhorn, *German*
OCM.

Alpha kai Omega, *Greek*
DFPCQ.

al piacere, *Italian*
DFT.

al più, *Italian*
DFT.

al rovescio, *Italian*
OCM.

als, *German*
OCM.

al segno, *Italian*
ICMM; OCM.

also, *German*
OCM.

als ob, *German*
DFWPN.

al solito, *Italian*
DFT.

alt, *German*
OCM.

alta, *Italian*
OCM.

al tedesco, *Italian*
DFT.

alter ego, *Latin*
DEP; DFPA; DFPCQ; DFT;
DFWPB; DFWPN; SPICE.

alter idem, *Latin*
DFPA; DFPCQ.

alter ipse amicus, *Latin*
DFPCQ; DFWPN.

alter kocker, *Yiddish*
JOY.

alternativo, *Italian*
OCM.

Alterthum, *German*
DFPCQ.

Altertum, *German*
DFWPN.

Altertumswissenschaft, *German*
DFWPN.

altezza, *Italian*
OCM.

altezza sonora, *Italian*
OCM/*altezza.*

Altflöte, *German*
OCM.

Altflügelhorn, *German*
OCM.

Altgeige, *German*
ICMM; OCM.

Althoboe, *German*
OCM.

Althorn, *German*
OCM.

altieramente, *Italian*
ICMM.

altiora peto, *Latin*
DFPCQ; DFWPN.

altiplano, *Spanish*
GG.

altissimo, *Italian*
DFWPN; ICMM; OCM.

altista, *Italian*
ICMM.

altiste, *French*
OCM.

Altklarinette, *German*
OCM.

Altkornett, *German*
OCM.

alto, *French*
OCM/*alto.*

alto, *Italian*
DFPCQ; DFWPN.

alto, *pl.* **alti,** *Italian*
DFWPB.

alto moderne, *French*
OCM/*alto.*

alto relievo, *Italian*
DFWPN.

alto rilievo, *Italian*
DEP; DFPA; DFWPB.

alto-rilievo, *Italian*
DA; DFT.

Altposaune, *German*
OCM.

altra, *Italian*
OCM.

altra volta, *Italian*
OCM.

altre, *Italian*
OCM/*altra*.

altri, *Italian*
OCM/*altro*.

altro, *Italian*
OCM.

Altschlüssel, *German*
ICMM.

altus, *Latin*
OCM.

alumna, *pl.* alumnae, *Latin*
DFWPN.

alumni, *Latin*
DFPCQ; DFWPN/*alumnus*.

alumnus, *Latin*
DFPCQ; DFWPN.

alumnus, *pl.* alumni, *Latin*
DFWPB.

alzati, *Italian*
OCM/*alzato*.

alzato, *Italian*
OCM.

am, *German*
OCM.

ama, *Japanese*
JLE.

amabile, *Italian*
DFT; DFWPN; OCM.

amado, *Japanese*
JLE.

Amagasaki, *Japanese*
JLE.

amain, *Yiddish*
JOY.

à main armée, *French*
DFPA.

amande, *French*
DFT.

amanori, *Japanese*
JLE.

amantium irae, *Latin*
DFPCQ; DFT.

amanuensis, *Latin*
DFPCQ; DFWPN.

amarevole, *Italian*
ICMM; OCM.

amarezza, *Italian*
OCM/*amarevole*.

amarezza, con, *Italian*
ICMM.

amargoso, *Spanish*
DFT.

amarissimamente, *Italian*
ICMM.

amarissimo, *Italian*
ICMM.

Amaterasu, *Japanese*
JLE.

amateur, *French*
DFPCQ; ICMM.

amau, *Hawaiian*
DFT.

ambiance, *French*
DFWPB.

ambitus, *Latin*
DFWPN; ICMM.

ambo, *Latin*
ICMM.

amboss, *German*
OCM.

ambulant, *French*
ICMM.

ambulatio, *Latin*
DA.

âme, *French*
OCM.

âme damnée, *French*
DFPA.

âme de boue, *French*
DFPA.

amende honorable, *French*
DEP.

amener, *French*
ICMM.

a mensa et thoro, *Latin*
DEP.

a mensa et toro, *Latin*
DFPA; DFPCQ.

amentia, *Latin*
DFWPN.

âme perdue, *French*
DFPA.

Americano, *Spanish*
DSTE.

à merveille, *French*
DFPA.

a mezza aria, *Italian*
ICMM.

a mezza di voce, *Italian*
ICMM.

a mezza voce, *Italian*
ICMM/*a mezza di voce.*

a mezzo voce, *Italian*
DFT.

am ha-aretz, *Yiddish*
JOY.

ami, *French*
DFT.

amicus curiae, *Latin*
DFPA; DFPCQ; DFT; DFWPN.

amicus curiæ, *Latin*
DEP.

amicus curiae, *pl.* amici curiae, *Latin*
DFWPB.

amicus humani generis, *Latin*
DFPA; DFPCQ.

amicus usque ad aras, *Latin*
DFPCQ.

ami (amie) de coeur, *French*
DFPA.

ami de cœur, *French*
DFT/*ami.*

ami de cour, *French*
DFPA; DFT/*ami.*

ami de table, *French*
DFT/*ami.*

ami du peuple, *French*
DFPA; DFT/*ami.*

ami en voie, *French*
DFT/*ami.*

amigo, *Spanish*
DFT; DFWPN; DSTE.

amir, *Arabic*
DFWPN.

à moitié, *French*
DFPA.

A moll, *German*
ICMM.

à mon avis, *French*
DFT.

Amontillado, *Spanish*
DFWPN; DFWPB.

amore, *Italian*
DFT; DFWPN; OCM.

amore, con, *Italian*
ICMM.

a moresco, *Italian*
ICMM.

amoretto, *Italian*
DFT.

amorevole, *Italian*
ICMM.

amorino, *Italian*
DFT.

amor nummi, *Latin*
DFPCQ.

amorosamente, *Italian*
OCM/*amoroso.*

amoroso, *Italian*
DEP; DFPCQ; DFT; DFWPN;
ICMM; OCM.

amor patriæ, *Latin*
DEP.

amor patriae, *Latin*
DFPA; DFPCQ; DFWPB.

amor vincit omnia, *Latin*
DFPA.

amour, *French*
DFWPB; DFWPN; OCM/*amore.*

amourette, *French*
DFT.

amourettes de veau, *French*
DFT/*amourette.*

amour propre, *French*
DEP; DFPA; DFT; DFWPN.

amour-propre, *French*
DFPCQ.

amparo, *Spanish*
DFT.

amphion, *Greek*
ICMM.

ampleur, *French*
OCM.

ampollosamente, *Italian*
ICMM.

amusement, *French*
ICMM.

an, *German*
OCM.

anabasis, *Greek*
DFWPN.

anabathmi, *Greek*
ICMM.

anakara, *Greek*
ICMM.

anakoluthon, *Greek*
DFWPN.

analytique, *French*
DA.

ananas, *French*
DFWPN.

ananes, *Greek*
ICMM.

anaqua, *Mexican Spanish*
DFT.

anathema, *Greek*
DFPCQ.

anathema sit!, *Latin*
DFPA.

anblasen, *German*
OCM.

anche, *French*
ICMM; OCM.

anche, *Italian*
OCM.

anchois, *French*
DFT; DFWPN.

anchois farcis, *French*
DFT/*anchois.*

ancia, *Italian*
OCM/*anche.*

ancien, *French*
DA.

ancienne noblesse, *French*
DFPA; DFPCQ; DFT.

ancien régime, *French*
DFPA; DFPCQ; DFT; DFWPB;
DFWPN.

ancón, *Mexican Spanish*
DFT.

ancona, *Italian*
DA.

ancora, *Italian*
DFT; OCM.

ancora una volta, *Italian*
DFT/*ancora.*

Andacht, *German*
OCM.

Andacht, mit, *German*
ICMM.

andale, *Spanish*
DSTE.

andalouse, *French*
OCM/*andaluz.*

andaluza, *Spanish*
OCM/*andaluz.*

andamento, *Italian*
ICMM; OCM.

andante, *Italian*
DFPA; DFPCQ; DFT; DFWPB;
DFWPN; ICMM; OCM.

andante cantabile, *Italian*
ICMM.

andante maestoso, *Italian*
ICMM.

andante ma non troppo, *Italian*
ICMM.

andantino, *Italian*
DFPCQ; DFT; DFWPB;
DFWPN; ICMM; OCM.

andare, *Italian*
ICMM.

andauernd, *German*
OCM.

ander, *German*
OCM.

andere, *German*
OCM/*ander.*

andno, *Italian*
OCM.

andon, *Japanese*
JLE.

andouillette, *French*
DFT.

anelantemente, *Italian*
ICMM.

anesis, *Greek*
ICMM.

Anfang, *German*
ICMM; OCM.

Anfang, vom, *German*
ICMM/*Anfang.*

Anfangsritornell, *German*
ICMM.

Angelica, *German*
ICMM.

angelique, *French*
ICMM/*Angelica.*

Angelus, *Latin*
DFWPN; DFWPB.

Angelus Domini, *Latin*
DFWPN.

angemessen, *German*
OCM.

angenehm, *German*
OCM.

angina pectoris, *Latin*
DFWPN.

angklung, *Javanese*
ICMM.

anglais, *French*
OCM.

anglaise, *French*
ICMM/*anglico*; OCM.

Angleterre, *French*
DFWPN.

anglicé, *Latin*
DEP.

anglice, *Latin*
DFPCQ.

anglico, *Italian*
ICMM.

angore, *Italian*
OCM.

angoscia, *Italian*
OCM.

angosciamento, *Italian*
ICMM.

angosciosissimamente, *Italian*
ICMM.

angreifen, *German*
ICMM; OCM.

Angst, *German*
DFWPB; DFWPN; LP; OCM.

ängstlich, *German*
OCM; OCM/*aengstlich.*

anguille, *French*
DFT.

anguille de mer, *French*
DFT/*anguille.*

anguis in herba, *Latin*
DFPA.

anhalten, *German*
OCM.

Anhang, *German*
ICMM; OCM.

an hua, *Chinese*
ACD.

anima, *Italian*
OCM.

anima, *Latin*
DFWPN.

anima, con, *Italian*
ICMM.

anima mundi, *Latin*
DFWPN.

animando, *Italian*
ICMM; OCM.

animato, *Italian*
DFPCQ; DFT; DFWPN; ICMM.

animé, *French*
OCM.

animelles, *French*
DFT.

animo, *Italian*
OCM.

animosamente, *Italian*
ICMM.

animoso, *Italian*
ICMM; OCM/*animo.*

animus, *Latin*
DFPCQ; DFWPN.

animus furandi, *Latin*
DFPA.

animus testandi, *Latin*
DFPA.

Anklang, *German*
ICMM.

anklingen, *German*
ICMM.

ankus, *Hindi*
DFT.

anlaufen, *German*
ICMM; OCM.

Anmut, *German*
OCM.

Anmuth, *German*
ICMM; OCM/*Anmut.*

année, *French*
DFWPN.

anno, *Latin*
DFT.

anno aetatis suae, *Latin*
DFPCQ; DFT/*anno*; DFWPN.

Anno Christi, *Latin*
DEP; DFPCQ.

Anno Domini, *Latin*
DFWPN.

Anno Domini (A. D.), *Latin*
DEP.

anno Domini, *Latin*
DFPA/*A. D.*; DFPA; DFT/*anno*;
DFWPB.

anno domini (A.D.), *Latin*
DFPCQ.

anno humanae salutis, *Latin*
DFPA.

Anno Mundi, *Latin*
DFWPN; DFPA.

anno mundi (A. M.), *Latin*
DEP.

anno mundi (A.M.), *Latin*
DFPCQ.

anno regni, *Latin*
DFWPN.

Anno Urbis Conditae, *Latin*
DFWPN; DFPA; DFT/*anno.*

anno urbis conditae (A.U.C.), *Latin*
DFPCQ.

annuit coeptis, *Latin*
DFPA; DFT.

annus, *Latin*
DFT; DFWPN.

annus magnus, *Latin*
DFT/*annus.*

Annus Mirabilis, *Latin*
DFWPN; DFPA; DFPCQ; DFT/
annus.

Año Nuevo, *Spanish*
DFWPN.

anreissen, *German*
OCM.

Ansatz, *German*
ICMM/*lip*; OCM.

anschauung, *German*
DFWPN.

Anschlag, *German*
ICMM/*touch*; OCM.

Anschluss, *German*
DFT; DFWPB; DFWPN.

anschmiegend, *German*
OCM.

anschwellend, *German*
OCM.

ansia, *Italian*
OCM.

anstatt, *German*
OCM.

anstimmen, *German*
OCM.

Anstrich, *German*
OCM/*Strich*; OCM.

ansu, *Japanese*
JLE.

ante, *Latin*
DEP; DFWPN.

ante bellum, *Latin*
DEP; DFPA; DFPCQ; DFT;
DFWPN.

ante Christum, *Latin*
DFT; DFWPN.

ante Christum (A.C.), *Latin*
DFPCQ.

ante cibum, *Latin*
DFPA/*a. c.*; DFT.

ante-cour, *French*
DA.

ante diem, *Latin*
DFT.

ante lucem, *Latin*
DFPA.

ante meridiem, *Latin*
DEP; DFPA/*a. m.*; DFT;
DFWPB; DFWPN.

ante meridiem (A.M.), *Latin*
DFPCQ.

antica, *Italian*
OCM.

antico, *Italian*
OCM.

antipasto, *Italian*
DFT; DFWPN.

antipasto, *pl.* antipasti, *Italian*
DFWPB.

anwachsend, *German*
OCM.

anzublasen, *German*
OCM.

à outrance, *French*
DFPA; DFT; DFWPN.

apache, *Spanish*
DSTE.

apaisé, *French*
OCM.

aparejador, *Spanish*
DA.

aparejo, *Spanish*
DFT; DSTE.

aparigerdor, *Spanish*
DA.

apartheid, *Afrikaans*
DFT; DFWPB.

à peine, *French*
OCM.

aperçu, *French*
DFPCQ; DFT; DFWPB;
DFWPN.

apéritif, *French*
DFT; DFWPB; DFWPN.

aperto, *Italian*
OCM.

a piacere, *Italian*
DFPA; DFT; DFT; ICMM.

à pied, *French*
DFPA.

à pierre fendre, *French*
DFT.

apikoros, *Yiddish*
JOY.

à plaisir, *French*
DFT.

aplomb, *French*
LB.

a poco a poco, *Italian*
DFPCQ; DFT.

à point, *French*
DFPA; DFT.

apologia, *Greek*
DFWPN.

apomnemoneumata, *Greek*
DFWPN.

a posse ad esse, *Latin*
DFPCQ.

a posteriori, *Latin*
DFPA; DFPCQ; DFT; DFWPB;
DFWPN.

apotheosis, *Greek*
DFPCQ.

apparat, *Russian*
DFWPB; MRWEW/*17*.

apparatchik, *Russian*
DFWPB.

apparatus criticus, *Latin*
DFPA; DFT.

apparatus criticus, *pl.* apparatus
critici, *Latin*
DFWPB.

appassionata, *Italian*
ICMM; OCM/*appassionato*.

appassionato, *Italian*
DFPCQ; DFT; OCM.

appel, *French*
DFT.

appena, *Italian*
OCM.

appenato, *Italian*
OCM.

applicatio, *Latin*
ICMM.

applicatur, *Latin*
ICMM.

appliqué, *French*
DA; DFWPB; DFWPN.

appoggiando, *Italian*
OCM.

appoggiato, *Italian*
DFPCQ; DFT; OCM/*appoggi-
ando*.

appoggiatura, *Italian*
DFPCQ; DFT; DFWPN; OCM.

appoggiatura, *pl.* appoggiature,
Italian
DFWPB.

appui, *French*
DA.

appuyé, *French*
OCM.

appuyée, *French*
OCM/*appuyé*.

après, *French*
DFWPN; OCM.

après coup, *French*
DFT.

après-midi, *French*
DFT; DFWPN.

Après-Midi D'Un Faune, *French*
DFWPN.

après moi le déluge, *French*
DFPA; DFPCQ; DFWPN.

après-ski, *French* + *Norwegian*
DFWPB.

a prima vista, *Italian*
DFPA; DFPCQ; DFWPN.

a primo, *Latin*
DFT.

a principio, *Latin*
DFT.

a priori, *Latin*
DEP; DFPA; DFPCQ; DFT;
DFWPB; DFWPN.

à propos, *French*
DFPA; DFPCQ; DFWPB.

à-propos, *French*
DFWPN.

apropos, *French*
DEP.

à propos de, *French*
DFPA.

a punta d'arco, *Italian*
ICMM; OCM.

aquí, *Spanish*
DFT; DFWPN.

aqua, *Latin*
DFPA/*aq.*; DFT.

aqua ardens, *Latin*
DFPA.

aqua benedicta, *Latin*
DFPCQ.

aqua fortis, *Latin*
DFPA; DFT/*aqua*; DFWPB;
DFWPN.

äqual, *German*
OCM.

aqua pura, *Latin*
DFPA/*aq.*; DFT/*aqua.*

aquardiente, *Spanish*
DSTE.

aqua regia, *Latin*
DFPA; DFPCQ; DFT/*aqua*;
DFWPB; DFWPN.

aquarelle, *French*
DFWPB; LP; OCM.

Aquarius, *Latin*
DFPCQ.

à quatre mains, *French*
DFT.

aqua vitæ, *Latin*
DEP.

aqua vitae, *Latin*
DFPA; DFPCQ; DFT/*aqua*;
DFWPB; DFWPN.

a quo, *Latin*
DFT; DFWPN.

à quoi bon?, *French*
DFPA.

arabeske, *German*
OCM.

arabesque, *French*
LB; LP; OCM.

arabesque à deux bras, *French*
LB/*arabesque.*

arabesque allongée, *French*
LB/*arabesque.*

arabesque allongée à terre, *French*
LB/*arabesque.*

arabesque à terre, *French*
LB/*arabesque.*

arabesque croisée, *French*
LB/*arabesque.*

arabesque croisée à deux bras,
French
LB/*arabesque.*

arabesque de face, *French*
LB/*arabesque.*

arabesque épaulée, *French*
LB/*arabesque.*

arabesque fondue, *French*
LB/*arabesque*; DFWPB.

arabesque ouverte, *French*
LB/*arabesque.*

arabesque ouverte croisée, *French*
LB/*arabesque.*

arabesque penchée, *French*
LB/*arabesque*; DFWPB.

arada, *Spanish*
OCM.

arado, *Spanish*
DFT.

aragonaise, *French*
OCM.

aragonesa, *Spanish*
OCM.

arbiter bibendi, *Latin*
DFPA; DFWPN.

arbiter elegantiae, *Latin*
DFT.

arbiter elegantiae (elegantiarum),
Latin
DFPA.

arbiter elegantiarum, *Latin*
DFPCQ; DFWPB; DFWPN.

arbiter literarum, *Latin*
DFPA.

arboretum, *Latin*
DFPCQ.

arbor vitae, *Latin*
DFWPN.

arc, *French*
DA.

arcanum (*pl.* **arcana**), *Latin*
DFPCQ.

arcata, *Italian*
OCM.

arcato, *Italian*
ICMM; OCM/*arcata.*

arc-boutant, *French*
DA; DFT.

Arc de Triomphe, *French*
DFWPN; DFT.

arc-doubleau, *French*
DA.

arc formeret, *French*
DA.

archet, *French*
OCM.

archi, *Italian*
OCM/*archet.*

archiviola, *Italian*
OCM.

arciliuto, *Italian*
OCM.

arciviola, *Italian*
OCM.

arciviola da gamba, *Italian*
OCM/*arciviola.*

arco, *Italian*
DFPCQ; DFT; ICMM; OCM.

arcus ecclesiae, *Latin*
DA.

ardemment, *French*
OCM.

ardente, *Italian*
DFT; ICMM; OCM.

ardentemente, *Italian*
DFT.

arditamente, *Italian*
ICMM.

arditezza, con, *Italian*
ICMM.

ardito, *Italian*
OCM.

ardore, *Italian*
OCM.

are, *French*
DFWPN.

à reculons, *French*
DFPA.

arena, *Spanish*
DFWPN.

areopagus, *Greek*
DFPCQ.

arête, *French*
GG.

argent, *French*
DFWPN.

argent comptant, *French*
DFPA/*a. c..*

argentum, *Latin*
DFWPN.

argille scagliose, *Italian*
GG.

argumenti gratia, *Latin*
DFPA.

argumentum, *Latin*
DFT.

argumentum ad absurdum, *Latin*
DFPCQ; DFT/*argumentum.*

argumentum ad baculum, *Latin*
DFPA/*argumentum baculinum*;
DFT/*argumentum*; DFWPN.

argumentum ad crumenam, *Latin*
DFPA; DFPCQ; DFT/*argumentum*; DFWPN.

argumentum ad hominem, *Latin*
DEP; DFPA; DFPCQ; DFT/
argumentum; DFWPN.

argumentum ad ignorantiam, *Latin*
DEP; DFPA; DFPCQ; DFT/
argumentum; DFWPN.

argumentum ad invidiam, *Latin*
DEP; DFPA; DFPCQ; DFT/
argumentum.

argumentum ad judicium, *Latin*
DEP; DFPA; DFPCQ; DFT/
argumentum; DFWPN.

argumentum ad misericordiam, *Latin*
DFPA; DFPCQ; DFT/*argumentum*; DFWPN.

argumentum ad populum, *Latin*
DFPA; DFPCQ; DFT/*argumentum*; DFWPN.

argumentum ad rem, *Latin*
DFPA; DFT/*argumentum*;
DFWPN.

argumentum ad verecundiam, *Latin*
DEP; DFPA; DFPCQ; DFT/
argumentum; DFWPN.

argumentum a fortiori, *Latin*
DFWPN.

argumentum a silentio, *Latin*
DFWPB.

argumentum baculinum, *Latin*
DFPA; DFT/*argumentum*.

argumentum ex concesso, *Latin*
DFWPN.

argumentum ex silentio, *Latin*
DFWPN.

aria, *Italian*
DFPCQ; DFT; DFWPN.

aria, *pl.* **arie,** *Italian*
DFWPB.

aria aggiunta, *Italian*
OCM/*aria*.

aria all'unisono, *Italian*
OCM/*aria*.

aria buffa, *Italian*
OCM/*aria*.

aria cantabile, *Italian*
DFWPN; OCM/*aria*.

aria concertata, *Italian*
OCM/*aria*.

aria d'abilità, *Italian*
OCM/*aria*.

aria da capo, *Italian*
DFWPN.

aria d'agilità, *Italian*
OCM/*aria*.

aria de chiesa, *Italian*
OCM/*aria*.

aria d'entrata, *Italian*
OCM/*aria*.

aria di bravura, *Italian*
DFWPN; OCM/*aria*.

aria di mezzo carattere, *Italian*
DFWPN; OCM/*aria*.

aria d'imitazione, *Italian*
OCM/*aria*.

aria di portamento, *Italian*
DFWPN; OCM/*aria*.

aria fugata, *Italian*
OCM/*aria*.

aria parlante, *Italian*
DFT; DFWPN; OCM/*aria*.

aria senza accompagnamento, *Italian*
OCM/*aria*.

aria tedesca, *Italian*
OCM/*aria*.

aries, *Latin*
DFPCQ.

arietta, *Italian*
DFPCQ; DFT; OCM.

arietta, *pl.* **ariette,** *Italian*
DFWPB.

ariette, *French*
OCM.

arigato, *Japanese*
DFT; JLE.

arioso, *Italian*
DFPCQ; DFT; DFWPB;
DFWPN; OCM.

ariston hudōr, *Greek*
DFPCQ.

ariston metron, *Greek*
DFPCQ.

a rivederci, *Italian*
DFPA; DFWPB.

arkose, *French*
GG.

arlecchinesco, *Italian*
ICMM; OCM.

arma, *Latin*
DFWPN.

arma accipere, *Latin*
DFPCQ.

arma dare, *Latin*
DFPCQ.

armadillo, *Spanish*
DSTE.

arma virumque cano, *Latin*
DFWPN.

armoire, *French*
ACD; DFT; DFWPB.

armonia, *Italian*
OCM.

armoniosamente, *Italian*
ICMM; OCM/*armonioso.*

armonioso, *Italian*
ICMM; OCM.

aroysgevorfen, *Yiddish*
JOY.

arpa, *Italian*
OCM.

arpège, *French*
OCM.

arpeggiare, *Italian*
OCM.

arpeggio, *Italian*
DFPCQ; DFT; DFWPN.

arpeggio, *pl.* **arpeggi,** *Italian*
DFWPB.

arpeggione, *Italian*
OCM.

arpent, *French*
DFT.

arpicordo, *Italian*
OCM.

arraché, *French*
OCM.

Arras, *French*
DFWPN.

arrastra, *Spanish*
DFT/*arrastre.*

arrastre, *Spanish*
DFT; DSTE/*236.*

arriba, *Spanish*
DFWPN.

arricciato/arricciatura/arriccio,
Italian
DFWPB.

arrière, en, *French*
LB.

arrière-garde, *French*
DFPA.

arrière pensée, *French*
DFPA; DFWPN.

arrivaderla, *Italian*
DFT.

arrivederci, *Italian*
DFPA/*a rivederci*; DFPCQ; DFT;
DFWPN.

arroba, *Spanish*
DFT.

arrondi, *French*
LB.

arrondissement, *French*
DFT; DFWPN.

arroyo, *Spanish*
DFT; DFWPB; DSTE; GG.

arroz, *Spanish*
DFT.

arroz con pollo, *Spanish*
DFPA; DFT/*pollo*; DFT.

ars, *Latin*
DFWPN.

ars amandi, *Latin*
DFWPN.

ars amatoria, *Latin*
DFWPN.

ars antiqua, *Latin*
ICMM; OCM.

ars est celare artem, *Latin*
DFPCQ; DFWPN.

ars gratia artis, *Latin*
DFPA; DFWPB; DFWPN.

arsis, *Greek*
OCM.

ars longa, vita brevis, *Latin*
DFPA; DFPCQ; DFWPN.

ars musica, *Latin*
ICMM.

ars nova, *Latin*
DFWPB; ICMM; OCM.

Ars Poetica, *Latin*
DFWPN.

art brut, l', *French*
LP.

artichaut, *French*
DFT; DFWPN.

articolato, *Italian*
OCM.

articulé, *French*
OCM.

articulus, *Latin*
DFPCQ.

artig, *German*
OCM.

artikuliert, *German*
OCM.

artiste, *French*
DFT; DFWPB.

artiste maudit, *French*
LP.

Artium Baccalaureus, *Latin*
DFWPN; DFPA/*A. B.*.

Artium Magister, *Latin*
DFWPN; DFPA/*A. M.*.

artium magister (A.M.), *Latin*
DFPCQ.

art moderne, *French*
DFWPB.

Art Nouveau, *French*
DA; DFT; DFWPB; LP.

arts d'agrément, *French*
DFT/*agrément*.

As, *German*
OCM.

AsAs, *German*
OCM.

a secco, *Italian*
DFWPB.

asequia, *Spanish*
DSTE/*acequia*.

Ases, *German*
OCM/*AsAs*.

Ashkenazi, *Yiddish*
HFY; JOY.

Ashkenazic, *Yiddish*
JOY/*Ashkenazi*.

Ashkenazim, *Hebrew*
DFWPN.

Ashkenazim, *Yiddish*
JOY/*Ashkenazi*.

así, *Spanish*
DFWPN.

asif, *Berber*
GG.

asinus ad lyram, *Latin*
DFPA.

askaulos, *Greek*
OCM.

asperge, *French*
DFT.

asperges me, *Latin*
ICMM.

aspergillum, *Latin*
ACD.

aspiratamente, *Italian*
OCM.

aspra, *Italian*
OCM/*aspro*.

aspro, *Italian*
OCM.

assai, *Italian*
DFPCQ; ICMM; OCM.

assai più, *Italian*
ICMM.

assegai, *Zulu*
DFT.

assemblage, *French*
DFWPB; LP.

assemblé, *French*
DFWPB.

assemblé battu, *French*
LB/*assemblé, pas*.

assemblé derrière, *French*
LB/*assemblé, pas*.

assemblé dessous, *French*
LB/*assemblé, pas*.

assemblé dessus, *French*
LB/*assemblé, pas*.

assemblé devant, *French*
LB/*assemblé, pas*.

assemblé élancé, *French*
  LB/*assemblé, pas.*

assemblé en arrière, *French*
  LB/*assemblé, pas.*

assemblé en avant, *French*
  LB/*assemblé, pas.*

assemblé en tournant, *French*
  LB/*assemblé, pas.*

assemblé, pas, *French*
  LB.

assemblé, petit, *French*
  LB/*assemblé, pas.*

assemblé porté, *French*
  LB/*assemblé, pas.*

assemblés de suite, *French*
  LB/*assemblé, pas.*

assemblé soutenu, *French*
  LB/*assemblé, pas.*

assemblé soutenu en tournant,
French
  LB/*assemblé, pas.*

assemblés sur les pointes, *French*
  LB/*assemblé, pas.*

assez, *French*
  ICMM; OCM.

assez lent, *French*
  ICMM.

assieme, *Italian*
  ICMM; OCM.

assiette, *French*
  DFT.

assiettes volantes, *French*
  DFT/*assiette.*

assise, *French*
  GG.

assoluta, *Italian*
  OCM.

asturiana, *Spanish*
  OCM/*asturiano.*

asturiano, *Spanish*
  OCM.

Asymphonie, *German*
  ICMM.

atelier, *French*
  DA; DFWPB; LP.

até logo, *Portuguese*
  DFPA.

Atempause, *German*
  OCM.

a tempo, *Italian*
  DFT; DFWPB; ICMM.

a tempo giusto, *Italian*
  DFT/*a tempo*; DFWPN.

a tempo primo, *Italian*
  ICMM.

a tempo rubato, *Italian*
  ICMM.

a tergo, *Latin*
  DFPA.

atole, *Mexican Spanish*
  DFT.

à toutes jambes, *French*
  DFPCQ.

à tout prix, *French*
  DFPA.

a tre, *Italian*
  ICMM.

à trois, *French*
  ICMM/*a tre.*

-atsh, *Yiddish*
  HFY.

attacca, *Italian*
  DFT; ICMM; OCM.

attacca subito, *Italian*
  DFPCQ; DFT/*attacca.*

attacco, *Italian*
  ICMM; OCM.

attaché, *French*
  DFPCQ; DFT; DFWPB;
  DFWPN.

attaque, *French*
  OCM.

attitude, *French*
  DFWPB; LB.

attitude à deux bras, *French*
  LB/*attitude.*

attitude à terre, *French*
LB/*attitude.*

attitude croisée, *French*
LB/*attitude.*

attitude de face, *French*
LB/*attitude.*

attitude devant, *French*
LB/*attitude.*

attitude effacée, *French*
LB/*attitude.*

attitude, en, *French*
LB.

attitude épaulée, *French*
LB/*attitude.*

attitude grecque, *French*
LB/*attitude.*

atto di cadenza, *Italian*
ICMM.

au, *French*
OCM.

aubade, *French*
DFT; DFWPN; ICMM; OCM.

aubergine, *French*
DFT.

au besoin, *French*
DFWPN.

au beurre, *French*
DFT/*beurre.*

au beurre fondu, *French*
DFT.

au beurre roux, *French*
DFT.

auch, *German*
OCM.

au contraire, *French*
DFPA; DFPCQ; DFT; DFWPB;
DFWPN.

au courant, *French*
DFPA; DFPCQ; DFT; DFWPB;
DFWPN.

Aucuba, *Japanese*
JLE.

audace, *French*
OCM.

au dessous, *French*
OCM.

audi alteram partem, *Latin*
DEP.

auf, *German*
OCM.

au fait, *French*
DEP; DFPA; DFT; DFWPB;
DFWPN; SPICE.

Aufeis, *German*
GG.

aufführen, *German*
OCM.

Aufführung, *German*
ICMM.

aufgeregt, *German*
OCM.

aufgeweckt, *German*
OCM.

aufhalten, *German*
OCM.

Aufklärung, *German*
DFT.

Auflage, *German*
OCM.

auflösen, *German*
OCM.

Auflösung, *German*
ICMM; OCM/*aufloösen.*

Auflösungszeichen, *German*
ICMM; OCM/*aufloösen.*

au fond, *French*
DFPA; DFT.

Aufschlag, *German*
OCM.

Aufschnitt, *German*
OCM.

Aufschwung, *German*
OCM.

Aufstrich, *German*
OCM.

Auftakt, *German*
ICMM; OCM.

auf Wiedersehen, *German*
DFT; DFWPB; DFPA.

Aufwuchs, *German*
GG.

Aufzug, *German*
OCM.

Augen, *German*
GG.

au grand sérieux, *French*
DFPA.

au gras, *French*
DFWPN.

au gratin, *French*
DFPA; DFT; DFT/*gratin*;
DFWPB; DFWPN.

au jus, *French*
DFPA; DFT/*jus*; DFT; DFWPN.

au lait, *French*
DFT/*lait*; DFT.

auletes, *Greek*
ICMM.

aulodia, *Italian*
ICMM.

au miroir, *French*
DFWPN.

a una corda, *Italian*
ICMM.

au naturel, *French*
DFPA; DFPCQ; DFT/*naturel*;
DFT; DFWPB; DFWPN.

au pair, *French*
DFPA.

au pied de la lettre, *French*
DFWPN; SPICE.

au pis aller, *French*
DFPA; DFT.

au point, *French*
DFPA.

au premier, *French*
DFT.

au premier coup, *French*
DFWPB; LP.

Aura, *Italian*
OCM.

aura popularis, *Latin*
DFPA; DFWPN.

aurea aetes, *Latin*
DFWPN.

aurea mediocritas, *Latin*
DFPA; DFPCQ; DFT; DFWPB;
DFWPN.

au revoir, *French*
DEP; DFPA; DFPCQ; DFT;
DFWPB; DFWPN; SPICE.

auri sacra fames, *Latin*
DEP.

aurora australis, *Latin*
DFWPB.

Aurora Borealis, *Latin*
DFPCQ; DFPA; DFWPB;
DFWPN.

aurum, *Latin*
DFT.

aus, *German*
OCM.

Ausdruck, *German*
DFT; ICMM; OCM.

au sérieux, *French*
DFPA; DFWPB.

Ausfüllgeiger, *German*
OCM.

Ausgabe, *German*
DFWPN; OCM.

ausgehalten, *German*
ICMM; OCM.

ausgelassen, *German*
ICMM.

aushalten, *German*
ICMM; OCM.

Aushaltung, *German*
ICMM.

Auslese, *German*
DFWPN.

au soleil, *French*
DFPA.

Auspex, *Latin*
DFWPN.

ausschlagen, *German*
OCM.

ausser, *German*
OCM.

äusserst, *German*
OCM.

aussi, *French*
OCM.

Austausch, *German*
GG.

Auszug, *German*
OCM.

aut Cæsar aut nullus, *Latin*
DEP.

Autobahn, *German*
DFWPN.

Autobahn, *pl.* **Autobahnen,** *German*
DFWPB.

auto da fé, *Portuguese*
DEP; DFWPN.

auto-da-fé, *Portuguese*
DFPA; DFT.

auto-da-fé, *pl.* **autos-da-fé,** *Portuguese*
DFWPB.

auto de fe, *Spanish*
DFPA; DFPCQ.

auto-de-fe, *Spanish*
DFT.

automaton, *Greek*
DFPCQ.

autore, *Italian*
DFT.

auto sacramental, *Spanish*
DFPA; ICMM.

autostrada, *Italian*
DFWPB.

autostrade, *Italian*
DFWPN.

autre, *French*
DFWPN; OCM.

autrefois, *French*
DFWPN.

autres, *French*
OCM/*autre.*

aux choux, *French*
DFT.

aux confitures, *French*
DFT.

aux cressons, *French*
DFT.

aux morilles, *French*
DFT.

aux oignons, *French*
DFT.

aux petits pois, *French*
DFT.

avant, *French*
DFPCQ; DFWPN; OCM.

avant-coureur, *French*
DEP.

avante, *Italian*
OCM/*avant.*

avant, en, *French*
LB.

avant-garde, *French*
DFPA; DFWPB; DFWPN; LP.

avanti, *Italian*
OCM/*avant.*

avant la lettre, *French*
DFPA.

avant propos, *French*
DFWPN.

avant-propos, *French*
DFPCQ.

avant-scène, *French*
ICMM.

ave atque vale, *Latin*
DFPA; DFWPB; DFWPN.

avec, *French*
DFWPN; OCM.

avec les pieds, *French*
ICMM.

Ave Maria, *Latin*
DFWPN; DFWPB; ICMM.

aven, *French*
GG.

averah, *Yiddish*
JOY.

a verbis ad verbera, *Latin*
DFWPN.

a vicenda, *Italian*
ICMM.

a vinculo matrimonii, *Latin*
DEP; DFPA.

avis, *Latin*
DFWPN.

a vista, *Italian*
ICMM.

avlakogene, *Russian*
GG.

avoirdupois, *Old French*
DFWPB; DFWPN.

à voix forte, *French*
ICMM.

à volonté, *French*
DFPA; DFT; ICMM.

a vostra salute, *Italian*
DFPA.

à votre santé, *French*
DFPA; DFT; DFWPN.

a votre santé, *French*
DFPCQ.

à vue, *French*
DFT; ICMM.

à vue d'oeil, *French*
DFPA; DFT/*à vue.*

a vuestra salud, *Spanish*
DFPA; DFPCQ; DFWPN.

awabi, *Japanese*
JLE.

axe, *French*
DA.

axiōmata, *Greek*
DFPCQ.

aydem, *Yiddish*
JOY.

ayer, *Spanish*
DFWPN.

ayu, *Japanese*
JLE.

ayudante, *Spanish*
DFT.

azafrán, *Spanish*
DFWPN.

azione, *Italian*
OCM.

azione sacra, *Italian*
ICMM.

azogue, *Spanish*
DFT.

azote, *Spanish*
DFT.

azul, *Spanish*
DFWPN.

azzurro, *Italian*
DFWPN.

B

Baal Shem, *Yiddish*
JOY.

baba, *French*
DFWPN.

baba, *Russian*
MRWEW/19.

baba au rhum, *French*
DFT/*baba.*

baborácka, *Czech*
ICMM.

baborák, *Czech*
ICMM.

babu, *Hindi*
DFT.

babushka, *Russian*
DFT; DFWPN; MRWEW/17.

baccalaureus legum, *Latin*
DFPA/*B.LL..*

baccalaureus musicae, *Latin*
ICMM.

baccalaureus pharmaciae, *Latin*
DFPA/*B. P..*

baccara(t), *French*
DFWPB.

baccarat, *French*
DFT; DFWPN.

bacchanale, *French*
DFWPN.

bacchanalia, *Greek*
DFWPN.

Bacchantes, *Greek*
DFWPN.

bacchetta, *Italian*
ICMM; OCM.

bacchette di legno, *Italian*
ICMM/*bacchetta.*

bacchette di spugna, *Italian*
ICMM/*bacchetta.*

Bacchuslied, *German*
ICMM.

Backfisch, *German*
DFT.

Bad, *German*
DFWPN.

badchanim, *Yiddish*
JOY/*badchen.*

badchen, *Yiddish*
JOY.

badchonim, *Hebrew*
OCM.

badia, *Italian*
DA.

badinage, *French*
DFT; DFWPB; OCM.

badinerie, *French*
DFWPB; ICMM; OCM/*badinage.*

bagasse, *French*
DFT.

bagatelle, *French*
DFPCQ; DFWPB; DFWPN;
ICMM; OCM.

Bagatelle, *German*
OCM.

bagel, *Yiddish*
DFWPN; HFY.

bagnio, *Italian*
DA.

baguette, *French*
DFT; DFWPN; GG; OCM.

baguettes de bois, *French*
OCM/*baguette*.

baguettes d'éponge, *French*
OCM/*baguette*.

Bahnhof, *German*
DFPCQ.

bahr, *Arabic*
GG.

baignoire, *French*
DA.

baile, *Spanish*
DFT; OCM.

baile flamenco, *Spanish*
DFWPN.

bain-marie, *French*
DFT; DFWPB; DFWPN.

baisser, *French*
ICMM; OCM.

bai-u, *Japanese*
JLE.

bajada, *Spanish*
GG.

baka (bomb), *Japanese*
JLE.

bakhshish, *Persian*
DFWPN.

baklava, *Russian*
DFWPN.

baksheesh, *Hindi*
DFT/*bakshish*.

baksheesh, *Persian*
DFWPB.

bakshish, *Hindi*
DFT.

balabatish, *Yiddish*
JOY/*balbatish*.

balabos, *Yiddish*
DFT.

balabustah, *Yiddish*
DFT.

balalaika, *Russian*
DFWPN; MRWEW/*17; OCM*.

balancement, *French*
ICMM.

balancé, pas, *French*
LB.

balançoire, en, *French*
LB.

balaneia, *Greek*
DA.

balbatim, *Yiddish*
JOY.

balbatish, *Yiddish*
JOY.

baldachino, *Italian*
DA.

balebatim, *Yiddish*
JOY.

baleboosteh, *Yiddish*
JOY/*baleboss*.

balebos, *Yiddish*
HFY.

baleboss, *Yiddish*
JOY.

baliki, *Russian*
DFT.

ballabile, *French*
LB.

ballabile, *Italian*
ICMM; OCM.

balladenmässig, *German*
OCM.

ballamatia, *Italian*
ICMM.

ballata, *Italian*
OCM.

ballatella, *Italian*
ICMM; OCM/*ballata.*

ballerina, *Italian*
DFWPN; ICMM.

ballerino, *Italian*
ICMM; OCM.

ballet, *French*
DFWPN; LB.

ballet blanc, *French*
DFWPB; LB.

ballet chanté, *French*
DFWPB.

ballet classique, *French*
LB.

ballet d'action, *French*
DFWPB; LB/*ballet.*

ballet romantique, *French*
LB.

Ballet Russe, *French*
DFWPN.

balletti, *Italian*
ICMM.

balletto, *Italian*
ICMM; OCM.

balli inglesi, *Italian*
ICMM.

balli ungaresi, *Italian*
ICMM.

ballo, *Italian*
OCM.

ballo furlano, *Italian*
OCM.

ballon, *French*
DFWPB; GG; LB.

ballonchio, *Italian*
ICMM.

ballon d'essai, *French*
DFPA; DFWPB; DFWPN.

ballonné, *French*
DFWPB; LB.

ballonné à trois temps, pas, *French*
LB/*ballonné, pas.*

ballonné composé, pas, *French*
LB/*ballonné, pas.*

ballonné, pas, *French*
LB.

ballotté, *French*
DFWPB.

ballotté, pas, *French*
LB.

balmalocha, *Yiddish*
JOY.

balmalucha, *Yiddish*
JOY.

bamanos, *Spanish*
DSTE/*vamos.*

bambino, *Italian*
DFT; DFWPN.

bambino, *pl.* **bambini,** *Italian*
DFWPB.

bamos, *Spanish*
DSTE/*vamos.*

bancha (tea), *Japanese*
JLE.

banco, *French from Italian*
DFWPB.

banco, *Italian*
DFWPN.

banco, *Spanish*
GG.

Band, *German*
DFWPN; OCM.

banda, *Italian*
ICMM.

banda turca, *Italian*
OCM.

Bände, *German*
OCM.

banderilla, *Spanish*
DFWPN; DSTE/*236.*

banderillero, *Spanish*
DFWPN; DSTE/*236.*

bandido, *Spanish*
DFT; DSTE.

bandito, *Italian*
DFPCQ.

bandola, *Spanish*
ICMM.

bandolero, *Spanish*
DFT.

bandoneon, *Spanish*
OCM.

bandore, *Spanish*
OCM.

bandurria, *Spanish*
DFWPN; ICMM.

bandurría, *Spanish*
OCM.

banquette, *French*
DA; DFT; DFWPN.

banya, *Hindi*
ICMM.

banzai, *adj., Japanese*
DFT; DFWPB; JLE.

Banzai, *interj., Japanese*
JLE.

baquero, *Spanish*
DSTE/*vaquero.*

bar, *French*
DFT.

barbarie, orgue de, *French*
OCM.

barba rossa, *Italian*
DFWPN.

barbeau, *French*
ACD; DFWPB.

barbera, *Italian*
DFT.

barbotine, *French*
DFWPB.

barbouillage, *French*
DFT.

barcarola, *Italian*
DFPCQ.

barcarolle, *French*
DFWPB; ICMM.

barcarula, *Italian*
ICMM.

barchan, *Russian*
GG.

barége, *French*
DFT.

barège, *French*
DFT/*barége.*

baren, *Japanese*
JLE.

bargello, *Italian*
DA.

bariolage, *French*
ICMM; OCM.

baripicni, *Modern Greek*
ICMM.

baripicni suoni, *Italian*
ICMM.

Barkarole, *German*
OCM.

barkhan, *Russian*
GG.

bar-mitzva, *Hebrew*
DFWPN.

Bar Mitzva, *Yiddish*
JOY.

bar mitzvah, *Hebrew*
DFT.

Bar Mitzvah, *Yiddish*
JOY.

bar mizvah (mitzvah, mitzwah),
Hebrew
DFPA.

barocco, *Italian*
OCM.

Barock, *German*
OCM/*barocco.*

baroque, *French*
OCM/*barocco.*

baroquerie, *French*
DFWPB.

barra, *Spanish*
DFT.

barracon, *Spanish*
DSTE.

barracuda, *Spanish*
DSTE.

barrage, *French*
GG.

barranca, *Spanish*
DFT/*barranco*; DSTE.

barranco, *Spanish*
DFT; GG.

barre, *French*
DFWPB; LB; OCM.

barrera, *Spanish*
DSTE//*236*.

barrio, *Spanish*
DFT.

Baruch, *Hebrew*
DFWPN.

baruch ha-Shem, *Yiddish*
HFY.

Baryton, *German*
OCM.

baryton-Martin, *French*
DFWPB.

bas, *French*
DFWPN.

bas bleu, *French*
DEP; DFPA; DFT; DFWPN.

bas-dessus, *French*
ICMM.

bas, en, *French*
LB.

basho, *Japanese*
JLE.

Baskische Tänze, *German*
OCM.

Baskische Trommel, *German*
OCM.

Bas Mitzva, *Yiddish*
JOY.

bas mitzvah, *Hebrew*
DFT.

Bas Mitzvah, *Yiddish*
JOY.

basques, *French*
OCM.

bas relief, *French*
DFPA.

bas-relief, *French*
DFT; DFWPB; DFWPN.

bass, *German*
OCM.

bassa, *Italian*
OCM.

bassa ottava, *Italian*
ICMM.

basse, *French*
OCM.

basse chantante, *French*
ICMM; OCM.

basse chiffrée, *French*
ICMM; OCM.

basse continue, *French*
OCM/*basse chiffrée*.

basse cour, *French*
DA.

basse danse, *French*
ICMM; OCM.

basse de flandres, *French*
OCM/*bumbass*; OCM.

basse de viole d'armour, *French*
OCM.

basse d'harmonie, *French*
OCM.

basse taille, *French*
ACD/*enamel*; DFWPN; ICMM.

basse-taille, *French*
DFWPB.

Bassettflöte, *German*
OCM.

bassetto, *Italian*
ICMM.

bassflicorno, *Italian*
OCM.

Bassflöte, *German*
OCM.

Bassflügelhorn, *German*
OCM.

bassi, *Italian*
OCM.

bassist, *German*
ICMM.

bassista, *Italian*
ICMM.

basso, *Italian*
DFPCQ; DFT; OCM/*bass*;
OCM.

basso al ottava, *Italian*
DFWPB.

basso buffo, *Italian*
DFPA; DFT/*basso*.

basso cantante, *Italian*
DFWPN; ICMM/*basse chantante*;
ICMM; OCM.

basso concertante, *Italian*
ICMM.

basso continuo, *Italian*
DFT/*basso*; DFWPB; DFWPN;
ICMM; OCM.

basso da camera, *Italian*
ICMM.

basson, *French*
OCM.

basson quinte, *French*
ICMM; OCM.

basson russe, *French*
OCM.

basso ostinato, *Italian*
DFT/*basso*; DFWPB; OCM.

basso profondo, *Italian*
DFT/*basso*; DFWPB; ICMM;
OCM.

basso profundo, *Italian*
DFWPN.

basso recitante, *Italian*
ICMM.

basso relievo, *Italian*
DFPCQ.

basso rilievo, *Italian*
DFPA; DFWPB.

basso-rilievo, *Italian*
DA; DFT.

basso ripieno, *Italian*
ICMM.

Bass-posaune, *German*
ICMM.

Bassposaune, *German*
OCM.

Bass-saite, *German*
OCM.

Basstrompete, *German*
OCM.

bassus, *Latin*
OCM.

bastarda, viola, *Italian*
OCM.

bastide, *French*
DA.

bastile, *French*
DA.

Bastille, *French*
DFPCQ; DFWPN.

batik, *Javanese*
DFWPB; DFWPN.

batiste, *French*
DFWPB; DFWPN.

batlan, *Yiddish*
JOY.

batlanim, *Yiddish*
JOY.

Bâton, *French*
DFPCQ.

battement, *French*
DFWPB; LB.

battement arrondi, *French*
LB/*battement*.

battement arrondi, grand, *French*
LB/*battement*.

battement battu, *French*
LB/*battement*.

battement dégagé, *French*
DFWPB; LB/*battement*.

battement développé, *French*
LB/*battement*.

battement fini piqué, grand, *French*
LB/*battement*.

battement fondu, *French*
LB/*battement*.

battement fouetté, *French*
LB/*battement*.

battement frappé, *French*
LB/*battement.*

battement glissé, *French*
LB/*battement.*

battement, grand, *French*
LB/*battement.*

battement jeté, grand, *French*
LB/*battement.*

battement jeté pointé, grand, *French*
LB/*battement.*

battement ouvert, grand, *French*
LB/*battement.*

battement, petit, *French*
LB/*battement.*

battement piqué, *French*
LB/*battement.*

battement raccourci, grand, *French*
LB/*battement.*

battement relevé, *French*
LB/*battement.*

battement retiré, *French*
LB/*battement.*

battements battus, petits, *French*
LB/*battement.*

battements en balançoire, *French*
LB/*battement.*

battements en cloche, *French*
LB/*battement.*

battements en cloche, grands, *French*
LB/*battement.*

battement soutenu, *French*
LB/*battement.*

battements serrés, *French*
LB/*battement.*

battements sur le cou-de-pied, petits,
French
LB/*battement.*

battement tendu, *French*
DFWPB; LB/*battement.*

battement tendu jeté, *French*
LB/*battement.*

battement tendu relevé, *French*
LB/*battement.*

batterie, *French*
ICMM; LB; OCM.

batterie de cuisine, *French*
DFT; DFWPB; DFWPN.

batterie, grande, *French*
LB/*batterie.*

batterie, petite, *French*
LB/*batterie.*

battimento, *Italian*
ICMM.

battitura, *Italian*
ICMM.

battre, *French*
OCM.

battre les cartes, *French*
DFT/*battre.*

battu, *French*
LB.

batture, *French*
DFT; GG.

battuta, *Italian*
DFPCQ; DFT; ICMM; OCM.

battute, *Italian*
OCM/*battuta.*

Bauer, *German*
DFT.

Bauernleier, *German*
OCM.

Bauernlied, *German*
ICMM.

Bauernsuppe, *German*
DFT.

Bauhaus, *German*
DFWPB.

bavardage, *French*
DFT.

bavarois, *French*
DFT.

bavaroise, *French*
DFWPN.

Bawren Leyer, *German*
OCM/*Bauernleier.*

bayle, *Spanish*
OCM/*baile;* OCM.

bayou, *Choctaw*
DFWPN.

b cancellatum, *Latin*
ICMM.

B dur, *German*
ICMM; OCM.

Be, *German*
OCM.

bearbeiten, *German*
OCM.

bearbeitet, *German*
ICMM.

Bearbeitung, *German*
ICMM.

béarnaise, *French*
DFWPB.

beatae memoriae, *Latin*
DFPA/*b. m.*; DFPA.

beati possidentes, *Latin*
DFT.

beau, *French*
DFWPN.

beau, *pl.* **beaux,** *French*
DFWPB.

beaucoup, *French*
OCM.

beaufait, *French*
ACD.

beau geste, *French*
DFPA; DFWPB; DFWPN.

beau idéal, *French*
DEP; DFPA; DFT; DFWPN.

beau monde, *French*
DEP; DFPA; DFPCQ; DFT;
DFWPB; DFWPN.

Beaune, *French*
DFWPN.

beauté du diable, *French*
DFPA.

Beauvais, *French*
ACD.

beaux arts, *French*
DFPA; DFWPN.

beaux-arts, *French*
DA; LP.

beaux arts *pl.,* *French*
DFWPB.

beaux esprits, *French*
DEP; DFPA; DFT; DFWPN/*bel
esprit.*

bébé, *French*
DFT.

bebend, *German*
OCM.

Bebung, *German*
DFWPB; ICMM; OCM.

bec, *French*
ICMM.

bécarre, *French*
DFT; OCM.

bécassine, *French*
DFT.

beccafico, *Italian*
DFT.

becco, *Italian*
ICMM.

becfigue, *French*
DFT.

béchamel, *French*
DFT; DFWPN.

bêche-de-mer, *French*
DFT.

Beck, *German*
OCM.

Becken, *German*
OCM.

bedächtig, *German*
OCM.

Bedarfsfall, *German*
OCM.

beddo, *Japanese*
JLE.

bedeutend, *German*
OCM.

bedrohlich, *German*
OCM.

begeistert, *German*
OCM.

begleiten, *German*
OCM.

begleitend, *German*
OCM/*begleiten.*

Begleitung, *German*
DFT; ICMM; OCM/*begleiten.*

behaglich, *German*
OCM.

behama, *Yiddish*
JOY/*behayma.*

behayma, *Yiddish*
JOY.

behayme, *Yiddish*
JOY/*behayma.*

behend, *German*
OCM.

behendig, *German*
OCM/*behend.*

Behendigkeit, *German*
OCM/*behend.*

beherzt, *German*
OCM.

beide, *German*
OCM.

beignet, *French*
DFT.

beignets de pommes, *French*
DFT/*beignet.*

beinahe, *German*
OCM.

Beispiel, *German*
OCM.

Beisser, *German*
ICMM/*mordent*; OCM.

bekko, *Japanese*
JLE.

beklemmt, *German*
ICMM; OCM.

beklommen, *German*
OCM/*beklemmt.*

bel, *Panjabi*
GG.

bel canto, *Italian*
DFPA; DFT; DFWPB; DFWPN;
OCM.

belduque, *Mexican Spanish*
DFT.

belebend, *German*
OCM.

belebt, *German*
OCM/*belebend.*

belebter, *German*
OCM/*belebend.*

bel esprit, *French*
DEP; DFPA; DFT; DFWPN.

bel étage, *French*
DA/*étage*; DFT.

bel-étage, *French*
DA.

Belieben, *German*
OCM.

beliebig, *German*
OCM/*Belieben.*

belladonna, *Italian*
DFWPN.

bella figlia dell'amore, *Italian*
DFWPN.

belle, *French*
DFPCQ; DFWPB.

belle âme, *French*
DFWPN.

belle époque, la, *French*
DFWPB.

Belle Époque, La, *French*
LP.

belle indifférence, *French*
DFPA; DFWPB.

belle peinture, *French*
DFWPB; LP.

belles lettres, *French*
DFPA.

belles-lettres, *French*
DFPCQ; DFT; DFWPN.

belles lettres, *pl.,* *French*
DFWPB.

bell gamba, *Italian*
OCM.

bellicosamente, *Italian*
ICMM; OCM.

bellicoso, *Italian*
OCM.

bello flagrante, *Latin*
DFPCQ.

bellum, *Latin*
DFWPN.

bellum internecinum, *Latin*
DFT.

bel paese, *Italian*
DFWPN.

belustigend, *German*
OCM.

bémol, *French*
ICMM; OCM.

bemolle, *Italian*
OCM.

ben, *Hebrew*
DFWPN.

ben, *Italian*
OCM.

ben, *Yiddish*
JOY.

bene, *Italian*
OCM/*ben*.

bene, *Latin*
DFWPN.

benedicite, *Latin*
DFT; DFWPB; DFWPN; ICMM.

Benedictus, *Latin*
DFWPB; ICMM; OCM.

beneficium clericale, *Latin*
DFPA.

bene merenti, *Latin*
DFPA/*b. m.*.

beneplacimento, *Italian*
OCM/*beneplacito*.

bene placito, *Italian*
ICMM.

beneplacito, *Italian*
OCM.

ben marcato, *Italian*
DFT.

bentsh, *Yiddish*
DFT; JOY.

ben venuto, *Italian*
DFT.

bequadro, *Italian*
OCM.

bequem, *German*
OCM.

bercement, *French*
OCM.

berceuse, *French*
ICMM; OCM.

bereite vor, *German*
OCM.

bereits, *German*
OCM.

beret, *French*
DFWPN.

béret, *French*
DFWPB.

berg, *Dutch*
GG.

bergamasca, *Italian*
ICMM; OCM/*bergomask*.

bergamasque, *French*
OCM/*bergomask*.

bergère, *French*
ACD; DFWPB.

bergerette, *French*
ICMM; OCM.

bergerie, *French*
DFWPB.

Bergreigen, *German*
ICMM.

Bergschrund, *German*
GG.

beriberi, *Singhalese*
DFT.

berlingozza, *Italian*
ICMM.

berm, *Dutch*
GG.

Bernstein, *German*
GG.

berrendo, *American Spanish*
DFT.

berretta, *Italian*
DFT.

berrettina, *Italian*
DFT.

berrettino, *Italian*
DFT/*berrettina.*

berrieh, *Yiddish*
JOY.

berro, *Spanish*
DFT.

beruhigen, *German*
OCM.

Bes, *German*
ICMM; OCM.

besant, *French*
DFWPN.

beschleunigen, *German*
OCM.

Bes din, *Yiddish*
JOY.

beseelt, *German*
OCM.

Bes Midrash, *Yiddish*
JOY.

besoin, *French*
DFWPN.

bestiarium, *Latin*
DFWPN.

bestimmt, *German*
OCM.

Bet din, *Yiddish*
JOY/*Bes din.*

bête, *French*
DEP.

betel, *Malay*
DFWPN.

betend, *German*
OCM.

bête noire, *French*
DEP; DFPA; DFPCQ; DFT/*bête*;
DFWPB; DFWPN.

beth, *Hebrew*
DFWPN.

Beth din, *Yiddish*
JOY/*Bes din.*

Beth Hamidrash, *Yiddish*
JOY.

Bet Midrash, *Yiddish*
JOY.

béton, *French*
DA.

betont, *German*
OCM.

Betonung, *German*
OCM/*betont.*

Betrübnis, *German*
OCM.

betrübt, *German*
OCM.

betterave, *French*
DFT.

betto, *Japanese*
JLE.

beurre, *French*
DFT; DFWPN.

beurré, *French*
DFT.

beurre fondu, *French*
DFT/*beurre.*

beurre noir, *French*
DFWPN.

beweglich, *German*
OCM.

bewegt, *German*
OCM.

Bewegung, *German*
OCM.

Bezifferter Bass, *German*
ICMM.

bezugo, *Spanish*
DFT.

bhabar, *Urdu*
GG/*Hindi.*

bhangar, *Urdu*
GG/*Hindi.*

bheesty, *Hindi*
DFT/*bhisti.*

bhel, *Panjabi*
GG.

bhil, *Bengali*
GG.

bhisti, *Hindi*
DFT.

bhit, *Sindhi*
GG.

bhur, *Urdu*
GG/*Hindi.*

bhuta, *Sanskrit*
DFWPN.

bialy, *Yiddish*
HFY; JOY.

bianca, *Italian*
OCM.

bianco, *Italian*
DFWPN.

bianco sangiovanni, *Italian*
LP.

bianco secco, *Italian*
DFWPN.

bianco sopra bianco, *Italian*
ACD.

bianco-sopra-bianco, *Italian*
DFWPB.

Bibelorgel, *German*
OCM.

bibelot, *French*
DFT; DFWPB; DFWPN.

Bibelregal, *German*
OCM/*Bibelorgel.*

biblioteca, *Italian*
DFWPN.

biblioteca, *Spanish*
DFWPN.

bibliotheca, *Latin*
DA; DFPCQ; DFWPN.

Bibliothek, *German*
DFT; DFWPN.

bibliothèque, *French*
DA; DFT; DFWPN.

bidet, *French*
ACD; DA; DFWPB; DFWPN.

Biedermeier, *German*
ACD; DFWPN.

bien, *French*
DFT; OCM.

bien aimée, *French*
DFWPN.

bien cuit, *French*
DFT.

bien entendu, *French*
DFPA.

bienvenue, *French*
DFT.

Bier, *German*
DFT.

bière, *French*
DFT.

Bierstube, *German*
DFT/*stube*; DFWPN.

bifteck, *French*
DFT.

bijou, *French*
DFPCQ; DFWPN.

bijouterie, *French*
ACD; DFT; DFWPB; DFWPN.

Bildung, *German*
DFWPN.

Bildungsroman, *German*
DFWPB.

billet, *French*
DFWPN.

billet doux, *French*
DEP; DFPA; DFPCQ; DFWPN.

billet-doux, *French*
DFT.

billet doux, *pl.* **billets doux,** *French*
DFWPB.

Bindung, *German*
ICMM.

Bindungszeichen, *German*
ICMM/*slur.*
biniou, *French*
OCM.
binnacle, *Dutch*
GG.
Biographia Literaria, *Latin*
DFWPN.
Birne, *German*
GG.
bis, *French*
ICMM; OCM.
bis, *German*
OCM.
bis, *Latin*
DFWPN.
bisagre, *American Spanish*
DFT.
bisbigliando, *Italian*
ICMM.
bisbigliato, *Italian*
OCM.
bischero, *Italian*
ICMM/*peg.*
biscroma, *Italian*
ICMM/*semiquaver*; OCM.
bise, *French*
DFWPN.
bisnaga, *Spanish*
DFT.
bisque, *French*
DFWPN.
bistecca, *Italian*
DFWPN.
bistro, *French*
DFWPB; DFWPN.
bitte, *German*
DFPCQ; DFT.
bittend, *German*
OCM.
biwa, *Japanese*
ICMM; JLE.
biznaga, *Spanish*
DFT/*bisnaga.*

bizzaro, *Italian*
OCM.
blagodaryu vas, *Russian*
DFPA.
blanc de blancs, *French*
DFWPB.
blanc-de-chine, *French*
ACD/*Tê-hua porcelain.*
blanc-de-Chine, *French*
DFWPB.
blanc fixe, *French*
LP.
blanchailles, *French*
DFT.
blanche, *French*
ICMM; OCM.
blanchir, *French*
DFWPN.
blanc mange, *French*
DFWPN.
blancmange, *Old French*
DFWPB.
blanquette, *French*
DFT; DFWPN.
blasé, *French*
DEP; DFPCQ; DFWPN.
Blaseinstrument, *German*
ICMM.
blasend, stark, *German*
OCM.
Bläser, *German*
DFT.
Blasinstrumente, *German*
OCM.
Blasmusik, *German*
ICMM; OCM.
blat, *Russian*
MRWEW/*18.*
Blaue Reiter, Der, *German*
LP.
Blech, *German*
OCM.
Blechinstrumente, *German*
ICMM.

Blechmusik, *German*
ICMM; OCM.

bleiben, *German*
OCM.

Blende, *German*
GG.

Blini, *Russian*
DFT; DFWPN.

blintz, *Yiddish*
HFY.

Blintze, *German*
DFT.

blintzeh, *Yiddish*
JOY.

blintzes, *Yiddish*
DFWPN.

Blitzkrieg, *German*
DFT; DFWPB; DFWPN.

blocage, *French*
DA.

Blockflöte, *German*
OCM.

blonde de veau, *French*
DFWPN.

bloss, *German*
OCM.

bluette, *French*
ICMM.

Blut und Boden, *German*
DFWPN.

Blut und Eisen, *German*
DFPA; DFPCQ; DFWPB;
DFWPN.

B moll, *German*
ICMM; OCM.

bnai, *Hebrew*
DFWPN.

B'nai B'rith, *Hebrew*
DFPA; DFWPN.

Bnai Brith, *Yiddish*
JOY.

boa noite, *Portuguese*
DFPA.

boa tarde, *Portuguese*
DFPA.

bobbe-myseh, *Yiddish*
JOY.

bobèche, *French*
DFT.

bobeleh, *Yiddish*
JOY / *bubeleh.*

bobkes, *Yiddish*
HFY.

boca, *Spanish*
DFWPN.

bocage, *French*
ACD.

bocal, *French*
ICMM.

bocanne, *French*
GG / *Canadian.*

bocca, *Italian*
GG.

bocca chiusa, *Italian*
ICMM; OCM.

bocca ridente, *Italian*
ICMM.

bocce, *Italian*
DFWPN.

bocchino, *Italian*
ICMM.

boccia, *Italian*
DFWPN.

bocco, *Italian*
ICMM / *bocal.*

boceto, *Spanish*
OCM.

boche, *French*
DFWPN.

Bockbier, *German*
DFWPN.

Bockfeife, *German*
ICMM.

Bodden, *German*
GG.

bodega, *Spanish*
DFWPB; DFWPN.

boeuf, *French*
DFT; DFWPN.

boeuf à la mode, *French*
DFWPN.

Bogen, *German*
DFT; OCM.

Bogenstrich, *German*
OCM/*Strich*; OCM/*Bogen.*

Bohême, *French*
DFWPN.

bohémien, *French*
OCM.

bohémienne, *French*
OCM/*bohémien.*

bois, *French*
DFWPN; OCM.

boisson, *French*
DFWPN.

boîte, *French*
DFWPN; OCM.

bolas, *Spanish*
DFWPN.

bolas *pl.,* *Spanish*
DFWPB.

bolero, *Spanish*
DFT; DFWPN; ICMM.

Bolsheviki, *Russian*
DFWPN.

bolson, *Spanish*
GG.

bombard, *Italian*
OCM.

bombarda, *Italian*
OCM/*bombard.*

bombarde, *Italian*
OCM/*bombard.*

bombardon, *French*
OCM.

bombe, *French*
DFT; DFWPB; DFWPN.

bombé, *French*
ACD; DFWPB.

bombe glacée, *French*
DFWPN.

bombe panachée, *French*
DFT/*bombe.*

bombe surprise, *French*
DFWPB.

bombix, *Greek*
ICMM.

bom dia, *Portuguese*
DFPA; DFT.

bon, *French*
DFT; DFWPN.

Bon, *Japanese*
JLE.

bona, *Latin*
DFWPN.

bonae fidei, *Latin*
DFWPN.

bonae fidei emptor, *Latin*
DFWPN.

bona fide, *Latin*
DEP; DFPA; DFWPN; SPICE.

bonâ fide, *Latin*
DFPCQ.

bona fides, *Latin*
DFT; DFWPN.

bon ami, *French*
DEP; DFPCQ; DFWPN.

bonang, *Javanese*
ICMM.

bonanza, *Spanish*
DFWPN.

bonbon, *French*
DFPCQ; DFWPN.

bonbonnière, *French*
DFT; DFWPB.

bonbonnières, *French*
ACD.

bonditt, *Yiddish*
JOY.

bon goût, *French*
DFPA.

bon gré, mal gré, *French*
DFPA.

bonheur-du-jour, *French*
ACD; DFWPB.

bonhomie, *French*
DEP; DFPCQ; DFT.

boni mores, *Latin*
DFPA.

bonis avibus, *Latin*
DFPA.

bon jour, *French*
DEP; DFWPN.

bonjour, *French*
DFPA; DFT.

bon marché, *French*
DFPA; DFT; DFWPB; DFWPN.

bon mot, *French*
DFPA; DFPCQ; DFT; DFWPN.

bon mot, *pl.* **bons mots,** *French*
DFWPB.

bonne, *French*
DEP.

bonne amie, *French*
DFPA.

bonne année, *French*
DFPA.

bonne bouche, *French*
DFT/*bouche*; DFT.

bonne chance, *French*
DFT.

bonne chance!, *French*
DFPA.

bonne nuit, *French*
DFPA.

bonne santé, *French*
DFPA.

bonnet de nuit, *French*
DFT.

bonsai, *Japanese*
DFT; DFWPB; JLE.

bons dias, *Portuguese*
DFPA.

bon-seki, *Japanese*
JLE.

bon soir, *French*
DEP; DFPA; DFPCQ.

bonsoir, *French*
DFT.

bon temps de la mesure, *French*
ICMM.

bon ton, *French*
DFPA; DFPCQ; DFT; DFWPN.

bonum commune, *Latin*
DFPA.

bonus, *Latin*
DFPCQ.

bon vivant, *French*
DFPA; DFPCQ; DFT; DFWPN.

bon vivant, *pl.* **bons vivants,** *French*
DFWPB.

bon viveur, *French*
DFT.

bon voyage, *French*
DFPCQ; DFT; DFWPB;
DFWPN.

bon voyage!, *French*
DFPA.

bonze, *Japanese*
JLE.

boobe-myseh, *Yiddish*
JOY/*bobbe-myseh*.

boolgoonyakh, *Yakutian*
GG.

bopkes, *Yiddish*
JOY/*bubkes*.

boquilla, *Spanish*
ICMM.

borasca, *Mexican Spanish*
GG.

bordello, *Italian*
DFT.

bordon, falso, *Italian*
ICMM.

bore, *French*
OCM/*bourrée*.

borracho, *Spanish*
DSTE.

borry, *French*
OCM/*bourrée*.

borsch, *Russian*
DFT.

borscht, *Russian*
DFWPN.

borzoi, *Russian*
DFWPN.

Böschung, *German*
GG.

bosquet, *French*
DA.

bossa nova, *Portuguese*
DFWPB.

botón, *Spanish*
DFT.

bouche, *French*
DFT; DFWPN.

bouche bée, *pl.* **bouches bées,** *French*
DFWPB.

bouchée, *French*
DFT; DFWPN.

bouchée aux huîtres, *French*
DFT/*bouchée.*

bouche fermée, *French*
ICMM/*bocca chiusa;* OCM.

bouche fermée, à, *French*
ICMM.

bouche fermée, *pl.* **bouches fermées,**
French
DFWPB.

bouchés, sons, *French*
OCM.

bouclé, *French*
DFWPN.

boudin, *French*
DFT; DFWPN; GG.

boudinage, *French*
GG.

boudin de lièvre, *French*
DFT/*boudin.*

boudiné, *French*
DFT.

boudin noir, *French*
DFT/*boudin.*

boudin ordinaire, *French*
DFT/*boudin.*

boudoir, *French*
DFT; DFWPB; DFWPN.

bouffant, *French*
DFT; DFWPN.

bouffe, *French*
OCM.

bouffes parisiens, *French*
OCM/*bouffe.*

bouffonistes, *French*
OCM.

bouffons, *French*
OCM.

bouffons, guerre des, *French*
ICMM; OCM.

bouillabaisse, *French*
DFT; DFWPB; DFWPN.

bouilli, *French*
DFT; DFWPB; DFWPN.

bouillie, *French*
DFT.

bouillon, *French*
DEP; DFT; DFWPN.

boulanger, *French*
DFWPN.

boulangerie, *French*
DFT.

boule, *French*
GG.

boulette, *French*
DFT.

boulettes de hachis, *French*
DFT/*boulette.*

bouquet d'herbes, *French*
DFWPN.

bouquet garni, *French*
DFWPB.

bouquin, cornet à, *French*
OCM.

bourdon, *French*
OCM.

bourdon de l'orgue, *French*
ICMM.

bourdon de musette, *French*
ICMM.

bourgeois, *French*
DFPCQ.

bourgeois(e), *French*
DFWPN.

Bourgeois Gentilhomme, *French*
DFWPN.

bourgeoisie, *French*
DFPCQ; DFWPN.

Bourgogne, *French*
DFWPN.

bourrée, *French*
ICMM; OCM.

boustrophedon, *Greek*
DFWPB; DFWPN.

boustrophēdon, *Greek*
DFPCQ.

bout, *French*
OCM.

boutade, *French*
ICMM; OCM.

bouteille, *French*
DFWPN.

boutique, *French*
DFWPN.

boutonnière, *French*
DFWPN.

bouts-rimés, *French*
DFT.

boyar, *Russian*
MRWEW/*18.*

boyau, *French*
OCM.

bozzetto, *pl.* **bozzetti,** *Italian*
DFWPB.

braccio, *Italian*
OCM.

brace, *French*
ICMM.

braguero, *Spanish*
DFT.

Brahma, *Sanskrit*
DFWPN.

Brahman, *Sanskrit*
DFWPN.

braisé, *French*
DFWPN.

braisière, *French*
DFWPN.

brandade, *French*
DFT.

brandade de morue, *French*
DFT/*brandade.*

branle, *French*
ICMM; OCM.

bransle, *French*
ICMM/*branle;* OCM/*branle.*

brantle, *French*
OCM.

bras, *French*
LB; OCM.

bras, à deux, *French*
LB.

bras au repos, *French*
LB.

bras bas, *French*
LB/*bras, positions de;* LB.

bras croisé, *French*
LB.

bras de lumière, *French*
ACD.

bras de lumière, *pl.* **bras de lumière,**
French
DFWPB.

bras, demi, *French*
LB.

bras en attitude, *French*
LB.

bras en couronne, *French*
LB.

brasero, *Spanish*
DFT.

bras, positions de, *French*
LB.

brassard, *French*
DFWPN.

Bratsche, *German*
ICMM; OCM.

bratwurst, *German*
DFT.

Brauhaus, *German*
DFWPN.

braul, *French*
OCM.

braule, *French*
OCM/*braul.*

Brautlied, *German*
ICMM; OCM.

brava, *Italian*
DFT.

bravado, *Spanish*
DSTE.

bravissimo, *Italian*
DFT; ICMM.

bravo, *Italian*
DEP; DFPCQ; DFT/*brava;*
ICMM.

bravo, *Spanish*
DSTE.

Bravour Arie, *German*
ICMM.

bravoure, *French*
OCM.

bravura, *Italian*
DFPCQ; DFWPN; ICMM; LP;
OCM.

brea, *Spanish*
GG.

breccia, *Italian*
DA; GG.

brecciola, *Italian*
GG.

breit, *German*
OCM.

bren, *Yiddish*
JOY.

brevet, *French*
DFPCQ.

brevi manu, *Latin*
DFPA.

Brie, *French*
DFWPN.

Brief, *German*
DFPCQ.

Briefmarke, *German*
DFPCQ.

brillant, *French*
OCM.

brillante, *French*
OCM/*brillant.*

brillante, *Italian*
DFPCQ; DFT; ICMM; OCM.

brindis, *Spanish*
DSTE/*236.*

brindisi, *Italian*
ICMM; OCM.

brio, *Italian*
DFT; DFWPB; DFWPN;
ICMM; OCM.

brioche, *French*
DFT; DFWPB; DFWPN.

bris, *Yiddish*
HFY; JOY/*brith.*

brisé, *French*
DFWPB; DFWPN; OCM.

brisé dessous, *French*
LB/*brisé, pas.*

brisé dessus, *French*
LB/*brisé, pas.*

brisée, *French*
ICMM/*turn.*

brisé, pas, *French*
LB.

brise-soleil, *French*
DA.

brisé télémaque, *French*
LB/*brisé volé, pas.*

brisé volé, *French*
DFWPB.

brisé volé en arrière, *French*
LB/*brisé volé, pas.*

brisé volé en avant, *French*
LB/*brisé volé, pas.*

brisé volé, pas, *French*
LB.

brith, *Yiddish*
JOY.

broche, *French*
DFT.

broche, *Yiddish*
JOY.

brochet, *French*
DFT.

brochette, *French*
DFT; DFWPN.

broderie à jour, *French*
DFT.

broderies, *French*
ICMM/*ornaments*; ICMM.

broletto, *Italian*
DA.

bronco, *Spanish*
DSTE.

brouillé, *French*
DFWPN.

(die) Brücke, *German*
DFWPB.

Brucke, Die, *German*
LP.

brûlé, *fem.* **brûlée,** *French*
DFWPB.

brûle-parfums, *pl.* **brûle-parfums,**
French
DFWPB.

brume, *French*
OCM.

Brummeisen, *German*
OCM.

Brummscheit, *German*
OCM.

brunette, *French*
ICMM.

bruscamente, *Italian*
OCM.

Brustwerk, *German*
OCM.

brut, *French*
DFT; DFWPB; DFWPN.

bu, *Japanese*
JLE.

bubbe, *Yiddish*
HFY.

bubbe-mayse, *Yiddish*
HFY.

bubee, *Yiddish*
HFY/*bubeleh*; JOY.

bubeleh, *Yiddish*
HFY; JOY.

bubkes, *Yiddish*
JOY.

buccina, *Italian*
ICMM.

buccolico, *Italian*
OCM.

Buchhandel, *German*
DFWPN.

bucolicum, *Latin*
DFWPN.

buée, *French*
OCM.

buena salud, *Spanish*
DSTE.

buenas noches, *Spanish*
DFPA; DFT.

buenas tardes, *Spanish*
DFPA; DFWPN.

buena suerte!, *Spanish*
DFPA.

buenos días, *Spanish*
DFPA; DFT; DFWPN.

buffa, *Italian*
OCM/*buffo*; OCM.

buffet d'orgue, *French*
OCM.

buffo, *Italian*
DFPCQ; DFT; DFWPB;
DFWPN; ICMM; OCM.

buffon, *French*
DFWPN.

buffone, *Italian*
ICMM.

buffonescamente, *Italian*
ICMM.

buffonesco, *Italian*
OCM.

Bugaku, *Japanese*
JLE.

Bügelhorn, *German*
OCM.

bugle à clefs, *French*
OCM/*bugle.*

bugle à pistons, *French*
OCM/*bugle.*

bugor, *Russian*
GG.

Buhaiu, *Rumanian*
OCM.

Bühnenfestspiel, *German*
OCM.

Bühnenweihfestspiel, *German*
OCM/*Bühnenfestspiel.*

Buké, *Japanese*
JLE.

buksheesh, *Anglo-Indian*
DFT/*bukshish.*

bukshish, *Anglo-Indian*
DFT.

bulba, *Yiddish*
JOY.

bulbanik, *Yiddish*
HFY.

bulbenik, *Yiddish*
JOY.

bulvan, *Yiddish*
JOY/*bulvon.*

bulvon, *Yiddish*
JOY.

Bund, *German*
DFWPN.

Bundesrat, *German*
DFWPN.

Bundesrepublik, *German*
DFWPN.

Bundestag, *German*
DFWPN.

Bundfrei, *German*
OCM.

Bunraku, *Japanese*
JLE.

buonaccordo, *Italian*
ICMM.

buona notte, *Italian*
DFPA; DFWPN.

buona sera, *Italian*
DFWPN.

buon fresco, *Italian*
DFWPB; LP; LP/*fresco.*

buon giorno, *Italian*
DFPA.

buon giórno, *Italian*
DFWPN.

Buon Natale, *Italian*
DFPA.

buraku, *Japanese*
JLE.

burakumin, *Japanese*
JLE.

Burg, *German*
DFWPN.

Bürgermeister, *German*
DFWPN.

burla, *Italian*
ICMM; OCM.

burlesca, *Italian*
ICMM/*burla*; OCM/*burla*; OCM/*burlesco.*

burlesco, *Italian*
OCM; OCM/*burla*:

burletta, *Italian*
DFT; DFWPN; ICMM; OCM/*burla*; OCM.

Burozem, *Russian*
GG.

burro, *Italian*
DFWPN.

burro, *Spanish*
DFWPB; DFWPN; DSTE.

burtchen, *Yiddish*
JOY.

bushido, *Japanese*
  JLE.
busna, *Italian*
  ICMM.
Butsu, *Japanese*
  JLE.
butsudan, *Japanese*
  JLE.
butte, *French*
  GG.
butte témoin, *French*
  GG.

buxum, *Latin*
  ICMM.
buxus, *Latin*
  ICMM.
buysine, *French*
  OCM.
bwana, *Swahili*
  DFT; DFWPB.
byōbu, *Japanese*
  JLE.

C

cabala, *Yiddish*
JOY.

cabaletta, *Italian*
DFT; DFWPN; ICMM; OCM.

caballad, *Spanish*
DFT/*caballada*.

caballada, *Spanish*
DFT.

caballero, *Spanish*
DFPCQ; DFT; DFWPN; DSTE.

caballo, *Spanish*
DFWPN; DSTE.

cabaña, *Spanish*
DA; DFWPN; DSTE.

cabaret, *French*
DFWPN.

cabbalah, *Yiddish*
JOY/*cabala*.

cabbaletta, *Italian*
OCM/*cabaletta*.

cabestro, *Spanish*
DFT.

cabeza, *Spanish*
DFWPN.

cabillaud, *French*
DFT.

cabillaud farci, *French*
DFT/*cabillaud*.

cabinet d'aisance, *French*
DFPA.

cabochon, *French*
ACD; DFT; GG.

cabrette, *French*
OCM.

cabriole, *French*
ACD; DFT; DFWPB; DFWPN;
LB.

cabriole à la seconde, *French*
LB/*cabriole*.

cabriole derrière, *French*
LB/*cabriole*.

cabriole devant, *French*
LB/*cabriole*.

cabriole fermée, *French*
LB/*cabriole*.

cabriole fouetté, *French*
LB/*cabriole*.

cabriole italienne, *French*
LB/*cabriole*.

cabriole ouverte, *French*
LB/*cabriole*.

caccia, *Italian*
DFT; ICMM; OCM.

cacciatore, *Italian*
DFT; DFWPN.

cachepot, *French*
DFT.

cachet, *French*
DFT.

cachuca, *Spanish*
DFWPN.

cachucha, *Spanish*
ICMM; OCM.

cacique, *Spanish*
DSTE.

cacoëthes, *Latin*
DFT.

cacoethes carpendi, *Latin*
DFPA.

cacoëthes carpendi, *Latin*
DFT/*cacoëthes*.

cacoethes loquendi, *Latin*
DFPA.

cacoëthes loquendi, *Latin*
DFT/*cacoëthes*.

cacoethes scribendi, *Latin*
DFPA; DEP.

cacoëthes scribendi, *Latin*
DFT/*cacoëthes*.

cadence, *French*
ICMM.

cadenza, *Italian*
DFPCQ; DFWPB; DFWPN;
OCM.

cadenza d'inganno, *Italian*
DFT; DFT/*inganno*.

cadenzato, *Italian*
OCM.

cadit quaestio, *Latin*
DFPA.

cadre, *French*
DFWPN.

caduceus, *Latin*
DFWPN.

caeca est invidia, *Latin*
DFPCQ.

caecum, *Latin*
DFPCQ.

caeteris paribus, *Latin*
DFPCQ; DFT.

café, *French*
DFT; DFWPN.

café au lait, *French*
DFPA; DFT/*café*; DFWPB;
DFWPN.

café filtre, *French*
DFWPB.

café noir, *French*
DFT/*café*; DFWPB; DFWPN.

Caffaggiolo, *Italian*
ACD.

caffè espresso, *Italian*
DFWPN.

cagnotte, *French*
DFT; DFWPB.

cahier, *French*
OCM.

cahier de chant, *French*
ICMM.

cahier de musique, *French*
ICMM.

caille, *French*
DFT.

cailles au truffes, *French*
DFT/*caille*.

ça ira, *French*
OCM.

caisse, *French*
ICMM; OCM.

caisse claire, *French*
OCM.

caisse grosse, *French*
OCM.

caisse plate, *French*
OCM.

caisse roulante, *French*
OCM.

caisse sourde, *French*
OCM.

cajon, *Spanish*
GG.

cala, *Spanish*
GG.

calabozo, *Spanish*
DSTE.

calamaro, *Italian*
DFT.

calando, *Italian*
DFPCQ; DFT; DFWPN; ICMM;
OCM.

calanque, *French*
GG.

calata, *Italian*
ICMM.

calcaire-grossière, *French*
DA.

calcando, *Italian*
OCM.

calendae, *Latin*
DFWPN.

caleta, *Spanish*
GG.

caliche, *American Spanish*
GG.

caliente, *Spanish*
DFWPN.

caliph, *Arabic*
DFWPN.

calmando, *Italian*
OCM/*calmato.*

calmato, *Italian*
DFT; DFWPN; OCM.

calme, *French*
OCM.

calore, *Italian*
OCM.

caloroso, *Italian*
DFT; DFWPN.

Calvados, *French*
DFWPN.

cam, *German*
GG.

camaïeu, *French*
DFT; LP.

camaraderie, *French*
DFWPN.

camarón, *Spanish*
DFT.

cambiare, *Italian*
OCM.

cambré, *French*
LB.

camera, *Italian*
DFPCQ; ICMM; OCM.

camera lucida, *Latin*
DFWPB; DFWPN; LP.

camera obscura, *Latin*
DFWPB; DFWPN; LP.

camino real, *Spanish*
DSTE.

camminando, *Italian*
OCM.

campagna, *Italian*
GG.

campana, *Italian*
ICMM; OCM.

campane, *Italian*
OCM/*campana.*

campanella, *Italian*
ICMM; OCM.

campanetta, *Italian*
ICMM; OCM.

campanile, *Italian*
DFWPN.

campo santo, *Spanish*
DSTE.

campus, *Latin*
DFWPN.

Campus Martius, *Latin*
DEP.

cañada, *Spanish*
DFT; GG.

canaigre, *Mexican Spanish*
DFT.

canapé, *French*
ACD; DFT; DFWPB; DFWPN.

canard, *French*
DFPCQ; DFT; DFWPN.

canard sauvage, *French*
DFT/*canard.*

canarie, *French*
ICMM.

canary, *Yiddish*
HFY.

cancan, *French*
ICMM.

cancion, *Spanish*
ICMM.

canción, *Spanish*
OCM.

cancrizans, *Latin*
ICMM.

cancrizante, *Italian*
ICMM.

candela, *Spanish*
GG.

candelia, *Spanish*
DFT.

caneton, *French*
DFT; DFWPN.

canne-de-roche, *French*
DFT.

cannelé, *French*
DFT.

cannelloni, *pl.*, *Italian*
DFWPB.

cannelon, *French*
DFT; DFWPN.

canon, *French*
OCM/*canon*.

cañon, *American Spanish*
GG.

cañon, *Spanish*
DFWPB; DSTE.

cañón, *Spanish*
DFWPN.

cañoncito, *Spanish*
DFT.

canone, *Italian*
DFPCQ; OCM/*canon*.

cantabile, *Italian*
DFPCQ; DFT; DFWPB;
DFWPN; ICMM; OCM.

Cantabrigiensis, *Latin*
DFPA/*cantab.*.

cantadour, *French*
ICMM.

cantando, *Italian*
DFT; OCM.

cantante, basso, *Italian*
OCM.

cantare a aria, *Italian*
ICMM.

cantata, *Italian*
DFPCQ; DFWPB; DFWPN;
ICMM; OCM.

cantate, *French*
OCM.

Cantate, *German*
OCM.

cantate Domino, *Latin*
DEP.

cantatore, *Italian*
DFT; ICMM.

cantatrice, *Italian*
DFT; DFWPB; ICMM; OCM.

cante flamenco, *Spanish*
OCM.

cante hondo, *Spanish*
ICMM; OCM.

canti carnascialeschi, *Italian*
OCM.

canticum, *Latin*
ICMM.

canti di carnivali, *Italian*
ICMM.

cantiga, *Spanish*
OCM.

cantilena, *Italian*
DFPCQ; DFT; DFWPB.

cantilena, *Latin*
ICMM.

cantilenare, *Italian*
ICMM.

cantilenas vulgares, *Spanish*
OCM.

cantilène, *French*
OCM.

87   **capo**

cantillatio, *Latin*
DFT; ICMM.

cantina, *Spanish*
DFT; DSTE.

cantino, *Italian*
ICMM.

cantiones sacrae, *Latin*
ICMM; OCM.

cantique, *French*
ICMM.

canto, *Italian*
DFPCQ; DFWPB; ICMM/*treble*;
ICMM; OCM.

canto armonio, *Italian*
ICMM.

canto fermo, *Italian*
OCM.

canto fermo, *pl.* canti fermi, *Italian*
DFWPB.

canto primo, *Italian*
ICMM.

canto recitativo, *Italian*
ICMM.

canto ripiendo, *Italian*
ICMM.

cantoris, *Latin*
DFT; OCM.

cantus, *Latin*
OCM.

cantus choralis, *Latin*
OCM.

cantus fictus, *Latin*
ICMM; OCM.

cantus figuratus, *Latin*
ICMM; OCM.

cantus firmus, *Latin*
ICMM; OCM.

cantus firmus, *New Latin*
DFT.

cantus fractus, *Latin*
ICMM.

cantus gregorianus, *Latin*
ICMM.

cantus mensurabilis, *Latin*
ICMM.

cantus mensuratus, *Latin*
OCM.

cantus planus, *Latin*
DFPA; ICMM; OCM.

cantus planus, *New Latin*
DFT.

canu penillion, *Welsh*
OCM.

canzona, *Italian*
OCM.

canzone, *Italian*
DFPCQ; DFT; DFWPN; ICMM;
OCM/*canzona*.

canzonetta, *Italian*
DFPCQ; ICMM; OCM/*canzonet*.

canzoni, *Italian*
OCM/*canzona*.

caoine, *Irish*
OCM.

capa, *Spanish*
DSTE/*237*.

cap à pie(d), *French*
DFWPN.

cap-a-pié, *Old French*
DFWPB.

cap-à-pie, *French*
DFPA; DFPCQ.

capella, *Italian*
DFPCQ; OCM/*cappella*.

Capelle, *German*
ICMM; OCM.

Capellmeister, *German*
OCM/*Capelle*.

Capellmeistermusik, *German*
OCM/*Capelle*.

capias, *Latin*
DFPA.

capitan, *Spanish*
DSTE.

capo, *Italian*
DFPCQ; DFWPN; ICMM;
OCM.

Capodaster, *German*
OCM/*capotasto*.

capodastère, *French*
OCM/*capotasto*.

capo d'astro, *Italian*
OCM/*capotasto*.

capodastro, *Italian*
OCM/*capotasto*.

Capo-di-Monte, *Italian*
ACD.

capo di tutti capi, *Italian*
DFT/*capo*.

caporal, *Spanish*
DFT; DSTE.

capotasto, *Italian*
DFT; ICMM; OCM.

capote, *Spanish*
DSTE/*237*.

cappella, *Italian*
OCM.

cappuccino, *Italian*
DFWPB.

câpre, *French*
DFT.

capriccio, *Italian*
DFPCQ; DFT; DFWPB;
DFWPN; ICMM; OCM.

capriccioso, *Italian*
DFPCQ; DFT; DFWPN; ICMM;
OCM.

capricieux, *French*
OCM/*capriccioso*.

caput, *Latin*
DEP; DFWPN.

caput mortuum, *Latin*
LP.

Caput Mundi, *Latin*
DFWPN; DFPA.

caquetoire, *French*
ACD.

cara, *Latin*
DFWPN.

cara, *Spanish*
DFWPN.

caracol, *French*
DA.

caractère, *French*
DFWPB.

caractère, danse de, *French*
LB.

carafe, *French*
DFWPN.

caramba, *Spanish*
DFT.

caramillo, *Spanish*
ICMM.

cara sposa, *Italian*
DFPCQ.

carattere, mezzo, *Italian*
ICMM.

carbonari, *Italian*
DEP.

carcelera, *Spanish*
OCM.

carciofi, *Italian*
DFWPN.

caressant, *French*
OCM.

caret, *Latin*
DFPCQ.

carezzando, *Italian*
OCM.

carezzevole, *Italian*
OCM/*carezzando*.

caries, *Latin*
DFPCQ.

carillon, *French*
OCM.

carillon à clavier, *French*
ICMM.

carillonneur, *French*
ICMM.

carisima, *Spanish*
DSTE.

carissima, *Italian*
DFWPN.

carità, *Italian*
DFT.

caritas, *Latin*
DFWPB.

carmagnole, *French*
ICMM.

carmagnole, *Italian*
OCM.

carmen, *Latin*
DFWPN; ICMM; OCM.

carne, *Italian*
DFWPN.

carne, *Spanish*
DFT.

carne de vaca, *Spanish*
DFT/*carne.*

carnero, *Spanish*
DFT.

caro, *Italian*
DFWPN.

carotte, *French*
DFT.

carpe diem, *Latin*
DEP; DFPCQ; DFT; DFWPB;
DFWPN.

carré, *French*
DFT.

carrée, *French*
ICMM; OCM.

carré, en, *French*
LB.

carrelet, *French*
DFT.

carta, *Latin*
DFWPN.

carte, *French*
DFPCQ; DFT.

carte blanche, *French*
DFPA; DFPCQ; DFT/*carte*;
DFWPB; DFWPN; SPICE.

carte de visite, *French*
DEP.

carte du jour, *French*
DFT/*carte.*

carte du vins [*sic*], *French*
DFT/*carte.*

cartel, *French*
DFPCQ; DFWPN.

cartellino, *pl.* **cartellini,** *Italian*
DFWPB.

Carthago delenda est, *Latin*
DFWPN.

carton pierre, *French*
DA.

cartouche, *French*
ACD; DFWPN; LP.

carus, *Latin*
DFWPN.

casa, *Italian*
DA; DFT.

casa, *Portuguese*
DFT.

casa, *Spanish*
DFT; DFWPN.

casa grande, *Spanish*
DSTE.

cascajo, *Spanish*
GG.

cascalho, *Portuguese*
GG.

casino, *Italian*
DFPCQ.

cassa, *Italian*
OCM.

cassa grande, *Italian*
ICMM; OCM.

cassa rullante, *Italian*
OCM.

Cassation, *German*
OCM/*Kassation.*

cassazione, *Italian*
OCM.

cassis, *French*
DFWPB.

cassone, *Italian*
ACD.

cassone, *pl.* **cassoni,** *Italian*
DFWPB.

castagnette, *Italian*
OCM.

castagnettes, *Italian*
OCM.

castañeta, *Spanish*
DFWPN.

Castelli, *Italian*
ACD.

castillane, *Spanish*
OCM.

castrati, *Italian*
DFWPN.

castrato, *Italian*
ICMM; OCM.

castrato, *pl.* **castrati,** *Italian*
DFWPB.

casus, *Latin*
DFWPN.

casus belli, *Latin*
DEP; DFPA; DFPCQ; DFT/
casus; DFWPB; DFWPN.

casus conscientiæ, *Latin*
DEP.

casus foederis, *Latin*
DFWPN.

casus fortuitus, *Latin*
DFPA.

catabasis, *Greek*
DFWPN.

catachresis, *Greek*
DFWPN.

catalán, *Spanish*
OCM.

catalane, *French*
OCM.

catalecta, *Greek*
DFWPN.

catalogue raisonné, *French*
DEP; DFPA; DFT; DFWPN.

catēgorēma, *Greek*
DFPCQ.

catexochen, *Greek*
DFT.

cathedra, *Latin*
DFWPN.

cattivo tempo, *Italian*
ICMM.

cauda, *Latin*
ICMM.

caudillo, *Spanish*
DFWPN.

causa, *Latin*
DFWPN.

causa causans, *Latin*
DFPCQ; DFT/*causa*; DFWPN.

causa causata, *Latin*
DFT/*causa*.

causa efficiens, *Latin*
DFWPN.

causa finalis, *Latin*
DFPA.

causa formalis, *Latin*
DFWPN.

causa materialis, *Latin*
DFWPN.

causa mortis, *Latin*
DFWPN.

causa proxima, *Latin*
DFWPN.

causa sine qua non, *Latin*
DFWPN.

causa sui, *Latin*
DFWPN.

cause célèbre, *French*
DFPA; DFPCQ; DFT; DFWPB;
DFWPN.

causeuse, *French*
ACD; DFT.

causse, *French*
GG.

ça va, *French*
DFWPN.

cavalier, *French*
LB.

cavalquet, *French*
ICMM.

ça va sans dire, *French*
DFWPN.

cavata, *Italian*
ICMM.

cavatina, *Italian*
DFPCQ; DFT; DFWPB; ICMM;
OCM.

caveat, *Latin*
DFPCQ; DFT; DFWPB;
DFWPN.

caveat actor, *Latin*
DFT/*caveat*; DFWPN.

caveat emptor, *Latin*
DFPA; DFPCQ; DFT/*caveat*;
DFWPB; DFWPN.

caveat venditor, *Latin*
DFPA; DFWPN.

caveat viator, *Latin*
DFT/*caveat*; DFWPN.

cave canem, *Latin*
DFPA; DFPCQ; DFT; DFWPN.

cavendo tutus, *Latin*
DEP.

cave quid dicis, quando, et cui, *Latin*
DEP.

cavetto, *Italian*
DFT.

cavo rilievo, *Italian*
DFWPB.

cavo-rilievo, *Italian*
DA; DFT.

cay, *Spanish*
GG.

cayo, *Spanish*
DFT.

cazo, *Spanish*
DFT.

C dur, *German*
ICMM.

céad míle fáilte, *Irish*
DFWPB.

céad míle fáilte!, *Irish*
DFPA.

cede Deo, *Latin*
DEP.

cédez, *French*
OCM.

ceilidh, *Scottish*
OCM.

ceja, *Spanish*
DFT; GG.

cela va sans dire, *French*
DFPCQ; DFWPN.

celere, *Italian*
OCM.

céleri, *French*
DFT.

celesta, *Italian*
OCM.

celeste, *Italian*
DFWPN.

céleste, *French*
OCM.

cellarino, *Italian*
DA.

celour, *French*
ACD.

cembalist, *Italian*
OCM.

cembalo, *Italian*
DFPCQ; DFT; DFWPN; OCM.

cembalo d'amore, *Italian*
OCM/*amore, amour.*

cencerro, *Spanish*
DFT.

cenote, *Mayan*
GG.

cenote, *Spanish*
DFT.

censor deputatus, *Latin*
DFPA.

censor morum, *Latin*
DFPCQ.

centavo, *Spanish*
DFWPN.

centime, *French*
DFWPN.

centon, *French*
OCM/*cento.*

centon, *Latin* [*sic*]
DFWPN.

centone, *Italian*
OCM/*cento.*

centone, *Latin* [*sic*]
ICMM.

central, *American Spanish*
DFT.

centum, *Latin*
DEP; DFWPN.

ceòl beag, *Scottish*
OCM.

ceòl meadhonach, *Scottish*
OCM.

ceòl mór, *Scottish*
OCM.

cepi corpus, *Latin*
DFPA.

cequia, *Spanish*
DSTE; DSTE/*acequia.*

cercar la nota, *Italian*
ICMM.

cerdana, *Spanish*
ICMM.

cerise, *French*
DFT; DFWPN.

certiorari, *Latin*
DEP; DFPA; DFWPN.

certosa, *Italian*
DA.

cervelas, *French*
OCM.

cervelle, *French*
DFT.

cervelles de veau en brochette,
French
DFT/*cervelle.*

Ces, *German*
ICMM; OCM.

C eses, *German*
OCM.

cesta, *Spanish*
DFWPN.

c'est à dire, *French*
DFPA; DFPCQ; DFWPN.

c'est-à-dire, *French*
DFT.

c'est ça, *French*
DFPA.

c'est dommage, *French*
DFPA; DFWPN.

c'est la guerre, *French*
DFPA; DFT; DFWPB.

c'est la vie, *French*
DFPA; DFWPB; DFWPN.

cetera, *Italian*
OCM.

ceteris paribus, *Latin*
DFPA; DFT; DFWPN.

cetra, *Italian*
ICMM.

cha, *Chinese*
DFT.

chacham, *Yiddish*
JOY/*chachem.*

chachem, *Yiddish*
DFT; JOY.

chachma, *Yiddish*
JOY.

chaconne, *French*
ICMM; OCM.

chacun à son goût, *French*
DFPA; DFPCQ; DFT; DFWPB;
DFWPN.

chadai, *Japanese*
JLE.

Chaim Yankel, *Yiddish*
HFY; JOY.

chaînés, tours, *French*
LB.

chairĕ, *Greek*
DFPCQ.

chaise longue, *French*
DFPA; DFT; DFWPN.

chaise-longue, *French*
DFWPB.

chalchihuitl, *Spanish*
GG.

chalepa ta kala, *Greek*
DFPCQ.

châlet, *French*
DFWPN.

chaleur, *French*
OCM.

chalil, *Hebrew*
ICMM.

chalileh, *Yiddish*
JOY / *cholilleh.*

challa, *Yiddish*
DFT; JOY.

challeh, *Yiddish*
JOY / *challa.*

chaloshes, *Yiddish*
JOY.

chalumeau, *French*
ICMM / *scialumo;* ICMM; OCM.

chalutz, *Yiddish*
JOY.

chalutzim, *Yiddish*
JOY / *chalutz.*

chamaco, *Spanish*
DSTE.

chambranle, *French*
DFT.

chambré, *French*
DFT; DFWPB.

chamisal, *American Spanish*
DFT.

champêtre, *French*
OCM.

champignon, *French*
DFT; DFWPN.

champlevé, *French*
ACD / *enamel;* DA; DFT.

Champville, *French*
DA.

changement battu, *French*
LB.

changement de pieds, *French*
LB.

changer de pied, *French*
LB.

changer, sans, *French*
LB.

changez, *French*
OCM.

Channukah, *Yiddish*
JOY / *Chanukah.*

chanoyu, *Japanese*
JLE.

chanson, *French*
DFWPN; ICMM; OCM.

chanson de geste, *French*
DFPA.

chanson des rues, *French*
ICMM.

chansonnette, *French*
ICMM.

chansonnier, *French*
DFWPN; ICMM.

chanson sans paroles, *French*
OCM.

chansons de geste, *French*
ICMM; OCM.

chansons de toile, *French*
DFPA.

chantant, *French*
OCM.

chanterelle, *French*
DFT; ICMM; OCM.

chanterres, *French*
ICMM.

chant funèbre, *French*
ICMM.

chantre, *French*
ICMM.

chant sacré, *French*
ICMM.

Chanukah, *Yiddish*
JOY.

chaori, *Hindi*
DA.

chapa, *Spanish*
DFT.

chaparejos, *Spanish*
DSTE.

chaparral, *Spanish*
DSTE.

chapeau chinois, *French*
ICMM.

chapeau de fer, *French*
GG.

chapeiro, *Portuguese*
GG.

chapelle, *French*
ICMM.

chapelle, maître de, *French*
ICMM.

chapon, *French*
DFT.

chaque, *French*
OCM.

char, *Hindi*
GG.

Charakterstück, *German*
OCM.

charbonnier, *French*
DFT.

charco, *Spanish*
DFT; GG.

charcuterie, *French*
DFT; DFWPB; DFWPN.

charcutier, *French*
DFT.

chargé(e), *French*
DFWPN.

chargé d'affaires, *French*
DFPA; DFPCQ; DFWPN.

chargé d'affaires, *pl.* chargés
d'affaires, *French*
DFWPB.

charger, se, *French*
OCM.

charivari, *French*
ICMM; OCM.

charlatan, *French*
DFPCQ.

charley, *Yiddish*
HFY.

charmante, *French*
DEP.

charpoy, *Anglo-Hindi*
DFT.

charpoy, *Anglo-Indian*
DFT.

charqui, *Spanish*
DFT.

charrette, *French*
DA.

charro, *Spanish*
DSTE.

charta, *Latin*
DFWPN.

Chartreuse, *French*
DFWPN.

chashitshu, *Japanese*
JLE.

Chasid, *Yiddish*
HFY; JOY.

Chasidim, *Yiddish*
JOY/*Chasid.*

chasse, *French*
DFT; ICMM.

chassé, *French*
DFT; DFWPB; DFWPN; LB/
chassé, pas; OCM.

chasse-café, *French*
DFT/*chasse.*

chasse, cor de, *French*
OCM.

chasse-cousins, *French*
DFT.

chassé croisé, *French*
DFWPN.

chassé-croisé, *French*
DFWPB.

chassée, *French*
LB/*chassé, pas.*

chassé en tournant, *French*
LB/*chassé, pas.*

chassen, *Yiddish*
JOY.

chasseneh, *Yiddish*
JOY.

chassé, pas, *French*
LB.

chassé passé en avant, *French*
LB/*chassé, pas.*

chassis, *French*
DFWPN.

chas vesholem, *Yiddish*
JOY.

château, *French*
DA; DFPCQ; DFT; DFWPN.

château, *pl.* châteaux, *French*
DFWPB.

châteaubriant, *French*
DFT.

château d'eau, *French*
DA.

chatelaine, *French*
ACD.

chatoyance, *French*
DFWPB.

chatoyant, *French*
DFT; DFWPB.

chatri, *Hindi*
DA.

chaud-froid, *French*
DFWPB; DFWPN.

chaudière, *French*
DFT.

chaudron, *French*
DFT.

chaussen, *Yiddish*
JOY/*chassen.*

chaver, *Yiddish*
JOY.

chazzen, *Yiddish*
JOY.

chazzer, *Yiddish*
JOY/*chozzer.*

chazzonim, *Yiddish*
JOY/*chazzen.*

che, *Italian*
OCM.

cheder, *Yiddish*
JOY.

chef d'attaque, *French*
ICMM; OCM.

chef de bataillon, *French*
DEP.

chef de cabinet, *French*
DFWPN.

chef de cuisine, *French*
DEP; DFPA; DFPCQ; DFT/*chef.*

chef d'oeuvre, *French*
DFPA; DFWPN.

chef-d'oeuvre, *French*
DFPCQ; DFT; LP.

chef d'oeuvre, *pl.* chefs d'oeuvre,
French
DFWPB.

chef-d'œuvre, *French*
DEP.

chef d'orchestre, *French*
DFT; ICMM.

Chelm, *Yiddish*
JOY.

cheneau, *French*
DA.

cheng, *Chinese*
ICMM; OCM.

chenier, *French*
GG.

cheppeh, *Yiddish*
JOY/*tcheppeh.*

cher, *French*
DFWPN.

cherchez la femme, *French*
DFPA; DFT; DFWPB; DFWPN.

chère amie, *French*
DEP; DFPA.

chéri, *fem.* chérie, *French*
DFWPB.

chérie, *French*
DFWPN.

Chernozem, *Russian*
GG.

che sarà sarà, *Italian*
DFPA; DFPCQ; DFT; DFWPN.

che sarà, sarà, *Italian*
DFWPB.

cheval, *French*
ACD.

chevalet, *French*
ICMM; OCM.

chevalier, *French*
DFPCQ.

chevaux, *French*
DA.

chevet, *French*
DA.

cheville, *French*
ICMM; ICMM/*peg*; OCM.

chevra, *Yiddish*
JOY.

chevrette, *French*
OCM.

chevreuil, *French*
DFT.

chevrotement, *French*
ICMM.

chez, *French*
DFWPB; DFWPN.

chianti, *Italian*
DFWPN.

chiao-tou, *Chinese*
ACD.

chiara, *Italian*
OCM/*chiaro.*

chiarentana, *Italian*
ICMM.

chiarezza, *Italian*
DFT.

chiarezza, con, *Italian*
ICMM.

chiarina, *Italian*
ICMM.

chiaro, *Italian*
OCM.

chiaroscuro, *Italian*
DEP; DFPCQ; DFT; DFWPB;
DFWPN; LP.

chiasmus, *Greek*
DFWPN.

chiasso, *Italian*
OCM.

chiave, *Italian*
OCM.

chiave maestro, *Italian*
ICMM.

chiavette, *Italian*
ICMM.

chiavi, *Italian*
ICMM.

chiavi trasportate, *Italian*
ICMM/*chiavette.*

Chiba, *Japanese*
JLE.

chic, *French*
DFWPN.

chica, *Spanish*
OCM.

chicalote, *Spanish*
DFT.

chicane, *French*
DFWPN.

chicle, *Spanish*
DSTE.

chico, *Spanish*
DSTE.

chicote, *Spanish*
DFT.

chiesa, *Italian*
ICMM; OCM.

chiffadera, *Spanish*
ICMM.

chiffonier [*sic*], *French*
ACD.

chiffonière [*sic*], *French*
ACD.

chiffonnier, *French*
DFT.

chiffonnier/chiffonnière, *French*
DFWPB.

chiffré, *French*
DFT.

chifonie, *French*
OCM.

-chik, *Yiddish*
HFY/*boychik*.

chile, *Spanish*
DSTE.

chile con carne, *Spanish*
DFT; DFWPN.

chili, *Spanish*
DSTE/*chile*.

chillul ha-shem, *Yiddish*
JOY/*chillul hashem*.

chillul hashem, *Yiddish*
JOY.

ch'in, *Chinese*
ICMM.

chinchilla, *Spanish*
DSTE.

Chinoiserie, *French*
LP; ACD; DFWPB.

chinor, *Hebrew*
ICMM.

chiquito, *Spanish*
DSTE.

chirimia, *Spanish*
ICMM.

chitarra, *Italian*
ICMM.

chitarra coll' arco, *Italian*
ICMM.

chitarrina, *Italian*
ICMM.

chitarrista, *Italian*
ICMM.

chitarrone, *Italian*
ICMM; OCM.

chittarone, *Italian*
OCM/*chitarrone*.

chiusa, *Italian*
OCM.

chiuso, *Italian*
OCM.

chivarras, *Mexican Spanish*
DFT.

chivarros, *Mexican Spanish*
DFT/*chivarras*.

chloppeh, *Yiddish*
JOY.

chmallyeh, *Yiddish*
JOY.

cho, *Japanese*
JLE.

chœur, *French*
OCM.

choleria, *Yiddish*
JOY.

cholilleh, *Yiddish*
JOY.

chometzdik, *Yiddish*
JOY.

chonin, *Japanese*
JLE.

Choral, *German*
OCM/*chorale*.

chorale partita, *Italian*
OCM.

choralmässig, *German*
ICMM.

Choral Vorspiel, *German*
OCM.

Chor-amt, *German*
ICMM.

choraulos, *Greek*
ICMM.

Chorbuch, *German*
ICMM.

chorda, *Latin*
ICMM.

chord a vido, *Italian*
ICMM.

choregraphe, *French*
LB.

choregraphie, *French*
LB.

chorikus, *Greek*
ICMM.

Chormässige Stimmung, *German*
OCM.

chorogi, *Japanese*
JLE.

choros, *Portuguese*
ICMM.

Chorstimmung, *German*
OCM.

Chorton, *German*
ICMM; OCM.

Chor Zinck, *German*
OCM.

chose, *French*
DFWPN.

Chosenese, *Japanese*
JLE.

chossen, *Yiddish*
JOY/*chassen.*

chotchke, *Yiddish*
JOY.

chotchkeleh, *Yiddish*
JOY/*chotchke.*

chou, *French*
DFT; DFWPN.

choucroute, *French*
DFT.

chou-fleur, *French*
DFWPN.

choufleur, *French*
DFT.

chou marin, *French*
DFT/*chou.*

choux de Bruxelles, *French*
DFT/*chou.*

chow fan, *Chinese*
DFT.

chozzer, *Yiddish*
JOY.

chozzerai, *Yiddish*
JOY.

Christe eleison, *Greek*
ICMM.

chromatique, *French*
OCM.

chromophonie, *French*
OCM.

chronique scandaleuse, *French*
DFPA.

chu, *Japanese*
JLE.

chuco, *Spanish*
GG.

chüeh, *Chinese*
ACD.

chulo, *Spanish*
DSTE/*237.*

chuppa, *Yiddish*
JOY.

chuppah, *Yiddish*
JOY/*chuppa.*

churrasco, *Spanish*
DFT.

chute, *French*
ICMM.

chutspa, *Yiddish*
JOY/*chutzpa.*

chutzpa, *Yiddish*
DFWPN; HFY; JOY.

chutzpadik, *Yiddish*
JOY/*chutzpa.*

chutzpah, *Hebrew*
DFT.

ciaccona, *Italian*
OCM.

ciao, *Italian*
DFT; DFWPB.

cicatrix, *Latin*
DFPCQ.

cicerone, *Italian*
DEP; DFPCQ; DFT; DFWPB;
DFWPN.

ci-devant, *French*
DEP; DFPA; DFT.

cienaga, *Spanish*
DSTE/*cienega.*

cienega, *Spanish*
DSTE.

cigány, *Hungarian*
OCM.

cigarrito, *Spanish*
DSTE.

cilindri, *Italian*
OCM/*cilindro.*

cilindro, *Italian*
OCM/*cylinder*; OCM.

cima, *Italian*
GG.

cimbalello, *Spanish*
ICMM.

cimbalo, *Spanish*
ICMM.

cimbalom, *Hungarian*
ICMM.

cimborio, *Spanish*
DA.

ciment fondu, *French*
DFWPB.

cincha, *Spanish*
DSTE/*cincho.*

cincho, *Spanish*
DSTE.

cinco, *Spanish*
DFWPN.

cinéaste, *French*
DFWPB.

cinelle, *Turkish*
ICMM.

cinelli, *Italian*
OCM.

cinéma-vérité, *French*
DFWPB.

cink, *German*
ICMM.

cinq, *French*
LB; OCM.

cinque, *Italian*
DFWPN; OCM.

cinquecento, *Italian*
DFT; LP.

cinque-pas, *French*
OCM/*cinque-pace.*

cinque-passi, *Italian*
OCM/*cinque-pace.*

cinquième, *French*
LB.

cinquième en avant, *French*
LB/*bras, positions de.*

cinquième en bas, *French*
LB/*bras, positions de.*

cinquième en haut, *French*
LB/*bras, positions de.*

cinquième position, *French*
LB/*pieds, cinq positions des*;
OCM.

cioè, *Italian*
OCM.

cipollata, *Italian*
DFWPB.

cipollino, *Italian*
DFWPB.

circa, *Latin*
DFPA/*ca.*; DFT; DFWPN.

circiter, *Latin*
DFT.

circulus in definiendo, *Latin*
DFWPN.

circulus in probando, *Latin*
DFPA; DFPCQ; DFT; DFWPN.

circulus vitiosus, *Latin*
DFPA; DFWPN.

circum, *Latin*
DFT.

ciré, *French*
DFWPB.

cire perdue, *French*
DFWPB.

cirque, *French*
GG.

cirque niveau, *French*
GG.

Cis, *German*
ICMM; OCM.

cis, *Latin*
DEP.

cis-, *Latin*
DFWPN.

Ciscis, *German*
ICMM.

Cis dur, *German*
ICMM.

ciseaux, *French*
LB.

ciseaux, pas de, *French*
LB.

ciselé, *French*
DFWPB.

Cisis, *German*
OCM.

Cis moll, *German*
ICMM.

cistella, *Italian*
ICMM.

cistre, *French*
OCM/*cister.*

cithare, *Italian*
ICMM.

citrioli, *Italian*
DFWPN.

città, *Italian*
DFWPN.

ciudad, *Spanish*
DFWPN.

civet, *French*
DFT.

civet de chevreuil, *French*
DFT/*civet.*

civetteria, *Italian*
ICMM; OCM.

civiliter, *Latin*
DFWPN.

claire, caisse, *French*
OCM.

clair-obscur, *French*
DFT.

clairon, *French*
OCM/*bugle*; OCM.

claque, *French*
ICMM.

claquebois, *French*
ICMM; OCM.

clarabella, *Italian*
OCM/*clarabel.*

claricembalo, *Italian*
OCM.

Clarin, *German*
ICMM.

Clarina, *German*
OCM.

Clarinblasen, *German*
ICMM.

clarinero, *Spanish*
ICMM.

clarinette alto, *French*
OCM.

clarinette basse, *French*
OCM/*clarinette alto.*

clarinette contrabasse, *French*
OCM/*clarinette alto.*

clarinetto, *Italian*
OCM.

clarinetto alto, *Italian*
OCM/*clarinetto.*

clarinetto basso, *Italian*
OCM/*clarinetto.*

clarinetto contrabasso, *Italian*
OCM/*clarinetto.*

clarinetto d'amore, *Italian*
OCM/*amore, amour.*

clarino, *Italian*
OCM.

clarino contrabasso, *Italian*
OCM.

clarion harmonique, *French*
ICMM.

clarone, *Italian*
OCM.

clàrsach, *Celtic*
OCM.

clarum et venerabile nomen, *Latin*
DEP.

Clausel, *German*
ICMM.

clausula, *Latin*
DFWPN; ICMM; OCM.

clausula, *pl.* **clausulae,** *Latin*
DFWPB.

clausula falsa, *Latin*
ICMM.

clausula peregrina, *Latin*
ICMM.

clausus, *Latin*
ICMM.

clave, *Latin*
ICMM.

clavecin, *French*
ICMM; OCM.

clavecin oculaire, *French*
OCM.

claveoline, *French*
ICMM.

claves curiae, *Latin*
DFWPN.

clavicembalo, *Italian*
ICMM/*cravicembalo*; OCM.

Clavier, *German*
ICMM; OCM/*Klavier.*

Clavier-auszug, *German*
ICMM.

clavier de récit, *French*
OCM.

clavier des bombardes, *French*
OCM.

Clavieren, *German*
ICMM.

Clavierübung, *German*
ICMM.

cliché, *French*
DFT; DFWPB; DFWPN.

clique, *French*
DFPCQ.

cloaca, *Latin*
DFPCQ.

cloaca maxima, *Latin*
DFPCQ.

cloche, en, *French*
LB.

cloches, *French*
OCM.

clochette, *French*
OCM.

cloisonné, *French*
ACD/*enamel*; DFT; DFWPB;
DFWPN.

cloisonnisme, *French*
LP.

clou, *French*
DFT.

cluse, *French*
GG.

cocchina, *Italian*
ICMM.

cochon, *French*
DFT.

cochon de lait, *French*
DFT/*cochon.*

cockamamy, *Yiddish*
HFY.

coda, *Italian*
DFPCQ; DFWPN; ICMM;
OCM.

code civil, *French*
DFWPN.

Code Napoléon, *French*
DFWPN.

codetta, *Italian*
DFT; DFWPN; ICMM; OCM.

codex, *Latin*
DFWPN.

Codex Justinianeus, *Latin*
DFWPN.

cœna Domini, *Latin*
DEP.

coeur, *French*
DFWPN.

cogito, ergo sum, *Latin*
DEP; DFPA; DFPCQ; DFT;
DFWPB; DFWPN.

cogli, *Italian*
OCM.

cognac, *French*
DFWPN.

cognomen, *Latin*
DFPCQ; DFWPN.

cognoscente, *Italian*
DFT; DFWPN.

cognoscenti, *Italian*
DFWPB; DFWPN/*cognoscente.*

Cohen, *Yiddish*
JOY/*Kohen*; JOY.

coi, *Italian*
OCM/*cogli.*

coif, *French*
DFWPN.

coiffeur, *French*
DEP; DFPCQ; DFT; DFWPN.

coiffeur, *fem.* **coiffeuse,** *French*
DFWPB.

coiffure, *French*
DEP; DFPCQ; DFT; DFWPB;
DFWPN.

Cointreau, *French*
DFWPN.

col, *French*
GG.

col, *Italian*
OCM.

colascione, *Italian*
OCM.

col basso, *Italian*
OCM/*col.*

colboy, *Yiddish*
HFY/*Chaim Yankel.*

col canto, *Italian*
DFT.

colina, *Spanish*
GG.

colk, *Dutch*
GG.

coll, *Italian*
OCM/*col.*

colla, *Italian*
OCM/*col.*

colla destra, *Italian*
DFT; ICMM.

collado, *Spanish*
GG.

collage, *French*
DFWPB; DFWPN; LP.

colla parte, *Italian*
DFPCQ; DFT; ICMM.

colla punta d'arco, *Italian*
ICMM.

colla punta dell' arco, *Italian*
OCM.

coll'arco, *Italian*
DFT; ICMM; OCM.

collarino, *Italian*
DA.

colla sinistra, *Italian*
DFT; ICMM.

colla voce, *Italian*
DFPCQ; DFT; ICMM; OCM/
col.

collé, *French*
LB; LP.

colle, *Italian*
OCM/*col.*

collectanea, *Latin*
DFT; DFWPN.

collectanea *pl., Latin*
DFWPB.

collegium, *Latin*
DFWPN.

collegium musicum, *Latin*
OCM.

col legno, *Italian*
DFWPB; ICMM; OCM.

collegno, *Italian*
DFT.

col legno dell' arco, *Italian*
ICMM.

colofonia, *Italian*
OCM/*colophony*; OCM.

colombage, *French*
DA.

colophane, *French*
ICMM; OCM/*colophony.*

colorado, *Spanish*
DFWPN.

coloratura, *Italian*
DFT; DFWPB; DFWPN;
ICMM; OCM.

colossus, *Latin*
DFPCQ.

colpo, *Italian*
OCM.

columbaria, *Greek* [*sic*]
DFWPN.

combien, *French*
DFWPN.

Comblanchien, *French*
DA.

come, *Italian*
OCM.

comédie de moeurs, *French*
DFWPN.

Comédie Française, *French*
DFWPN.

comédie humaine, *French*
DFWPN.

(la) comédie humaine, *French*
DFWPB.

comédie larmoyante, *French*
DFWPB.

come prima, *Italian*
DFT; OCM/*come.*

comes, *Latin*
ICMM; ICMM.

come sopra, *Italian*
DFT; ICMM; OCM/*come.*

come stà, *Italian*
OCM/*come.*

comique, *French*
OCM.

comitas inter communitates, *Latin*
DFWPN.

comitas inter gentes, *Latin*
DFWPN.

comitia, *Latin*
DFPCQ.

commandite, *French*
DFT.

comme, *French*
OCM.

comme ci comme ça, *French*
DFT.

comme ci, comme ça, *French*
DFPA; DFWPN.

commedia dell' arte, *Italian*
DFPA; DFWPB; DFWPN; OCM.

comme il faut, *French*
DEP; DFPA; DFPCQ; DFT;
DFWPB; DFWPN; SPICE.

comment allez-vous, *French*
DFT.

comment ça va, *French*
DFT.

comment ça va?, *French*
DFPA.

commère, *French*
OCM.

commissar, *Russian*
DFWPN.

commissariat, *Russian*
DFWPN.

commissionnaire, *French*
DFPCQ.

commode, *French*
ACD.

commodo, *Italian*
DFPCQ; DFT; ICMM; OCM.

commune bonum, *Latin*
DFPCQ.

communi consensu, *Latin*
DEP; DFPA.

communiqué, *French*
DFT; DFWPB; DFWPN.

communn gàidhealach, *Scottish*
OCM.

comodo, *Italian*
OCM.

cómo está, *Spanish*
DFT.

cómo le va, *Spanish*
DFT.

compadre, *Spanish*
DFT; DSTE.

compagnia del gonfalone, *Italian*
OCM.

compagnon de voyage, *French*
DEP; DFPCQ.

compañero, *Spanish*
DFT.

comparses, *French*
ICMM.

compère, *French*
OCM.

compiacevole, *Italian*
ICMM; OCM.

Compiègne, *French*
DFWPN.

complainte, *French*
ICMM.

completorium, *Latin*
ICMM.

componiert, *German*
OCM.

composé, *French*
OCM.

composé, pas, *French*
LB.

compositeur, *French*
DFT.

compos mentis, *Latin*
DEP; DFPCQ; DFT; DFWPB;
DFWPN.

compote, *French*
DFT; DFWPN.

comprimario, *Italian*
OCM.

compris, *French*
DFWPN.

compter, *French*
OCM.

compte rendu, *French*
DFPA; DFWPN.

comte, *French*
DEP; DFWPN.

comtesse, *French*
DEP.

con, *Italian*
DFWPN; OCM.

con, *Spanish*
DFWPN.

con abbandono, *Italian*
DFT.

con affetto, *Italian*
ICMM.

con amore, *Italian*
DEP; DFPA; DFPCQ; DFT;
DFT/*amore*; DFWPB; DFWPN;
ICMM.

con anima, *Italian*
DFPCQ; ICMM.

con brio, *Italian*
DFT; DFWPB; ICMM.

con calore, *Italian*
DFT/*calore*; DFT.

concento, *Italian*
ICMM.

concentus, *Latin*
OCM.

concertante, *Italian*
DFPCQ; DFT; DFWPB; ICMM;
OCM.

concertata, aria, *Italian*
OCM.

concertata messa, *Italian*
ICMM.

concertati madrigali, *Italian*
ICMM.

concertato, *Italian*
ICMM; OCM.

concert d'orgue, *French*
OCM.

concertina, *Italian*
OCM.

concertino, *Italian*
DFT; ICMM; OCM.

105   **confutatis**

Concertmeister, *German*
DFT; OCM/*concert master.*

concerto, *Italian*
DFPCQ; DFT; DFWPN.

concerto, *pl.* concerti, *Italian*
DFWPB.

concerto a solo, *Italian*
ICMM.

concerto, di, *Italian*
ICMM/*concertato.*

concerto di chiesa, *Italian*
ICMM.

concerto doppio, *Italian*
ICMM.

concerto grosso, *Italian*
DFPA; ICMM.

concerto grosso, *pl.* concerti grossi,
Italian
DFWPB.

concerto spirituale, *Italian*
ICMM.

concerts du conservatoire, *French*
OCM.

Concertstück, *German*
OCM.

concha, *Spanish*
DSTE.

concierge, *French*
DFPCQ; DFT; DFWPB.

concièrge, *French*
DFWPN.

conciergerie, *French*
DA.

concitato, *Italian*
ICMM; OCM.

concombre, *French*
DFT.

concours, *French*
DA; LP.

con diligenza, *Italian*
DFPA.

conditio sine qua non, *Latin*
DFPA; DFPCQ.

con dolcezza, *Italian*
DFT.

con dolore, *Italian*
DEP; DFPA; DFT.

condominium, *Latin*
DFPCQ.

condottiere, *pl.* condottieri, *Italian*
DFWPB.

conductus, *Latin*
ICMM; OCM.

con espressione, *Italian*
DFT.

confer, *Latin*
DFWPB; DFWPN.

confessio fidei, *Latin*
DFWPN.

confidante, *French*
ACD.

confiserie, *French*
DFWPB.

confiseur, *French*
DFWPB.

confit, *French*
DFWPB.

confiteor, *Latin*
DFT; DFWPB; OCM.

confiture, *French*
DFT.

confitures, *French*
DFWPN.

con forza, *Italian*
DFT.

confrère, *French*
DEP; DFPCQ; DFT; DFWPB;
DFWPN.

confrérie de la passion, *French*
OCM.

con fuoco, *Italian*
DFT; DFWPN.

con furia, *Italian*
DFPA.

confutatis, *Latin*
OCM.

conga, *Spanish*
OCM.

con grazia, *Italian*
DFT.

congregatio de propaganda fide,
Latin
DFWPN.

con gusto, *Italian*
DFT.

con impeto, *Italian*
DFT/*impeto*; DFT.

conjugium, *Latin*
DFWPN.

con molta passione, *Italian*
DFPA.

con molto passione [*sic*], *Italian*
DFT.

con moto, *Italian*
DFT/*moto*; DFT; DFWPB;
DFWPN; ICMM.

connaisseur, *French*
DFPCQ; DFWPN.

conoscente, *Italian*
DFPCQ.

con ottava, *Italian*
ICMM.

con ottava ad libitum, *Italian* +
Latin
ICMM.

con permesso, *Italian*
DFPCQ; DFT.

con precipitazione, *Italian*
OCM/*precipitato*.

con prestezza, *Italian*
DFT.

conquistador, *Spanish*
DFT; DSTE.

conquistador, *pl.* conquistadores,
Spanish
DFWPB.

conquistadores, *Spanish*
DFWPN.

con semplicità, *Italian*
DFT.

consensus facit legem, *Latin*
DEP.

consensus gentium, *Latin*
DFWPN.

conservatoire, *French*
OCM/*conservatorio*.

conservatorio, *Italian*
ICMM; OCM.

conserver, *French*
OCM.

consilium abeundi, *Latin*
DFPA.

consistoire, *French*
DFWPN.

consistorium, *Latin*
DFWPN.

consolatio, *Latin*
DFWPN.

consommé, *French*
DFT; DFWPB; DFWPN.

consommé de tête de veau, *French*
DFT/*consommé*.

con sordini, *Italian*
DFPCQ.

con sordino, *Italian*
DFT; DFWPB; ICMM; OCM.

conspectus, *Latin*
DFPCQ.

con spirito, *Italian*
DEP; DFT; DFWPB.

consummatum est, *Latin*
DFPA; DFT.

conte, *French*
DFWPN; OCM.

conté crayon, *French*
DA.

conteur, *French*
DFWPN.

continuato, *Italian*
DFT.

continuo, *Italian*
DFWPB; OCM.

contra, *Latin*
DFPCQ; DFWPN.

contrabasso, *Italian*
DFPCQ; DFT; DFWPN; ICMM;
OCM.

contrabbasso, *Italian*
DFT/*contrabasso.*

contra bonos mores, *Latin*
DFPA; DFPCQ; DFT; DFWPB;
DFWPN.

contrada dei nobili, *Italian*
DFPCQ.

contradanza, *Italian*
OCM/*country dance*; OCM.

contradictio in adjecto, *Latin*
DFWPN.

contra-fagotto, *Italian*
DFPCQ.

contrafagotto, *Italian*
DFT; OCM.

contra jus commune, *Latin*
DFWPN.

contralto, *Italian*
DFPCQ/*alto.*

contralto, *pl.* **contralti,** *Italian*
DFWPB.

contra naturam, *Latin*
DFWPN.

contrapás, *Catalan*
ICMM.

contrapposto, *Italian*
DFWPB; LP.

contrappunto alla mente, *Italian*
OCM.

contrappunto doppio, *Italian*
ICMM.

contrapunctus, *Latin*
ICMM.

contrassoggetto, *Italian*
ICMM.

contrattempo, *Italian*
ICMM.

contre basse, *French*
DFWPN.

contrebasse, *French*
ICMM; OCM.

contrebasson, *French*
ICMM; OCM.

contrecoup, *French*
DFT.

contredanse, *French*
DFWPN; ICMM; OCM/*country
dance*; OCM.

contretemps, *French*
DFT; DFWPN; LB.

controversiae, *Latin*
DFWPN.

con variazioni, *Italian*
DFPCQ.

con velocità, *Italian*
ICMM/*veloce.*

convenance, *French*
DFT.

conversazione, *Italian*
DEP; DFPCQ.

conversio, *Latin*
ICMM.

copeck, *Russian*
DFWPN.

coperto, *Italian*
ICMM; OCM.

copla, *Spanish*
OCM.

Coppel, *German*
OCM.

coprifoco, *Italian*
OCM/*coprifuoco.*

coprifuoco, *Italian*
OCM.

coq, *French*
DFT.

coq au vin, *French*
DFWPN.

coq de bruyère, *French*
DFT/*coq.*

coq de combat, *French*
DFT/*coq.*

coq d'Inde, *French*
DFT/*coq.*

coquetterie, *French*
DFWPN.

coquillage, *French*
ACD; DA; DFT; DFWPB.

coquille, *French*
DFT; DFWPN.

coquilles de moules, *French*
DFT/*coquille.*

cor, *French*
ICMM; OCM.

coram judice, *Latin*
DFPA; DFWPN.

coram non judice, *Latin*
DFPA.

coram populo, *Latin*
DFWPN.

cor anglais, *French*
DFT; ICMM; OCM.

coranto, *Italian*
OCM/*courante;* OCM.

cor à pistons, *French*
OCM.

cor chromatique, *French*
OCM.

corda, *Italian*
DFT; DFWPN; OCM.

cordatura, *Italian*
ICMM.

corde, *French*
OCM.

corde, *Italian*
OCM/*corda.*

corde à jour, *French*
ICMM; OCM.

corde à vide, *French*
ICMM; OCM/*corde à jour.*

cor de basset, *French*
ICMM; OCM.

cor de chasse, *French*
ICMM; OCM.

corde fausse, *French*
ICMM.

cordelle, *French*
DFT.

cor de nuit, *French*
OCM.

cor de postillon, *French*
ICMM.

cor des alpes, *French*
OCM; OCM/*Alpenhorn.*

cor de vaches, *French*
ICMM.

cor d'harmonie, *French*
OCM.

cordillera, *Spanish*
DSTE; GG.

cordon bleu, *French*
DFPA; DFPCQ; DFT; DFWPB.

cordon militaire, *French*
DFPCQ.

cordon rouge, *French*
DFWPB.

cordon sanitaire, *French*
DFPA; DFPCQ; DFWPB;
DFWPN.

corea, *Spanish*
OCM.

corista, *Italian*
OCM.

corista di camera, *Italian*
OCM/*corista.*

corista di coro, *Italian*
OCM/*corista.*

cor mixte, *French*
OCM.

cornado, *Spanish*
DSTE//*237.*

cornamusa, *Italian*
OCM/*bagpipe family.*

cornemuse, *French*
OCM.

cornet à bouquin, *French*
OCM.

cornet d'harmonie, *French*
OCM.

cornetta, *Italian*
OCM.

cornetta segnale, *Italian*
OCM/*bugle*; OCM.

cornettino, *Italian*
OCM.

cornetto, *Italian*
OCM.

Cornett-ton, *German*
OCM.

corno, *Italian*
DFPCQ; DFT; OCM.

corno alto, *Italian*
OCM.

corno a macchina, *Italian*
OCM.

corno a mano, *Italian*
OCM.

corno a pistoni, *Italian*
OCM.

corno basso, *Italian*
OCM; OCM/*corno alto.*

corno cromatico, *Italian*
OCM.

corno da caccia, *Italian*
ICMM; OCM.

corno di bassetto, *Italian*
DFPCQ; DFT/*corno*; ICMM;
OCM.

corno dolce, *Italian*
OCM.

corno inglese, *Italian*
DFT/*corno*; ICMM; OCM.

cornone, *Italian*
OCM.

corno torto, *Italian*
OCM.

corno ventile, *Italian*
OCM.

cornucopia, *Latin*
DFPCQ.

cornu copiae, *Latin*
DFWPN.

coro, *Italian*
OCM.

corolla, *Latin*
DFWPN.

corona, *Latin*
DFWPN.

coronado, *Spanish*
DFWPN.

coro primo, *Italian*
ICMM.

corps, *French*
DFT; LB.

corps de ballet, *French*
DFPA; DFT/*corps*; DFWPB;
DFWPN; ICMM; LB.

corps de garde, *French*
DEP.

corps de rechange, *French*
OCM.

corps de voix, *French*
ICMM.

corps diplomatique, *French*
DEP; DFPA; DFPCQ; DFWPB.

corpus, *Latin*
DFT; DFWPN.

Corpus Christi, *Latin*
DFWPN.

corpus delicti, *Latin*
DEP; DFPCQ; DFT/*corpus*;
DFWPB; DFWPN.

corpus iuris canonici, *Latin*
DFPCQ.

corpus iuris civilis, *Latin*
DFPCQ.

corpus juris, *Latin*
DFWPB; DFWPN.

corpus juris canonici, *Latin*
DFPA/*c. j. can.*; DFWPN.

corpus juris civilis, *Latin*
DFPA/*c. j. civ.*; DFWPN.

corregidor, *Spanish*
DFPCQ.

corrente, *Italian*
ICMM; ICMM/*courante*; OCM;
OCM/*courante.*

corrida, *Spanish*
DFWPN; DSTE/*237; DSTE.*

corrida de toros, *Spanish*
DFPA; DFT/*toro.*

corriente, *Spanish*
DSTE.

corrigenda, *Latin*
DFPA; DFPCQ; DFWPN.

corrigendum, *Latin*
DFT; DFWPN.

corsage, *French*
DFWPN.

cor simple, *French*
OCM.

corta, *Italian*
OCM/*corto.*

cortège, *French*
DFPCQ; DFWPB; DFWPN;
OCM.

cortex, *Latin*
DFPCQ.

corto, *Italian*
OCM.

coryphaeus, *Greek*
DFWPN.

coryphæus, *Latin*
OCM.

coryphée, *French*
DFT; DFWPB.

cosa, *Spanish*
DFWPN.

cosacca, *Italian*
OCM/*cosacco.*

cosacco, *Italian*
OCM.

cosa nostra, *Italian*
DFPA.

cosaque, *French*
DFT; ICMM; OCM.

cosí-cosí [*sic*], *Italian*
DFWPN.

così così, *Italian*
DFPA.

cosí fan tutte [*sic*], *Italian*
DFWPN.

così fan tutte, *Italian*
DFPA.

così fan tutti, *Italian*
DFT.

costumier, *French*
DFWPB.

côte, *French*
DFWPN.

coteau, *Canadian French*
GG.

Côte d'Azur, *French*
DFWPN.

côté, de, *French*
LB.

Côte d' Ivoire, *French*
DFWPN.

Côte d'Or, *French*
DFWPN.

côtelette, *French*
DFT.

côtelette de filet, *French*
DFT/*côtelette.*

côtelette en papillote, *French*
DFT/*papillote*; DFT/*côtelette.*

côtelettes, *French*
OCM.

coterie, *French*
DFPCQ; DFWPN.

côtes de bœuf, *French*
DFT.

cothurnus, *Latin*
DFWPN.

couac, *French*
ICMM.

cou-de-pied, *French*
LB.

cou-de-pied, sur le, *French*
LB/*cou-de-pied.*

coulamment, *French*
OCM.

coulé, *French*
DFT; DFWPB; OCM.

coulee, *French*
GG (*twice*).

coulée, *French*
DFT.

couleur de rose, *French*
SPICE.

coulisse, *French*
GG; OCM.

couloir, *French*
GG.

coumarin, *Spanish*
DSTE.

coup, *French*
DFPCQ; DFT.

coup d'archet, *French*
DFT; ICMM; OCM.

coup de bourse, *French*
DFPA.

coup d'éclat, *French*
DFPA.

coup de dès, *French*
DFT/*coup.*

coup de fond, *French*
DFT/*coup.*

coup de foudre, *French*
DFPA.

coup de glotte, *French*
DFWPN; OCM.

coup de grâce, *French*
DEP; DFPA; DFPCQ; DFT/
coup; DFWPB; DFWPN.

coup de main, *French*
DFPA; DFPCQ; DFWPB;
DFWPN.

coup de maître, *French*
DFPA; DFWPN.

coup d'épée, *French*
DFPA.

coup de plume, *French*
DFPA; DFWPN.

coup de soleil, *French*
DEP.

coup d'essai, *French*
DFPA; DFWPB; DFWPN.

coup d'état, *French*
DEP; DFPA; DFPCQ; DFT/
coup; DFWPB; DFWPN.

coup de tête, *French*
DFPA.

coup de théâtre, *French*
DFPA; DFPCQ; DFT/*coup*;
DFWPN.

coup d'oeil, *French*
DFPA; DFT/*coup*; DFWPB;
DFWPN.

coup d'œil, *French*
DEP.

coupé, *French*
DFT; DFWPB; DFWPN; LB;
OCM.

coupé ballotté, *French*
LB/*coupé, pas.*

coupé brisé, *French*
LB/*coupé, pas.*

coupé chassé en tournant, *French*
LB/*coupé, pas.*

coupé dessous, *French*
LB/*coupé, pas.*

coupé dessus, *French*
LB/*coupé, pas.*

coupé en tournant, *French*
LB/*coupé, pas.*

coupé fouetté raccourci, *French*
LB/*coupé, pas.*

coupé jeté en tournant, *French*
LB/*coupé, pas.*

coup en passant, *French*
DFWPB.

coupé, pas, *French*
LB.

coupure, *French*
DFT; OCM.

courante, *French*
ICMM; OCM.

courge, *French*
DFT.

courge à la moelle, *French*
DFT/*courge.*

couronne, en, *French*
LB.

courroie, *French*
OCM.

court-bouillon, *French*
DFT.

couru, *French*
LB.

couscous, *Arabic*
DFWPB.

couture, *French*
DFWPB; DFWPN.

couturier, *French*
DFT; DFWPN.

couturier, *fem.* **couturière,** *French*
DFWPB.

couturière, *French*
DFT.

couvert, *French*
DFWPB; OCM.

couverte, *French*
OCM/*couvert.*

coyote, *Spanish*
DSTE.

crabe, *French*
DFT.

cracovienne, *French*
OCM.

cramignon, *French*
OCM.

craquelé, *French*
DFT.

craquelure, *French*
LP.

cravicembalo, *Italian*
ICMM.

crécelle, *French*
OCM.

crèche, *French*
LP.

crede Deo, *Latin*
DFPCQ.

crede experto, *Latin*
DFPA.

credenda, *Latin*
DFPCQ.

credenza, *Italian*
ACD/*credence;* DFWPN.

credo, *Latin*
DFWPN; ICMM; OCM.

crembalum, *Latin*
OCM.

crème [*sic*], *French*
DFWPN.

crème, *French*
DFT.

crème à la glace, *French*
DFT/*crème.*

crème brûlèe, *French*
DFWPB.

crème de la crème, *French*
DFPA; DFT/*crème;* DFWPB.

crème de la crême [*sic*], *French*
DFPCQ; DFWPN.

crème de menthe [*sic*], *French*
DFWPN.

crème de menthe, *French*
DFT/*crème.*

crème fouettée, *French*
DFT/*crème.*

crème glacée, *French*
DFT/*crème.*

cremona, *Italian*
ICMM.

créole, *French*
DFWPN.

crêpe, *French*
DFT; DFT; DFWPB; DFWPN.

crêpe de Chine, *French*
DFT/*crêpe;* DFWPB; DFWPN.

crêpe lisse, *French*
DFWPB.

crêpes suzette, *French*
DFT/*crêpe;* DFWPN.

crépon, *French*
DFT; DFWPB.

crescendo, *Italian*
DFPCQ; DFT; DFWPB;
DFWPN; ICMM; OCM.

cresson, *French*
DFT.

crêt, *French*
GG.

creta, *Latin*
GG.

crevasse, *French*
GG.

crève-cœur, *French*
DFT.

crevette, *French*
DFT.

cri de coeur, *French*
DFWPB.

cri du coeur, *French*
DFPA.

crimen innominatum, *Latin*
DFWPN.

crimen laesae majestatis, *Latin*
DFPCQ.

crime passionel [*sic*], *French*
DFWPN.

crime passionnel, *French*
DFWPB.

cristallo, *Italian*
ACD.

critique, *French*
DA; DFPCQ; DFWPN.

croche, *French*
ICMM/*quaver*; ICMM; OCM.

crochet, *French*
DFWPN.

croisé, *French*
LB.

croisé derrière, *French*
LB/*croisé*.

croisé devant, *French*
LB/*croisé*.

croisée, *French*
LB/*croisé*.

croisé en arrière, *French*
LB/*croisé*.

croisé en avant, *French*
LB/*croisé*.

croiser, *French*
OCM.

croissant, *French*
DFT; DFWPB; DFWPN.

croix botonée, *French*
DA/*cross*.

Croix de Guerre, *French*
DFWPN; DFPA; DFT/*croix*;
DFWPB.

croix, en, *French*
LB.

croix fourchée, *French*
DA/*cross*.

croix pattée, *French*
DA/*cross*.

croix pommée, *French*
DA/*cross*.

croix sonore, *French*
OCM.

croma, *Italian*
ICMM/*quaver*; OCM.

cromatica, *Italian*
OCM/*cromatico*.

cromatico, *Italian*
OCM.

cromatico, corno, *Italian*
OCM.

Cromatische Harmonika, *German*
OCM.

cromorne, *French*
OCM.

croquante, *French*
DFT.

croque-en-bouche, *French*
DFT/*croquembouche*.

croquembouche, *French*
DFT.

croquette, *French*
DFWPN.

croquis, *French*
DA; LP.

crotales, *French*
OCM.

crotalum, *Latin*
ICMM.

114

crotola, *Spanish*
OCM.
croupier, *French*
DFWPB; DFWPN.
croustade, *French*
DFT; DFWPN.
croûte, *French*
DFT; DFWPB.
croute calcaire, *French*
GG.
croûton, *French*
DFT.
croutons, *French*
DFWPN.
cru, *French*
DFWPB.
crucifixus, *Latin*
ICMM; OCM.
crudités *pl., French*
DFWPB.
crux, *Latin*
DFPCQ.
crux ansata, *Latin*
DFPA.
crux criticorum, *Latin*
DFPA.
crux interpretum, *Latin*
DFPA.
crux mathematicorum, *Latin*
DFPA.
cruz, *Spanish*
DFWPN.
crystallo ceramie, *French*
ACD.
csárdás, *Hungarian*
OCM/*Czardas*; OCM.
cuadrilla, *Spanish*
DFWPN; DSTE/*237*.
cuarta, *Spanish*
DSTE.
cuatro, *Spanish*
DFWPN.
cubile ferarum, *Latin*
DFPCQ.

cucaracha, *Spanish*
DFWPN.
cuchilla, *Spanish*
GG.
cucina, *Italian*
DFWPN.
cuesta, *Spanish*
DFT; DSTE; GG.
cui, *Latin*
DFWPN.
cui bono, *Latin*
DEP; DFPCQ; DFT; DFWPB;
DFWPN.
cui bono?, *Latin*
DFPA.
cuidado, *Spanish*
DSTE.
cui malo, *Latin*
DFPCQ; DFT.
cui malo?, *Latin*
DFPA.
cuisine, *French*
DFPCQ; DFT; DFWPN.
cuisine bourgeoise, *French*
DFT/*bourgeois*; DFT/*cuisine*.
cuisinier, *French*
DFWPN.
cuisse, *French*
DFT.
cuissot, *French*
DFT.
cuit à point, *French*
DFPA/*à point*; DFT/*à point*;
DFT.
cuivre, *French*
OCM.
cuivré, *French*
ICMM; OCM.
cul-de-four, *French*
DA.
cul-de-lampe, *French*
DA.
cul-de-sac, *French*
DA; DFPA; DFPCQ; DFT;
DFWPB; DFWPN; GG.

culotte, *French*
DFT; DFWPN.

culpa, *Latin*
DFWPN.

culpae poena par esto, *Latin*
DFWPN.

cum, *Latin*
DFT.

cum grano salis, *Latin*
DFPA; DFPCQ; DFT; DFWPB;
DFWPN.

cum laude, *Latin*
DFPA; DFT; DFWPB; DFWPN.

cum notis variorum, *Latin*
DFT; DFWPN.

cum sancto spiritu, *Latin*
OCM.

cum tacent, clamant, *Latin*
DFWPN.

cuñado, *Spanish*
DSTE.

cupo, *Italian*
OCM.

cura, *Latin*
DFWPN.

cura, *Spanish*
DSTE.

curé, *French*
DFWPN.

curettage, *French*
DFWPB.

curette, *French*
DFWPB.

curia, *Latin*
DFWPN.

curia domini, *Latin*
DFWPN.

curia regis, *Latin*
DFPA; DFWPN.

curioso, *Italian*
DFT.

currente calamo, *Latin*
DFPA.

curriculum, *Latin*
DFPCQ.

curriculum vitae, *Latin*
DFPA; DFWPB; DFWPN.

cursus honorum, *Latin*
DFPA.

custodes, *Latin*
DFWPN/*custos.*

custos, *Latin*
DFPCQ; DFWPN; ICMM.

custos morum, *Latin*
DFPCQ; DFWPN.

Custos Privati Sigilli,
DFPA.

Custos Rotulorum, *Latin*
DFPA.

Custos Sigilli, *Latin*
DFPA.

cuvée, *French*
DFT; DFWPB; DFWPN.

Cyklus, *German*
OCM.

cymanfa ganu, *Welsh*
OCM.

cyma recta, *Latin*
ACD; DFT.

cyma reversa, *Latin*
ACD; DFT.

cymbales, *French*
OCM.

cymbalum orale, *Latin*
OCM.

cymbasso, *Italian*
OCM.

Cymbelstern, *German*
ICMM.

cythare, *French*
ICMM.

Czakane, *German*
OCM.

czar, *Russian*
DFWPN.

Czardas, *Hungarian*
OCM; ICMM.

czarevitch, *Russian*
  DFWPB.
czarina, *Russian*
  DFWPN.

czarowitz, *Russian*
  DFWPN.

D

d', *French*
DFWPN.

da, *Italian*
OCM.

da, *Russian*
DFWPN; MRWEW/*18.*

da ballo, *Italian*
DFT; ICMM.

d'abord, *French*
DFWPN.

da camera, *Italian*
DFPA; ICMM.

da capo, *Italian*
DFPA; DFPCQ; DFT; DFWPB;
DFWPN; ICMM; ICMM/*capo*;
OCM.

da capo al fine, *Italian*
DFPA; DFT/*da capo*; ICMM.

da capo al segno, *Italian*
DFT/*da capo.*

da capo e poi la coda, *Italian*
ICMM.

da capo sin' al segno, *Italian*
ICMM.

da cappello, *Italian*
DFT.

d'accord, *French*
DFPCQ; DFT; DFWPN; ICMM.

d'accordo, *Italian*
ICMM.

dacha, *Russian*
DFWPB; MRWEW/*18.*

da chiesa, *Italian*
DFT/*da cappello.*

dachnik, *Russian*
MRWEW/*19.*

Dachshund, *German*
DFWPN.

da dextram misero, *Latin*
DFPCQ.

Daibutsu, *Japanese*
JLE.

daikon, *Japanese*
JLE.

daimio, *Japanese*
DFWPB; JLE.

daimon, *Greek*
DFWPN.

daimyo, *Japanese*
JLE.

Dai Nippon, *Japanese*
JLE.

dairi, *Japanese*
JLE.

dai-sho, *Japanese*
JLE.

dai-sho-no-soroimono, *Japanese*
JLE.

Dalai Lama, *Tibetan*
DFWPN.

dallage, *French*
DA.

dal segno, *Italian*
DFT; DFWPB; ICMM; OCM.

dal segno alla fine, *Italian*
ICMM.

dambo, *Bantu*
GG.

dame, *French*
DFWPN.

damnum absque injuria, *Latin*
DFPA.

Dämpfer, *German*
OCM.

dan, *Japanese*
JLE.

dance du ventre, *French*
DFPA.

danke, *German*
DFT.

danke schön, *German*
DFPA; DFT/*danke.*

Danklied, *German*
ICMM.

dansant, *French*
DFT.

danse, *French*
DFT; LB; OCM.

danse comique, *French*
LB.

danse de caractère, *French*
LB.

danse d'école, *French*
DFWPB.

danse de demi-caractère, *French*
LB.

danse de vertige, *French*
DFWPB.

danse du ventre, *French*
DFWPB; DFWPN.

Danse Macabre, *French*
DFWPN; DFPA; DFT/*danse*;
DFWPB.

danse noble, *French*
LB.

danseur, *French*
DFT; LB.

danseur, *fem.* danseuse, *French*
DFWPB.

danseur noble, *French*
DFWPB; LB.

danseur, premier, *French*
LB.

danseuse, *French*
DFT; LB.

danseuse, première, *French*
LB.

danza, *Italian*
OCM.

danza española, *Spanish*
OCM.

danza tedesca, *Italian*
OCM.

danzon, *Spanish*
OCM.

danzonetta, *Spanish*
OCM/*danzon.*

da prima, *Italian*
ICMM.

dariole, *French*
DFT.

darne, *French*
DFT.

darshan, *Yiddish*
JOY.

darshanim, *Yiddish*
JOY.

daruma, *Japanese*
JLE.

darunter, *German*
OCM.

das, *German*
OCM/*der.*

Dasein, *German*
DFWPN.

Dasia-notierung, *German*
ICMM.

décollement

dasselbe, *German*
  OCM.
dasvidanya, *Russian*
  DFWPN.
data, *Latin*
  DFPCQ.
daube, *French*
  DFT.
Dauer, *German*
  ICMM; OCM.
dauernd, *German*
  OCM.
Dauphin, *French*
  DFWPB; DFWPN; DFT.
daven, *Yiddish*
  HFY; JOY.
dayan, *Yiddish*
  JOY.
dayanim, *Yiddish*
  JOY / *dayan.*
dayen, *Yiddish*
  JOY / *dayan.*
dayyan, *Yiddish*
  JOY / *dayan.*
dazu, *German*
  OCM.
D dur, *German*
  ICMM.
de, *Dutch*
  DFWPN.
de, *French*
  DFWPN; OCM.
de, *Latin*
  DFWPN.
de, *Spanish*
  DFWPN.
de ambitu, *Latin*
  DFWPN.
débâcle, *French*
  DFWPN.
debile, *Italian*
  OCM.
débile, *French*
  OCM.

déboîté, pas, *French*
  LB.
debole, *Italian*
  OCM.
de bonis propriis, *Latin*
  DFPA.
debouchment, *French*
  GG.
debouchure, *French*
  GG.
déboulés, *French*
  LB.
débris, *French*
  DFPCQ; DFWPN.
début, *French*
  DFPCQ; DFWPN; OCM.
débutant, *French*
  DFPCQ.
décalage, *French*
  DFT.
decani, *Latin*
  DFT; ICMM; OCM.
déchant, *French*
  OCM.
décidé, *French*
  OCM.
decime, *French*
  DFWPN.
deciso, *Italian*
  DFT; ICMM; OCM.
Decke, *German*
  GG; ICMM.
Deckenkarren, *German*
  GG.
declamando, *Italian*
  OCM.
declamato, *Italian*
  OCM / *declamando.*
déclassé, *French*
  DFT; DFWPN.
déclassé, *fem.* déclassée, *French*
  DFWPB.
décollement, *French*
  GG.

décolletage, *French*
DFT; DFWPB; DFWPN.

décolleté, *French*
DFT; DFWPN.

décolletée, *French*
DFWPB.

décor, *French*
DFWPN.

décoration, *French*
ICMM.

découpage, *French*
DFWPB.

découpler, *French*
OCM.

decrescendo, *Italian*
DFT; DFWPN; ICMM; OCM.

decresciuto, *Italian*
OCM/*decrescendo.*

dedans, en, *French*
LB.

de droit, *French*
DFPA.

deësis, *Greek*
DFWPB.

de facto, *Latin*
DEP; DFPA; DFPCQ; DFT;
DFWPB; DFWPN.

de fait, *French*
DFPA.

défaut, *French*
OCM.

défense de fumer, *French*
DFT.

Defensor Fidei, *Latin*
DFPA.

deficit, *Latin*
DFPCQ.

de fide, *Latin*
DFPA; DFT; DFWPN.

defitsitny, *Russian*
MRWEW/*19.*

dégagé, *French*
DFPCQ; DFT; DFWPN.

dégagé, *fem.* **dégagée,** *French*
DFWPB.

dégagé en tournant, *French*
LB.

dégagé, pas, *French*
LB.

dégager, *French*
LB.

de gustibus (non est disputandum),
Latin
DFWPB.

de gustibus non est disputandum,
Latin
DFPCQ; DFT; DFWPN.

déhanchement, *French*
DFWPB.

dehors, *French*
OCM.

dehors, en, *French*
LB.

Dei gratia, *Latin*
DEP; DFPCQ; DFT; DFPA;
DFWPN.

de integro, *Latin*
DFPA; DFWPN.

déjà vécu, *French*
DFPA.

déjà vu, *French*
DFPA; DFT; DFWPB; LP.

déjeuner, *French*
DFT; DFWPN.

déjeûner [*sic*]**,** *French*
DFPCQ.

de jure, *Latin*
DEP; DFPA; DFPCQ; DFT;
DFWPB; DFWPN.

de la, *French*
OCM.

delator temporis acti, *Latin*
DFPA.

dele, *Latin*
DFWPN.

delenda est Carthago, *Latin*
DFWPN.

délicatesse, *French*
DFT.

delicato, *Italian*
DFT; DFWPN; OCM.

délié, *French*
OCM.

delirio, *Italian*
OCM.

delirium tremens, *Latin*
DFPA; DFPCQ; DFWPB;
DFWPN.

delizioso, *Italian*
OCM.

dell, *German*
GG.

de luxe, *French*
DFWPN.

dem, *German*
OCM/*der.*

démancher, *French*
OCM.

démarche, *French*
DFT; DFWPN.

dementia, *Latin*
DFT; DFWPN.

dementia praecox, *Latin*
DFPA; DFT/*dementia*; DFWPB;
DFWPN.

dementia senilis, *Latin*
DFPA.

demi, *French*
DFT; LB; OCM.

demi-, *French*
DFWPN.

demi-bras, *French*
LB.

demi-caractère, *French*
DFWPB.

demi-contretemps, *French*
LB.

demi-détourné, *French*
LB.

demie-tasse [*sic*]**,** *French*
DFWPN.

demi-hauteur, *French*
LB.

demi-jeu, *French*
OCM.

demi-mondaine, *French*
DFT.

demimondaine, *French*
DFT/*demi-mondaine.*

demi-monde, *French*
DFPCQ; DFT; DFWPB;
DFWPN.

demimonde, *French*
DFT/*demi-monde.*

demiourgos, *Greek*
DFWPN.

demi-pause, *French*
OCM.

demi-plié, *French*
LB.

demi-pointe, *French*
DFWPB.

demi-pointes, sur les, *French*
LB.

demi-position, *French*
LB.

demi-rond de jambe, *French*
LB.

demi-rond de jambe à terre, *French*
LB/*demi-rond de jambe.*

demi-seconde position, *French*
LB.

demissus vultum, *Latin*
DFPCQ.

demi-tasse, *French*
DFPA; DFWPB.

demi-ton, *French*
OCM.

demi-tour, *French*
LB.

demi-voix, *French*
OCM.

démodé, *French*
DFT; DFWPB; LP.

demoiselle, *French*
GG.

de mortuis, *Latin*
SPICE.

de mortuis nil nisi bonum, *Latin*
DEP; DFWPN.

dēmos, *Greek*
DFPCQ.

demüthig, *German*
OCM/*demütig.*

demütig, *German*
OCM.

den, *German*
OCM/*der.*

de nada, *Spanish*
DFWPN.

De Natura Rerum, *Latin*
DFWPN.

de nihilo nihil, *Latin*
DFPA; DFT.

Denkschrift, *German*
DFWPN.

dennoch, *German*
OCM.

dénouement, *French*
DFPCQ; DFT; DFWPB;
DFWPN.

de nouveau, *French*
DFT; DFWPN.

de novo, *Latin*
DEP; DFPA; DFPCQ; DFT;
DFWPB; DFWPN.

Deo duce, *Latin*
DEP.

Deo ducente, *Latin*
DFPCQ.

Deo favente, *Latin*
DFPCQ; DFPA; DFWPN.

Deo gratias, *Latin*
DEP; DFPCQ; DFT; DFPA.

Deo juvante, *Latin*
DFPCQ; DFPA.

deo volente, *Latin*
DFPA; DFWPB; DFWPN.

Deo volente, *Latin*
DEP.

Deo volente (D.V.), *Latin*
DFPCQ.

département, *French*
DFWPN.

de pied en cap, *French*
DFPA.

dépôt, *French*
DFPCQ.

De Profundis, *Latin*
DFWPN; DEP; DFPCQ; DFT;
DFWPB.

dépucellage, *French*
DFWPB.

der, *German*
OCM.

de race, *French*
DFPA.

derb, *German*
OCM.

de rebus, *Latin*
DFWPN.

de règle, *French*
DFWPB.

De Rerum Natura, *Latin*
DFWPN.

der Führer, *German*
DFT.

de rigueur, *French*
DFPA; DFT; DFWPB; DFWPN;
SPICE.

dernier, *French*
DFWPN.

dernier cri, *French*
DFT; DFWPN.

(le) dernier cri, *French*
DFWPB.

dernier cri, le, *French*
LP.

dernier ressort, *French*
DEP.

déroulé, *French*
LB.

derrière, *French*
DFT; LB.

derselbe, *German*
OCM.

des, *French*
OCM.

Des, *German*
ICMM; OCM.

descendant, en, *French*
LB.

Des dur, *German*
ICMM.

Deses, *German*
OCM.

déshabillé, *French*
DFPCQ; DFT; DFWPB;
DFWPN.

desiderata, *Latin*
DFWPN.

desideratum, *Latin*
DEP; DFT; DFWPN.

desideratum, *pl.* **desiderata,** *Latin*
DFPCQ.

Desideria, *Latin*
DFWPN.

desiderio, *Italian*
OCM.

designatum, *Latin*
DFWPN.

desinvolto, *Italian*
OCM.

desinvoltura, *Italian*
OCM/*desinvolto.*

Des moll, *German*
ICMM.

dessin, *French*
DFT.

dessous, *French*
LB; OCM.

dessous des cartes, *French*
DFT.

dessus, *French*
DFT; ICMM/*treble*; LB; OCM.

dessus de table, *French*
DFWPB.

dessus de viole, *French*
OCM.

desto, *Italian*
DFT; OCM.

destra, *Italian*
DFT; OCM/*destro.*

destra mano, *Italian*
DFT/*destra.*

destro, *Italian*
OCM.

de suite, *French*
OCM.

desunt caetera/desunt cetera, *Latin*
DFWPB.

détaché, *French*
DFT; DFWPB; DFWPN;
ICMM/*staccato*; ICMM; OCM.

détente, *French*
DFT; DFWPB; DFWPN.

determinato, *Italian*
OCM.

detinet, *Latin*
DFPA.

détiré, temps, *French*
LB.

détonner, *French*
DFT.

détour, *French*
DFPCQ.

détourné, *French*
LB.

détourné d'adage, *French*
LB/*détourné.*

detritus, *Latin*
DFPCQ.

de trop, *French*
DEP; DFPA; DFPCQ; DFT;
DFWPB; DFWPN; SPICE.

deus, *Latin*
DFWPN.

deus ex machina, *Latin*
DFPA; DFPCQ; DFT; DFWPN.

deus ex machina, *fem.* dea ex machina, *Latin*
DFWPB.

deus misereatur, *Latin*
OCM.

Deus tecum, *Latin*
DFWPN.

Deus vobiscum, *Latin*
DEP; DFT; DFWPN.

deutlich, *German*
OCM.

Deutsch, *German*
DFPCQ; OCM.

Deutsche, *German*
OCM.

Deutsche Demokratische Republik, *German*
DFPA/*D.D.R.*.

Deutscher Tanz, *German*
OCM/*Deutsche.*

Deutschland über alles, *German*
DFT; DFWPN.

deux, *French*
LB; OCM.

deuxième, *French*
LB; OCM.

deux temps, *French*
OCM.

deux-temps, *French*
DFWPB.

devant, *French*
LB.

développé, *French*
DFWPB.

développé en fondu, *French*
LB/*développé, temps.*

développement, *French*
OCM/*development.*

développé passé, *French*
LB/*développé, temps.*

développé, temps, *French*
LB.

devotissimo suo, *Italian*
DFPCQ.

devoto, *Italian*
OCM.

devozione, *Italian*
OCM.

dharma, *Sanskrit*
DFT; DFWPN.

di, *Italian*
OCM.

día, *Spanish*
DFWPN.

diable, *French*
DFWPN.

diablerie, *French*
DFWPB.

diablo, *Spanish*
DSTE.

diabolus in musica, *Latin*
DFWPB.

diaconicon, *Greek*
ICMM.

diagonale, *French*
DFWPB.

diagonale, en, *French*
LB.

diagramma, *Greek*
ICMM.

dialogo, *Italian*
ICMM.

dialogue intérieur, *French*
DFWPN.

diamanté, *French*
DFWPB.

dianoia, *Greek*
DFWPN.

diapason, *Greek*
ICMM.

diapason à bouche, *French*
OCM/*diapason.*

diapason à branches, *French*
OCM/*diapason.*

diapason normal, *French*
DFT.

diapente, *German*
OCM.

diapente, *Greek*
ICMM.

diaphonia, *Greek*
ICMM.

dia polla, *Greek*
DFPCQ.

diario, *Spanish*
DFWPN.

diaspora, *Greek*
DFWPN.

diastole, *Greek*
ICMM.

diatesseron, *Greek*
ICMM.

diaulia, *Greek*
ICMM.

di bravura, *Italian*
DFPA; DFT.

di buon'ora, *Italian*
DFPCQ.

Dichtung, *German*
OCM.

Dichtung und Wahrheit, *German*
DFPCQ; DFWPN.

dick, *German*
OCM.

dictum, *Latin*
DEP; DFPCQ.

dictum sapienti sat est, *Latin*
DFPCQ.

dictyotheton, *Greek*
DA.

die, *German*
OCM/*der.*

die, *Latin*
DFPCQ.

dieci, *Italian*
OCM.

die geistige Welt, *German*
DFT.

Die Götterdämmerung, *German*
DFPA.

dies, *Latin*
DFT; DFWPN.

dies a quo, *Latin*
DFWPN.

dies ater, *Latin*
DFPA.

die schöne Welt, *German*
DFT.

dièse, *French*
ICMM; OCM.

dieselbe, *German*
OCM.

dies faustus, *Latin*
DFPA; DFPCQ.

dies infaustus, *Latin*
DFPA; DFPCQ.

Dies Irae, *Latin*
DFT/*dies*; DFWPN; DEP;
DFPA; DFPCQ; DFWPB;
ICMM; OCM.

diésis, *French*
ICMM.

diesis, *German*
OCM.

diesis, *Greek*
ICMM.

diesis, *Italian*
ICMM.

diesis chromatica, *Greek*
ICMM.

dies non [*sic*], *Latin*
DEP.

dietro, *Italian*
OCM.

Dieu, *French*
DFWPN.

Dieu et mon droit, *French*
DFPCQ; DFT; DFWPB;
DFWPN; DEP.

Dieu vous garde, *French*
DFPCQ.

diez, *Spanish*
DFWPN.

Die Zauberflöte, *German*
DFWPN.

diferencias, *Spanish*
ICMM.

differentia, *Latin*
DFWPN.

difficile, *French*
DFT.

difficilia quae pulcra, *Latin*
DFPCQ.

difficilior lectio potior, *Latin*
DFWPB.

di giorno, *Italian*
DFPCQ.

dii penates, *Latin*
DFWPN.

di leggiero, *Italian*
ICMM.

dilettante, *Italian*
DEP; DFPCQ; LP.

diligente, *Italian*
DFWPB.

diluendo, *Italian*
DFT; DFWPN; OCM.

dilungando, *Italian*
OCM.

diminuendo, *Italian*
DFPCQ; DFT; DFWPB;
DFWPN; ICMM; OCM.

di molto, *Italian*
DFPCQ; DFT; ICMM; OCM.

dinde, *French*
DFT.

dinde en daube, *French*
DFT/*dinde.*

dindon, *French*
DFT; DFWPN.

dindonneaux, *French*
DFWPN.

diner [*sic*], *French*
DEP.

dîner, *French*
DFT.

dinero, *Spanish*
DFT; DFWPN; DSTE.

di notte, *Italian*
DFPCQ.

di nuovo, *Italian*
DFPA; OCM.

di più in più, *Italian*
DFPCQ.

Directoire, *French*
DFWPB.

directorium chori, *Latin*
OCM.

direttore, *Italian*
DFT.

diritta, *Italian*
ICMM.

Dirndl, *German*
DFWPB; DFWPN.

Dis, *German*
ICMM; OCM.

discantus supra librum, *Latin*
OCM.

Discant Zinck, *German*
OCM.

discere docendo, *Latin*
DFPCQ; DFWPN.

discobolus, *Greek*
DFWPN.

discothèque, *French*
DFT; DFWPB.

discretezza, *Italian*
OCM/*discrezione.*

discreto, *Italian*
OCM.

discrezione, *Italian*
OCM.

disinvolto, *Italian*
OCM.

Disis, *German*
OCM.

disjecta membra, *Latin*
DEP; DFT.

Diskant, *German*
ICMM/*treble.*

Dis moll, *German*
ICMM.

disperato, *Italian*
OCM.

127 **dolendo**

distanza, *Italian*
OCM.
distinctio, *Latin*
ICMM.
distingué, *French*
DEP; DFT; DFWPN.
distinto, *Italian*
OCM.
distrait, *French*
DEP; DFT; DFWPN.
dit, *French*
DFT; DFWPN.
dithyramb, *Greek*
ICMM.
dithyrambe, *French*
OCM.
ditirambo, *Italian*
OCM.
diva, *Italian*
DFT; DFWPN.
divertimento, *Italian*
DFPCQ; ICMM; OCM.
divertimento, *pl.* divertimenti, *Italian*
DFWPB.
divertissement, *French*
DFPCQ; DFT; DFWPB;
DFWPN; ICMM/*divertimento*;
LB; OCM.
divisés, *French*
OCM.
divisi, *Italian*
DFT; ICMM; OCM/*divisés.*
divisio, *Latin*
ICMM.
divotamente, *Italian*
OCM/*divoto.*
divoto, *Italian*
OCM.
dix, *French*
OCM.
do, *Italian*
OCM.
do, *Japanese*
JLE.

do'brii ve'tcher, *Russian*
DFWPN.
dobriy den, *Russian*
DFPA.
dobriy vecher, *Russian*
DFPA.
dobroe utro, *Russian*
DFWPN.
dobroye utro, *Russian*
DFPA.
docendo discimus, *Latin*
DFWPN.
docendo discitur, *Latin*
DFWPN.
doch, *German*
OCM/*do.*
Doctor Divinitatis, *Latin*
DFPA/*D.D..*
doctor legum, *Latin*
DFPA.
doglia, *Italian*
OCM/*do.*
doigt, *French*
OCM/*do.*
doit, *French*
OCM/*do.*
doivent, *French*
OCM/*doit.*
dojo, *Japanese*
JLE.
dolce, *Italian*
DEP; DFPCQ; DFT; DFWPN;
OCM.
dolce far niente, *Italian*
DFPA; DFPCQ; DFT/*dolce*;
DFWPB; DFWPN; SPICE.
dolcemente, *Italian*
DFT.
dolce stil nuovo, *Italian*
DFPA.
dolce vita, *Italian*
DFT; DFWPB.
dolendo, *Italian*
ICMM.

dolente, *Italian*
DFWPN; OCM.

dolore, *Italian*
OCM.

doloroso, *Italian*
DEP; DFPCQ; DFT; DFWPN.

Dolzflöte, *German*
OCM.

Domine Deus, *Latin*
OCM.

Domine Jesu, *Latin*
OCM.

domingo, *Spanish*
DFWPN.

domino, *Italian*
DEP.

domino optimo maximo, *Latin*
DFWPN.

dominus, *Latin*
DFWPN.

Dominus providebit, *Latin*
DFPCQ.

Dominus vobiscum, *Latin*
DEP; DFPCQ; DFT; DFPA;
DFWPN.

domra, *Russian*
OCM.

domus aurea, *Latin*
DFPA.

domus Dei, *Latin*
DFWPN.

Domus Procerum, *Latin*
DFPA; DFT.

Don, *Spanish*
DFT; DFPCQ.

Dona, *Portuguese*
DFT.

Doña, *Spanish*
DFT.

dona eis, *Latin*
OCM.

dona nobis, *Latin*
OCM.

donemus, *Latin*
OCM.

Donna, *Italian*
DFT; DFWPN.

donnée, *French*
DFT.

Donner, *German*
DFWPN.

dopo, *Italian*
DFT; OCM.

Dopolavoro, *Italian*
DFWPN.

doppel, *German*
OCM.

Doppel B, *German*
OCM.

Doppel-Be, *German*
OCM.

Doppelchor, *German*
OCM.

Doppelfagott, *German*
OCM.

Doppelflöte, *German*
OCM.

Doppelfuge, *German*
OCM.

Doppelgänger, *German*
DFT.

Doppelhorn, *German*
OCM.

Doppelkreuz, *German*
OCM.

doppeln, *German*
OCM.

Doppelschlag, *German*
ICMM/*turn*; OCM.

Doppeltaktnote, *German*
OCM.

doppelt so schnell, *German*
OCM.

doppess, *Yiddish*
HFY; JOY.

doppio, *Italian*
DFT; OCM.

129   **doyen**

oppio bemolle, *Italian*
OCM/*doppio*.

oppio diesis, *Italian*
OCM/*doppio*.

oppio movimento, *Italian*
DFT/*doppio*; ICMM; OCM/
doppio.

oppio pedale, *Italian*
ICMM.

oppio tempo, *Italian*
ICMM.

orado, *Spanish*
DFWPN.

orbank, *Afrikaans*
GG.

l'orsay, *French*
DFWPN.

orsum, *Latin*
DFPCQ.

os, *Spanish*
DFWPN.

os à dos, *French*
LB.

os-à-dos, *French*
DFPA.

os au public, *French*
LB.

ossier, *French*
DFT; DFWPN.

Dosvidanio, *Russian*
DFWPN.

lo svidaniya, *Russian*
DFT.

lo svidanya, *Russian*
DFPA.

otaku, *Japanese*
JLE.

ouane, *French*
DFT.

ouanier, *French*
DFT.

ouble, *French*
LB; OCM/*double*.

doublé, *French*
DFT; ICMM; ICMM/*turn*; LB.

double bémol, *French*
OCM/*double*.

doublé cadence, *French*
ICMM.

double corde, *French*
ICMM.

double croche, *French*
ICMM/*semiquaver*; ICMM.

double-croche, *French*
OCM/*double*.

double dièse, *French*
OCM/*double*.

double entendre, *French*
DFPA; DFT/*double entente*;
DFWPB; DFWPN; SPICE.

double entente, *French*
DFPA; DFPCQ; DFT; DFWPN.

doublette 2, *French*
OCM.

doublure, *French*
DFT.

douce, *French*
DFWPN; OCM.

doucement, *French*
DFT; DFWPN.

douceur, *French*
DEP.

doucine, *French*
DA.

douleur, *French*
OCM.

do ut des, *Latin*
DFPA; DFT.

do ut facias, *Latin*
DFPA.

doux, *French*
DFWPN; OCM.

doxa, *Greek*
DFWPN.

doyen, *French*
DFT.

drabant, *Polish*
OCM.

drachma, *Greek*
DFWPN.

dramatis personæ, *Latin*
DEP.

dramatis personae, *Latin*
DFPA; DFPCQ; DFT; DFWPB;
DFWPN.

drame lyrique, *French*
OCM.

dramma giocoso, *Italian*
ICMM.

dramma lirico, *Italian*
OCM.

dramma per musica, *Italian*
ICMM; OCM.

drammatico, *Italian*
OCM.

drängend, *German*
OCM.

Drang nach Osten, *German*
DFPA; DFT; DFWPB.

drapeau tricolore, *French*
DFT/*drapeau.*

draperie mouillée, *French*
DFWPB.

draykop, *Yiddish*
JOY.

draykopf, *Yiddish*
JOY.

dreck, *Yiddish*
HFY; JOY.

Dreher, *German*
ICMM.

Drehleier, *German*
OCM.

drei, *German*
OCM.

Dreikanter, *German*
GG.

dreinfach, *German*
OCM.

dreinfahren, *German*
OCM.

dreitaktig, *German*
OCM.

dreml, *Yiddish*
HFY.

dressage, *French*
DFWPB.

dringend, *German*
OCM.

dritte, *German*
OCM.

drohend, *German*
OCM.

droit, *French*
DFWPN; OCM.

droit du seigneur, *French*
DFWPN.

droite, *French*
OCM/*droit.*

droite, à, *French*
LB.

Druse, *German*
GG.

druzhinnik, *Russian*
MRWEW/*18.*

du, *French*
OCM.

duce, *Italian*
DFT; DFWPB; DFWPN.

duces tecum, *Latin*
DFWPN.

duchesse, *French*
ACD; DFWPB.

duda, *Polish*
OCM.

Dudelkasten, *German*
ICMM.

Dudelkastensack, *German*
ICMM.

Dudelsack, *German*
ICMM/*Dudelkastensack;* OCM.

due, *Italian*
DFPCQ; DFT; DFWPN; OCM.

ieña, *Spanish*
DFT.

ieño, *Spanish*
DFT; DSTE.

iett, *German*
OCM/*duet.*

iettino, *Italian*
DFPCQ.

ietto, *Italian*
DFPCQ; OCM/*duet.*

ie volte, *Italian*
DFPCQ; DFT/*due*; DFT/*volta.*

iftig, *German*
OCM.

i jour, *French*
DFT.

ilce, *Spanish*
DSTE.

ilce domum, *Latin*
DFPCQ.

ilce quod utile, *Latin*
DFWPN.

ilcian, *German*
OCM.

imka, *Russian*
ICMM.

imka, *Slavonic*
OCM.

imky, *Slavonic*
OCM/*dumka.*

impf, *German*
OCM.

im spiro, spero, *Latin*
DEP.

im vivimus, vivamus, *Latin*
DEP.

inkel, *German*
OCM.

io, *French*
OCM/*duet.*

io, *Italian*
DFT; DFWPB; OCM/*duet.*

io concertante, *Italian*
ICMM.

duolo, *Italian*
OCM.

duomo, *Italian*
DFT; DFWPN.

dur, *French*
DFT.

Dur, *German*
OCM; ICMM; ICMM/*major.*

dura mater, *Latin*
DFPCQ; DFWPN.

duramente, *Italian*
DFT; ICMM; OCM.

durch, *German*
OCM.

durchaus, *German*
OCM.

durchdringend, *German*
OCM.

Durchführung, *German*
OCM; OCM/*development.*

durchkomponiert, *German*
ICMM; OCM.

durchweg, *German*
OCM.

dureté, *French*
OCM.

durezza, *Italian*
OCM.

duro, *Italian*
OCM.

düster, *German*
OCM.

duttile, trombone, *Italian*
OCM.

duvet, *French*
DFWPB; DFWPN.

dux, *Latin*
ICMM; OCM.

dy, *Swedish*
GG.

dybbuk, *Yiddish*
JOY.

dynamis, *Greek*
DFWPN.

dzhlob, *Yiddish*
   JOY.

E

e, *Italian*
DFWPN; OCM.

e, *Latin*
DFWPN.

eau, *French*
DFT; DFWPN.

eau de Cologne, *French*
DFWPB; DEP; DFWPN.

eau de vie, *French*
DEP; DFPA; DFPCQ; DFT/*eau*;
DFWPN.

eau de vie, *pl.* **eaux de vie,** *French*
DFWPB.

eau forte, *pl.* **eaux fortes,** *French*
DFWPB.

eau rougie, *French*
DFT/*eau.*

eau sucrée, *French*
DFT/*eau.*

ebenfalls, *German*
OCM.

ébéniste, *French*
ACD; DFWPB.

ébénisterie, *French*
DFWPB.

ebenso, *German*
OCM/*ebenfalls.*

écarté, *French*
DFT/*écart*; LB.

ecce, *Latin*
DFT.

Ecce Homo, *Latin*
DFT/*ecce*; DEP; DFPA; DFPCQ;
DFWPB; DFWPN.

ecce signum, *Latin*
DFPCQ; DFWPB; DFWPN.

ecclesia, *Latin*
DFWPN.

échappé, *French*
DFWPB; DFWPN; OCM.

échappé battu, *French*
LB/*échappé, temps.*

échappé changé, *French*
LB/*échappé, temps.*

échappée de lumière, *French*
DFT/*échappée.*

échappé royale, *French*
LB/*échappé, temps.*

échappé sans changer, *French*
LB/*échappé, temps.*

échappé sauté, grand, *French*
LB/*échappé, temps.*

échappé sauté, petit, *French*
LB/*échappé, temps.*

échappé sur les pointes, *French*
LB/*échappé, temps.*

échappé, temps, *French*
LB.

écharpe, *French*
OCM.

échelette, *French*
OCM.

echelle, *French*
DA.

échelle, *French*
DFT; ICMM; OCM.

échelle chromatique, *French*
ICMM.

échelle diatonique, *French*
ICMM.

echelon, *French*
DFPCQ.

échelon, *French*
ICMM.

Echoklavier, *German*
OCM.

éclair, *French*
DFWPN.

éclat, *French*
DFWPN.

éclatant, *French*
OCM.

eco, *Italian*
OCM.

école, *French*
DFT; DFWPB; LB; OCM.

ecole militaire, *French*
DEP.

école normale, *French*
DFWPN.

ecole polytechnique, *French*
DEP.

école primaire, *French*
DFWPN.

e contra, *Latin*
DFPA; DFT; DFWPN.

e contrario, *Latin*
DFPA; DFT.

e converso, *Latin*
DFPA.

écorché, *French*
LP.

écossaise, *French*
OCM.

écoulement, *French*
GG.

écrasement, *French*
DFT.

écraseur, *French*
DFT.

écrevisse, *French*
DFT; DFWPN.

écritoire, *French*
DFWPB.

écru, *French*
DFT; DFWPB.

écuelle, *French*
ACD.

ed, *Italian*
OCM.

edel, *German*
OCM.

edel, *Yiddish*
JOY.

edelkeit, *Yiddish*
JOY.

Edelweiss, *German*
DFWPN.

editio princeps, *Latin*
DFPA; DFPCQ; DFT; DFWPN.

editio princeps, *pl.* editiones
principes, *Latin*
DFWPB.

editus, *Latin*
DFWPN.

E dur, *German*
ICMM.

effacé, *French*
LB.

effacé derrière, *French*
LB/*effacé, effacée.*

effacé devant, *French*
LB/*effacé, effacée.*

effacée, *French*
LB/*effacé.*

effacé en arrière, *French*
LB/*effacé, effacée.*

effacé en avant, *French*
LB/*effacé, effacée.*

effets d'orage, *French*
OCM.

effleurage, *French*
DFWPB.

effleurer, *French*
OCM.

ef haristo, *Modern Greek*
DFT.

égal, *French*
OCM.

égale, *French*
OCM.

egalité, *French*
DFPCQ.

égalité, *French*
DFT; DFWPN.

église, *French*
DFWPN.

églogue, *French*
OCM.

ego, *Latin*
DFWPB; DFWPN.

eguaglianza, *Italian*
ICMM.

eguale, *Italian*
OCM.

egualemente, *Italian*
ICMM/*eguaglianza.*

eidola, *Greek*
DFWPN.

eidōlon, *Greek*
DFPCQ.

eidos, *Greek*
DFWPN.

eidyllion, *Greek*
DFWPN.

Eifer, *German*
OCM.

eifrig, *German*
OCM.

eikon, *Greek*
DFWPN.

eikōn, *Greek*
DFPCQ.

Eile, *German*
OCM.

eilen, *German*
OCM.

eilig, *German*
OCM.

ein, *German*
OCM.

eine, *German*
OCM.

einfach, *German*
OCM.

Einfacher Choral, *German*
ICMM.

einige, *German*
OCM.

Einkanter, *German*
GG.

Einleitung, *German*
ICMM.

Einleitungspiel, *German*
ICMM/*Einleitungssatz.*

Einleitungssatz, *German*
ICMM.

einlenken, *German*
OCM.

einmal, *German*
OCM.

einredenish, *Yiddish*
JOY.

Einsang, *German*
ICMM.

Einschnitt, *German*
ICMM.

einstimmig, *German*
OCM.

eintritt, *German*
OCM.

ein wenig schneller, *German*
DFT.

einzeln, *German*
OCM.

eirēann go brat, *Gaelic*
DFT.

Eis, *German*
ICMM; OCM.

Eisen und Blut, *German*
DFPA; DFWPB.

Eisis, *German*
ICMM; OCM.

ejido, *Spanish*
DFT.

ejusdem generis, *Latin*
DFPCQ.

el, *Spanish*
DFWPN.

-el, *Yiddish*
HFY.

élan, *French*
DFT; DFWPN; OCM.

élancé, *French*
LB.

élancer, *French*
LB.

élan vital, *French*
DFWPB; DFWPN; GG; LP.

élargir, *French*
OCM.

elatton horos, *Greek*
DFWPN.

El Dorado, *Spanish*
DFPCQ; DFWPN.

eldorado, *Spanish*
DFWPB.

élégant, *French*
DFT.

elegantemente, *Italian*
DFT; OCM.

elegantia, *Latin*
DFWPN.

elegantiae arbiter, *Latin*
DFWPB.

elegia, *Italian*
OCM.

elegiaco, *Italian*
OCM/*elegia.*

élégie, *French*
OCM.

eleutheria, *Greek*
ICMM.

elevatio, *Latin*
OCM.

élévation, *French*
DFWPB; LB.

élévation, temps d', *French*
LB.

elevato, *Italian*
OCM.

elevazione, *Italian*
OCM.

élève, *French*
DFWPN; OCM.

elixir vitae, *Latin*
DFPA; DFPCQ; DFT; DFWPN.

El Libertador, *Spanish*
DFWPN.

Elohim, *Hebrew*
DFWPN.

Elohim, *Yiddish*
JOY.

éloigner, *French*
OCM.

émaillerie à jour, *French*
DFWPB.

emakimono, *Japanese*
JLE.

emboîté en tournant, *French*
LB/*emboîté, pas.*

emboîté, pas, *French*
LB.

emboîté sur les pointes, *French*
LB/*emboîté, pas.*

embouchure, *French*
DFPCQ; DFWPB; DFWPN;
GG; ICMM/*lip*; OCM.

emeritus, *Latin*
DEP; DFPCQ; DFT; DFWPN.

meritus, *pl.* emeriti, *Latin*
DFWPB.

migré, *French*
DFT; DFWPN.

migré, *fem.* émigrée, *French*
DFWPB.

minence grise, *French*
DFPA.

mir, *Arabic*
DFT.

moll, *German*
ICMM.

mozione, *Italian*
OCM.

mpfindung, *German*
OCM.

mphase, *French*
OCM.

mphase, *German*
OCM.

mplastrum, *Latin*
DFT.

mployé, *French*
DFPCQ.

mporté, *French*
OCM.

mpressé, *French*
DFT; OCM.

mptor, *Latin*
DFWPN.

mu, *French*
OCM.

n, *French*
DFWPN; OCM.

n, *Spanish*
DFWPN.

n avant!, *French*
DEP.

n badinant, *French*
ICMM.

n bloc, *French*
DFPA; DFT; DFWPN.

en brochette, *French*
DFT; DFT/*brochette*; DFWPB;
DFWPN.

en brosse, *French*
DFPA.

en cabochon, *French*
DFT/*cabochon*; DFT; GG.

encabritada, *Spanish*
DFT.

en camaïeu, *French*
DFWPB.

en casserole, *French*
DFWPB; DFWPN.

encastré, *French*
DFT.

enceinte, *French*
DFT; DFWPN.

enchaînez, *French*
OCM.

enchaînement, *French*
DFWPB; LB; OCM.

en chantant, *French*
ICMM.

enchanté, *French*
DFT.

encheiridion, *Greek*
DFWPN.

enchilada, *Spanish*
DFT.

enciente [*sic*], *French*
DEP.

enclume, *French*
OCM.

encoignure, *French*
ACD.

encore, *French*
DFPCQ; DFT; DFWPN; ICMM;
OCM.

en dedans, *French*
DFWPB.

en dehors, *French*
DFWPB.

en dernier ressort, *French*
DFPA.

en déshabillé, *French*
DEP; DFPA; DFT; DFWPN.

Endrumpf, *German*
GG.

en échelle, *French*
DFT.

en echelon, *French*
GG.

energia, *Italian*
OCM.

energicamente, *Italian*
DFT.

energico, *Italian*
DFT; DFWPN.

en face, *French*
LP.

en fait, *French*
DFWPN.

en famille, *French*
DEP; DFPA; DFT.

enfans perdus [*sic*], *French*
DEP.

enfant, *French*
DFT.

enfant prodigue, *French*
DFWPN.

enfants perdus, *French*
DFPA.

enfant terrible, *French*
DFPA; DFPCQ; DFT/*enfant*;
DFWPN.

enfant terrible, *pl.* **enfants terribles,**
French
DFWPB.

enfant trouvé, *French*
DFWPN.

enfasi, *Italian*
OCM.

enfaticamente, *Italian*
DFT; OCM/*enfatico*.

enfatico, *Italian*
OCM.

enfer, *French*
DFWPN.

en fête, *French*
DFT.

enfilade, *French*
DA.

en flèche, *French*
DFT/*flèche*.

engagé, *French*
DFWPB; LP.

en garde, *French*
DFWPB.

Engelstimme, *German*
OCM.

enger, *German*
OCM.

Engführung, *German*
ICMM; ICMM/*stretto*.

Englisches Horn, *German*
OCM.

engobe, *French*
DFWPB.

en grand, *French*
DFT.

en grande tenue, *French*
DFPA.

en grande toilette, *French*
DFPA; DFT.

en grand seigneur, *French*
DFT/*seigneur*; DFT.

enjambement, *French*
DFWPB; DFWPN.

enlèvement, *French*
LB.

enlevez, *French*
OCM.

enluminure, *French*
DFT.

en masse, *French*
DEP; DFPA; DFPCQ; DFT;
DFWPN.

ennui, *French*
DEP; DFPCQ; DFT; DFWPN.

en papillote, *French*
DFWPN.

en papillotes, *French*
DFPA; DFT.

en passant, *French*
DEP; DFPA; DFPCQ; DFT;
DFWPB; DFWPN.

en plein, *French*
ACD/*enamel*; DFWPB.

en plein air, *French*
DFPA; DFT/*en plein*; LP.

en plein jour, *French*
DFPA; DFWPN.

en prise, *French*
DFWPB.

en queue, *French*
DFPA.

en rapport, *French*
DFT/*rapport*; LP.

en règle, *French*
DEP.

en route, *French*
DEP; DFPCQ; DFT; DFWPB;
DFWPN; SPICE.

ens, *Late Latin*
DFT.

ens, *Latin*
DFWPN.

ensalada, *Spanish*
OCM.

ensaladas, *Spanish*
ICMM.

en scène, *French*
DFT.

ensemble, *French*
DFPCQ; DFWPN; LB; LP;
OCM.

en sourdine, *French*
DFWPB.

en suite, *French*
DEP; DFT; DFWPB.

en surtout, *French*
DFPA.

entelecheia, *Greek*
DFPA.

entendre, *French*
OCM.

entente, *French*
DFT; DFWPB; DFWPN.

Entente Cordiale, *French*
DFWPN; DEP; DFPA.

entente demi-cordiale, *French*
DFPA.

en tête-à-tête, *French*
DFT.

entfernt, *German*
OCM.

entoner, *French*
ICMM.

entourage, *French*
DA; DFT; DFWPN.

en tout, *French*
DEP.

en tout cas, *French*
DFPA.

en-tout-cas, *French*
DFT.

entr'acte, *French*
DFPA; DFPCQ; DFT; DFWPB;
ICMM; OCM.

entrada, *Spanish*
ICMM; OCM.

entrain, *French*
OCM.

entrata, *Italian*
DFT; OCM.

en travesti, *French*
DFWPB.

entrechat, *French*
DFT; DFWPB; DFWPN; LB;
OCM.

entrechat cinq, *French*
LB/*entrechat*.

entrechat cinq fermé, *French*
LB/*entrechat*.

entrechat cinq ouvert, *French*
LB/*entrechat*.

entrechat cinq ramassé, *French*
LB/*entrechat*.

entrechat de volée, *French*
LB.

entrechat dix, *French*
LB/*entrechat.*

entrechat huit, *French*
LB/*entrechat.*

entrechat quatre, *French*
LB/*entrechat.*

entrechat sept, *French*
LB/*entrechat.*

entrechat six, *French*
LB/*entrechat.*

entrechat six de volée, *French*
LB/*entrechat de volée.*

entrechat trois, *French*
LB/*entrechat.*

entrecôte, *French*
DFT; DFWPB.

entredeux, *French*
DFWPB.

entrée, *French*
DFPCQ; DFWPB; DFWPN;
ICMM; LB; OCM.

entrelacé, *French*
LB.

entremés, *Spanish*
OCM.

entremet, *French*
DFWPN.

entremets, *French*
DFT; DFWPB.

entre nous, *French*
DEP; DFPA; DFPCQ; DFT;
DFWPN; SPICE.

entrepôt, *French*
DEP; DFWPN.

entrepreneur, *French*
DFWPN.

entrepreneur, *fem.* **entrepreneuse,**
French
DFWPB.

entresol, *French*
DA; DFT; DFWPN.

Entrückung, *German*
OCM.

entschieden, *German*
OCM.

entschlafen, *German*
ICMM.

entschlossen, *German*
OCM.

entusiasmo, *Italian*
OCM.

Entwurf, *German*
ICMM.

envelopée [*sic*], *French*
LB.

en vérité, *French*
DEP.

envoi, *French*
DA; DFWPN.

en voiture, *French*
DFWPN.

envoyé, *French*
DEP.

eo die, *Latin*
DFWPN.

eo nomine, *Latin*
DFWPN.

épater le bourgeois, *French*
LP.

épaulé, épaulée, *French*
LB.

épaulement, *French*
DFWPB; LB.

epea pteroenta, *Greek*
DFPCQ.

épée, *French*
DFWPB.

éperlan, *French*
DFT.

epi, *French*
DA.

épice, *French*
DFT; DFWPN.

Epicidion, *German*
ICMM.

Epicoris, *Yiddish*
JOY.

epidiapente, *Greek*
OCM.

pigramme, *French*
DFT.

pinard, *French*
DFT.

pinette, *French*
OCM.

piskopos, *Greek*
DFWPN.

pisteme, *Greek*
DFWPN.

pistola, *Latin*
DFWPN.

pitalamio, *Italian*
ICMM/*epithalamium.*

pithalame, *French*
ICMM/*epithalamium.*

pithalamion, *Greek*
DFWPN.

pithalamium, *Latin*
DFPCQ.

pitonium, *Latin*
ICMM.

pluribus unum, *Latin*
DEP; DFPA; DFPCQ; DFT;
DFWPN.

ponge, baguette d', *French*
OCM.

pos, *Greek*
DFWPN.

ppes, *Yiddish*
HFY; JOY.

pure, *French*
DA.

quabile, *Italian*
OCM.

quabilmente, *Italian*
DFT.

quale, *Italian*
OCM.

ques, *Latin*
DFWPN.

équilibre, *French*
LB.

équivaut, *French*
OCM.

e (ex) re nata, *Latin*
DFPA.

Eretz Israel, *Yiddish*
JOY/*Eretz Yisroel.*

Eretz Yisrael, *Yiddish*
JOY/*Eretz Yisroel.*

Eretz Yisroel, *Yiddish*
JOY.

ergeron, *French*
GG.

ergo, *Latin*
DFPCQ; DFT; DFWPB;
DFWPN.

ergon, *Greek*
DFWPN.

ergriffen, *German*
OCM.

erhaben, *German*
OCM.

êrh hsien, *Chinese*
ICMM.

Erhöhungs-zeichen, *German*
ICMM.

Erin go bragh, *Gaelic*
DFWPN.

Erin go bragh, *Irish*
DFPA; DFT.

erin go bragh, *Pseudo-Irish*
DFWPB.

erleichterung, *German*
OCM.

erlöschend, *German*
OCM.

Ermangelung, *German*
OCM.

ermattend, *German*
OCM.

ermattet, *German*
OCM/*ermattend.*

erniedrigen, *German*
OCM.

Erniedrigung, *German*
ICMM.

eroica, *Italian*
DFWPN; OCM/*eroico.*

eroico, *Italian*
DFT; OCM.

erotica, *Italian*
DFT.

erotikon, *Greek*
OCM.

errare est humanum, *Latin*
DEP; DFPCQ.

errare humanum est, *Latin*
DFPA; DFWPN.

errata, *Latin*
DFPA; DFWPN/*erratum.*

erratum, *Latin*
DFWPN.

erratum, *pl.* **errata,** *Latin*
DFPCQ.

Ersatz, *German*
DFWPB; DFWPN; OCM.

erschüttert, *German*
OCM.

erst, *German*
OCM.

erste, *German*
OCM/*erst.*

ersterbend, *German*
OCM.

erstickt, *German*
OCM.

erweitert, *German*
OCM.

Erzähler, *German*
ICMM; OCM.

Erziehungsroman, *German*
DFWPB.

erzürnt, *German*
OCM.

Es, *German*
OCM.

esaltato, *Italian*
OCM.

esalté, *French*
OCM.

esatta, *Italian*
OCM/*esatto.*

esatto, *Italian*
OCM.

escargot, *French*
DFT; DFWPB.

escargots, *French*
DFWPN.

escarpment, *French*
GG.

escritoire, *French*
DFWPN.

escritoire, *Old French*
DFWPB.

esecuzione, *Italian*
OCM.

esercizi, *Italian*
OCM/*esercizio.*

esercizio, *Italian*
OCM.

Eses, *German*
OCM.

Es moll, *German*
ICMM.

esonare, *Italian*
ICMM.

esotica, *Italian*
OCM/*esotico.*

esotico, *Italian*
OCM.

espada, *Spanish*
DFWPN; DSTE/*237.*

espadrille, *Spanish*
DFWPN.

Espagne, *French*
OCM.

espagnol, *French*
OCM.

espagnola, *Italian*
OCM/*espagnolo.*

espagnole, *French*
OCM/*espagnol.*

espagnolette, *French*
ACD.

espagnolo, *Italian*
OCM.

espagnuola, *Italian*
OCM/*espagnolo.*

espagnuola, all', *Italian*
ICMM.

espagnuolo, *Italian*
OCM/*espagnolo.*

espalier, *French*
DA.

española, *Spanish*
OCM.

esperanza, *Spanish*
DFWPN.

espirando, *Italian*
ICMM; OCM.

espressione, *Italian*
DFPCQ; DFT; OCM.

espressivo, *Italian*
DFPCQ; DFT; DFWPN; OCM.

espresso, *Italian*
DFWPB.

espringale, *French*
ICMM.

esprit, *French*
DFT; DFWPN.

esprit de corps, *French*
DEP; DFPA; DFPCQ; DFT/
esprit; DFWPB; SPICE.

esprit d'escalier, *French*
DFWPB; DFWPN.

esprit gaulois, *French*
DFWPN.

esquisse, *French*
DA; ICMM/*sketch*; ICMM;
OCM; OCM/*sketch.*

esquisse-esquisse, *French*
DA.

esraj, *Hindi*
ICMM.

esse, *Latin*
DFT; DFWPN.

esse est percipi, *Latin*
DFWPN.

essence, l', *French*
LP.

esse quam videri, *Latin*
DFPCQ.

essodio, *Italian*
ICMM.

está bien, *Spanish*
DFWPN.

Estados Unidos, *Spanish*
DFWPN.

estaminet, *French*
DA.

estampida, *French*
OCM/*estampie.*

estampie, *French*
OCM.

estinguendo, *Italian*
ICMM; OCM.

estinto, *Italian*
ICMM; OCM.

est modus in rebus, *Latin*
DEP; DFPCQ; DFWPN.

estocada, *Spanish*
DSTE/*237.*

estompé, *French*
OCM.

esto perpetua, *Latin*
DEP.

estoque, *Spanish*
DSTE/*237.*

estravaganza, *Italian*
OCM.

estremamente, *Italian*
OCM.

estribillo, *Spanish*
OCM.

estudiantina, *Spanish*
OCM/*estudiantino.*

estudiantino, *Spanish*
OCM.

esturgeon, *French*
DFT.

es tut mir leid, *German*
DFT.

esultazione, *Italian*
OCM.

et, *French*
DFWPN; OCM/*Lat.*

et, *Latin*
DFWPN.

Eta, *Japanese*
JLE.

étage, *French*
DA.

étagère, *French*
ACD; DFT; DFWPB.

et aliae, *Latin*
DFPA/*et alii*; DFT/*et alii.*

et alii, *Latin*
DFPA; DFT; DFWPN.

étang, *French*
GG.

état, *French*
DFWPN.

Etats Unis, *French*
DFWPN.

et caetera, *Latin*
DFWPN.

et cetera, *Latin*
DFPA; DFPCQ; DFWPN.

et cum spiritu tuo, *Latin*
DFT.

éteindre, *French*
OCM.

étendre, *French*
LB.

étendue, *French*
ICMM; OCM.

ethica, *Latin*
DFWPN.

et hoc genus omne, *Latin*
DFPCQ.

et incarnatus, *Latin*
ICMM.

et incarnatus est, *Latin*
OCM.

et in spiritum sanctum, *Latin*
OCM.

et in unum dominum, *Latin*
OCM.

étoile, *French*
DFT; LB.

étoile de mer, *French*
DFT/*étoile.*

étouffé, *French*
ICMM.

étouffer, *French*
OCM.

et passim, *Latin*
DFWPN.

être, *French*
DFWPN.

et resurrexit, *Latin*
ICMM; OCM.

et sequens, *Latin*
DFT; DFWPN.

et sequentes, *Latin*
DFPA; DFT.

et sequentia, *Latin*
DFPA/*et sequentes*; DFT/*et
sequentes*; DFWPN.

et similia, *Latin*
DFT.

ettachordo, *Italian*
ICMM.

et tu Brute, *Latin*
DFWPN.

et tu, Brute, *Latin*
DEP; DFPCQ; DFWPB; DFT.

étude, *French*
DFT; DFWPB; DFWPN; OCM.

etude de concert, *French*
DFT/*étude.*

études, *French*
ICMM.

étudiant, *French*
DFWPN.

étui, *French*
ACD; ICMM.

étuvée, *French*
DFT.

et uxor, *Latin*
DFPA; DFWPN.

et vir, *Latin*
DFPA.

et vitam, *Latin*
ICMM.

etwas, *German*
OCM.

etwas langsamer, *German*
ICMM.

etymon, *Greek*
DFPCQ; DFWPN.

euge, *Greek*
DFPCQ.

Euphonion, *German*
OCM.

eureka, *Greek*
DFWPN.

eurus, *Latin*
DFPCQ.

évasé, *French*
DA.

éveillé, *French*
OCM.

evirato, *Italian*
ICMM; OCM.

evocación, *Spanish*
OCM.

evolutio, *Latin*
ICMM.

ewige Jude, der, *German*
DFPCQ.

ex, *Latin*
DFPCQ; DFWPN.

ex abundantia, *Latin*
DFPCQ.

exactement, *French*
OCM.

ex aequo, *Latin*
DFPA.

ex animo, *Latin*
DFPA; DFPCQ.

ex auctoritate mihi commissa, *Latin*
DEP.

ex capite, *Latin*
DEP; DFPA; DFPCQ; DFWPN.

ex cathedra, *Latin*
DFPA; DFPCQ; DFT; DFWPB;
DFWPN; SPICE.

ex cathedrâ, *Latin*
DEP.

excelsior, *Latin*
DEP; DFPA; DFPCQ; DFT;
DFWPN.

exceptio probat regulam, *Latin*
DEP; DFPCQ; DFWPN.

exceptis excipiendis, *Latin*
DFPCQ.

excerpta, *Latin*
DEP; DFPCQ.

ex concessis, *Latin*
DFWPN.

ex concesso, *Latin*
DEP; DFPA.

ex contractu, *Latin*
DFPA.

ex curia, *Latin*
DFPA; DFPCQ; DFWPN.

ex curiâ, *Latin*
DEP.

excursus, *Latin*
DFPCQ.

ex delicto, *Latin*
DFPA; DFWPB.

exeat, *Latin*
DFPA; DFWPN.

exegetes, *Latin*
DFWPN.

exemplar, *Latin*
DFPCQ.

exempli gratia, *Latin*
DFPA; DFT; DFWPB; DFWPN.

exempli gratiâ, *Latin*
DEP.

exempli gratia (e.g. or ex. gr.), *Latin*
DFPCQ.

exemplum, *Latin*
DFT; DFWPN.

Exequien, *German*
ICMM.

exercices à la barre, *French*
LB.

exercices au milieu, *French*
LB.

exeunt, *Latin*
DFT; DFWPB; DFWPN.

exeunt omnes, *Latin*
DEP; DFPA; DFT/*exeunt*;
DFWPB; DFWPN.

ex facie, *Latin*
DFT.

ex facto, *Latin*
DFWPN.

ex gratia, *Latin*
DFPA.

ex grege, *Latin*
DFPA.

ex hypothesi, *Latin*
DFPA; DFPCQ.

exit, *Latin*
DEP; DFPCQ; DFT; DFWPB.

exitus acta probat, *Latin*
DEP.

ex libris, *Latin*
DFPA; DFT; DFWPB; DFWPN.

ex more, *Latin*
DEP; DFWPN.

ex necessitate rei, *Latin*
DEP; DFPA; DFPCQ.

ex nihilo, *Latin*
DFWPN.

ex nihilo nihil fit, *Latin*
DEP; DFPCQ; DFT.

ex officio, *Latin*
DEP; DFPA; DFPCQ; DFT;
DFWPB; DFWPN; SPICE.

exordium, *Latin*
DFPCQ.

ex parte, *Latin*
DEP; DFPA; DFT; DFWPN.

ex pede herculem, *Latin*
DFPA.

experientia docet, *Latin*
DFPCQ.

experientia docet stultos, *Latin*
DEP.

experimentum crucis, *Latin*
DEP.

experto crede, *Latin*
DFPA; DFWPN.

expertus, *Latin*
DEP.

explication de texte, *French*
DFPA; DFWPB.

explicit, *Latin*
DFPA.

exposé, *French*
DEP; DFPCQ: DFT; DFWPB;
DFWPN.

ex post facto, *Latin*
DEP; DFPA; DFPCQ; DFT;
DFWPN.

ex post facto/expostfacto, *Latin*
DFWPB.

expressif, *French*
OCM.

expressis verbis, *Latin*
DEP.

ex professo, *Latin*
DEP.

ex propriis, *Latin*
DFT.

ex quocunque capite, *Latin*
DFWPN.

ex relatione, *Latin*
DFPA.

ex (e) silentio, *Latin*
DFPA.

ex silentio, *Latin*
DFWPB.

ex tempore, *Latin*
DEP; DFPA; DFPCQ; DFT;
DFWPN.

ex tempore/extempore, *Latin*
DFWPB.

extempore, *Latin*
  LP.
extension, *French*
  LB.
extra muros, *Latin*
  DFPA; DFPCQ; DFT.
extrêmement, *French*
  OCM.

ex uno disce omnes, *Latin*
  DEP; DFPCQ; DFWPN.
ex voluntate, *Latin*
  DFWPN.
ex voto, *Latin*
  DFPA; DFT; DFWPN.
ezcudantza, *Spanish*
  OCM.

F

fa, *Italian*
OCM.

faber suæ fortunæ, *Latin*
DEP.

fabliau, *French*
DFT.

fabliau, *Old French*
DFWPN.

fabula, *Latin*
DFWPN.

fabula palliata, *Latin*
DFPA.

fabula togata, *Latin*
DFPA.

fac, *Latin*
DFWPN.

façade, *French*
DFPCQ; DFT; DFWPN.

face, de, *French*
LB.

face, en, *French*
LB.

facetiae, *Latin*
DFPCQ.

facetiæ, *Latin*
DEP.

facettes, *French*
DA.

Fach, *German*
OCM.

facile, *French*
DFT; OCM.

facile, *Italian*
DFT; OCM.

facilement, *French*
OCM.

facile princeps, *Latin*
DEP.

facilis descensus Averni, *Latin*
DFPCQ.

facilis est descensus, *Latin*
DFPCQ.

facilità, *Italian*
OCM.

facilmente, *Italian*
OCM/*facilement*.

Fackeltanz, *German*
OCM.

façon de parler, *French*
DFWPN.

façonné, *French*
DFWPB.

facta, *Latin*
DFWPN/*factum*.

fac totum, *Latin*
DEP.

factotum, *Latin*
DFPCQ; DFWPB; DFWPN.

factum, *Latin*
DFWPN.

factura 150

factura, *Spanish*
DSTE.

fadama, *Hausa*
GG.

fa dièse, *French*
ICMM.

fadinho, *Portuguese*
OCM.

fado, *Portuguese*
OCM.

faïence, *French*
DFT; DFWPB; DFWPN.

faex populi, *Latin*
DFWPN.

fa fictum, *Latin*
OCM.

fagioli, *Italian*
DFWPN.

Fagott, *German*
OCM; ICMM.

fagottino, *Italian*
ICMM.

fagotto, *Italian*
DFPCQ; DFWPN; OCM/*fagott.*

fagotto contra, *Italian*
ICMM.

fagottone, *Italian*
ICMM.

Fahlband, *German*
GG.

Fahlerz, *German*
GG.

Fahlore, *German*
GG.

Fahnen-marsch, *German*
ICMM.

fahren, *German*
OCM.

faible, *French*
OCM.

faience, *French*
ACD; DFT.

faience anglais, *French*
ACD/*faience.*

faience Japonnée, *French*
ACD/*faience.*

faience parlante, *French*
ACD/*faience.*

faience populaire, *French*
ACD/*faience.*

faience porcelaine, *French*
ACD/*faience.*

faillé, *French*
DFWPN.

faille, *French*
DFWPB.

failli, pas, *French*
LB.

fáilte, *Irish*
DFWPB.

faire, *French*
DFWPN; OCM.

faire le salon, *French*
DFWPN.

faisan, *French*
DFT.

fait, *French*
DFWPN.

fait accompli, *French*
DFPA; DFPCQ; DFT; DFWPB;
DFWPN.

faites, *French*
OCM.

faites vos jeux, *French*
DFWPB.

faja, *Spanish*
DSTE//*237.*

fakir, *Hindi*
DFT; DFWPN.

falaise, *French*
GG.

Fall, *German*
OCM.

Falle, *German*
OCM/*Fall.*

falsetto, *Italian*
DFPCQ; DFWPB; DFWPN;
ICMM; OCM.

falsobordone, *Italian*
ICMM; OCM; OCM/*faburden.*

fama, *Latin*
DFPCQ; DFWPN.

fama volat, *Latin*
DFT.

famille jaune, *French*
ACD; DFWPB.

famille noire, *French*
ACD; DFWPB.

famille rose, *French*
ACD; DFWPB.

famille verte, *French*
ACD; DFWPB.

fanático, *Spanish*
DFT.

fandango, *Spanish*
DFWPB; DFWPN; ICMM;
OCM.

fandanguillo, *Spanish*
ICMM.

fantaisie, *French*
ICMM/*fantasia*; OCM.

fantasia, *Italian*
DFWPB; OCM.

Fantasiestück, *German*
OCM.

fantasque, *French*
OCM/*fantastico.*

fantastico, *Italian*
OCM.

fantastisch, *German*
OCM/*fantastico.*

farandole, *French*
DFT; ICMM.

farandole, *Spanish*
OCM.

Farbe, *German*
OCM.

Farbe-ton, *German*
ICMM/*Tonfarbe.*

farbissen, *Yiddish*
JOY.

farbisseneh, *Yiddish*
JOY/*farbissen.*

farbissener, *Yiddish*
JOY/*farbissen.*

farblondjet, *Yiddish*
JOY.

farce, *French*
DFT; DFWPN.

farchadat, *Yiddish*
JOY.

farci, *French*
DFWPB; DFWPN.

fare, *Latin*
DFWPN.

farfufket, *Yiddish*
HFY.

farmisht, *Yiddish*
HFY.

far niente, *Italian*
DFT; DFWPN.

farpatshket, *Yiddish*
HFY.

farpotshket, *Yiddish*
JOY.

farruca, *Spanish*
OCM.

farshtinkener, *Yiddish*
HFY; JOY.

fartootst, *Yiddish*
JOY.

fartootsteh, *Yiddish*
JOY/*fartootst.*

fartootster, *Yiddish*
JOY/*fartootst.*

fartumelt, *Yiddish*
HFY.

fartutst, *Yiddish*
HFY.

fas, *Latin*
DFWPN.

fasces, *Latin*
DFPCQ; DFWPN.

fascia, *Latin*
DFPCQ.

fascie, *Italian*
ICMM.

fas est ab hoste doceri, *Latin*
DEP.

Fassung, *German*
OCM.

fast, *German*
OCM.

fasti, *Latin*
DFWPN.

fastoso, *Italian*
OCM.

fata morgana, *Latin*
DFPCQ.

fata Morgana, *Italian*
DEP; DFWPB.

fata obstant, *Latin*
DFWPN.

fatihah, *Arabic*
DFT.

fatrasie, *French*
DFWPN.

fatum, *Latin*
DFWPN.

fatuus, *Latin*
DFWPN.

fausset, *French*
OCM.

fausse tortue, *French*
DFT.

fauteuil, *French*
ACD; DEP; DFT; DFWPB.

(Les) Fauves, *French*
DFWPB.

fauvisme, *French*
DFWPB.

faux, *French*
DFWPN.

faux ami, *French*
DFPA.

faux amis, *French*
DFWPB.

fauxbourdon, *French*
ICMM; OCM/*faburden*; OCM.

faux pas, *French*
DEP; DFPA; DFPCQ; DFT/
faux; DFWPB; DFWPN; SPICE.

faygele, *Yiddish*
HFY/*feygele.*

faygeleh, *Yiddish*
JOY.

F dur, *German*
ICMM.

fe, *Spanish*
DFWPN.

fec(it), *Latin*
DFWPB.

fecit, *Latin*
DEP; DFPA; DFPCQ; DFT;
DFWPN; LP.

fedele, *Italian*
ICMM.

fedora, *French*
DFWPN.

feh, *Yiddish*
JOY.

feierlich, *German*
OCM.

Feis, *Gaelic*
DFWPN.

fei ts'ui, *Chinese*
GG.

feldpartita, *German*
OCM.

Feldrohr, *German*
ICMM.

feldsher, *Russian*
MRWEW/*18.*

Feldton, *German*
ICMM.

Feld-trompete, *German*
ICMM.

felice, *Italian*
OCM.

felix, *Latin*
DFWPN.

felix culpa, *Latin*
DFT.

femme, *French*
DFT; DFWPN.

femme couverte, *French*
DFPA.

femme de chambre, *French*
DEP.

femme fatale, *French*
DFPA; DFWPB; DFWPN.

fendu, *French*
DFT.

fenêtre, *French*
GG.

fêng ling, *Chinese*
ICMM.

fenouil, *French*
DFT.

Fenster, *German*
GG.

fermamente, *Italian*
OCM.

fermata, *Italian*
DFT; ICMM; ICMM/*pause*;
OCM.

fermate, *German*
OCM/*fermata*.

ferme, *French*
OCM.

fermé, fermée, *French*
LB.

fermé(e), *French*
DFWPN.

fermer, *French*
OCM.

fermezza, *Italian*
OCM.

fermo, *Italian*
OCM.

ferne, *German*
OCM.

Fernflöte, *German*
OCM.

Fernwerk, *German*
OCM.

feroce, *Italian*
OCM.

ferrum, *Latin*
DFWPN.

fertig, *German*
OCM.

fertigkeit, *German*
DFT.

fervente, *Italian*
OCM.

fervidamente, *Italian*
OCM/*fervido*.

fervido, *Italian*
OCM.

fervore, *Italian*
OCM/*fervido*.

Fes, *German*
ICMM; OCM.

Feses, *German*
OCM.

Fest, *German*
OCM.

festa, *Italian*
OCM.

festa teatrale, *Italian*
DFWPB.

festina lente, *Latin*
DFPA; DFPCQ; DFT; DFWPN.

festivamente, *Italian*
DFT.

festivo, *Italian*
OCM.

festlich, *German*
OCM.

festoso, *Italian*
OCM.

Festschrift, *German*
DFWPB; DFWPN.

Festspiel, *German*
OCM.

fête, *French*
DFPCQ; DFT; DFWPB;
DFWPN.

fête champêtre, *French*
DEP.

fettucini, *Italian*
DFT.

fetus, *Latin*
DFPCQ.

feu de joie, *French*
DEP.

Feuer, *German*
OCM.

Feuerstein, *German*
GG.

feuille d'album, *French*
OCM.

feuilletage, *French*
DFWPN.

feuilleton, *French*
DFPCQ; DFWPN.

feurig, *German*
OCM.

fève, *French*
DFT.

fève de marais, *French*
DFT/*fève.*

feygele, *Yiddish*
HFY.

fez, *Turkish*
DFWPN.

fiacco, *Italian*
OCM.

fiamme, *Italian*
GG.

fiancée, *French*
DFWPN.

fianchetto, *Italian*
DFWPB.

fiat, *Latin*
DFPCQ; DFWPN.

fiata, *Italian*
OCM.

fiate, *Italian*
OCM/*fiata.*

fiat lux, *Latin*
DFPA; DFPCQ; DFT; DFWPB;
DFWPN.

fiato, *Italian*
OCM.

fiat voluntas tua, *Latin*
DFPA.

ficelles, *French*
DFWPN.

Fidei Defensor, *Latin*
DFPA; DFT; DFWPN.

fidei defensor (F.D.), *Latin*
DFPCQ.

fideliter, *Latin*
DFWPN.

fides, *Latin*
DFWPN.

fides Punica, *Latin*
DFPCQ.

Fidus Achates, *Latin*
DFPA; DEP; DFPCQ; DFWPB;
DFWPN; DFT.

Fiedel, *German*
ICMM.

fier, *French*
OCM.

fieramente, *Italian*
DFT.

fière, *French*
OCM/*fier.*

fierezza, *Italian*
OCM.

fieri facias, *Latin*
DFPA.

fiero, *Italian*
OCM.

fiesta, *Spanish*
DFT; DFWPB; DFWPN.

fifer, *Yiddish*
HFY; JOY.

Figuralmusik, *German*
OCM/*musica figurata.*

figurant, *French*
DFT.

155

fiorito

figurante, *Italian*
ICMM.

figura obliqua, *Latin*
ICMM.

figurato, *Italian*
OCM/*figural*.

figure, *French*
LB.

figuré, *French*
OCM/*figural*.

figuriert, *German*
OCM/*figural*; OCM.

filar il suono, *Italian*
DFT/*filar la voce*.

filar il tuono, *Italian*
ICMM.

filar la voce, *Italian*
DFT; OCM.

filer, *French*
LB.

filer la voix, *French*
OCM/*filar la voce*.

filer le son, *French*
OCM/*filar la voce*.

filet, *French*
DFT; DFWPB; DFWPN.

filet mignon, *French*
DFWPB; DFWPN.

filius nullius, *Latin*
DFWPN.

fille, *French*
DFWPN.

fille de joie, *French*
DFPA; DFWPN.

fils, *French*
DEP; DFWPN.

filtre, *French*
DFWPB.

fin, *French*
DFT; DFWPN; OCM.

fin, *Italian*
OCM.

fin, *Yiddish*
JOY.

finale, *Italian*
DFPCQ; DFWPB.

financière, *French*
DFWPN.

fin de siècle, *French*
DFPA; DFT/*fin*; DFWPB;
DFWPN; LP.

fine, *Italian*
DFPCQ; DFT; DFWPN; ICMM;
OCM.

fine (champagne), *French*
DFWPB.

fine champagne, *French*
DFWPN.

fines herbes, *French*
DFWPN.

fines herbes, *pl.*, *French*
DFWPB.

Fingerfertigkeit, *German*
OCM.

Fingersatz, *German*
OCM.

fin gourmet, *French*
DFWPB.

finif, *Yiddish*
JOY.

finiff, *Yiddish*
JOY.

finis, *Latin*
DEP; DFPCQ; DFWPB;
DFWPN.

finis coronat opus, *Latin*
DEP; DFPCQ.

finnif, *Yiddish*
JOY.

fino, *Italian*
ICMM; OCM.

fioco, *Italian*
DFT.

fioreggiante, *Italian*
DFT.

fiorette, *Italian*
ICMM/*ornaments*.

fiorito, *Italian*
DFT.

fioritura, *Italian*
DFT; OCM.

fioritura, *pl.* **fioriture,** *Italian*
DFWPB.

fioriture, *Italian*
DFPCQ; ICMM/*ornaments*;
ICMM.

firn, *German*
GG.

Firnspiegel, *German*
GG.

Fis, *German*
OCM.

fiscus, *Latin*
DFWPN.

Fis, Fisis, *German*
ICMM.

Fisis, *German*
OCM.

fistula panis, *Latin*
ICMM.

fjäll, *Swedish*
GG.

fjard, *Swedish*
GG.

fjeld, *Norwegian*
GG.

fjeldbotn, *Norwegian*
GG.

fjeldmark, *Norwegian*
GG.

fjord, *Norwegian*
DFT; DFWPB; GG.

fl(oruit), *Latin*
DFWPB.

flacon, *French*
DFT.

flacon d'odeur, *French*
DFT/*flacon.*

Fladen, *German*
GG.

flageolet, *French*
OCM.

flageolet notes, *French*
OCM.

Flageolett, *German*
OCM.

Flageolettöne, *German*
OCM/*flageloett.*

flageolet tones, *French*
OCM/*flageolet notes.*

flagrans, *Latin*
DFWPN.

flagrante bello, *Latin*
DEP; DFPA; DFPCQ.

flagrante delicto, *Latin*
DEP; DFPA; DFPCQ; DFT;
DFWPB; DFWPN.

flambé, *French*
ACD; DFT; DFWPB.

flamenco, *Spanish*
DFT; DFWPB; DFWPN; OCM.

flan, *Spanish*
DFT.

flânerie, *French*
DFT.

flatté, *French*
ICMM.

flattément, *French*
ICMM.

flatter, *French*
OCM.

Flatterzunge, *German*
OCM.

flatus, *Latin*
DFPCQ.

flautando, *Italian*
ICMM; OCM.

flautato, *Italian*
OCM/*flautando.*

flautendo, *French*
OCM.

flauti, *Italian*
OCM.

flautina, *Italian*
ICMM; OCM.

flauto, *Italian*
DFPCQ; OCM.

flauto a becco, *Italian*
OCM.

flauto amabile, *Italian*
OCM.

flauto d'amore, *Italian*
OCM/*amore, amour*; OCM.

flauto d'echo, *Italian*
DFWPB.

flauto d'eco, *Italian*
OCM.

flauto diritto, *Italian*
OCM.

flauto dolce, *Italian*
OCM.

flautone, *Italian*
ICMM; OCM.

flauto piccolo, *Italian*
DFPCQ; ICMM; OCM.

flauto traverso, *Italian*
OCM.

flayshedig, *Yiddish*
JOY.

flayshig, *Yiddish*
JOY.

flebile, *Italian*
DFPCQ; DFT; OCM.

flebilmente, *Italian*
DFT; OCM/*flebile*.

flèche, *French*
DA; DFT.

flèche d'amour, *French*
GG.

fléchir, *French*
LB.

Fleckschiefer, *German*
GG.

Fledermaus, *German*
DFWPN.

flehend, *German*
OCM.

flessibile, *Italian*
OCM.

flessibiltà, *Italian*
OCM/*flessibile*.

fleur, *French*
DFT; DFWPN.

fleur de lis, *French*
DFPCQ; DFWPN.

fleur-de-lis, *French*
DA; DFT/*fleur*; GG.

fleur de lys, *French*
DFPA.

fleuret, *French*
DFT.

fleuron, *French*
DFT.

flic-flac, *French*
LB.

flic-flac en tournant, *French*
LB/*flic-flac*.

flicorni, *Italian*
OCM/*flicorno*.

flicorno, *Italian*
OCM.

fliessend, *German*
OCM.

Floetz, *German*
GG.

Flora Danica, *Latin*
ACD/*Copenhagen*.

florida, *Spanish*
DFWPN.

florilegium, *Latin*
DFWPN.

floruit, *Latin*
DFPA; DFT; DFWPN.

Flöte, *German*
OCM.

flottant, *French*
OCM.

flotter, *French*
OCM.

flüchtig, *German*
OCM.

Fluegelhorn, *German*
ICMM.

Flügel, *German*
ICMM; OCM.

Flügelhorn, *German*
DFT; OCM.

fluido, *Italian*
OCM.

flüssig, *German*
OCM.

flûte, *French*
OCM.

flûté, *French*
OCM.

flûte à bec, *French*
ICMM; OCM.

flûte à cheminée, *French*
OCM.

flûte allemande, *French*
ICMM.

flûte alto, *French*
OCM.

flûte à pavillon, *French*
OCM.

flûte d'amour, *French*
ICMM; OCM; OCM/*amore,
amour.*

flûte d'angleterre, *French*
OCM.

flûte douce, *French*
OCM.

Flysch, *German*
GG.

F moll, *German*
ICMM.

foco, *Italian*
OCM.

focosamente, *Italian*
DFT.

focoso, *Italian*
DFT; OCM.

Foehn, *German*
GG.

Föhn, *German*
DFWPN.

föhrde, *Danish*
GG.

foie, *French*
DFT.

foie de veau, *French*
DFT/*foie.*

foie gras, *French*
DFT/*foie*; DFWPB.

foies gras, *French*
DFWPN.

fois, *French*
OCM.

Folge, *German*
OCM.

folgen, *German*
OCM.

folia, *Portuguese*
ICMM.

folía, *Portuguese*
OCM.

folie de grandeur, *French*
DFWPN.

folio verso, *Latin*
DFT.

folks-mensh, *Yiddish*
JOY.

follia, *Portuguese*
ICMM/*folia.*

follía, *Portuguese*
OCM/*folia.*

fonda, *Spanish*
DFPCQ.

fondant, *French*
DFWPB; DFWPN.

fondé(e), *French*
DFWPN.

fondo d'oro, *Italian*
DFWPB.

fonds d'orgue, *French*
OCM.

fondu, *French*
LB.

fondue, *French*
DFT; DFWPB; DFWPN; LB/
fondu.

fonfer, *Yiddish*
HFY; JOY.

fons et origo, *Latin*
DFPA.

fons et origo malorum, *Latin*
DFPA.

fonte, *French*
DFWPN.

force de frappe, *French*
DFPA.

force majeure, *French*
DFPA; DFT; DFWPB; DFWPN.

förde, *Danish*
GG.

forensis, *Latin*
DFWPN.

forlana, *Italian*
ICMM; OCM.

forlane, *French*
OCM.

formaggio, *Italian*
DFWPN.

format de poche, *French*
OCM.

formes libres *pl.*, *French*
DFWPB.

Formkreis, *German*
GG.

fors, *Swedish*
GG.

fort, *French*
DFWPN.

fort, *German*
OCM.

forte, *French*
DFWPB.

forte, *Italian*
DFPA; DFPCQ; DFT; DFWPN;
ICMM; OCM.

forte forte, *Italian*
DFT/*forte.*

forte-piano, *Italian*
DFT/*forte.*

forte possible, *Italian*
DFT/*forte.*

fortfahren, *German*
OCM.

fortissimo, *Italian*
DFPCQ; DFT; DFWPN; OCM.

Fortrücken, *German*
ICMM.

Fortsetzung, *German*
OCM.

fortuna caeca est, *Latin*
DFWPN.

fortuna fortes juvat, *Latin*
DFWPN.

fortuna sequatur, *Latin*
DFPCQ.

forza, *Italian*
DFT; OCM.

forzando, *Italian*
DFPCQ; DFT.

foso, *Spanish*
GG.

Fossildiagenese, *German*
GG.

fou, *French*
DFWPN.

fouetté, *French*
DFWPB; DFWPN; LB; OCM.

fouetté, demi, *French*
LB/*fouetté.*

fouetté, grand, *French*
LB/*fouetté.*

fouetté, petit, *French*
LB/*fouetté.*

fouetté en l'air, *French*
LB/*fouetté.*

fouetté en tournant, petit, *French*
LB/*fouetté.*

fouetté raccourci, *French*
LB/*fouetté.*

fouetté rond de jambe en tournant, *French*
LB/*fouetté.*

fougueuse, *French*
OCM/*fougueux.*

fougueux, *French*
OCM.

four, *French*
DFWPN.

fourchette, *French*
DFT; DFWPB; DFWPN.

fourragère, *French*
DFT.

foyer, *French*
DFWPN.

fra, *Italian*
DEP; DFWPN.

fracas, *French*
DFPCQ.

fraîche, *French*
OCM/*frais.*

frais, *French*
OCM.

fraise, *French*
DFT; DFWPN.

Fraktur, *German*
DFWPB; DFT.

framboise, *French*
DFT; DFWPN.

franc, *French*
DFWPN; OCM.

français, *French*
OCM.

française, *French*
ICMM; OCM/*français*; OCM.

franchezza, *Italian*
OCM.

franchise, *French*
OCM/*franchezza.*

frangipane, *French*
DFWPN.

frappé, *French*
DFT; DFWPB; DFWPN; LB.

frapper, *French*
OCM.

Frau, *German*
DFPCQ; DFWPB; DFWPN;
DFT.

Frauenchor, *German*
OCM.

Fräulein, *German*
DFPCQ; DFWPB; DFWPN.

freddamente, *Italian*
DFT.

freddo, *Italian*
OCM.

fredon, *French*
ICMM.

fredonner, *French*
OCM.

fregiatura, *Italian*
DFT.

frei, *German*
OCM.

freie, *German*
OCM/*frei.*

Freiekombination, *German*
OCM.

frenetica, *Italian*
OCM/*frenetico.*

frenetico, *Italian*
OCM.

frère, *French*
DFWPN.

frescamente, *Italian*
DFT.

fresco, *Italian*
DFWPB; DFWPN; OCM.

fresco secco, *Italian*
DFWPB; LP/*fresco*; LP.

fress, *Yiddish*
JOY.

fresser, *Yiddish*
DFT; JOY.

fretta, *Italian*
ICMM; OCM.

fuimus

Freude, *German*
OCM.

freudig, *German*
DFT.

friandise, *French*
DFT.

fricassé, *French*
DFWPN.

fricassée, *French*
DFWPB; ICMM.

frijol, *Spanish*
DFT; DSTE.

frijole, *Spanish*
DFT/*frijol*; DSTE/*frijol.*

frijoles, *Spanish*
DFWPN.

frisch, *German*
DFT; OCM.

frit, *French*
DFT; DFWPN.

fritos, *Spanish*
DFWPN.

fritto misto, *Italian*
DFWPB.

friture, *French*
DFT.

fröhlich, *German*
OCM.

froid, *French*
OCM.

fromage, *French*
DFWPN.

fronton, *French*
DA.

frontón, *Spanish*
DFWPN.

Frosch, *German*
OCM.

frosk, *Yiddish*
JOY.

frottage, *French*
LP.

frottola, *Italian*
DFT; ICMM; OCM.

frottole, *Italian*
OCM/*frottola.*

Fruchtschiefer, *German*
GG.

früher, *German*
OCM.

Frühlingslied, *German*
OCM.

frum, *Yiddish*
JOY.

frummeh, *Yiddish*
JOY/*frum.*

frummer, *Yiddish*
JOY/*frum.*

frustra, *Latin*
DFPCQ; DFWPN.

fu, *Chinese*
ACD.

fuchi, *Japanese*
JLE.

fuehrer, *German*
DFT/*führer.*

fuga, *Italian*
DFPCQ; DFT; OCM.

fuga doppia, *Italian*
DFPCQ.

fugato, *Italian*
DFPCQ; DFWPN; ICMM.

fughetta, *Italian*
DFPCQ; DFT; DFWPN; ICMM.

fugit hora, *Latin*
DFPCQ.

fugu, *Japanese*
JLE.

fugue, *French*
OCM.

führend, *German*
OCM.

Führer, *German*
DFWPN; DFT.

Führer, der, *German*
DFWPB.

fuimus, *Latin*
DFPCQ.

fuit Ilium, *Latin*
DFPCQ.

fuji, *Japanese*
JLE.

Fukuoka, *Japanese*
JLE.

fulji, *Arabic*
GG.

Füllflöte, *German*
OCM.

Fülligstimmen, *German*
OCM.

Füllstimme, *German*
OCM.

fumage, *French*
DFWPB.

fun, *Japanese*
JLE.

funèbre, *French*
OCM.

funebre, *Italian*
OCM/*funèbre.*

fünf, *German*
OCM.

funori, *Japanese*
JLE.

fuoco, *Italian*
DFT; OCM.

für, *German*
OCM.

furia, *Italian*
OCM.

furibondo, *Italian*
OCM/*furioso.*

furieusement, *French*
OCM/*furieux.*

furieux, *French*
OCM.

furiosamente, *Italian*
DFT.

furioso, *Italian*
DFPCQ; DFWPN; OCM.

furiosus, *Latin*
DFWPN.

furlano, *Italian*
ICMM/*forlana*; OCM/*forlana.*

furore, *Italian*
DFPCQ; OCM.

furor loquendi, *Latin*
DFPA; DFPCQ.

furor poeticus, *Latin*
DFPA; DFPCQ.

furor scribendi, *Latin*
DFPA; DFPCQ.

Furor Teutonicus, *Latin*
DFPA.

furoshiki, *Japanese*
JLE.

fusa, *Latin*
OCM.

fusain, *French*
DFT.

fusarole, *Italian*
DA.

fusée, *French*
ICMM.

fusella, *Latin*
ICMM.

Fusshang, *German*
GG.

fusuma, *Japanese*
JLE.

futon, *Japanese*
JLE.

fuyant, *French*
OCM.

G

Gabelklavier, *German*
OCM.

gaffe, *French*
DFWPN.

gagaku, *Japanese*
JLE.

gagliarda, *Italian*
OCM.

gai, *French*
OCM.

gaia, *Italian*
OCM/*gaio.*

gaiement, *French*
OCM/*gai.*

gaijin, *Japanese*
JLE.

gaillard, *French*
OCM.

gaillarde, *French*
ICMM.

gaio, *Italian*
OCM.

gaita, *Spanish*
OCM.

gajamente, *Italian*
DFT.

gajo, *Italian*
OCM.

galamment, *French*
OCM/*galant.*

galant, *French*
DFWPB; OCM.

galantemente, *Italian*
DFT.

Galanterien, *German*
ICMM; OCM.

galanteries, *French*
OCM/*galanterien.*

Galanter Stil, *German*
ICMM/*gallant style*; OCM/*style galant*; OCM.

galantine, *French*
DFWPB.

galbe, *French*
DFT; DFWPB.

galimathias, *French*
ICMM.

Galitzianer, *Yiddish*
JOY.

gallegada, *Spanish*
OCM.

galliard, *French*
ICMM.

galop, *French*
DFWPB.

galoubet, *French*
OCM.

galus, *Yiddish*
JOY/*galut.*

galut, *Yiddish*
JOY.

gamba, *Italian*
OCM; OCM/*braccio.*

gambang, *Javanese*
ICMM.

Gambe, *German*
ICMM.

gambusino, *Spanish*
DSTE.

gamelan, *Javanese*
ICMM.

gamine, *French*
DFWPN.

gamma, *Greek*
ICMM.

gamme, *French*
ICMM/*scale;* OCM.

ganascione, *Italian*
ICMM.

gancho, *Spanish*
DFT.

Gan Eden, *Yiddish*
JOY.

gangar, *Norwegian*
OCM.

ganov, *Yiddish*
DFWPN.

ganz, *German*
OCM.

ganze Note, *German*
ICMM/*semibreve.*

Ganzetaktnote, *German*
OCM.

gaon, *Yiddish*
JOY.

garbanzo, *Spanish*
DSTE.

garbanzos, *Spanish*
DFWPN.

Garbenschiefer, *German*
GG.

garbo, *Italian*
OCM.

garbure, *French*
DFT.

garçon, *French*
DEP; DFPCQ; DFT; DFWPN.

garde du corps, *French*
DEP.

garde mobile, *French*
DEP.

garder, *French*
OCM.

gardez la foi, *French*
DFPCQ.

gare, *French*
DA.

gargouillade, *French*
LB.

gargulho, *Portuguese*
GG.

gariglione, *Italian*
ICMM.

garni, *French*
DFT; DFWPB; DFWPN.

garniture de cheminée, *French*
ACD.

garrocha, *Spanish*
DSTE/*237.*

Gassenhauer, *German*
OCM.

gassi, *Arabic*
GG.

gastronome, *French*
DFWPB.

gâteau, *French*
DFT; DFWPN.

gâteau, *pl.* **gâteaux,** *French*
DFWPB.

gâte-sauce, *French*
DFT.

gauche, *French*
DFT; DFWPB; DFWPN; OCM.

gauche, à, *French*
LB.

gaucherie, *French*
DFPCQ; DFT; DFWPB;
DFWPN.

gaucho, *Spanish*
DFT; DFWPB; DFWPN.

Gaudeamus igitur, *Latin*
DFWPN; DFT; DFWPB.

gaudioso, *Italian*
DFT.

gaufrette, *French*
DFWPB.

gavage, *French*
DFT.

gavotta, *Italian*
DFPCQ.

gavotte, *French*
DFWPB; ICMM; OCM.

gazpacho, *Spanish*
DFWPB; DFWPN.

G dur, *German*
ICMM.

gebentsht, *Yiddish*
JOY/*bentsh*.

gebentshteh, *Yiddish*
JOY/*bentsh*.

gebentshter, *Yiddish*
JOY/*bentsh*.

Gebet, *German*
OCM.

Gebrauch, *German*
OCM.

Gebrauchsmusik, *German*
ICMM; OCM.

gebunden, *German*
ICMM/*legato*; OCM.

gedact, *German*
OCM.

gedämpft, *German*
DFT; OCM.

gedeckt, *German*
OCM.

gedehnt, *German*
OCM.

Gedicht, *German*
OCM.

Gefallen, *German*
OCM.

gefällig, *German*
OCM.

gefilte [fish], *Yiddish*
DFWPN; JOY.

Gefühl, *German*
DFT; OCM.

gefulte [fish], *Yiddish*
JOY.

gegen, *German*
OCM.

Gegengesang, *German*
ICMM.

gehalten, *German*
OCM.

gehaucht, *German*
OCM.

geheimnisvoll, *German*
OCM.

Gehena, *Yiddish*
JOY/*Gehenna*.

gehend, *German*
DFT; ICMM; OCM.

Gehenna, *Yiddish*
JOY.

gehörig, *German*
OCM.

Geige, *German*
ICMM; OCM.

Geigen, *German*
OCM.

Geigenprinzipal, *German*
OCM/*Geigen*.

geisha, *Japanese*
DFT; DFWPB; DFWPN; JLE.

Geist, *German*
OCM.

Geisterharfe, *German*
OCM.

geistlich, *German*
OCM.

gekneipt, *German*
OCM.

gekoppelt, *German*
OCM.

gelassen, *German*
OCM.

gelato, *Italian*
DFWPN.

geläufig, *German*
OCM.

Geld, *German*
DFPCQ.

gelée, *French*
DFT; DFWPN.

gelée de groseille, *French*
DFT/*gelée.*

Gellenflöte, *German*
ICMM.

gelt, *Yiddish*
HFY; JOY.

gemächlich, *German*
OCM.

Gemara, *Yiddish*
JOY.

gemässigt, *German*
OCM.

Gematria, *Yiddish*
JOY.

gemebondo, *Italian*
OCM/*gemendo.*

gemendo, *Italian*
OCM.

gemessen, *German*
OCM.

Gemshorn, *German*
ICMM.

gemüt(h), *German*
OCM.

gemütlich, *German*
DFWPN; DFWPB.

Gemütlichkeit, *German*
DFWPN.

genannt, *German*
OCM.

genau, *German*
OCM.

gendarme, *French*
DFT; DFWPN; GG.

gendarmerie, *French*
DFWPN.

gendarmes, *French*
DFPCQ.

gender, *Javanese*
ICMM.

génépi, *French*
DFT.

general-bass, *German*
OCM.

generalissimo, *Italian*
DFPCQ; DFWPB.

generoso, *Italian*
OCM.

genius loci, *Latin*
DEP; DFPA; DFPCQ; DFT;
DFWPB.

genou, *French*
LB.

genre, *French*
DFT; LP.

genro, *Japanese*
JLE.

gens d'armes, *French*
DEP.

gens de condition, *French*
DFPA.

gens d'église, *French*
DFPA.

gens de guerre, *French*
DFPA.

gens de lettres, *French*
DFPA.

gens de loi, *French*
DFPA.

gens de peu, *French*
DFPA.

gens de robe, *French*
DFPA.

gens du bien, *French*
DFPA.

gens du monde, *French*
DFPA.

gentil, *French*
OCM.

gentile, *Italian*
DFT; OCM.

gentilhomme, *French*
DFPCQ.

gentille, *French*
OCM/*gentil.*

genus, *Latin*
ICMM.

genus homo, *Latin*
DFPA.

Gerader Zinck, *German*
OCM.

Geröllton, *German*
GG.

gerührt, *German*
OCM.

Ges, *German*
ICMM; OCM/*gentil.*

Gesamtausgabe, *German*
ICMM; OCM.

gesangvoll, *German*
OCM.

geschlagen, *German*
OCM.

geschleift, *German*
OCM.

geschlossen, *German*
OCM.

Geschmack, *German*
OCM.

geschwind, *German*
ICMM; OCM.

Ges dur, *German*
ICMM.

Gesellschaft, *German*
DFT.

Geses, *German*
OCM.

geshmat, *Yiddish*
JOY.

geshmott, *Yiddish*
JOY.

gesprochen, *German*
OCM.

gesso, *Italian*
DA; DFT; DFWPB; LP.

gesso duro, *Italian*
DA.

gesso grosso, *Italian*
DFWPB.

gesso sottile, *Italian*
DFWPB.

Gestalt, *German*
DFT; DFWPB; LP.

Gestapo, *German*
DFPA; DFT; DFWPN.

gesteigert, *German*
OCM.

gestopft, *German*
OCM.

gestossen, *German*
OCM.

Gesundheit, *German*
DFT; DFWPB; DFWPN.

gesundheit, *Yiddish*
JOY.

get, *Yiddish*
JOY.

geta, *Japanese*
JLE.

geteilt, *German*
OCM/*getheilt.*

getheilt, *German*
ICMM; OCM.

getragen, *German*
OCM.

gevald, *Yiddish*
JOY/*gevalt.*

Gevalt, *Yiddish*
HFY; JOY.

gewichtig, *German*
OCM.

gewidmet, *German*
OCM.

gewöhnlich, *German*
OCM.

gezogen, *German*
OCM.

gezunthayt, *Yiddish*
HFY.

ghat, *Hindi*
GG.

ghee, *Anglo-Indian*
DFT.

ghi, *Anglo-Indian*
DFT/*ghee.*

ghiribizzo, *Italian*
OCM.

ghiribizzoso, *Italian*
DFT.

ghironda, *Italian*
ICMM.

gi, *Japanese*
JLE.

giallo antico, *Italian*
DFT.

gibelotte, *French*
DFT.

gibier, *French*
DFT.

gibier à plume, *French*
DFT/*gibier.*

gibier de potence, *French*
DFT/*gibier.*

giga, *Italian*
DFPCQ; OCM.

gigelira, *Italian*
ICMM.

giglio, *Italian*
DA.

gigot, *French*
DFT; DFWPB; DFWPN.

gigue, *French*
ICMM; OCM.

gilet, *French*
DFWPB.

gilgul, *Yiddish*
JOY.

ginete, *Spanish*
DFT.

gingko, *Japanese*
JLE.

ginkgo, *Japanese*
JLE.

ginkgo (nut), *Japanese*
JLE.

giobu, *Japanese*
ACD.

giochevole, *Italian*
DFT.

gioco, *Italian*
OCM.

giocondo, *Italian*
DFT; OCM.

giocondoso, *Italian*
OCM/*giocondo.*

giocoso, *Italian*
DFPCQ; DFT; ICMM; OCM.

gioia, *Italian*
OCM.

gioiosamente, *Italian*
OCM/*gioioso.*

gioioso, *Italian*
OCM.

gioja, *Italian*
OCM/*gioia.*

giojosamente, *Italian*
OCM/*gioioso.*

giojoso, *Italian*
DFPCQ; OCM/*gioioso.*

gioviale, *Italian*
DFT; OCM.

giovialità, *Italian*
OCM/*gioviale.*

Gipfelflur, *German*
GG.

girandole, *French*
ACD.

giri, *Japanese*
JLE.

Gis, *German*
ICMM; OCM.

gisement, *French*
GG.

Gisis, *German*
OCM.

gitana, *Spanish*
OCM/*gitano.*

gitano, *Spanish*
DFPCQ; OCM.

giù, *Italian*
OCM.

giubilio, *Italian*
OCM/*giubilo.*

giubilo, *Italian*
OCM.

giulivo, *Italian*
OCM.

giumarrite, *Italian*
GG.

giuoco, *Italian*
OCM; OCM/*gioco.*

giusta, *Italian*
OCM/*giusto.*

giustamente, *Italian*
DFT; OCM.

giusto, *Italian*
DFT; ICMM; OCM.

gja, *Icelandic*
GG.

glace, *French*
DFT.

glacé, *French*
DFT; DFWPB; DFWPN.

glacière, *French*
DFT; GG.

glacier remanié, *French*
GG.

glänzend, *German*
OCM.

Glasharmonika, *German*
OCM.

Glasspiel, *German*
OCM.

Glasstabharmonika, *German*
OCM.

glatt, *German*
OCM.

glatt kosher, *Yiddish*
HFY.

gleich, *German*
OCM.

Gleiche Stimmen, *German*
OCM/*equal voices.*

gleitend, *German*
OCM.

Gletscherschlucht, *German*
GG.

gli, *Italian*
OCM.

Glimmer, *German*
GG.

glingbu, *Tibetan*
ICMM.

glint, *Norwegian*
GG.

glissade, *French*
DFWPB; LB.

glissade changée, *French*
LB/*glissade.*

glissade derrière, *French*
LB/*glissade.*

glissade devant, *French*
LB/*glissade.*

glissade en arrière, *French*
LB/*glissade.*

glissade en avant, *French*
LB/*glissade.*

glissade précipitée, *French*
LB/*glissade.*

glissade sur les pointes, *French*
LB/*glissade.*

glissando, *Italian*
DFPA; DFT; DFWPN; ICMM; OCM.

glissando, *pl.* **glissandi,** *Pseudo-Italian*
DFWPB.

glissant, *French*
OCM/*glisser.*

glissé, *French*
LB.

glisser, *French*
LB; OCM.

glissicare, *Italian*
OCM.

glitch, *Yiddish*
JOY.

glitsh, *Yiddish*
HFY.

Glöckchen, *German*
OCM.

Glocke, *German*
OCM.

Glocken, *German*
ICMM; OCM/*Glocke.*

Glockenspiel, *German*
DFT; OCM.

gloria, *Latin*
DFT; ICMM.

gloria in excelsis, *Latin*
DEP; DFPCQ.

gloria in excelsis (deo), *Latin*
DFT/*gloria.*

Gloria in Excelsis Deo, *Latin*
OCM.

Gloria Patri, *Latin*
DFPCQ; DEP.

glottis, *Greek*
ICMM.

glühend, *German*
OCM.

Glühwein, *German*
DFWPB.

gnocchi, *Italian*
DFWPN; GG.

Gnomenreigen, *German*
OCM.

gnōthi kairon, *Greek*
DFPCQ.

gnothi seauton, *Greek*
DFPA.

go, *Japanese*
JLE.

gobang, *Japanese*
JLE.

gobi, *Mongolian*
GG.

gobo, *Japanese*
JLE.

godiveau, *French*
DFT.

goldeneh medina, *Yiddish*
JOY.

golem, *Yiddish*
JOY.

gommeux, *French*
DFT.

go-moku, *Japanese*
JLE.

gomokuzogan, *Japanese*
JLE.

gondola, *Italian*
DFWPB.

gondoliera, *Italian*
OCM.

gonef, *Yiddish*
HFY; JOY/*gonif.*

gonif, *Yiddish*
DFT; JOY.

goniff, *Yiddish*
DFWPN.

gonov, *Yiddish*
JOY/*gonif.*

gopak, *Russian*
OCM.

gorge de pigeon, *French*
DFPA.

gorge-de-pigeon, *French*
DFT.

gorgheggio, *Italian*
DFT; OCM.

gorilka, *Russian*
MRWEW/*19.*

Gott, *Yiddish*
JOY.

Gottenyu, *Yiddish*
JOY.

Götterdämmerung, *German*
DFWPB.

gouache, *French*
DFT; DFWPB; DFWPN; LP.

gouffre, *French*
GG.

goumi, *Japanese*
JLE.

gour, *French*
GG.

gourmand, *French*
DFPCQ; DFT.

gourmand, *fem.* **gourmande,** *French*
DFWPB.

gourmandise, *French*
DFT; DFWPB.

gourmet, *French*
DFT; DFWPB.

goût, *French*
DFPCQ; DFT.

goût de chant, *French*
OCM.

goûter, *French*
DFT.

goût raffiné, *French*
DFT/*goût.*

goutte, *French*
DFT.

goutte à goutte, *French*
DFPA; DFT/*goutte.*

goy, *Yiddish*
DFT; JOY.

goy, *pl.* **goyim,** *Hebrew*
DFWPB.

goyim, *Yiddish*
JOY/*goy.*

goyish, *Yiddish*
JOY/*goy.*

goz, *Arabic*
GG.

gozlen, *Yiddish*
JOY/*gozlin.*

gozlin, *Yiddish*
JOY.

Graben, *German*
GG.

gracias, *Spanish*
DFT.

gracieuse, *French*
OCM/*gracieux.*

gracieux, *French*
OCM.

gradatamente, *Italian*
OCM.

gradatim, *Latin*
DEP; DFPCQ.

gradevole, *Italian*
OCM.

gradin, *French*
DA.

gradine, *French*
DA.

gradito, *Italian*
OCM.

graduale, *Latin*
ICMM.

graduellement, *French*
OCM.

gradus, *Latin*
DFPCQ.

gradus ad Parnassum, *Latin*
DFPA; DFPCQ; DFT; OCM.

graffiti, *Italian*
DFT; DFWPN.

graffito, *pl.* **graffiti,** *Italian*
DFWPB.

grama, *Spanish*
DSTE.

gran, *Italian*
OCM.

granadina, *Spanish*
OCM.

gran cassa, *Italian*
ICMM; OCM; OCM/*cassa grande.*

grand, *French*
LB; OCM.

grand bourdon, *French*
ICMM.

grand bugle, *French*
OCM/*bugle.*

grand choeur, *French*
ICMM.

grand chœur, *French*
OCM.

grand cru, *French*
DFWPB.

grand détaché, *French*
OCM.

grande, *French*
LB/*grand*; OCM/*It*; OCM/*grand.*

grande dame, *French*
DFPA; DFWPN.

grande flûte, *French*
OCM.

grande parure, *French*
DFPA.

grandezza, *Italian*
OCM.

grandioso, *Italian*
DFPCQ; DFT; ICMM; OCM.

gran-disegno, *Italian*
LP.

grandisonante, *Italian*
OCM.

grand jeu, *French*
ICMM; OCM.

grand mal, *French*
DFWPB.

grand orchestre, *French*
OCM.

grand orgue, *French*
ICMM; OCM.

grand-positif-récit, *French*
OCM/*g.p.r..*

Grand Prix, *French*
DFWPB; DFWPN.

grand prix de Rome, *French*
OCM.

Grand-Récit, *French*
OCM/*G.R..*

grand seigneur, *French*
DFPA.

grand tamburo, *Italian*
OCM.

gran gusto, *Italian*
OCM.

gran tamburo, *Italian*
OCM/*tamburo grande.*

gran turismo, *Italian*
DFWPB.

grappa, *Italian*
DFWPB.

gras, *French*
DFT.

grasseyé, *French*
DFT.

Grat, *German*
GG.

gratias, *Latin*
OCM.

gratias agere, *Latin*
DFPCQ.

gratin, *French*
DFT; DFWPN.

gratinée, *French*
DFWPN.

gratis, *Latin*
DFPCQ; DFWPN.

graub, *Yiddish*
JOY.

grauber, *Yiddish*
JOY.

graubyon, *Yiddish*
JOY.

Graupel, *German*
GG.

Grauwacke, *German*
GG.

grave, *Italian*
DFT; ICMM; OCM/*Fr.*

gravement, *French*
OCM.

gravemente, *Italian*
OCM/*gravement.*

gravicembalo, *Italian*
ICMM; OCM.

gravità, *Italian*
OCM.

Graywacke, *German*
GG.

grazia, *Italian*
OCM.

grazie, *Italian*
DFT.

graziös, *German*
OCM.

graziosamente, *Italian*
DFT; OCM/*grazia.*

grazioso, *Italian*
DFPCQ; DFT; OCM/*grazia.*

grelots, *French*
OCM.

grenouille, *French*
DFWPN.

Grenz, *German*
GG.

gridzheh, *Yiddish*
JOY.

Griff, *German*
OCM.

Griffbrett, *German*
OCM.

grillé, *French*
DFT.

grimmig, *German*
OCM.

gringo, *Spanish*
DFT; DFWPB; DFWPN; DSTE.

griotte, *French*
GG.

grippe, *French*
DFPCQ.

grisaille, *French*
ACD; DFWPB; DFWPN; LP.

grob, *German*
OCM.

groente, *Dutch*
DFT.

groppo, *Italian*
ICMM/*gruppo.*

gros, *French*
DFT; OCM.

gros-bois, *French*
OCM.

groseille, *French*
DFT.

groseille à maquereau, *French*
DFT/*groseille.*

groseille verte, *French*
DFT/*groseille.*

grosgrain, *French*
DFWPB.

gros point, *French*
DFWPB.

gros poisson, *French*
DFT/*gros.*

gross, *German*
OCM.

grosse, *French*
OCM/*gros.*

grosse, *German*
OCM/*gross.*

grosse caisse, *French*
ICMM; OCM.

Grosse Flöte, *German*
OCM.

Grosses Orchester, *German*
OCM.

Grosse Trommel, *German*
ICMM; OCM.

Grossflöte, *German*
OCM.

grossi, *Italian*
OCM/*grosso.*

grosso, *Italian*
DFT; OCM.

gros tambour, *French*
OCM.

grotesk, *German*
OCM.

grottesca, *pl.* **grottesche,** *Italian*
DFWPB.

grottesco, *Italian*
OCM.

groupe, *French*
ICMM/*turn*.

Grundstimmen, *German*
OCM.

Grundthema, *German*
OCM.

grupetto, *Italian*
ICMM/*gruppo*.

gruppetto, *Italian*
DFPCQ; DFT; ICMM/*turn*;
OCM.

gruppo, *Italian*
ICMM.

Grus, *German*
GG.

guajira, *Spanish*
ICMM; OCM.

guano, *Spanish*
DFT.

guaracha, *Spanish*
ICMM; OCM.

guarapo, *American Spanish*
DFT.

guarracha, *Spanish*
OCM/*guaracha*.

guazzo, *Italian*
DFT.

Guéridon, *French*
ACD; LP.

guero, *Spanish*
DSTE.

guerre, *French*
DFT.

guerre à l'outrance, *French*
DEP.

guerre à mort, *French*
DEP; DFPA.

guerre à outrance, *French*
DFPA.

guerre des bouffons, *French*
OCM.

guerriera, *Italian*
OCM/*guerriero*.

guerriero, *Italian*
OCM.

guerrilla, *Spanish*
DFPCQ; DFT.

guglia, *Italian*
DA.

guia, *Spanish*
DSTE.

guilloche, *French*
ACD; DFWPB.

guillotine, *French*
DFT; DFWPB; DFWPN.

guimbarde, *French*
OCM.

guimpe, *French*
DFWPN.

guingette, *French*
DFT.

guipure, *French*
DFWPN.

guistezza, *Italian*
OCM.

guitare, *French*
ICMM.

guitare d'amour, *French*
OCM/*amore, amour*; OCM.

guitarra, *Spanish*
ICMM.

gula, *Italian*
DA.

gulag, *Russian*
MRWEW/*17*.

gumi, *Japanese*
JLE.

gun, *Japanese*
JLE.

gunsel, *Yiddish*
HFY.

guri bori, *Japanese*
JLE.

175

gyttja

guru, *Hindi*
 DFWPB.
guru, *Sanskrit*
 DFWPN.
guslee, *Russian*
 OCM/*gusli.*
gusli, *Russian*
 OCM.
gusto, *Italian*
 DFPCQ; OCM.
gustosamente, *Italian*
 DFT.
gustoso, *Italian*
 DFPCQ; DFT.
gut, *German*
 OCM.

Guten Abend, *German*
 DFPCQ; DFT.
Gute Nacht, *German*
 DFPA; DFT.
Guten Morgen, *German*
 DFPA; DFPCQ; DFT.
guten Tag, *German*
 DFT.
Gut Shabbes, *Yiddish*
 HFY.
guzla, *Bulgarian*
 ICMM.
Gymnasium, *German*
 DFT.
gyttja, *Swedish*
 GG.

H

Habanera, *Spanish*
OCM; ICMM.

habatsu, *Japanese*
JLE.

Habdala, *Yiddish*
JOY.

Habdalah, *Yiddish*
JOY / *Habdala.*

habeas corpus, *Latin*
DFPA; DFPCQ; DFWPB;
DFWPN.

habeas corpus ad prosequendum,
Latin
DFPCQ.

habeas corpus ad respondendum,
Latin
DFPCQ.

habeas corpus ad satisfaciendum,
Latin
DFPCQ.

Haber-rohr, *German*
ICMM.

habet, *Latin*
DFPCQ.

habilis, *Latin*
DFWPN.

habitant, *French*
DFT.

habu, *Japanese*
JLE.

habutai, *Japanese*
JLE.

hacendado, *Spanish*
DSTE.

hachis, *French*
DFT.

hachma, *Yiddish*
JOY / *chachma.*

hacienda, *Spanish*
DFPCQ; DFT; DFWPB;
DFWPN; DSTE.

Hackbrett, *German*
ICMM; OCM.

Hadassah, *Hebrew*
DFWPN.

Hadassah, *Yiddish*
JOY.

hadj, *Arabic*
DFT.

Hadji, *Arabic*
DFWPN; DFT.

Haff, *German*
GG.

Haftarah, *Yiddish*
JOY.

Haftorah, *Yiddish*
JOY.

Hagadah, *Yiddish*
HFY.

Haggadah, *Hebrew*
DFWPN.

Haggadah, *Yiddish*
JOY.

hagi, *Japanese*
JLE.

haham, *Yiddish*
JOY/*chachem.*

hahnebüchen, *German*
OCM.

Hahnentrapp, *German*
OCM.

haikai, *Japanese*
JLE.

haiku, *Japanese*
DFT; DFWPB; DFWPN; JLE.

haimish, *Yiddish*
JOY.

haimisheh, *Yiddish*
JOY/*haimish.*

haimisher, *Yiddish*
JOY/*haimish.*

haj, *Arabic*
DFT/*hadj.*

haji, *Arabic*
DFT/*hadji.*

hak a chainik, *Yiddish*
JOY/*hok a tchynik.*

hakama, *Japanese*
JLE.

Hakenharfe, *German*
OCM.

Hakodate, *Japanese*
JLE.

Halakah, *Yiddish*
JOY.

Halakha, *Yiddish*
JOY.

halava, *Yiddish*
JOY.

halavah, *Yiddish*
JOY/*halvah*; JOY.

halb, *German*
OCM.

Halbe, *German*
OCM; OCM/*halb.*

Halbenote, *German*
OCM/*Halbe.*

Halbe-pause, *German*
OCM.

Halbetaktnote, *German*
OCM.

Halbprinzipal, *German*
OCM.

Halbsopran, *German*
OCM.

Halbtenor, *German*
OCM.

Haldenhang, *German*
GG.

halevai, *Yiddish*
JOY.

hälfte, *German*
OCM.

halla, *Yiddish*
JOY.

hallelujah, *Hebrew*
DFWPN.

hallelujah, *Yiddish*
HFY.

hallen, *German*
OCM.

halling, *Norwegian*
ICMM; OCM.

Halt, *German*
OCM.

halten, *German*
OCM.

halutz, *Yiddish*
JOY/*chalutz.*

halva, *Russian*
DFWPN.

halva, *Yiddish*
HFY.

halvah, *Yiddish*
JOY.

Hamamatsu, *Japanese*
JLE.

hamantash, *Yiddish*
JOY.

hamartia, *Greek*
DFWPB; DFWPN.

hammada, *Arabic*
GG.

Hammerklavier, *German*
ICMM.

Hanacca, *German*
OCM.

hanaise, *French*
OCM/*Hanacca.*

Hanakisch, *German*
OCM/*Hanacca.*

hanami, *Japanese*
JLE.

hanamichi, *Japanese*
JLE.

hanashika, *Japanese*
JLE.

Hand, *German*
OCM.

Hände, *German*
OCM/*Hand.*

Handharmonika, *German*
OCM.

Handregistrierung, *German*
OCM.

Handtrommel, *German*
OCM.

haniwa, *Japanese*
JLE.

Hannuka, *Yiddish*
JOY/*Hanuka.*

Hanuka, *Yiddish*
JOY/*Chanukah*; JOY.

Hanukkah, *Yiddish*
JOY/*Chanukah.*

haole, *Hawaiian*
DFT.

haori, *Japanese*
JLE.

hao t'ung, *Chinese*
ICMM.

hapax legomenon, *Greek*
DFPA; DFT; DFWPN.

hapax legomenon, *pl.* hapax
legomena, *Greek*
DFWPB.

happi-coat, *Japanese*
JLE.

harai goshi, *Japanese*
JLE.

hara-kiri, *Japanese*
DFT; DFWPB; JLE.

hardangerfele, *Norwegian*
OCM.

hardi, *French*
OCM.

hardiment, *French*
OCM/*hardi.*

hareng, *French*
DFT.

hareng frais, *French*
DFT/*hareng.*

hareng fumé, *French*
DFT/*hareng.*

hareng pec, *French*
DFT/*hareng.*

Harfe, *German*
ICMM; OCM.

haricot, *French*
DFPCQ; DFWPN.

haricot de mouton, *French*
DFWPN.

haricots verts, *French*
DFT; DFWPN.

harmonie, *French*
OCM.

harmonie, basse d', *French*
OCM.

harmonie, cor d', *French*
OCM.

harmonie, cornet d', *French*
OCM.

Harmoniemusik, *German*
OCM.

harmonie, trompette d', *French*
OCM.

Harmonika, *German*
OCM.

harmonique, *French*
OCM.

harmonische Töne, *German*
OCM.

harpchorde, *French*
ICMM.

harpe à crochets, *French*
OCM.

Hart, *German*
OCM.

Harte, *German*
OCM./*Hart*; ICMM.

Hartschiefer, *German*
GG.

hasardé, *French*
DFT.

Hasenpfeffer, *German*
DFT.

Hashem, *Yiddish*
JOY.

hashigakari, *Japanese*
JLE.

hasid, *Hebrew*
DFWPN.

Hasid, *Yiddish*
JOY.

hasidim, *Hebrew*
DFWPN/*hasid*.

Hasidim, *Yiddish*
JOY.

Haskala, *Yiddish*
JOY.

Haskalah, *Yiddish*
JOY.

hassen, *Yiddish*
JOY/*chassen*.

hasseneh, *Yiddish*
JOY.

Hassid, *Yiddish*
JOY/*Chasid*; JOY.

Hassidic, *Yiddish*
JOY.

Hassidim, *Yiddish*
JOY; JOY/*Chasid*.

hasta la vista, *Spanish*
DFPA; DFWPB; DSTE.

hasta luego, *Spanish*
DFPA; DFT; DFWPB; DFWPN.

hasta mañana, *Spanish*
DFPA; DFT.

hastig, *German*
OCM.

has vesholem, *Yiddish*
JOY/*chas vesholem*.

hatamoto, *Japanese*
JLE.

Hatikva, *Yiddish*
JOY/*Hatikvah*.

Hatikvah, *Yiddish*
JOY.

haud ignota loquor, *Latin*
DFPCQ.

haud passibus æquis, *Latin*
DEP.

Haupt, *German*
OCM.

Hauptstimme, *German*
OCM.

Hauptthema, *German*
OCM.

Hauptwerk, *German*
ICMM; OCM.

Hausfrau, *German*
DFT; DFWPB; DFWPN.

Hausmaler, *German*
ACD.

haut, *French*
OCM.

haut, en, *French*
LB.

hautbois, *French*
DFWPN; ICMM; OCM.

hautbois d'amour, *French*
OCM; OCM/*amore, amour*.

hautboy, *French*
OCM.

haute, *French*
OCM/*haut*; OCM.

haute bourgeoisie, *French*
DFPA; DFT.

haute coiffure, *French*
DFPA.

haute couture, *French*
DFPA; DFWPB; DFWPN.

haute cuisine, *French*
DFPA; DFWPB.

haute danse, *French*
OCM.

hauteur, *French*
DFPCQ; DFT; LB; OCM.

haut goût, *French*
DFPA; DFT.

haut-relief, *French*
DFT.

haut ton, *French*
DFPA.

havanaise, *French*
OCM.

Havdala, *Yiddish*
JOY/*Habdala.*

havelina, *Spanish*
DSTE.

havsband, *Swedish*
GG.

hayashi, *Japanese*
JLE.

hazzan, *Hebrew*
OCM.

hazzan, *Yiddish*
JOY/*chazzen.*

hazzen, *Yiddish*
JOY.

H dur, *German*
ICMM.

hechima, *Japanese*
JLE.

Heckelclarina, *German*
OCM.

Heckelklarinette, *German*
OCM/*Heckelclarina.*

Heckelphone, *German*
OCM.

hectare, *French*
DFPCQ; DFWPN.

heder, *Yiddish*
HFY; JOY/*cheder.*

heftig, *German*
OCM.

hegira, *Arabic*
DFT.

hegira/hejira, *Latin from Arabic*
DFWPB.

Heian, *Japanese*
JLE.

Heil, *German*
DFWPN.

heimin, *Japanese*
JLE.

heiss, *German*
OCM.

heiter, *German*
OCM.

Heldentenor, *German*
ICMM; OCM.

hell, *German*
OCM.

Hellflöte, *German*
OCM.

Herabstrich, *German*
OCM.

Heraufstrich, *German*
OCM.

herbarium, *Latin*
DFPCQ.

Herbstlied, *German*
OCM.

hernach, *German*
OCM.

héroïque, *French*
OCM.

heroisch, *German*
OCM/*héroïque.*

Herr, *German*
DFPCQ; DFT; DFWPN.

Herstrich, *German*
OCM.

Herunterstimmen, *German*
OCM.

Herunterstrich, *German*
OCM.

hervidero, *Spanish*
GG.

hervorgehoben, *German*
OCM.

hervorragend, *German*
OCM.

herzhaft, *German*
OCM.

herzig, *German*
OCM.

herzlich, *German*
OCM/*herzhaft.*

Hes, *German*
OCM.

hetaera, *Greek*
DFWPN.

hetaera, *pl.* **hetaerae,** *Greek*
DFWPB.

hetaira, *Greek*
DFWPN.

heu!, *Latin*
DFPCQ.

heurēka, *Greek*
DFPCQ.

hexameron, *Greek*
ICMM.

Hexentanz, *German*
OCM.

hexerei, *German*
DFT.

hiba (arborvitae), *Japanese*
JLE.

hibachi, *Japanese*
DFT; JLE.

hibakusha, *Japanese*
JLE.

hic et ubique, *Latin*
DFPA; DFPCQ; DFT; DFWPB.

hichiriki, *Japanese*
ICMM.

hic iacet, *Latin*
DFPCQ; DFT/*hic jacet.*

hic jacet, *Latin*
DEP; DFPA; DFT; DFWPB;
DFWPN.

hic sepultus, *Latin*
DFPA.

hidalgo, *Spanish*
DFPCQ; DFWPN; DSTE.

hidalguia, *Spanish*
DFPCQ.

Hief-horn, *German*
ICMM.

hier, *German*
OCM.

hierophon, *Greek*
ICMM.

Hillul Hashem, *Yiddish*
JOY/*Hatikvah.*

Hillul ha-Shem, *Yiddish*
JOY/*Hillul Hashem.*

Himeji, *Japanese*
JLE.

hinin, *Japanese*
JLE.

hinoki, *Japanese*
JLE.

hinsterbend, *German*
OCM.

Hinstrich, *German*
OCM.

Hinterland, *German*
GG.

hippophorbos, *Greek*
ICMM.

Hirado, *Japanese*
JLE.

hiragana, *Japanese*
JLE.

Hiroshima, *Japanese*
JLE.

Hirt, *German*
OCM.

hirtlich, *German*
DFT.

His, *German*
ICMM; OCM.

hitschiriki, *Japanese*
ICMM.

hitsu-no-koto, *Japanese*
ICMM.

hityokiri, *Japanese*
ICMM.

Hizen, *Japanese*
JLE.

Hizen (porcelain), *Japanese*
JLE.

H moll, *German*
ICMM.

Hoboe, *German*
OCM.

hoc age, *Latin*
DFPCQ.

Hochdruckstimmen, *German*
OCM.

Hochkammerton, *German*
OCM.

höchst, *German*
OCM.

Hochzeitsmarsch, *German*
OCM.

Hochzeitszug, *German*
OCM.

hocket, *French*
OCM.

hodie, non cras, *Latin*
DFPCQ.

hogan, *Navaho*
DFT.

Hohlflöte, *German*
OCM.

hoi! hoi!, *Spanish*
DSTE/*237.*

hoi polloi, *Greek*
DFPA; DFPCQ; DFT; DFWPB;
DFWPN.

hok, *Yiddish*
HFY.

hok a tchynik, *Yiddish*
JOY.

hokku, *Japanese*
DFWPN; JLE.

holi, *Hindi*
DFT.

hollandais, *French*
DFT.

hollandaise, *fem., French*
DFT/*hollandais.*

Holz, *German*
OCM.

Holzbläser, *German*
OCM.

Holzblasinstrumente, *German*
ICMM; OCM.

Holzflöte, *German*
OCM.

Holzharmonika, *German*
ICMM; OCM.

Holzschlägel, *German*
OCM.

Holztrompete, *German*
ICMM; OCM.

homard, *French*
DFT; DFWPN.

hombre, *Spanish*
DFT; DFWPN; DSTE.

homentash, *Yiddish*
HFY.

hometzdik, *Yiddish*
JOY/*chometzdik.*

homme, *French*
DFWPN.

homme d'affaires, *French*
DFPA.

homme de bien, *French*
DFPA.

homme de guerre, *French*
DFPA.

homme de lettres, *French*
DFPA.

homme de paille, *French*
DFPA.

homme d'épée, *French*
DFPA.

homme d'esprit, *French*
DFPA; DFPCQ; DFWPN.

homme d'état, *French*
DFPA; DFPCQ.

homme de théâtre, *French*
DFPA.

homme du monde, *French*
DFPA.

homme du peuple, *French*
DFPA.

homme moyen sensuel, *French*
DFPA.

homo, *Latin*
DFT; DFWPN.

homo covivens, *Latin*
DFPA.

homo faber, *Latin*
DFWPN.

homo ferus, *Latin*
DFPA.

homo ludens, *Latin*
DFPA; DFWPB.

homo sapiens, *Latin*
DFT/*homo*; DFPA; DFWPB;
DFWPN.

honda, *Spanish*
DSTE.

hondo, *Spanish*
GG; OCM.

honi soit qui mal y pense, *French*
DFPCQ.

hon(n)i soit qui mal y pense, *French*
DFWPN.

honnête homme, *French*
DFPA.

honorarium, *Latin*
DFPCQ.

honoris causa, *Latin*
DFT; DFWPB.

honoris gratia, *Latin*
DFT/*honoris causa.*

hoodoo, *African*
GG.

hoo-ha, *Yiddish*
JOY.

Hook, *German*
ICMM.

hookah, *Arabic*
DFWPN.

hoolee, *Hindi*
DFT/*holi.*

hopak, *Russian*
OCM.

Hopser, *German*
ICMM; OCM.

hoquet, *French*
OCM.

Hörner, *German*
OCM.

Hornquinten, *German*
ICMM.

Hornstein, *German*
GG.

horresco referens, *Latin*
DEP.

horribile dictu, *Latin*
DFPA; DFPCQ; DFT; DFWPB;
DFWPN.

horribile visu, *Latin*
DFT.

hors concours, *French*
DA/*concours*; DA; DFPA; DFT;
LP.

hors d'affaire, *French*
DFWPN.

hors de combat, *French*
DEP; DFPA; DFPCQ; DFT;
DFWPN.

hors de commerce, *French*
DFPA.

hors de concours, *French*
DFWPN.

hors de propos, *French*
DFPA; DFWPN.

hors de saison, *French*
DFPA.

hors d'oeuvre, *French*
DFPA.

hors d'œuvre, *French*
DFT.

hors d'oeuvre, *pl.* hors d'oeuvre,
French
DFWPB.

hors d'oeuvres, *French*
DFWPN.

hors la loi, *French*
DFPA.

Horst, *German*
GG.

hortus conclusus, *Latin*
DFPA; DFWPB.

hosanna, *Hebrew*
OCM.

hôtel, *French*
DA.

Hôtel de Ville, *French*
DA; DEP.

hôtel Dieu, *French*
DA.

hôtel garni, *French*
DFPA.

hôtel meublé, *French*
DFPA.

Hotzeplotz, *Yiddish*
JOY.

howdah, *Arabic*
DFWPN.

hoya, *Spanish*
GG.

hozzer, *Yiddish*
JOY.

hsiao, *Chinese*
ICMM.

hubris, *Greek*
DFWPN.

hübsch, *German*
OCM.

huchet, *French*
ICMM.

hu ch'in, *Chinese*
ICMM.

huerfano, *Spanish*
GG.

huero, *Spanish*
DSTE.

huit, *French*
OCM.

huitain, *French*
DFWPN.

Humaniora, *Latin*
DFT.

humanum est errare, *Latin*
DFPCQ.

Humoreske, *German*
ICMM; OCM.

humoresque, *French*
OCM.

hüpfend, *German*
OCM.

huppa, *Yiddish*
JOY / *chuppa.*

huppe, *Yiddish*
JOY.

hurtig, *German*
DFT; ICMM; OCM.

husteron proteron, *Greek*
DFPCQ.

huître, *French*
DFT; DFWPN.

huîtres en coquille, *French*
DFWPN.

hutspa, *Yiddish*
JOY.

hutzpah, *Yiddish*
DFT; JOY.

hybris, *Greek*
DFWPN.

Hydraulicon, *German*
ICMM.

hydraulikon, *Greek*
OCM.

hypathoides, *Greek*
ICMM.

hyper, *Greek*
ICMM.

hypo, *Greek*
ICMM.

hypoaeolian, *Greek*
OCM.

hypodorian, *Greek*
OCM/*hypoaeolian.*

hypoionian, *Greek*
OCM/*hypoaeolian.*

hypolocrian, *Greek*
OCM/*hypoaeolian.*

hypolydian, *Greek*
OCM/*hypoaeolian.*

hypomixolydian, *Greek*
OCM/*hypoaeolian.*

hypophrygian, *Greek*
OCM/*hypoaeolian.*

hysteron proteron, *Greek*
DFPA; DFT; DFWPN.

I

i, *Italian*
OCM.

iacta alea est, *Latin*
DFWPN.

iacta est alea, *Latin*
DFPCQ.

iaido, *Japanese*
JLE.

ibérien, *French*
OCM.

ibérienne, *French*
OCM/*ibérien*.

ibidem, *Latin*
DFT; DFWPN.

ibidem (ibid.), *Latin*
DFPCQ.

ich, *German*
DFWPN.

Ich dien, *German*
DFPA; DFPCQ.

ich dien', *German*
DFWPN.

ICHTHYS, *Greek*
DFPA.

ici, *French*
DFWPN.

ici on parle français, *French*
DFPA.

icthys, *Greek*
DFWPN.

id, *Latin*
DFWPB.

idée fixe, *French*
DFPA; DFPCQ; DFT; DFWPN;
OCM.

idée fixe, *pl.* **idées fixes,** *French*
DFWPB.

idée maîtresse, *French*
DFPA.

idée mère, *French*
DFWPN.

idées reçues *pl.*, *French*
DFWPB.

idem, *Latin*
DFPCQ; DFT; DFWPN.

ideo, *Latin*
DFWPN.

id est, *Latin*
DFT; DFWPB; DFWPN.

id est (i.e.), *Latin*
DFPCQ.

id genus omne, *Latin*
DFPCQ.

Iesus Nazarenus Rex Iudaeorum,
Latin
DFWPN.

ignis fatuus, *Latin*
DFPA; DFPCQ; DFT; DFWPN.

ignis fatuus, *pl.* **ignes fatui,** *Latin*
DFWPB.

ignoramus, *Latin*
DFPCQ.

ignorantia legis neminem excusat,
Latin
DFPCQ.

ignoratio elenchi, *Latin*
DFPA; DFT.

I-go, *Japanese*
JLE.

ikebana, *Japanese*
JLE.

il, *French*
DFWPN.

il, *Italian*
DFWPN; OCM.

Il Duce, *Italian*
DFT; DFWPN.

il faut, *French*
DFWPN; OCM.

Ilium fuit, *Latin*
DFPCQ.

illuminati, *Latin*
DFPCQ; DFWPN.

illuminato, *pl.* **illuminati,** *Italian*
DFWPB.

il n'y a pas de quoi, *French*
DFT.

il penseroso, *Italian*
DFWPN.

il y a, *French*
DFWPN.

imago, *Latin*
DFWPB.

imam, *Arabic*
DFWPB; DFWPN.

imam, *Persian*
DFT.

iman, *Arabic*
DFWPN.

Imari, *Japanese*
JLE.

imboccatura, *Italian*
ICMM/*lip.*

imbroglio, *Italian*
DFWPN; ICMM.

imitazione, aria d', *Italian*
OCM.

immer, *German*
OCM.

immer schlimmer, *German*
DFT; DFWPN.

imo pectore, *Latin*
DFPCQ; DFT.

impair, *French*
OCM.

impasto, *Italian*
DFWPB; DFWPN; LP.

impaziente, *Italian*
OCM.

impazientemente, *Italian*
DFT; OCM/*impaziente.*

impedimenta, *Latin*
DFPCQ.

imperator, *Latin*
DFPCQ.

imperioso, *Italian*
DFT; OCM.

imperium in imperio, *Latin*
DEP.

Imperium Romanum, *Latin*
DFPA.

impeto, *Italian*
DFT; OCM.

impétueux, *French*
OCM.

impetuosamente, *Italian*
OCM/*impetuoso.*

impetuosità, *Italian*
OCM/*impetuoso.*

impetuoso, *Italian*
DFT; OCM.

impetus, *Latin*
DFPCQ.

imponente, *Italian*
OCM.

imponierend, *German*
OCM.

impos animi, *Latin*
DFPA.

impresario, *Italian*
DFPCQ.

impresario, *pl.* **impresarii,** *Italian*
DFWPB.

imprimatur, *Latin*
DFPA; DFPCQ; DFWPB;
DFWPN.

imprimatura, *Italian*
DFWPB; LP.

imprimé, *French*
DFWPB.

imprimi permittitur, *Latin*
DFPA.

imprimi potest, *Latin*
DFPA.

imprimis, *Latin*
DFPCQ.

impromptu, *French*
ICMM.

improperia, *Latin*
ICMM.

improvisatore [*sic*], *Italian*
OCM.

improvvisata, *Italian*
DFT.

improvvisatore, *Italian*
DFPCQ; DFT.

im voraus, *German*
OCM.

in absentia, *Latin*
DFPA; DFPCQ; DFWPB;
DFWPN.

in actu, *Latin*
DFPA; DFWPN.

in aeternum, *Latin*
DFPA; DFPCQ; DFWPN.

in alt, *Italian*
DFT/*in alto*; ICMM.

in altissimo, *Italian*
DFT; ICMM.

in altissimo, *Latin*
OCM/*in alt*.

in alto, *Italian*
DFT.

in articulo mortis, *Latin*
DEP.

in bianco, *Italian*
DFPCQ.

incalcando, *Italian*
OCM.

incalzando, *Italian*
OCM.

in camera, *Latin*
DFPA; DFPCQ; DFT; DFWPB;
DFWPN.

in capite, *Latin*
DFPA; DFPCQ.

incarnatus, *Latin*
ICMM.

incipit, *Latin*
DFPA; DFT.

inciso, *Italian*
OCM.

incliné, *French*
LB:

inclinée, *French*
LB/*incliné*.

incognita, *Latin*
DFPCQ.

incognito, *Italian*
DFPCQ.

incominciando, *Italian*
OCM.

incommunicado, *Spanish*
DSTE.

in concreto, *Latin*
DFPA.

inconnu, *French*
DFT.

inconnu(e), *French*
DFWPN.

incordamento, *Italian*
DFT.

incubus, *Latin*
DFPCQ.

incubus, *pl.* **incubi,** *Latin*
DFWPB.

incunabula, *Latin*
DFWPN.

incunabula *pl.,* *Latin*
DFWPB.

in curia, *Latin*
DFPCQ.

in curiâ, *Latin*
DEP.

in custodia legis, *Latin*
DFPA.

indebolendo, *Italian*
OCM.

indeciso, *Italian*
OCM.

Index Expurgatorius, *Latin*
DFT; DFWPN; DEP; DFPA;
DFPCQ; DFWPB.

Index Librorum Prohibitorum, *Latin*
DFPA; DFT; DFWPN; DFWPB.

index locorum, *Latin*
DFPA.

index nominum, *Latin*
DFPA.

index rerum, *Latin*
DFPA; DFPCQ; DFT.

index verborum, *Latin*
DFPA; DFT.

indicato, *Italian*
OCM.

in dies, *Latin*
DFPCQ.

in dubiis, *Latin*
DFPCQ.

in dubio, *Latin*
DFPA; DFT.

in eadem conditione, *Latin*
DFPCQ.

inégales, notes, *French*
ICMM.

in equilibrio, *Latin*
DFPCQ.

in esse, *Latin*
DFPA; DFPCQ; DFT.

in excelsis, *Latin*
DFT.

in extenso, *Latin*
DFT.

in extremis, *Latin*
DEP; DFPA; DFPCQ; DFT;
DFWPB; DFWPN; SPICE.

in facie curiae, *Latin*
DFPA; DFT.

in facto, *Latin*
DFWPN.

in fieri, *Latin*
DFPA.

in flagrante (delicto), *Latin*
DFWPN.

in flagrante delicto, *Latin*
DFPA; DFPCQ; DFT; DFWPB;
SPICE.

in fore, *Latin*
DFPCQ.

in foro conscientiae, *Latin*
DFPA.

in foro conscientiæ, *Latin*
DEP.

in foro externo, *Latin*
DFPA.

in foro interno, *Latin*
DFPA.

infra, *Italian*
OCM.

infra, *Latin*
DFT; DFWPB; DFWPN.

infra dig, *Latin*
SPICE.

infra dig(nitatem), *Latin*
DFWPB; DFWPN.

infra dignitatem, *Latin*
DFPA; DFT/*infra.*

infra dignitatem (infra dig.), *Latin*
DFPCQ.

in fretta, *Italian*
DFT.

in futuro, *Latin*
DEP; DFPA; DFPCQ.

inganno, *Italian*
DFPCQ; DFT; ICMM.

in genere, *Latin*
DFT.

ingenue, *French*
DFWPN.

ingénue, *French*
DFT; DFWPB.

inglese, *Italian*
OCM.

in gremio legis, *Latin*
DFPA.

in hoc signo vinces, *Latin*
DFPCQ; DFT; DFWPN.

in infinito, *Latin*
DFPCQ.

in infinitum, *Latin*
DFPA; DFT.

in initio, *Latin*
DFPA; DFPCQ.

initio, *Latin*
DFT.

in jure, *Latin*
DFWPN.

inlayo, *Japanese*
JLE.

in loco, *Latin*
DFPA; DFPCQ; DFT.

in loco citato, *Latin*
DFPA; DFT/*in loco*; DFWPN.

in loco parentis, *Latin*
DEP; DFPA; DFPCQ; DFT/*in loco*; DFWPN; SPICE.

in malam partem, *Latin*
DFWPN.

in medias res, *Latin*
DEP; DFPA; DFPCQ; DFT; DFWPB; DFWPN.

in mediis rebus, *Latin*
DFPCQ; DFT; DFWPN.

in medio, *Latin*
DFT.

in memoriam, *Latin*
DEP; DFPA; DFPCQ; DFT; DFWPB; DFWPN.

in mitn derinnen, *Yiddish*
JOY.

in mitske derinnen, *Yiddish*
JOY.

in modo di, *Italian*
OCM.

innamorato, *Italian*
DFPCQ.

innig, *German*
ICMM; OCM.

inno, *Italian*
OCM.

innocenza, *Italian*
OCM.

in nomine, *Latin*
DFPA; DFT; ICMM; OCM.

in nomine Domini, *Latin*
DFPA; DFT/*in nomine*; DFWPN.

in notis, *Latin*
DFT.

in nubibus, *Latin*
DFPA.

in nuce, *Latin*
DFPA.

innuendo, *Latin*
DFPCQ.

in ova, *Latin*
DFPCQ.

in ovo, *Latin*
DEP; DFPA; DFT.

in pace, *Latin*
DEP; DFPA; DFPCQ.

in partibus, *Latin*
DFT/*in partibus infidelium*.

in partibus infidelium, *Latin*
DEP; DFPA; DFT.

in perpetuam rei memoriam, *Latin*
DEP.

in perpetuo, *Latin*
DFWPN.

in perpetuum, *Latin*
DEP; DFPA; DFPCQ; DFT;
DFWPN.
in persona, *Latin*
DFT.
in personam, *Latin*
DFT.
in posse, *Late Latin*
DFT.
in posse, *Latin*
DFPA; DFPCQ.
in potentia, *Latin*
DFT.
in praesenti, *Latin*
DFPCQ; DFT.
in praesentia, *Latin*
DFT.
in principio, *Latin*
DFPA; DFT.
in propria persona, *Latin*
DFPA.
in propriâ personâ, *Latin*
DEP.
in puris naturalibus, *Latin*
DFPA.
inquiet, *French*
OCM.
inquieto, *Italian*
OCM/*inquiet.*
in re, *Latin*
DEP; DFPA; DFPCQ; DFT.
in rem, *Latin*
DEP; DFT.
in rerum natura, *Latin*
DFPA.
in rerum naturâ, *Latin*
DEP.
inro, *Japanese*
JLE.
in saecula saeculorum, *Latin*
DFPA; DFT.
insalata, *Italian*
DFWPN.

in se, *Latin*
DFT; DFWPN.
in secco, *Italian*
DFWPB.
in secula seculorum, *Latin*
DFPCQ.
Inselberg, *German*
GG.
insensibilmente, *Italian*
DFT.
insensible, *Italian*
OCM.
insieme, *Italian*
OCM.
insignia, *Latin*
DFPCQ.
in situ, *Latin*
DEP; DFPA; DFPCQ; DFT;
DFWPB; DFWPN; LP.
in solidum (solido), *Latin*
DFPA.
insomnia, *Latin*
DFPCQ.
insouciance, *French*
DFPCQ; DFT; DFWPN.
insouciant, *French*
DFWPN.
in specie, *Latin*
DFPA.
inständig, *German*
OCM.
instante, *Italian*
OCM.
instar omnium, *Latin*
DFPCQ; DFT.
in statu quo, *Latin*
DEP; DFPA; DFT; DFWPN.
instrument à cordes, *French*
ICMM.
instrument à vent, *French*
ICMM.
instrumento da fiato, *Italian*
ICMM.

instrumento da penna, *Italian*
ICMM.

instrumento da percotimento, *Italian*
ICMM.

instrumento da tasto, *Italian*
ICMM.

insula, *Italian*
DA.

intaglio, *Italian*
ACD; DFWPN.

intaglio rilevato, *Italian*
DFT.

intarsia, *Italian*
ACD.

intavolatura, *Italian*
ICMM/*tablature*; OCM/*tablature*.

integer valor notarum, *Latin*
ICMM.

intelligentsia, *Russian*
DFT; DFWPN.

in tenebris, *Latin*
DFPA; DFPCQ; DFT.

inter, *Latin*
DFT.

inter alia, *Latin*
DEP; DFPA; DFPCQ; DFT/
inter; DFWPB; DFWPN.

inter alios, *Latin*
DFT/*inter*.

interea, *Latin*
DFPCQ.

intermède, *French*
OCM/*intermezzo*.

intermedio, *Italian*
OCM/*intermezzo*.

intermezzo, *Italian*
DFPCQ; DFT; DFWPN; OCM.

intermezzo, *pl.* **intermezzi,** *Italian*
DFWPB.

inter nos, *Latin*
DEP; DFPA; DFPCQ; DFWPN.

inter pares, *Latin*
DFWPN.

inter pocula, *Latin*
DFPCQ.

interregnum, *Latin*
DFPCQ.

in terrorem, *Latin*
DFPA.

inter se, *Latin*
DFPA; DFPCQ; DFT/*inter*.

inter vivos, *Latin*
DFPA; DFT/*inter*.

intestatus, *Latin*
DFPCQ.

intime, *French*
DFWPN; OCM.

intimiste, *French*
DFWPB.

intimo, *Italian*
OCM/*intime*.

intonaco, *Italian*
LP/*fresco*.

in toto, *Latin*
DEP; DFPA; DFPCQ; DFT;
DFWPN; SPICE.

intrada, *Italian*
ICMM.

intrada, *Spanish*
OCM.

intra muros, *Latin*
DFPA; DFPCQ; DFT; DFWPN.

in transitu, *Latin*
DEP.

intrepidezza, *Italian*
OCM/*intrepido*.

intrepido, *Italian*
OCM.

introduzione, *Italian*
DFPCQ; OCM.

introitus, *Latin*
ICMM.

in usu, *Latin*
DFT.

in utero, *Latin*
DFPA; DFT; DFWPB.

in vacuo

in vacuo, *Latin*
DFPCQ; DFT/*vacuo*; DFT;
DFWPB.
in ventre, *Latin*
DFPA; DFT.
invictus, *Latin*
DFWPN.
in vino veritas, *Latin*
DFPA; DFPCQ; DFT; DFWPB;
DFWPN.
invitatorium, *Latin*
ICMM.
in vitro, *Latin*
DFPA; DFT.
in vivo, *Latin*
DFPA; DFT; DFWPB.
ippon, *Japanese*
JLE.
ipse, *Latin*
DFWPN.
ipse dixit, *Latin*
DFPA; DFPCQ; DFT; DFWPN.
ipsissima verba, *Latin*
DFPA; DFPCQ; DFT; DFWPN.
ipsissima verba *pl.*, *Latin*
DFWPB.
ipsissimis verbis, *Latin*
DFT; DFWPN.
ipso facto, *Latin*
DFPA; DFPCQ; DFT; DFWPB;
DFWPN.
ipso jure, *Latin*
DFPA; DFPCQ; DFT; DFWPB;
DFWPN.
ira, *Italian*
OCM.
ira furor brevis est, *Latin*
DFPCQ.
irato, *Italian*
DFT.
irhzer, *Berber*
GG.
irofa, *Japanese*
JLE.

iroha, *Japanese*
JLE.
ironicamente, *Italian*
OCM/*ironico*.
ironico, *Italian*
OCM.
irresoluto, *Italian*
OCM.
isblink, *Danish*
GG.
Ishihara (test), *Japanese*
JLE.
ishime, *Japanese*
JLE.
islancio, con, *Italian*
OCM.
ispravnik, *Russian*
DFT.
issei, *Japanese*
JLE.
ista, *Spanish*
DSTE.
istesso, *Italian*
DFT; OCM.
istoriato, *Italian*
ACD.
istrumento d'acciaio, *Italian*
OCM.
ita est, *Latin*
DFPCQ; DFWPN.
itai-itai, *Japanese*
JLE.
ite missa est, *Latin*
DFT.
ite, missa est, *Latin*
DFPA; DFWPN.
iter, *Latin*
DFWPN.
iterum, *Latin*
DFPCQ; DFT.
Ito sukashi, *Japanese*
JLE.
itzebu, *Japanese*
JLE.

ius canonicum, *Latin*
DFPCQ.
ius civile, *Latin*
DFPCQ.
ius et norma loquendi, *Latin*
DFPCQ.
ius gentium, *Latin*
DFPCQ.
ius militare, *Latin*
DFPCQ.

ius municipale, *Latin*
DFPCQ.
Izvestia, *Russian*
DFWPN.
izvestyia, *Russian*
DFWPN.
izzat, *Hindi*
DFT.

J

ja, *German*
DFWPN.

jabo, *Spanish*
OCM.

jaburan, *Japanese*
JLE.

jacal, *Spanish*
DSTE.

jacara, *Spanish*
OCM/*xacara.*

jácara, *Spanish*
OCM.

j'accuse, *French*
DFPA; DFWPB.

Jacquerie, *French*
DFT.

Jacques Bonhomme, *French*
DFWPN.

jacta alea est, *Latin*
DFPA.

jacta est alea, *Latin*
DFT; DFWPB; DFWPN.

Jagdhorn, *German*
OCM.

Jäger, *German*
OCM.

Jägerhorn, *German*
ICMM.

Jahresringe, *German*
GG.

jai alai, *Basque*
DFT.

jai-alai, *Basque*
DFWPN.

jalatarang, *Hindi*
ICMM.

jaleo, *Spanish*
ICMM; OCM.

jalousie, *French*
DA.

Jalousieschweller, *German*
OCM.

jambe, *French*
LB.

jambon, *French*
DFT; DFWPN.

jamón, *Spanish*
DFT.

janitscharen, *Turkish*
ICMM.

Janitscharenmusik, *German*
OCM/*Janissary music.*

janken, *Japanese*
JLE.

januis clausis, *Latin*
DFPA.

japonaiseries, *French*
DFWPN.

jaquima, *Spanish*
DFT; DSTE.

jarabe, *Spanish*
DFT; ICMM.

jardin, *French*
DFT.

jardinière, *French*
ACD; DFT; DFWPB; DFWPN.

Jaspis, *German*
GG.

javalina, *Spanish*
DSTE.

je, *German*
OCM.

jebel, *Arabic*
GG.

jefe, *Spanish*
DSTE.

jefe politico, *Spanish*
DSTE/*jefe.*

jehad, *Arabic*
DFT/*jihad.*

je m'en fous, *French*
DFT.

je ne sais quoi, *French*
DFPA; DFPCQ; DFT; DFWPN.

je-ne-sais-quoi, *French*
DFWPB.

je suis prêt, *French*
DFT.

Jesus, hominum Salvator (I.H.S.), *Latin*
DFPCQ.

Jesus Nazarenus Rex Judaeorum, *Latin*
DFWPN.

jet d'eau, *French*
DA; DEP.

jeté, *French*
DFWPB; DFWPN.

jeté, grand, *French*
LB/*jeté, pas.*

jeté, pas, *French*
LB.

jeté, petit, *French*
LB/*jeté, pas.*

jeté bateau, *French*
LB/*jeté, pas.*

jeté battu, *French*
DFWPB; LB/*jeté, pas.*

jeté de côté, *French*
LB/*jeté, pas.*

jeté dessous, *French*
LB/*jeté, pas.*

jeté dessus, *French*
LB/*jeté, pas.*

jetée, *French*
DFT.

jeté en arrière, grand, *French*
LB/*jeté, pas.*

jeté en arrière, petit, *French*
LB/*jeté, pas.*

jeté en attitude, *French*
LB/*jeté, pas.*

jeté en avant, grand, *French*
LB/*jeté, pas.*

jeté en avant, petit, *French*
LB/*jeté, pas.*

jeté en tournant, *French*
LB/*jeté, pas.*

jeté en tournant entrelacé, grand, *French*
LB/*jeté, pas.*

jeté en tournant par demi-tours, *French*
LB/*jeté, pas.*

jeté en tournant par terre, *French*
LB/*jeté, pas.*

jeté entrelacé, *French*
LB/*jeté, pas.*

jeté enveloppé, *French*
LB/*jeté, pas.*

jeté fermé, *French*
LB/*jeté, pas.*

jeté fermé de côté, *French*
LB/*jeté, pas.*

jeté fouetté, grand, *French*
LB/*jeté, pas.*

jeté passé, *French*
LB/*jeté, pas.*

jeté renversé, grand, *French*
  LB/*jeté, pas.*

jetés battements, *French*
  LB/*jeté, pas.*

jeté sur les pointes, *French*
  LB/*jeté, pas.*

jeté volé de côté, *French*
  LB/*jeté, pas.*

jeu, *French*
  DFT; DFWPN; ICMM; OCM.

jeu de clochettes, *French*
  OCM.

jeu de hasard, *French*
  DFT/*jeu.*

jeu de mots, *French*
  DEP; DFPA; DFPCQ; DFT/*jeu.*

jeu de mots, *pl.* **jeux de mots,**
French
  DFWPB.

jeu d'esprit, *French*
  DEP; DFPA; DFPCQ; DFT/*jeu*;
  DFWPN.

jeu d'esprit, *pl.* **jeux d'esprit,** *French*
  DFWPB.

jeu de théâtre, *French*
  DFPA; DFPCQ; DFT/*jeu.*

jeu de timbers, *French*
  OCM.

jeu du hasard, *French*
  DFT/*jeu.*

jeune fille, *French*
  DFWPB.

jeunesses musicales, *French*
  OCM.

jeu ordinaire, *French*
  OCM.

jeux, *French*
  OCM.

jeux d'anches, *French*
  ICMM.

(les) jeux sont faits, *French*
  DFWPB.

jheel, *Hindi*
  GG.

jhil, *Hindi*
  GG.

jigotai, *Japanese*
  JLE.

jihad, *Arabic*
  DFT.

jimigaki, *Japanese*
  JLE.

jingu, *Japanese*
  JLE.

jinja, *Japanese*
  JLE.

jinkai senjitsu, *Japanese*
  JLE.

jinrickisha, *Japanese*
  DFWPN.

jinricksha, *Japanese*
  JLE.

jinrikisha, *Japanese*
  JLE.

jinriksha, *Japanese*
  JLE.

jito, *Japanese*
  JLE.

jiu jitsu, *Japanese*
  DFT.

jiu-jitsu, *Japanese*
  DFWPB; JLE.

Joch, *German*
  GG.

Jodel, *French*
  OCM.

Jodel, *German*
  ICMM; OCM.

Jodo, *Japanese*
  JLE.

Johannes fac totum, *Latin*
  DFPA.

joie de vivre, *French*
  DFPA; DFT; DFWPB; DFWPN.

jokul, *Icelandic*
  GG.

jökulhlaup, *Icelandic*
  GG.

joli, *French*
DFT.

joli(e), *French*
DFWPN.

jomon, *Japanese*
JLE.

jongleur, *French*
ICMM; OCM.

jornada, *Spanish*
DFT; DSTE.

joro, *Japanese*
JLE.

joruri, *Japanese*
JLE.

jota, *Spanish*
ICMM; OCM.

jouer, *French*
OCM.

jour, *French*
DFT; DFWPN.

jour gras, *French*
DFPA.

jour maigre, *French*
DFPA; DFT/*maigre.*

journal intime, *French*
DFT.

joyeuse, *French*
OCM/*joyeux.*

joyeux, *French*
OCM.

Joyeux Noël, *French*
DFPA.

jubé, *French*
DA.

jubelnd, *German*
OCM.

Jubilate, *Latin*
ICMM; OCM.

jubili, *Latin*
OCM.

Judenharfe, *German*
OCM.

Judesmo, *Yiddish*
JOY.

judo, *Japanese*
DFT; DFWPB; JLE.

judoka, *Japanese*
JLE.

Jugendstil, *German*
LP.

jujitsu, *Japanese*
JLE.

julienne, *French*
DFT; DFWPN.

jumelle, *French*
DFT.

Jungfrau, *German*
DFWPN.

Junker, *German*
DFT; DFWPN.

Junkerei, *German*
DFT.

junshi, *Japanese*
JLE.

junta, *Spanish*
DFT; DFWPB; DFWPN; DSTE.

junto, *Spanish*
DFWPN.

Juppiter tonans, *Latin*
DFPA.

jure, *Latin*
DFT; DFWPN.

jure belli, *Latin*
DFPA.

jure divino, *Latin*
DEP; DFPA.

jure humano, *Latin*
DEP; DFPA.

jure uxoris, *Latin*
DFPA.

juris, *Latin*
DFWPN.

juris peritus, *Latin*
DFPA; DFT.

Juris Utriusque Doctor, *Latin*
DFT.

jus, *French*
DFT.

jus, *Latin*
    DFT; DFWPN.
jus ad rem, *Latin*
    DFPA.
jus belli, *Latin*
    DFWPN.
jus canonicum, *Latin*
    DFPA; DFT/*jus*; DFWPN.
jus civile, *Latin*
    DEP; DFPA; DFT/*jus*; DFWPN.
jus civitatis, *Latin*
    DFPA.
jus civitatus, *Latin*
    DFWPN.
jus commercii, *Latin*
    DFPA.
jus commune, *Latin*
    DFT/*jus*.
jus devolutionis, *Latin*
    DFPA.
jus divinum, *Latin*
    DFT/*jus*.
jus et norma loquendi, *Latin*
    DFPA; DFT/*jus*.
jusgado, *Spanish*
    DSTE/*juzgado*.
jus gentium, *Latin*
    DFPA; DFT/*jus*; DFWPB;
    DFWPN.
jus gladii, *Latin*
    DFPA.
jus hereditatis, *Latin*
    DFPA.
jus in re, *Latin*
    DFT/*jus*.
jus mariti, *Latin*
    DFPA; DFT/*jus*.
jus mercatorum, *Latin*
    DFPA.
jus naturae, *Latin*
    DFPA.

jus necationis, *Latin*
    DFPA.
jus pignoris, *Latin*
    DFT/*jus*.
jus possessionis, *Latin*
    DFPA; DFT/*jus*.
jus postliminii, *Latin*
    DFT/*jus*.
jus primae noctis, *Latin*
    DFPA; DFT.
jus proprietatis, *Latin*
    DFPA; DFT/*jus*.
jus publicum, *Latin*
    DFPA.
jusqu'à, *French*
    OCM.
jus regium, *Latin*
    DFT/*jus*.
jus relictae, *Latin*
    DFPA.
jus sanguinis, *Latin*
    DFPA; DFT/*jus*.
jus soli, *Latin*
    DFT/*jus*.
jus suffragii, *Latin*
    DFPA.
juste, *French*
    OCM.
juste milieu, *French*
    DEP; DFWPN.
juste-milieu, *French*
    DFT.
jus ubique docendi, *Latin*
    DFPA.
juzgado, *Spanish*
    DSTE.
j'y suis, j'y reste, *French*
    DFPA.

K

kabab, *Hindi*
DFT.

kabab, *Persian*
DFT.

kabala, *Yiddish*
JOY.

kabane, *Japanese*
JLE.

kabbala, *Yiddish*
JOY.

kabbalah, *Yiddish*
JOY / *cabala.*

kabtsen, *Yiddish*
HFY.

kabtzen, *Yiddish*
JOY.

kabtzonim, *Yiddish*
JOY / *kabtzen.*

Kabuki, *Japanese*
JLE; DFWPB; DFWPN.

kabuto gane, *Japanese*
JLE.

kabuzuchi, *Japanese*
JLE.

Kaddish, *Yiddish*
JOY.

kadsura, *Japanese*
JLE.

Kaffeeklatsch, *German*
DFT; DFWPN.

kaffiyeh, *Arabic*
DFT.

kafir, *Arabic*
DFT.

kago, *Japanese*
JLE.

kagoshima, *Japanese*
JLE.

kagura, *Japanese*
JLE.

kai, *Maori*
DFT.

kai, *Polynesian*
DFT.

kairon gnothi, *Greek*
DFPA.

kairon gnōthi, *Greek*
DFPCQ.

kai su, teknon, *Greek*
DFPA.

kakemono, *Japanese*
DFT; DFWPB; JLE.

kaki, *Japanese*
JLE.

Kakiemon, *Japanese*
JLE; ACD.

kakke, *Japanese*
JLE.

kakko, *Japanese*
ICMM.

kalamaika, *Hungarian*
ICMM.
kalikeh, *Yiddish*
JOY.
kalleh, *Yiddish*
JOY.
kalyike, *Yiddish*
HFY.
kamaina, *Hawaiian*
DFT.
Kamakura, *Japanese*
JLE.
kamashimo zashi, *Japanese*
JLE.
kambara (earth), *Japanese*
JLE.
kami, *Japanese*
DFT; JLE.
kamikaze, *Japanese*
DFWPB; DFWPN; JLE.
Kammer, *German*
OCM.
Kammermusik, *German*
ICMM.
Kammerton, *German*
ICMM; OCM/*cammerton.*
Kampf, *German*
DFWPN.
kana, *Japanese*
JLE.
kana-majiri, *Japanese*
JLE.
kanamono, *Japanese*
JLE.
kanazawa, *Japanese*
JLE.
kanji, *Japanese*
JLE.
kankar, *Hindi*
GG.
Kanon, *German*
OCM; OCM/*canon.*
kan pei, *Chinese*
DFT.

kantele, *Finnish*
ICMM; OCM.
kanten, *Japanese*
JLE.
kaolin, *Chinese*
LP.
kao-lin, *Chinese*
ACD/*porcelain.*
kaolin(e), *Chinese*
DFWPN.
Kapelle, *German*
DFT; DFWPN; ICMM/*Capelle;*
OCM.
Kapellmeister, *German*
DFT; ICMM; OCM/*Kapelle.*
Kapellmeistermusik, *German*
OCM/*Kapelle.*
Kapellton, *German*
OCM.
kapora, *Yiddish*
JOY/*kaporeh.*
kaporeh, *Yiddish*
JOY.
Kapoyr, *Yiddish*
JOY.
kapusti, *Russian*
DFWPN.
kaputt, *German*
DFWPB; DFWPN.
kar, *Swiss German*
GG.
karate, *Japanese*
DFWPB; JLE.
karateka, *Japanese*
JLE.
karewa, *Kashmiri*
GG.
karez, *Baluchi*
GG.
kari, *French*
DFT.
kari à l'indienne, *French*
DFT/*kari.*

karma, *Sanskrit*
DFT; DFWPB; DFWPN.

Karren, *German*
GG.

Karrenfeld, *German*
GG.

Karst, *German*
GG.

Karst Fenster, *German*
GG.

Kartell, *German*
DFT.

kasha, *Russian*
DFWPN.

kasheh, *Yiddish*
JOY.

kasher, *Hebrew*
DFWPN.

kashira, *Japanese*
JLE.

kashrut, *Yiddish*
JOY.

Kassation, *German*
OCM.

Kastagnetten, *German*
OCM.

kata, *Japanese*
JLE.

katakana, *Japanese*
JLE.

katana, *Japanese*
DFT; JLE.

Katayama, *Japanese*
JLE.

kat' exochen, *Greek*
DFWPN.

kat' exochēn, *Greek*
DFPCQ.

katharsis, *Greek*
DFWPN.

katsu, *Japanese*
JLE.

katsuo, *Japanese*
JLE.

katsura, *Japanese*
JLE.

katsura (tree), *Japanese*
JLE.

katsuramono, *Japanese*
JLE.

Katzenjammer, *German*
DFWPB; DFWPN.

Katzenmusik, *German*
OCM.

kaum, *German*
OCM.

kauri, *Maori*
GG.

kavir, *Persian*
GG.

kawaguchi, *Japanese*
JLE.

kaya, *Japanese*
JLE.

kayn ayn hore, *Yiddish*
HFY.

kayn aynhoreh, *Yiddish*
JOY.

kebab, *Turkish*
DFWPB.

keck, *German*
OCM.

keffiyeh, *Arabic*
DFT.

Kegel Karst, *German*
GG.

kegon, *Japanese*
JLE.

Kehraus, *German*
ICMM.

kehrreim, *German*
ICMM/*refrain*.

keineswegs, *German*
OCM.

Kempeitai, *Japanese*
JLE.

ken, *Japanese*
JLE.

kendo, *Japanese*
JLE.

keren, *Hebrew*
ICMM.

kerux, *Greek*
ICMM.

kesa-gatame, *Japanese*
JLE.

kess-kess, *Arabic*
GG.

keyaki, *Japanese*
JLE.

khal, *Bengali*
GG.

khaloshes, *Yiddish*
JOY/*chaloshes*; JOY.

khaluts, *Yiddish*
HFY.

khan, *Tatar*
DFT.

khan, *Turkish*
DFWPN.

khana, *Hindi*
DFT.

kharakteristika, *Russian*
MRWEW/*18*.

khari, *Bengali*
GG.

khasi, *Sanskrit*
DFWPN.

khasseneh, *Yiddish*
JOY.

khaukhem, *Yiddish*
JOY.

khaukhma, *Yiddish*
JOY.

khaver, *Yiddish*
JOY; JOY/*chaver*.

khavyar, *Russian*
DFWPN.

khazen, *Yiddish*
HFY.

khazer, *Yiddish*
HFY.

kheneg, *Arabic*
GG.

khmer, *Persian*
DFWPN.

khor, *Arabic*
GG.

khud, *Hindi*
GG.

khuligan, *Russian*
MRWEW/*hooligan*.

khushi, *Hindi*
DFT.

khushi, *Persian*
DFT.

kiaki, *Japanese*
JLE.

kibbitz, *Yiddish*
JOY/*kibitz*.

kibbitzer, *Yiddish*
JOY/*kibitzer*.

kibbutz, *Hebrew*
DFT; DFWPN.

kibbutz, *Yiddish*
JOY.

kibbutz, *pl.* kibbutzim, *Hebrew*
DFWPB.

kibbutzim, *Yiddish*
JOY/*kibbutz*.

kibbutznik, *Hebrew*
DFT.

kibei, *Japanese*
JLE.

kibitz, *Yiddish*
DFT; JOY.

kibitzer, *Yiddish*
DFWPN; HFY; JOY.

kichel, *Yiddish*
JOY.

Kicks, *German*
ICMM.

Kiddush, *Yiddish*
JOY.

Kiddush Hashem, *Yiddish*
JOY.

Kiddush ha-Shem, *Yiddish*
JOY/*Kiddush Hashem.*

Kielflügel, *German*
OCM.

kies, *German*
GG.

Kieselguhr, *German*
GG.

kiku, *Japanese*
JLE.

Kikuchi, *Japanese*
JLE.

kikumon, *Japanese*
DFT; JLE.

kikyo, *Japanese*
JLE.

kimchi, *Korean*
DFT.

ki-mon, *Japanese*
JLE.

kimono, *Japanese*
DFWPB; JLE.

k'in, *Chinese*
ICMM/*ch'in.*

kin, *Japanese*
JLE.

Kind, *German*
OCM.

kind, *Yiddish*
HFY.

Kindchen, *German*
GG.

Kinder, *German*
OCM/*Kind.*

kinder, *Yiddish*
JOY.

kinderlach, *Yiddish*
JOY.

Kinderstück, *German*
OCM.

kindlich, *German*
OCM.

kine-ahora, *Yiddish*
JOY/*kineahora*; JOY/*kayn aynhoreh.*

kineahora, *Yiddish*
JOY/*kayn aynhoreh*; JOY.

kinnor, *Hebrew*
ICMM.

kiosque, *Turkish*
DFWPN.

kipuka, *Hawaiian*
GG.

Kirche, *German*
OCM.

Kirchencantate, *German*
OCM.

kiri, *Japanese*
JLE.

kirigami, *Japanese*
JLE.

kirimon, *Japanese*
DFT; JLE.

kirin, *Japanese*
JLE.

Kirsche, *German*
DFWPN.

Kirschwasser, *German*
DFWPN.

kishka, *Yiddish*
JOY.

kishke, *Yiddish*
HFY.

kishkes, *Yiddish*
DFWPN.

kismet, *Turkish*
DFT; DFWPN.

Kissentanz, *German*
OCM.

kithara, *Greek*
ICMM.

Kitsch, *German*
DFWPB; LP.

kittel, *Yiddish*
JOY.

klagend, *German*
OCM.

kläglich, *German*
OCM/*klagend.*

Klang, *German*
ICMM.

Klangfarbe, *German*
ICMM/*timbre*; ICMM; OCM.

klap, *Yiddish*
JOY/*klop.*

Klappen-flügelhorn, *German*
ICMM.

Klappenhorn, *German*
ICMM; OCM.

Klapperstein, *German*
GG.

Klapp-trompete, *German*
ICMM.

klar, *German*
OCM.

Klarinette, *German*
ICMM; OCM.

Klarinetten, *German*
OCM/*Klarinette.*

Klavarskribo, *German*
OCM.

Klaviatur, *German*
OCM.

Klaviaturharmonika, *German*
OCM.

Klavier, *German*
DFWPN; ICMM; OCM.

Klaviertiger, *German*
DFWPB.

klein, *German*
OCM.

Kleinbass, *German*
ICMM.

Kleinbassgeige, *German*
ICMM.

Klein Discant Zink, *German*
OCM.

Kleine Altposaune, *German*
ICMM.

Kleine Flöte, *German*
OCM.

Kleine Trommel, *German*
OCM.

Kleinflöte, *German*
OCM/*Kleine Flöte.*

klezmer, *Yiddish*
JOY.

klingen, *German*
OCM.

Klippe, *German*
GG.

kloof, *Afrikaans*
GG.

klop, *Yiddish*
JOY.

klotz, *Yiddish*
JOY/*klutz.*

klutz, *Yiddish*
DFT; HFY; JOY.

k'naker, *Yiddish*
HFY.

Knarre, *German*
OCM.

knaydl, *Yiddish*
JOY.

kneifend, *German*
OCM.

knesset, *Hebrew*
DFWPN.

knetcher, *Yiddish*
JOY.

Knickpunkt, *German*
GG.

knippel, *Yiddish*
JOY/*knippl.*

knippl, *Yiddish*
JOY.

knish, *Yiddish*
JOY.

knishes, *Yiddish*
JOY.

k'nocker, *Yiddish*
JOY.

Knotenschiefer, *German*
GG.

koan, *Japanese*
JLE.

koban, *Japanese*
JLE.

kobang, *Japanese*
JLE.

kobe, *Japanese*
JLE.

kobtzen, *Yiddish*
JOY.

kobu, *Japanese*
JLE.

koch alayn, *Yiddish*
JOY / *kochalayn.*

kochalayn, *Yiddish*
HFY; JOY.

kochi, *Japanese*
JLE.

kochleffl, *Yiddish*
JOY.

kodogu, *Japanese*
JLE.

kofu, *Japanese*
JLE.

kogai, *Japanese*
JLE.

Kohen, *Yiddish*
JOY.

koi, *Japanese*
JLE.

koi-cha, *Japanese*
JLE.

koine, *Greek*
DFWPB.

koiné, *Greek*
DFWPN.

koji, *Japanese*
JLE.

kojiri, *Japanese*
JLE.

ko-katana, *Japanese*
JLE.

kokeshi, *Japanese*
JLE.

kokett, *German*
OCM.

Kokka, *Japanese*
JLE.

koku, *Japanese*
JLE.

kokura, *Japanese*
JLE.

kokyu, *Japanese*
ICMM.

Kolk, *German*
GG.

kolkhoz, *Russian*
DFT; MRWEW / *17.*

kolleh, *Yiddish*
JOY / *kalleh.*

kollo, *Japanese*
ICMM.

Kol Nidre, *Yiddish*
HFY; JOY.

Kölnisch(es) Wasser, *German*
DFWPN.

kolomyika, *Polish*
OCM.

Kolophon, *German*
OCM.

kolyika, *Yiddish*
JOY / *kalikeh.*

komban-wa, *Japanese*
DFT.

Kombination, *German*
OCM.

Kombinationstöne, *German*
ICMM / *resultant tones.*

kombu, *Japanese*
JLE.

komisch, *German*
OCM.

komponiert, *German*
OCM.

komponiren, *German*
ICMM.

Komponist, *German*
ICMM.

Komsomol, *Russian*
DFPA; DFWPN.

Konditorei, *German*
DFWPN.

koniak, *Japanese*
JLE.

König und Kaiser, *German*
DFPCQ.

konjak, *Japanese*
JLE.

konnichi-wa, *Japanese*
DFT.

Kontrabass, *German*
DFWPN; ICMM; OCM.

Kontrabassklarinette, *German*
OCM.

Kontrabasstuba, *German*
OCM.

Kontrafagott, *German*
ICMM; OCM.

Kontrasbassposaune, *German*
OCM.

Konzert, *German*
OCM.

Konzertmeister, *German*
ICMM.

Konzertstück, *German*
DFWPN.

kopdrayenish, *Yiddish*
JOY.

kopek, *Russian*
DFWPN.

kopje, *Dutch*
GG.

Koppel, *German*
OCM.

koppie, *Afrikaans*
GG.

koptzen, *Yiddish*
JOY/*kabtzen.*

Koran, *Arabic*
DFWPN.

Korin, *Japanese*
JLE.

Kornett, *German*
OCM.

koro, *Japanese*
JLE.

kos, *Hungarian*
ICMM.

kosher, *Yiddish from Hebrew*
DFT.

kosher, *Yiddish*
DFWPN; JOY.

Kostenka, *Serbo-Croatian*
OCM.

kotatsu, *Japanese*
JLE.

koto, *Japanese*
ICMM; JLE.

kouiaviak, *Polish*
OCM.

koum, *French*
GG.

koved, *Yiddish*
JOY.

kovid, *Yiddish*
JOY.

koza, *Japanese*
JLE.

kozo, *Japanese*
JLE.

kozuka, *Japanese*
JLE.

Kraft, *German*
OCM.

kräftig, *German*
DFT.

kragERöite, *Norwegian*
GG.

krakovienne, *French*
ICMM.

krakowiak, *Polish*
OCM/*cracovienne.*

krantz, *Afrikaans*
GG.

krasnaya zvezda, *Russian*
DFPA.
krater, *Greek*
ACD.
Krebsgang, *German*
OCM.
Krebskanon, *German*
OCM; OCM/*canon.*
krechtz, *Yiddish*
JOY.
Kreis, *German*
DFWPN; OCM.
krenk, *Yiddish*
JOY.
kreplach, *Yiddish*
JOY.
kreplakh, *Yiddish*
HFY.
kreplech, *Yiddish*
JOY.
Kreuz, *German*
ICMM; ICMM; OCM.
krewain, *Thai*
ICMM.
krich arein in di bayner, *Yiddish*
JOY.
Krieg, *German*
DFPCQ; OCM.
Krishna, *Sanskrit*
DFWPN.
krona, *Swedish*
DFWPN.
krone, *Danish*
DFWPN.
krone, *Norwegian*
DFWPN.
krotovina, *Russian*
GG.
Krumhorn, *German*
ICMM.
Krummbogen, *German*
OCM.
Krummbügel, *German*
OCM/*Krummbogen.*

Kshatriya, *Sanskrit*
DFT.
ktema es aei, *Greek*
DFPA.
ku, *Chinese*
ACD.
kuan hua, *Chinese*
DFWPN.
Kubo, *Japanese*
JLE.
Kuchen, *German*
DFWPN.
kudos, *Greek*
DFT; DFWPN.
kudzu, *Japanese*
JLE.
kuei, *Chinese*
ACD.
Kuge, *Japanese*
JLE.
kugel, *Yiddish*
JOY.
Kuh-horn, *German*
ICMM.
kujawiak, *Polish*
OCM/*kujiaviak*; OCM/*kouiaviak.*
kujiaviak, *Polish*
OCM.
kulak, *Russian*
MRWEW/*17.*
Kultur, *German*
DFT; DFWPB; DFWPN.
kumamoto, *Japanese*
JLE.
kumaso, *Japanese*
JLE.
kumite, *Japanese*
JLE.
Kümmel, *German*
DFWPN.
kung fu, *Chinese*
DFT.
Kuni Lemmel, *Yiddish*
JOY.

Kunst, *German*
DFPCQ; DFT; OCM.

Kunst Harmonium, *German*
OCM.

Kunstlied, *German*
ICMM; OCM.

Kunye Leml, *Yiddish*
HFY.

Kupfernickel, *German*
GG.

kura, *Japanese*
JLE.

kure, *Japanese*
JLE.

Kurhaus, *German*
DA.

kurikata, *Japanese*
JLE.

kuromaku, *Japanese*
JLE.

Kuroshio, *Japanese*
JLE.

kuroshio (extension), *Japanese*
JLE.

kuroshio (system), *Japanese*
JLE.

kuroshiwo, *Japanese*
JLE.

Kursaal, *German*
DA.

kuruma, *Japanese*
JLE.

Kurume, *Japanese*
JLE.

kurveh, *Yiddish*
JOY.

kurz, *German*
OCM.

kurze, *German*
OCM/*kurz.*

Kurzer Vorschlag, *German*
OCM.

kussir, *Turkish*
ICMM.

Kutani, *Japanese*
JLE.

kuzushi, *Japanese*
JLE.

kvass, *Russian*
DFT; MRWEW/*18.*

kvell, *Yiddish*
DFT; HFY; JOY.

kvetch, *Yiddish*
JOY.

kvetcherkeh, *Yiddish*
JOY.

kvetsh, *Yiddish*
HFY.

kvitch, *Yiddish*
JOY.

kwaiken, *Japanese*
JLE.

kwazoku, *Japanese*
JLE.

kyogen, *Japanese*
JLE.

kyoto, *Japanese*
JLE.

Kyrie, *Greek*
OCM.

Kyrie Eleison, *Greek*
DFWPN; DFPA; DFT.

kyrie eleïson, *Greek*
DFWPB.

kyu, *Japanese*
JLE.

kyudo, *Japanese*
JLE.

L

l', *French*
OCM.

l', *Italian*
OCM.

la, *French*
DFWPB; DFWPN; OCM.

la, *Italian*
DFWPN; OCM.

la, *Spanish*
DFWPN.

laagte, *Afrikaans*
GG.

la belle dame sans merci, *French*
DFT.

la belle époque, *French*
DFPA.

la bémol, *French*
ICMM.

Labialstimme, *German*
OCM.

la bonne bouche, *French*
DFPA.

labor limae, *Latin*
DFPCQ.

labor omnia vincit, *Latin*
DFPCQ.

lächelnd, *German*
OCM.

lâcher, *French*
OCM.

la comédie larmoyante, *French*
DFPA.

la commedia è finita, *Italian*
DFT.

la condition humaine, *French*
DFPA.

lacrimae rerum, *Latin*
DFT.

lacrimosa, *Latin*
ICMM.

lacrimoso, *Italian*
OCM.

lacuna, *Latin*
DFPCQ; DFWPN.

lacunae, *Latin*
LP.

ladino, *Spanish*
DSTE.

Ladino, *Yiddish*
JOY.

la dolce vita, *Italian*
DFPA.

la donna é mobile, *Italian*
DFPA; DFT/*Donna*.

la douce France, *French*
DFPA.

ladron, *Spanish*
DSTE.

laesa majestas, *Latin*
DFPA.

la fortune passe partout, *French*
DFT.

lag baomer, *Yiddish*
JOY.

Lage, *German*
ICMM; OCM.

lagg, *Swedish*
GG.

lagnappe, *Louisiana French*
DFT/*lagniappe.*

lagnevole, *Italian*
OCM/*lagnoso.*

lagniappe, *Louisiana French*
DFT.

lagnoso, *Italian*
OCM.

La Grande Voleuse, *French*
DFPA.

lagrimando, *Italian*
OCM.

lagrimoso, *Italian*
DFPCQ; DFT; OCM/*lacrimoso*;
OCM/*lagrimando.*

laguna, *Spanish*
DSTE; GG.

lagune, *French*
GG.

lahar, *Javanese*
GG.

la haute politique, *French*
DFPA; DFT.

lai, *French*
OCM.

lai, *Old French*
DFWPN.

laisser, *French*
OCM.

laisser-aller, *French*
DFPCQ; DFT.

laisser faire, *French*
DFPCQ.

laisser-faire, *French*
DFT.

laissez aller, *French*
DFPA; DFWPN.

laissez-aller/laisser-aller, *French*
DFWPB.

laissez dire, *French*
DFPA.

laissez faire, *French*
DFPA; DFWPN; SPICE.

laissez-faire/laisser-faire, *French*
DFWPB.

laissez passer, *French*
DFPA.

lait, *French*
DFT; DFWPN.

laitance, *French*
DFT.

lait coupé, *French*
DFT/*lait.*

laitue, *French*
DFT; DFWPN.

l'allegro, *Italian*
DFPCQ.

lama, *Tibetan*
DFT; DFWPB; DFWPN.

la majeur, *French*
ICMM.

lambrequin, *French*
ACD.

lamé, *French*
DFT; DFWPB; DFWPN.

lamentabile, *Italian*
DFPCQ; OCM/*lamentando.*

lamentando, *Italian*
DFT; OCM.

lamentazione, *Italian*
OCM.

lamentevole, *Italian*
DFPCQ; DFT; OCM/*lamentando.*

lamento, *Italian*
ICMM; OCM/*lamentazione.*

lamentoso, *Italian*
DFT; OCM/*lamentando.*

la mineur, *French*
ICMM.

215 **lapsus**

lampons, *French*
ICMM.
lamproie, *French*
DFT.
la nation boutiquière, *French*
DFT.
lancio, *Italian*
OCM.
Ländler, *German*
DFWPB; ICMM; OCM.
ländlich, *German*
OCM.
landsman, *Yiddish*
JOY.
lang, *German*
OCM.
langage, *French*
DFT.
Langer Vorschlag, *German*
OCM.
langleik, *Icelandic*
OCM.
langoureusement, *French*
OCM/*langoureux*.
langoureux, *French*
OCM.
langouste, *French*
DFT; DFWPB; DFWPN.
langsam, *German*
ICMM; OCM.
langspil, *Icelandic*
OCM.
langue, *French*
DFT; DFWPN.
langue de chat, *French*
DFWPN.
langue-de-chat, *pl.* **langues-de-chat,**
French
DFWPB.
langue d'oc, *French*
DFPA; DFT/*langue*; DFWPN;
OCM.
langue d'oïl, *French*
DFPA; DFT/*langue*; DFWPN;
OCM/*langue d'oc*.

langue maternelle, *French*
DFT/*langue*.
languemente, *Italian*
OCM/*languendo*.
languendo, *Italian*
DFPCQ; OCM.
languente, *Italian*
DFPCQ; DFT; OCM/*languendo*.
languettes, *French*
ICMM.
langueur, *French*
OCM.
langue verte, *French*
DFT/*langue*.
languidamente, *Italian*
DFT; OCM/*languido*.
languido, *Italian*
OCM.
languissant, *French*
OCM.
languore, *Italian*
OCM.
la nouvelle cuisine, *French*
DFPA.
Lanzentanz, *German*
OCM.
la pa, *Chinese*
ICMM.
lapereau, *French*
DFT.
la petite bourgeoisie, *French*
DFPA.
lapin, *French*
DFT; DFWPN.
lapin au kari, *French*
DFT/*lapin*.
lapis lazuli, *Latin*
DFPCQ; DFWPB; LP.
lapis-lazuli, *Italian*
DFWPN.
la plaza de toros, *Spanish*
DFPA.
lapsus, *Latin*
DFT.

lapsus calami, *Latin*
DFPA; DFPCQ; DFT/*lapsus*;
DFWPB; DFWPN.

lapsus linguae, *Latin*
DFPA; DFPCQ; DFT/*lapsus*;
DFWPB; DFWPN.

lapsus linguæ, *Latin*
DEP.

lapsus memoriae, *Latin*
DFPA; DFPCQ; DFT/*lapsus*;
DFWPB; DFWPN.

lapsus memoriæ, *Latin*
DEP.

lapsus pennae, *Latin*
DFWPN.

lar, *Latin*
DFT.

la règle du jeu, *French*
DFPA.

lares et penates, *Latin*
DFPA; DFPCQ; DFT/*lar*;
DFWPN.

lar familiaris, *Latin*
DFT/*lar*.

largamente, *Italian*
DFT; ICMM; OCM.

large, *French*
OCM.

largement, *French*
OCM.

l'argent, *French*
DFWPN.

largeur, *French*
OCM.

larghetto, *Italian*
DFPCQ; DFT; DFWPB;
DFWPN; ICMM; OCM.

larghezza, *Italian*
OCM.

larghissimo, *Italian*
DFT.

largo, *Italian*
DFPCQ; DFT; DFWPB;
DFWPN; ICMM; OCM.

largo, *Spanish*
DSTE.

larigo, *Spanish*
DFT.

la ringrazio, *Italian*
DFT.

larmier, *French*
DA.

l'art de vivre, *French*
DFPA.

L'Art Nouveau, *French*
DFPA.

l'art pour l'art, *French*
DFWPN.

lasagne, *Italian*
DFWPN.

lasciare, *Italian*
OCM.

lassú, *Hungarian*
OCM.

latet anguis in herba, *Latin*
DEP; DFPCQ; DFT.

latigo, *Spanish*
DSTE.

latine, *Latin*
DFT.

latke, *Yiddish*
JOY.

lato sensu, *Latin*
DFT.

latte, *Italian*
DFWPN.

latticinio, *Italian*
ACD.

latticino, *Italian*
ACD.

laud, *Spanish*
OCM.

laúd, *Spanish*
ICMM.

laudamus te, *Latin*
OCM.

laudator temporis acti, *Latin*
DFPA; DFPCQ; DFT; DFWPN.

laudator temporis acti, *pl.* **laudatores temporis acti,** *Latin*
DFWPB.

laudi spirituali, *Italian*
ICMM; OCM.

Lauf, *German*
ICMM.

Laufwerk, *German*
OCM.

lau lau, *Hawaiian*
DFWPN.

laus Deo, *Latin*
DFPCQ; DFWPN.

laut, *German*
OCM.

Laute, *German*
ICMM; OCM.

Lautenclavicymbel, *German*
ICMM.

Lautenmacher, *German*
OCM.

la volta, *Italian*
ICMM.

la volte, *Italian*
ICMM.

lavoro di commesso, *Italian*
DFPA.

lay, *French*
OCM/*lai.*

lazo, *Spanish*
DSTE.

l'chaim, *Hebrew*
DFT.

L'chayim, *Yiddish*
HFY; JOY.

le, *French*
DFWPN; OCM.

le beau monde, *French*
DEP; DFPCQ; DFT.

lebendig, *German*
OCM.

Lebensabend, *German*
DFT.

Leben Sie wohl, *German*
DFPA; DFWPN.

Lebensraum, *German*
DFPA; DFWPB; DFWPN.

lebhaft, *German*
DFT; ICMM; OCM.

le bon genre, *French*
DFPA.

leche, *Spanish*
DFT.

leçon, *French*
LB.

lectio difficilior, *Latin*
DFWPN.

lector benevole, *Latin*
DFPCQ.

le demi-monde, *French*
DFPA.

Lederhosen *pl.,* *German*
DFWPB.

le dernier cri, *French*
DFPA.

le dernier mot, *French*
DFPA.

le dessous des cartes, *French*
DFPA.

le droit des gens, *French*
DFPA.

leer, *German*
OCM.

le fin mot, *French*
DFT.

legabile, *Italian*
OCM/*legato.*

legadero, *American Spanish*
DFT.

legalis homo, *Latin*
DFPA.

legando, *Italian*
OCM/*legato.*

legatissimo, *Italian*
DFT; DFWPN.

legato, *Italian*
DFPCQ; DFT; DFWPB;
DFWPN; ICMM; OCM.

legatura, *Italian*
DFT; ICMM/*slur*; OCM.

légature, *French*
ICMM/*slur*.

legatus a latere, *Latin*
DFPA.

Legende, *German*
ICMM.

lege, quaeso, *Latin*
DFT.

léger, *French*
OCM.

légère, *French*
OCM/*léger*.

légèrement, *French*
ICMM.

leggero, *Italian*
OCM/*leggiero*.

leggiadretto, *Italian*
OCM/*leggiadro*.

leggiadro, *Italian*
OCM.

leggieramente, *Italian*
DFPCQ.

leggiero, *Italian*
DFPCQ; DFT; DFWPN; ICMM;
OCM.

leggio, *Italian*
OCM.

legibus solutus, *Latin*
DFPA.

Légion d'Honneur, *French*
DFWPN.

legno, *Italian*
OCM.

le grand mal, *French*
DFPA.

Le Grand Monarque, *French*
DFPA.

le grand monde, *French*
DFPA.

le grand prix, *French*
DFPA.

le grand siècle, *French*
DFPA.

legua, *Spanish*
DFT.

legumi, *Italian*
DFWPN.

le haut monde, *French*
DFPA.

Lehm, *German*
GG.

lei, *Chinese*
ACD.

lei, *Hawaiian*
DFT; DFWPB.

Leichengesang, *German*
ICMM.

leicht, *German*
OCM.

leichtfertig, *German*
OCM.

Leichtigkeit, *German*
OCM.

Leid, *German*
OCM.

Leidenschaft, *German*
OCM/*Leid*.

leidenschaftlich, *German*
DFT.

Leier, *German*
ICMM.

leineag, *Scottish*
ICMM/*luinig*.

Leinentrommel, *German*
OCM.

leise, *German*
OCM.

leisten, *German*
OCM.

Leitaccord, *German*
ICMM.

leitmotif, *German*
DFT.

Leitmotiv, *German*
DFWPB; DFWPN; ICMM;
OCM/*leading motif*; OCM; DFT/
leitmotif.

Leitmotive, *German*
OCM/*leading motif.*

le juste milieu, *French*
DFPA.

le juste-milieu, *French*
DFT.

l'élan vital, *French*
DFPA.

Le Métro, *French*
DFWPN.

le monde, *French*
DFT.

le monde savant, *French*
DFT/*le monde.*

le mot juste, *French*
DFPA; DFT.

Le Moyen Age, *French*
DFPA.

lendler, *Yiddish*
JOY.

lene, *Italian*
OCM.

leno, *Italian*
OCM/*lene.*

lent, *French*
OCM.

lentamente, *Italian*
DFT.

lentando, *Italian*
DFPCQ; DFT.

lentille, *French*
DFT.

lento, *Italian*
DFPCQ; DFT; DFWPN; ICMM;
OCM.

lento assai, *Italian*
DFT/*lento.*

lento molto, *Italian*
DFT/*lento.*

l'envoi, *French*
DFT.

le petit caporal, *French*
DFPA; DFT.

le petit coin, *French*
DFPA.

le petit monde, *French*
DFPCQ.

le premier pas, *French*
DFT.

le premier venu, *French*
DFT.

le roi est mort, vive le roi, *French*
DFT.

le roi le veut, *French*
DFT.

le roi s'avisera, *French*
DFT.

les, *French*
DFWPN; OCM.

les affaires font les hommes, *French*
DFPCQ.

le Salon, *French*
DFT/*salon.*

les amis du vin, *French*
DFPA.

le savoir-faire, *French*
DFPCQ.

le savoir-vivre, *French*
DFPCQ.

les convenances, *French*
DFPA; DFT.

lèse majesté, *French*
DFPA.

lèse-majesté, *French*
DFT; DFWPB; DFWPN.

lesginka, *Russian*
OCM.

les jeux sont faits, *French*
DFT.

l'esprit de suite, *French*
DFPA.

lesquercade, *French*
OCM.

les savants, *French*
DFT/*savant.*

les scènes à faire, *French*
DFPA.

lesto, *Italian*
OCM.

l'état c'est moi!, *French*
DFPCQ.

L'état, c'est moi, *French*
DFWPN.

le tout ensemble, *French*
DEP; DFPA; DFPCQ; DFT.

lettre, *French*
DFT.

lettre de cachet, *French*
DFPA; DFT/*lettre.*

lettre de change, *French*
DFPA; DFT/*lettre.*

lettre de créance, *French*
DFPA; DFT/*lettre.*

lettre de crédit, *French*
DFT/*lettre.*

lettre de récréance, *French*
DFWPN.

letz, *Yiddish*
JOY.

letzt, *German*
OCM.

leuto, *Italian*
ICMM.

levare, *Italian*
OCM.

levari facias, *Latin*
DFPA.

levaya, *Yiddish*
JOY.

levee, *French*
GG.

levezza, *Italian*
OCM.

levraut, *French*
DFT.

lex, *Latin*
DFT.

lex loci, *Latin*
DFPA; DFT/*lex.*

lex mercatoria, *Latin*
DFT/*lex.*

lex mercatorum, *Latin*
DFT/*lex.*

lex non scripta, *Latin*
DFPA; DFPCQ.

lex scripta, *Latin*
DFPA; DFPCQ; DFT/*lex.*

lex talionis, *Latin*
DFPA; DFT/*lex*; DFWPB;
DFWPN.

lex terrae, *Latin*
DFPA; DFT/*lex.*

lex terræ, *Latin*
DEP.

lezginka, *Russian*
OCM.

l'havdil, *Yiddish*
JOY.

l'homme, *French*
DFWPN.

li, *Chinese*
ACD.

liaison, *French*
DFPCQ; OCM.

liberamente, *Italian*
DFT; ICMM; OCM.

libertà, *Italian*
OCM.

libertas, *Latin*
DFPCQ.

liberté, egalité, fraternité [*sic*]**,** *French*
DFWPN.

liberté, égalité, fraternité, *French*
DFPA.

libido, *Latin*
DFWPN.

libitum, *Latin*
OCM.

libre, *French*
OCM.

librement, *French*
ICMM/*liberamente*; OCM/*libre.*

libret, *French*
DFT.

libretti, *Italian*
DFWPN/*libretto.*

libretto, *Italian*
DFPCQ; DFWPN; ICMM;
OCM.

libretto, *pl.* **libretti,** *Italian*
DFWPB.

libris clausis, *Latin*
DFPA.

licenza, *Italian*
DFT; OCM.

licet, *Latin*
DFT.

lidia, *Spanish*
DSTE/*237.*

lié, *French*
ICMM/*legato*; OCM.

Liebchen, *German*
DFT; DFWPN.

Liebe, *German*
OCM.

Liebesgeige, *German*
ICMM; OCM.

Liebesoboe, *German*
OCM.

Lieblichflöte, *German*
OCM.

Lieblich Gedact, *German*
ICMM; OCM.

Lied, *German*
DFPCQ; DFWPB; ICMM; OCM.

Lieder, *German*
DFWPB; ICMM; OCM/*Lied.*

Liederkranz, *German*
DFWPN.

Liederkreis, *German*
ICMM.

Liederspiel, *German*
ICMM.

Liedertafel, *German*
ICMM; OCM.

Liedertanz, *German*
ICMM.

Liedform, *German*
ICMM.

Lied ohne Worte, *German*
OCM.

lieto, *Italian*
OCM.

lieu, *French*
DFWPN.

lieve, *Italian*
OCM.

lièvre, *French*
DFT.

ligne, *French*
LB.

lignum vitae, *Latin*
ACD; DFWPN.

limae labor, *Latin*
DFPCQ.

limande, *French*
DFT.

limma, *Greek*
ICMM.

limon, *French*
GG.

ling lung, *Chinese*
ACD.

lingua Adamica, *Latin*
DFPA.

lingua franca, *Italian*
DFPCQ; DFWPB.

lingua franca, *Latin*
DFPA; DFPCQ; DFWPN.

lingua volgare, *Italian*
DFPCQ.

Liniensystem, *German*
ICMM/*stave.*

linke Hand, *German*
OCM.

liquet, *Latin*
DFWPN.

liqueur, *French*
DFWPN.

lira, *Italian*
DFWPN; OCM/*lyra*; OCM.

lira organizzata, *Italian*
DFWPB; OCM.

lirico, *Italian*
OCM.

lirone, *Italian*
OCM.

lirone perfetto, *Italian*
OCM/*lirone*.

lis, *Latin*
DFWPN.

liscia, *Italian*
OCM/*liscio*.

liscio, *Italian*
OCM.

lis litem generat, *Latin*
DFPA.

lis pendens, *Latin*
DFPA; DFT.

lisse, *French*
DFWPB.

lis sub iudice, *Latin*
DFPCQ.

lis sub judice, *Latin*
DFPA.

l'istesso, *Italian*
OCM.

l'istesso tempo, *Italian*
ICMM.

lit de justice, *French*
DFPA.

litem lite resolvere, *Latin*
DFPA.

lite pendente, *Latin*
DFPA; DFPCQ; DFT.

literae humaniores, *Latin*
DFPCQ; DFWPN.

literati, *Latin*
DFPCQ; DFT; DFWPN.

literati *pl.,* *Italian*
DFWPB.

literatim, *Latin*
DFPCQ; DFT.

litotes, *Greek*
DFWPN.

litterae humaniores, *Latin*
DFPA; DFT; DFWPN.

litterae humaniores *pl.,* *Latin*
DFWPB.

littérateur, *French*
DFPCQ; DFT; DFWPN.

littérateur, *fem.* **littératrice,** *French*
DFWPB.

Litvak, *Yiddish*
HFY; JOY.

liuto, *Italian*
DFPCQ; ICMM; OCM.

livre, *French*
OCM.

livre à clef, *French*
DFWPN.

livres d'heures, *French*
DFPA.

llama, *Spanish*
DSTE.

llano, *Spanish*
DSTE.

Llano Estacado, *Spanish*
DSTE.

lobo, *Spanish*
DSTE.

locale, *French*
DFPCQ.

loca supra citato, *Latin*
DFT/*loco*.

loc(o) cit(ato), *Latin*
DFWPB.

loch in kop, *Yiddish*
JOY.

loci, *Latin*
DFWPN/*locus*.

loco, *Italian*
DFT; ICMM; OCM.

loco, *Latin*
DFT.

loco, *Spanish*
DSTE.

loco citato, *Latin*
DFPA; DFT/*loco*; DFWPN.

loco citato (loc. cit.), *Latin*
DFPCQ.

loco laudato, *Latin*
DFT/*loco*.

loco parentis, *Latin*
DFWPB; DFWPN.

(in) loco parentis, *Latin*
DFWPB.

loco parentis, in, *Latin*
SPICE.

locum tenens, *Latin*
DFPA; DFT.

locus, *Latin*
DFT; DFWPN.

locus, *pl.* **loci,** *Latin*
DFWPB.

locus citatus, *Latin*
DFT/*locus*.

locus classicus, *Latin*
DFPA; DFT/*locus*; DFWPN.

locus classicus, *pl.* **loci classici,** *Latin*
DFWPB.

locus communis, *Latin*
DFPA; DFT/*locus*.

locus communis, *pl.* **loci communes,**
Latin
DFWPB.

locus criminis, *Latin*
DFPA; DFT/*locus*.

locus delicti, *Latin*
DFPA; DFT/*locus*; DFWPN.

locus in quo, *Latin*
DFPA; DFT/*locus*.

locus poenitentiae, *Latin*
DFPA; DFT/*locus*.

locus sigilli, *Latin*
DEP; DFPA; DFT/*locus*.

locus standi, *Latin*
DFPA; DFT/*locus*.

Loess, *German*
GG.

Loess Kindchen, *German*
GG.

loessoïde, *Dutch*
GG.

loggia, *Italian*
DFWPN.

logion, *Greek*
DFT.

logiste, *French*
DA.

logos, *Greek*
DFWPN.

logos echei, *Greek*
DFPCQ.

loin, *French*
OCM.

lointain, *French*
OCM/*loin*.

loksh, *Yiddish*
JOY.

loma, *Spanish*
DFT; DSTE; GG.

lombarda, *Italian*
ICMM.

lomita, *Spanish*
DFT.

longa, *Latin*
ICMM.

longe, *French*
DFT.

long spiel, *Icelandic*
ICMM.

lonja, *Spanish*
DA.

lontano, *Italian*
OCM.

loquitur, *Latin*
DFT; DFWPN.

los, *German*
OCM.

los, *Spanish*
DFWPN.

Löss, *German*
GG.

Louis-d'or, *French*
DFWPN.

Louis Quatorze, *French*
DFT.

Louis Quinze, *French*
DFT.

Louis Seize, *French*
DFT.

Louis Treize, *French*
DFT.

loukoum, *Turkish*
DFT.

lourd, *French*
OCM.

lourde, *French*
OCM/*lourd.*

loure, *French*
ICMM; OCM.

lox, *Yiddish*
HFY.

L'shone toyve, *Yiddish*
HFY.

lubricum linguae, *Latin*
DFWPN.

luce di sotto, *Italian*
DFWPB.

lucus a non lucendo, *Latin*
DFT; DFWPN.

lues, *Latin*
DFT.

lues commentatoria, *Latin*
DFPA.

lues venerea, *Latin*
DFT/*lues.*

luftig, *German*
OCM.

luftmensh, *Yiddish*
JOY.

luftmentsh, *Yiddish*
HFY.

Luftwaffe, *German*
DFWPN.

lugubre, *French*
OCM.

lugubre, *Italian*
OCM.

luinig, *Scottish*
ICMM.

luli kebab, *Russian*
DFWPN.

lumen fidei, *Latin*
DFWPN.

lumière, *French*
DFWPN.

lumina civitatis, *Latin*
DFPCQ.

lumineux, *French*
OCM.

lump, *Yiddish*
JOY.

lune, *French*
DFWPN.

lunga, *Italian*
OCM/*lungo.*

lunga pausa, *Italian*
ICMM.

lungo, *Italian*
OCM.

luogo, *Italian*
OCM.

lupus in fabula, *Latin*
DFT.

lur, *Danish*
OCM.

l'usage du monde, *French*
DFT.

lusigando, *Italian*
OCM.

lusingando, *Italian*
DFPCQ; ICMM; OCM.

Lust, *German*
OCM.

Lustig, *German*
OCM/*Lust*; ICMM.

lustrum, *Latin*
DFPCQ.

lusus naturae, *Latin*
DFPA.

luth, *French*
OCM.
luthier, *French*
ICMM; OCM.
lutto, *Italian*
OCM.
luttuosamente, *Italian*
DFT.
luttuoso, *Italian*
DFT.
lux, *Latin*
DFWPN.
lux in tenebris, *Latin*
DFT.

lycée, *French*
DFT; DFWPB; DFWPN.
lyra, *German*
OCM.
lyre, *German*
OCM.
lyre, en, *French*
LB.
lyrique, *French*
OCM.
lyrisch, *German*
OCM/*lyrique.*
Lyrisches Stück, *German*
OCM.

M

ma, *Italian*
OCM.

maarev, *Yiddish*
JOY/*mairev*; JOY.

maariv, *Yiddish*
JOY/*mairev*.

macabre, *French*
DFWPN.

macchia, *Italian*
DFWPB.

macchina, *Italian*
OCM.

macédoine, *French*
DFT; DFWPN.

machalath, *Hebrew*
ICMM.

macher, *Yiddish*
JOY.

ma chère, *French*
DEP; DFPA/*ma chérie*.

ma chérie, *French*
DFPA.

machetayneste, *Yiddish*
JOY.

machete, *Portuguese*
ICMM.

machete, *Spanish*
DFT; DFWPB; DFWPN; DSTE.

machetuneste, *Yiddish*
JOY.

machetunim, *Yiddish*
JOY.

machine à vent, *French*
OCM.

macho, *Spanish*
DFWPB.

machol, *Hebrew*
ICMM.

mächtig, *German*
OCM.

machuten, *Yiddish*
JOY.

machutin, *Yiddish*
JOY.

macigno, *Italian*
GG.

macle, *French*
GG.

macramé, *Turkish*
DFWPB.

maculatum, *Latin*
DFWPN.

Mädchen, *German*
DFPCQ; DFT; DFWPN.

madeleine, *French*
DFT.

mademoiselle, *French*
DFT; DFWPB; DFWPN.

madère, *French*
DFT.

Madonna, *Italian*
DFPCQ; DFWPN; DFWPB.

madre, *Italian*
DFWPN.

madre, *Spanish*
DFT; DFWPN.

madriale, *Italian*
OCM.

madrigali spirituali, *Italian*
OCM.

madrileña, *Spanish*
OCM.

madrilène, *French*
OCM/*madrileña.*

madroña, *Spanish*
DSTE.

maestà, *Italian*
OCM.

maestade, *Italian*
OCM/*maestà.*

maestosamente, *Italian*
DFT.

maestoso, *Italian*
DFPCQ; DFT; ICMM; OCM.

maestrale, *Italian*
ICMM; OCM.

maestro, *Italian*
DFT; DFWPN; ICMM; OCM.

maestro, *pl.* **maestri,** *Italian*
DFWPB.

maestro, *Spanish*
DSTE.

maestro di cappella, *Italian*
DFPA; DFWPB.

maffia, *Italian*
DFWPN.

mafia, *Italian*
DFT; DFWPN.

mafioso, *Italian*
DFT.

magada, *Greek*
ICMM.

magas, *Greek*
ICMM.

Magen David, *Yiddish*
JOY/*Mogen David.*

maggid, *Yiddish*
JOY.

maggiolata, *Italian*
OCM.

maggiore, *Italian*
DFPCQ; ICMM/*major*; ICMM;
OCM.

magi, *Persian*
DFWPN/*Lat-magus.*

magister, *Latin*
DFT; DFWPN.

Magister Artium, *Latin*
DFT/*magister.*

magister artium (M.A.), *Latin*
DFPCQ.

magister bibendi, *Latin*
DFPA.

magister ceremoniarum, *Latin*
DFPA.

magister dixit, *Latin*
DFT/*magister.*

magna, *Italian*
OCM/*magno*; OCM.

Magna Carta, *Latin*
DFPA.

Magna Charta, *Latin*
DFPCQ; DFWPN.

magna cum laude, *Latin*
DFPA; DFT; DFWPN.

magna est veritas, et prevalebit,
Latin
DEP.

magnífico, *Spanish*
DFWPN.

Magnificat, *Latin*
DFWPB; DFWPN; ICMM.

magno, *Italian*
OCM.

magnum bonum, *Latin*
DEP; DFPCQ.

magnum in parvo, *Latin*
DFT.

magnum opus, *Latin*
DFPA; DFPCQ; DFT; DFWPB;
DFWPN; SPICE.

magnus Apollo, *Latin*
DEP.

magoridi, *Hindi*
ICMM.

magot, *French*
DFWPN.

magrepha, *Hebrew*
ICMM.

maguey, *Spanish*
DSTE.

magus, *Persian through Latin*
DFWPN.

Magus, *pl.* Magi, *Latin*
DFWPB.

Mahabharata, *Sanskrit*
DFWPN.

mahalo, *Hawaiian*
DFT.

maharaja, *Hindi*
DFT.

maharaja, *Sanskrit*
DFT.

Maharajah, *Hindi*
DFWPN.

Maharanee, *Hindi*
DFWPN; DFWPB.

maharani, *Hindi*
DFT.

Mahatma, *Sanskrit*
DFWPN; DFT; DFWPB.

mahayana, *Sanskrit*
DFT.

Mahdi, *Arabic*
DFWPN.

mahhol, *Hebrew*
ICMM/*machol.*

mahjong, *Chinese*
DFT.

mah nishtana, *Yiddish*
JOY.

mah nishtannah, *Yiddish*
JOY.

mah nishtanu, *Yiddish*
JOY.

mahout, *Hindi*
DFWPN.

mai, *Japanese*
JLE.

mai a, *Hawaiian*
DFWPN.

Maigelein, *German*
ACD.

maigre, *French*
DFT.

maiko, *Japanese*
JLE.

mailloche, *French*
OCM.

maillot, *French*
LB.

main, *French*
DFWPN; LB; OCM.

main droite, *French*
OCM/*m.d..*

mains, *French*
OCM/*main.*

maiolica, *Italian*
ACD.

mairev, *Yiddish*
JOY.

mairie, *French*
DA.

mais, *French*
OCM.

maison, *French*
DFT; DFWPB; DFWPN.

maison de jeu, *French*
DFPA.

maître, *French*
DFT; OCM.

maître de ballet, *French*
LB.

maître de ballet, *fem.* **maîtresse de ballet,** *French*
DFWPB.

maître de chapelle, *French*
ICMM.

maître de danse, *French*
DFT/*maître*.

maître d'hôtel, *French*
DFPA; DFPCQ; DFT; DFWPB; DFWPN.

maîtrise, *French*
ICMM; OCM.

majestätisch, *German*
OCM.

majestueuse, *French*
OCM/*majestueux*.

majestueux, *French*
OCM.

majeur, *French*
ICMM/*major*; OCM.

majolica, *Italian*
ACD; DFWPB; DFWPN.

major domo, *Latin*
DFPCQ; DFWPN.

majordomo, *Spanish*
DSTE/*mayordomo*.

major domus, *Latin*
DFPA.

majusculae, *Latin*
DFPCQ; DFT.

makhutin, *Yiddish*
HFY.

makimono, *Japanese*
DFT; DFWPB; JLE.

makkes, *Yiddish*
JOY.

mal, *French*
DFT.

Mal, *German*
OCM.

malades imaginaires, *French*
DFPCQ.

maladie du pays, *French*
DFPA; DFWPN.

maladresse, *French*
DFPCQ.

maladroit, *French*
DFWPN.

mala fide, *Latin*
DFPCQ; DFT.

mala fides, *Latin*
DFPA; DFT.

malagueña, *Spanish*
ICMM; OCM.

malahini, *Hawaiian*
DFT.

malakh, *Yiddish*
HFY.

mala praxis, *Latin*
DFPA.

mal à propos, *French*
DEP; DFPA; DFPCQ; DFT; DFWPB.

malapropos, *French*
DFWPN.

mal de mer, *French*
DFPA; DFT/*mal*; DFWPB; DFWPN.

mal du pays, *French*
DFPA.

mal (maladie) du siècle, *French*
DFPA.

Malerisch, *German*
LP.

malgré lui, *French*
DFWPN.

malgré moi, *French*
DFWPN.

malgré nous, *French*
DFPCQ.

malgré soi, *French*
DFPCQ.

malgré tout, *French*
DFWPN.

mali exempli, *Latin*
DFPA; DFPCQ.

malinconia, *Italian*
OCM.

malinconico, *Italian*
OCM/*malinconia.*

malizia, *Italian*
OCM.

malpais, *Spanish*
DSTE.

malum, *Latin*
DFT.

malum in se, *Latin*
DFT/*malum.*

malum prohibitum, *Latin*
DFT/*malum.*

mamale, *Yiddish*
HFY.

mama-loshen, *Yiddish*
JOY.

mama-loshn, *Yiddish*
HFY.

mama-san, *Japanese*
JLE.

mamma mia, *Italian*
DFPA.

mamushi, *Japanese*
JLE.

mamzarim, *Yiddish*
JOY/*momzer.*

man, *Italian*
OCM.

mana, *Japanese*
JLE.

mana, *Maori*
DFWPB.

manada, *Spanish*
DFT; DSTE.

managana, *Spanish*
DSTE.

mañana, *Spanish*
DFT; DFWPB; DFWPN; DSTE.

mancando, *Italian*
DFPCQ; DFT; OCM.

mancante, *Italian*
OCM/*mancando.*

mancanza, *Italian*
OCM/*mancando.*

manche, *French*
ICMM.

manchega, *Spanish*
OCM/*mancando.*

mandala, *Sanskrit*
LP.

mandamus, *Latin*
DFPCQ; DFWPN.

mandorla, *Italian*
DFT.

mandriale, *Italian*
OCM/*mancando.*

manécanterie, *French*
OCM/*mancando.*

manége [*sic*], *French*
DFPCQ.

manège, *French*
DA.

manège, en, *French*
LB.

Manes, *Latin*
DFPCQ.

manet, *Latin*
DFT.

mangiare, *Italian*
DFWPN.

mani, *Italian*
OCM/*mano*; OCM/*mancando.*

manibus pedibusque, *Latin*
DFPCQ.

manica, *Italian*
OCM/*mancando.*

manico, *Italian*
OCM/*mancando.*

manicorde, *French*
ICMM.

manicotti, *Italian*
DFWPN.

Manier, *German*
ICMM.

Manieren, *German*
ICMM/*ornaments*; OCM/*man-cando.*

manieroso, *Italian*
DFWPB.

manioc, *Portuguese*
DFWPN.

mannequin, *French*
DFWPB.

Männer, *German*
OCM/*mancando.*

Männergesangverein, *German*
ICMM.

mano, *Italian*
OCM/*mancando.*

mano, *Spanish*
DFT.

mano destra, *Italian*
OCM/*m.d..*

manqué, *French*
LP.

manqué, *fem.* **manquée,** *French*
DFWPB.

mantilla, *Spanish*
DFWPB; DFWPN.

mantra, *Sanskrit*
DFWPB; DFWPN.

Manualkoppel, *German*
OCM; OCM/*m.k..*

manubrio, *Italian*
ICMM.

manubrium, *Latin*
ICMM/*manubrio.*

manu forti, *Latin*
DFPA.

manu propria, *Latin*
DFPA.

manzanilla, *Spanish*
DFWPB.

manzanita, *Spanish*
DSTE.

mao tai, *Chinese*
DFT.

maquereau, *French*
DFT.

maquette, *French*
DFWPB; LP.

maquillage, *French*
DFWPB.

marabout, *French*
DFT.

maraca, *Spanish*
DFWPN.

marajuana, *Spanish*
DSTE/*marihuana.*

maraschino, *Italian*
DFWPN.

marbré, *French*
DFT.

marcando, *Italian*
OCM.

marcato, *Italian*
DFPCQ; DFT; ICMM; OCM/
marcando.

marche, *French*
ICMM/*march*; OCM.

marche aux flambeaux, *French*
OCM.

Märchen, *German*
DFT; DFWPN; OCM.

Märchen, *pl.* **Märchen,** *German*
DFWPB.

marcia, *Italian*
DFPCQ; ICMM/*march*; OCM.

marcia funebre, *Italian*
DFPCQ.

Mardi Gras, *French*
DFWPB; DFPA; DFWPN.

mare clausum, *Latin*
DFPA.

mare liberum, *Latin*
DFPA.

mare magnum, *Latin*
DFPA.

Mare Nostrum, *Latin*
DFPA; DFWPB.

marginalia, *Latin*
DFT.

mariachi, *Mexican*
DFWPN.

mariage, *French*
DFT.

mariage de conscience, *French*
DFPA; DFT/*mariage*.

mariage de convenance, *French*
DFPA; DFT/*mariage*; DFT/
convenance; DFWPB; DFWPN.

mariage de la main gauche, *French*
DFPA; DFT/*mariage*.

mariage de politique, *French*
DFPA.

mariage d'inclination, *French*
DFT/*mariage*.

marihuana, *Spanish*
DSTE.

marijuana, *Spanish*
DSTE/*marihuana*.

marimba, *Spanish*
DFWPN.

marinade, *French*
DFWPN.

mariné(e), *French*
DFWPN.

marin gräns, *Swedish*
GG.

markiert, *German*
OCM.

markig, *German*
OCM.

marli, *French*
DFWPN.

marmite, *French*
DFT; DFWPN.

marouflage, *French*
LP.

marque, *French*
DFWPB.

marqué, *French*
OCM.

marque de fabrique, *French*
DFPA.

marquer, *French*
LB.

marqueterie, *French*
DFWPN.

marquis, *French*
DFWPN.

marquise, *French*
ACD; DFWPN.

Marrano, *Yiddish*
JOY.

marron, *French*
DFT; DFWPN.

marron d'inde, *French*
DFT/*marron*.

marron glacé, *pl.* marrons glacés,
French
DFWPB.

marrons glacés, *French*
DFWPN.

Marsala, *Italian*
DFWPN.

Marsch, *German*
ICMM/*march*; OCM.

marschmässig, *German*
OCM.

Marseillaise, *French*
DFWPN.

marteau, *French*
OCM.

martelé, *French*
ICMM; OCM.

martellando, *Italian*
OCM.

martellato, *Italian*
DFT; DFWPB; ICMM/*martelé*;
OCM/*martellando*.

martellement, *French*
ICMM.

marziale, *Italian*
DFPCQ; DFT; OCM.

Marzipan, *German*
DFWPN.

masa, *Spanish*
DFT.

mascara, *Spanish*
DFWPB.

mascarade, *French*
OCM.

mascherone, *Italian*
DFWPB.

Maschinenpauken, *German*
OCM.

Mashiach, *Yiddish*
JOY; JOY/*meshiach.*

mashrogiytha, *Hebrew*
ICMM.

masjid, *Arabic*
DFT.

Maskenspiel, *German*
OCM/*masque.*

maskilin, *Yiddish*
JOY.

masque, *French*
OCM.

massé, *French*
DFT; DFWPB; DFWPN.

massepain, *French*
DFT.

masseur, *French*
DFWPN.

masseur, *fem.* masseuse, *French*
DFWPB.

masseuse, *French*
DFWPN.

massier, *French*
DA.

mässig, *German*
DFT; ICMM; OCM.

massima, *Italian*
OCM/*massimo.*

massimo, *Italian*
OCM.

matador, *Spanish*
DFT; DFWPN; DSTE/*237.*

matassins, *French*
ICMM; OCM.

mate, *Spanish*
DSTE.

maté, *Spanish*
DFT; DFWPB.

matelassé, *French*
DFT.

matelote, *French*
DFT; DFWPN.

matelotte, *Dutch*
ICMM.

matelotte, *French*
OCM.

mater, *Latin*
DFWPN.

mater familias, *Latin*
DFPA.

materfamilias, *Latin*
DEP; DFPCQ; DFT; DFWPB;
DFWPN.

materia medica, *Latin*
DFWPB.

materia prima, *Latin*
DFPA.

matet, *Spanish*
DSTE/*metate.*

matete, *Spanish*
DSTE/*metate.*

matière, *French*
DFWPB; LP.

matmid, *Yiddish*
JOY.

matsu, *Japanese*
JLE.

matsuri, *Japanese*
JLE.

matsuyama, *Japanese*
JLE.

mattachins, *French*
OCM.

mattinata, *Italian*
DFT; OCM.

matze, *Hebrew*
DFT.

matzo, *Hebrew*
DFT/*matze.*

matzo, *Yiddish*
HFY; JOY.

matzoh, *Yiddish*
JOY.

matzos, *Yiddish*
DFWPN.

Maultrommel, *German*
OCM.

Maul-trommel, *German*
ICMM.

mauresco, *Spanish*
OCM.

mauresque, *French*
OCM.

mauvaise honte, *French*
DEP; DFPCQ; DFWPN.

mauvais goût, *French*
DFPA; DFPCQ.

mauvais ton, *French*
DFPCQ.

maven, *Yiddish*
HFY.

mavin, *Yiddish*
DFT; JOY.

maxima, *Latin*
ICMM; OCM.

maxima cum laude, *Latin*
DFWPB; DFWPN.

maxixe, *Portuguese*
DFT.

maxixe, *Spanish*
OCM.

maya, *Sanskrit*
DFT.

mayordomo, *Spanish*
DSTE.

mazagran, *French*
DFT.

mazapán, *Spanish*
DFWPN.

mazel, *Yiddish*
DFT; HFY; JOY.

Mazel tov, *Yiddish*
HFY; DFT/*mazel*; JOY.

mazik, *Yiddish*
JOY.

mazuma, *Yiddish*
DFWPN; JOY.

mazurka, *Polish*
DFWPB; OCM.

mazzel-tov, *Yiddish*
DFWPN.

me, *French*
OCM.

me, *Italian*
OCM.

mea culpa, *Latin*
DFPA; DFT; DFWPB; DFWPN.

mea maxima culpa, *Latin*
DFPCQ; DFWPB; DFWPN.

mebos, *Japanese*
JLE.

mecate, *Spanish*
DSTE.

mechaieh, *Yiddish*
JOY.

mechuleh, *Yiddish*
JOY.

medaille, *French*
DA.

medaka, *Japanese*
JLE.

medano, *Spanish*
GG.

meden agan, *Greek*
DFPA; DFT; DFWPN.

mēden agan, *Greek*
DFPCQ.

medesimo, *Italian*
OCM.

medesimo tempo, *Italian*
ICMM.

medina, *Yiddish*
HFY/*Columbus'*; JOY.

medium, per, *Latin*
ICMM.

Meerschaum, *German*
DFWPN; GG.

mega biblion, mega kakon, *Greek*
DFPA; DFPCQ.

megilla, *Yiddish*
HFY.

megillah, *Yiddish*
DFT; JOY.

mehr, *German*
OCM.

mehrere, *German*
OCM.

Meiji, *Japanese*
JLE.

mein Gott, *German*
DFT.

Mein Herr, *German*
DFPA; DFPCQ; DFT.

mei ping, *Chinese*
ACD.

Meistersinger, *German*
DFWPN; ICMM.

me iudice, *Latin*
DFPCQ.

me judice, *Latin*
DFPA; DFT; DFWPB; DFWPN.

melamed, *Yiddish*
HFY; JOY.

mélange, *French*
DFPCQ; DFT; DFWPN; GG.

mélange de genres, *French*
DFWPN.

melanzana, *Italian*
DFWPN.

mêlé, *French*
DFT.

Melech Ham'lochim, *Yiddish*
JOY.

mêlée, *French*
DFPCQ; DFT; DFWPN; GG.

melikaria, *Greek*
GG.

melisma, *Greek*
ICMM; OCM.

melismata, *Greek*
OCM.

Melismatisch, *German*
ICMM.

mélopée, *French*
OCM.

melopoea, *Greek*
ICMM.

melos, *Greek*
ICMM.

membretto, *Italian*
DA.

membrum virile, *Latin*
DFWPN.

même, *French*
OCM.

memento mori, *Latin*
DEP; DFPA; DFPCQ; DFT;
DFWPB; DFWPN; LP.

mémoire, *French*
DFWPN.

memorabilia, *Latin*
DFPCQ.

memsahib, *Anglo-Indian*
DFT.

men, *Italian*
OCM.

ménage, *French*
DFPCQ; DFT; DFWPB;
DFWPN.

ménage à trois, *French*
DFPA; DFT/*ménage*; DFWPB.

mench, *Yiddish*
JOY/*mensh.*

ménestrandie, *French*
OCM/*ménestrier.*

ménestrel, *French*
OCM.

ménestrel de bouche, *French*
OCM/*ménestrel.*

ménestrel de guerre, *French*
OCM/*ménestrel.*

ménestrier, *French*
OCM.

Mengwacke, *German*
GG.

meno, *Italian*
OCM.

meno mosso, *Italian*
DFT/*meno*; ICMM.

Menorah, *Hebrew*
DFWPN.

menorah, *Yiddish*
HFY; JOY.

mensa et toro, *Latin*
DFT.

Mensch, *German*
DFWPN.

mensh, *Yiddish*
JOY.

mens legis, *Latin*
DEP; DFPA.

mens rea, *Latin*
DFPA; DFT; DFWPB.

mens sana in corpore sano, *Latin*
DEP; DFPCQ; DFT; DFWPB;
DFWPN.

menthe, *French*
DFT.

mention, *French*
DA.

mentsh, *Yiddish*
HFY.

menu, *French*
DFPCQ.

menuet, *French*
ICMM/*minuet*; OCM/*minuet*.

Menuett, *German*
OCM/*minuet*.

menu gibier, *French*
DFT; DFT/*gibier*.

menuisier, *French*
ACD.

menuki, *Japanese*
JLE.

menu peuple, *French*
DFPA.

meo periculo, *Latin*
DFPA.

meo voto, *Latin*
DFT; DFWPN.

merci, *French*
DFT; DFWPN.

merci beaucoup, *French*
DFPA.

merde, *French*
DFWPN.

mer de glace, *French*
GG.

mère, *French*
DFWPN.

meringue, *French*
DFWPN.

merlan, *French*
DFT.

merum sal, *Latin*
DFPA; DFPCQ; DFT.

merveilleux, *French*
DFWPN.

merz, *German*
LP.

mesa, *Spanish*
DFT; DFWPN; DSTE; GG.

mésalliance, *French*
DEP.

mescal, *American Spanish*
DFT.

mescal, *Spanish*
DSTE/*mezcal*.

meschal, *Spanish*
DSTE/*mezcal*.

mescol, *Spanish*
DSTE/*mezcal*.

mesdemoiselles, *French*
DFT.

meseta, *Spanish*
GG.

meshiach, *Yiddish*
JOY.

meshpocheh, *Yiddish*
JOY/*mishpocheh*.

meshugah, *Hebrew*
DFT.

meshuggah, *Yiddish*
DFWPN.

meshugge, *Yiddish*
HFY; JOY.

meshumad, *Yiddish*
JOY.

mesilla, *Spanish*
DFT; GG.

mesquit, *Spanish*
DSTE/*mesquite.*

mesquite, *Spanish*
DSTE.

mesquits, *Spanish*
DSTE/*mesquite.*

messa di voce, *Italian*
DFPCQ; DFT; DFWPB;
DFWPN; ICMM; OCM.

messa per i defunti, *Italian*
OCM.

messe des morts, *French*
OCM/*messa per i defunti.*

Messing, *German*
OCM.

mestizo, *Spanish*
DFT; DFWPN.

mestizo, *fem.* **mestiza,** *Spanish*
DFWPB.

mesto, *Italian*
DFPCQ; ICMM; OCM.

mesure, *French*
ICMM/*time*; OCM.

mesure à trois temps, *French*
ICMM/*triple time.*

metà, *Italian*
OCM.

metabole, *Greek*
ICMM.

metabolism, *Greek*
ICMM.

metake, *Japanese*
JLE.

metanoia, *Greek*
DFWPN.

metate, *Spanish*
DFT; DSTE.

méthode, *French*
LB.

métier, *French*
DFT; DFWPB; DFWPN; LP.

mètre, *French*
ICMM/*meter.*

Metrik, *German*
ICMM/*meter.*

metro, *Italian*
ICMM/*meter.*

métronome, *French*
OCM/*metronome.*

metronomo, *Italian*
OCM/*metronome.*

metsieh, *Yiddish*
JOY.

mettere, *Italian*
OCM.

mettre, *French*
OCM/*mettere.*

meubles, *French*
DFT; DFWPN.

meubles d'occasion, *French*
DFPA.

meum et tuum, *Latin*
DFT; DFWPB.

meu senhor, *Portuguese*
DFPCQ.

mezcal, *Spanish*
DSTE.

mezuzah, *Yiddish*
JOY.

mezuze, *Yiddish*
HFY.

mezza, *Italian*
ICMM; OCM.

mezza-Maiolica, *Italian*
ACD.

mezza voce, *Italian*
DFPA; DFWPB.

mezzo, *Italian*
DFPCQ; DFT; ICMM; OCM.

mezzo carattere, aria di, *Italian*
OCM.

mezzo forte, *Italian*
DFPA; DFT/*mezzo.*

mezzo-forte, *Italian*
DFPCQ; DFWPN; ICMM.

mezzo piano, *Italian*
DFPA; DFT/*mezzo.*

mezzo-piano, *Italian*
DFPCQ; DFWPN; ICMM.

mezzo-relievo [*sic*]**,** *Italian*
DFWPN.

mezzo rilievo, *Italian*
DFWPB.

mezzo-rilievo, *Italian*
DA; DFT.

mezzo soprano, *Italian*
DFWPB.

mezzo termine, *Italian*
DFT/*mezzo.*

mezzo voce, *Italian*
DFT/*mezzo.*

mezzo-voce, *Italian*
DFPCQ.

mezzuza, *Yiddish*
JOY.

mi, *French*
OCM.

mi, *Italian*
ICMM; OCM.

miai, *Japanese*
JLE.

mi bemol, *French*
ICMM.

mi contra fa, *Italian*
ICMM.

Midi, *French*
DFT/*midi*; DFT.

mi diese, *French*
ICMM.

midrash, *Yiddish*
JOY.

miesse meshina, *Yiddish*
JOY.

mignard, *French*
DFT.

mignardise, *French*
DFT.

mignon, *French*
DFWPN.

mijnheer, *Dutch*
DFT.

mijoter, *French*
DFT.

Mikado, *Japanese*
DFWPB; DFT; JLE.

mikan, *Japanese*
JLE.

Mikimoto, *Japanese*
JLE.

mikva, *Yiddish*
DFT; JOY.

mikvah, *Yiddish*
JOY.

mikveh, *Yiddish*
JOY.

milchedig, *Yiddish*
JOY.

milchik, *Yiddish*
JOY.

miles gloriosus, *Latin*
DFPA; DFT; DFWPN.

milieu, *French*
DFT; DFWPB; DFWPN; GG;
LP; OCM.

milieu, au, *French*
LB.

militaire, *French*
OCM.

militär, *German*
OCM/*militaire.*

militare, *Italian*
OCM/*militaire.*

Militärtrommel, *German*
OCM.

millefiori, *Italian*
ACD; DFWPB.

millefleurs, *French*
DFWPB.

millier, *French*
DFT.

milpa, *Spanish*
DSTE.

mimer, *French*
LB.

mimesis, *Greek*
DFWPN.

mimosa, *Spanish*
DSTE.

minaccevole, *Italian*
OCM.

minaccevolmente, *Italian*
DFT; OCM/*minaccevole.*

minacciando, *Italian*
DFT; ICMM.

Minamata (disease), *Japanese*
JLE.

mincha, *Yiddish*
JOY.

minder, *German*
OCM.

minestrone, *Italian*
DFT; DFWPB; DFWPN.

mineur, *French*
ICMM; ICMM/*minor*; OCM.

mingei, *Japanese*
JLE.

minhah, *Yiddish*
JOY.

minima, *Latin*
ICMM; OCM.

Minne, *German*
OCM.

Minnesänger, *German*
DFWPN; ICMM/*Minnesingers.*

Minnesingers, *German*
OCM.

minore, *Italian*
DFPCQ; ICMM/*minor*; ICMM;
OCM.

minuetto, *Italian*
DFPCQ; ICMM/*minuet*; OCM/
minuet.

minuge, *Italian*
ICMM.

minusculae, *Latin*
DFT.

minutia, *pl.* **minutiae,** *Latin*
DFWPB.

minutiae, *Latin*
DFPCQ.

minyan, *Yiddish*
JOY.

minyen, *Yiddish*
HFY.

minyon, *Yiddish*
JOY.

mirabile dictu, *Latin*
DFPA; DFPCQ; DFT; DFWPB;
DFWPN.

mirabile visu, *Latin*
DFPA; DFPCQ; DFT; DFWPB;
DFWPN.

mirabilia, *Latin*
DFPCQ.

mirliton, *French*
ICMM; OCM.

miroton, *French*
DFT; DFWPN.

mirum, *Latin*
DFPCQ.

mise, *French*
OCM.

mise a la masse [*sic*], *French*
GG.

mise en scène, *French*
DFPA; DFPCQ; DFT; DFWPB;
DFWPN.

miserabile dictu, *Latin*
DFPA; DFT.

miserabile vulgus, *Latin*
DFPA.

miserable vulgus, *Latin*
DFT.

misère, *French*
DFT.

miserere, *Latin*
ICMM.

miserere nobis, *Latin*
DFPCQ.

miséricorde, *French*
DFWPN.

mishegaas, *Yiddish*
JOY/*mishegoss.*

mishegoss, *Yiddish*
JOY.

mishling, *Yiddish*
HFY.

Mishnah, *Yiddish*
JOY.

mishpocheh, *Yiddish*
JOY.

mishpokhe, *Yiddish*
HFY.

miso, *Japanese*
JLE.

Missa, *Latin*
DFT; DFWPN.

Missa bassa, *Latin*
DFT/*Missa.*

Missa cantata, *Latin*
DFT/*Missa*; DFWPB.

Missa catechumenorum, *Latin*
DFT/*Missa.*

Missa fidelium, *Latin*
DFT/*Missa.*

missa lecta, *Latin*
OCM.

missa parodia, *Latin*
ICMM/*parody mass.*

missa privata, *Latin*
OCM.

missa pro defunctis, *Latin*
OCM.

missa quarti toni, *Latin*
OCM.

missa sine nomine, *Latin*
OCM.

Missa solemnis, *Latin*
DFT/*Missa*; DFWPB.

missa solennis, *Latin*
OCM.

missa supra voces musicales, *Latin*
OCM.

misterioso, *Italian*
DFT.

mistero, *Italian*
OCM.

mistico, *Italian*
OCM.

misura, *Italian*
DFPCQ; ICMM/*time*; OCM.

misurato, *Italian*
DFPCQ; DFT.

mit, *German*
DFWPN; OCM.

mitleidig, *German*
OCM.

mitsukurina, *Japanese*
JLE.

mitsumata, *Japanese*
JLE.

Mittagessen, *German*
DFT/*Mittagsessen.*

Mittagsessen, *German*
DFT.

Mitte, *German*
OCM.

Mitteleuropa, *German*
DFWPN.

mittimus, *Latin*
DFPA; DFPCQ; DFT.

mit Vershiebung, *German*
ICMM/*una corda.*

mitzva, *Yiddish*
JOY.

mitzvah, *Yiddish*
JOY.

mitzvoth, *Yiddish*
JOY.

Miyagawanella, *Japanese*
JLE.

mizrach, *Yiddish*
JOY.

mizrachi, *Yiddish*
JOY.

mo, *Swedish*
GG.
mobile perpetuum, *Latin*
DFPA; DFT; DFWPN.
mobile vulgus, *Latin*
DFPA.
mochi, *Japanese*
JLE.
mochila, *Spanish*
DSTE.
mocho, *Spanish*
DSTE.
modello, *pl.* modelli, *Italian*
DFWPB.
moderado, *Spanish*
DFPCQ.
moderato, *Italian*
DFPCQ; DFT; DFWPN; ICMM;
OCM.
moderato cantabile, *Italian*
DFPA.
modéré, *French*
OCM/*moderato.*
modestie, *French*
DFT.
modicum, *Latin*
DFPCQ.
modinha, *Portuguese*
OCM.
modiste, *French*
DFT; DFWPN.
modo, *Italian*
OCM.
modus, *Latin*
DFT.
modus lascivus, *Latin*
OCM.
modus operandi, *Latin*
DEP; DFPA; DFPCQ; DFT/
modus; DFWPN.
modus operandi, *pl.* modi operandi,
Latin
DFWPB.
modus ponens, *Latin*
DFT/*modus.*

modus tollens, *Latin*
DFT/*modus.*
modus vivendi, *Latin*
DFPA; DFT/*modus*; DFWPB;
DFWPN.
moel, *Yiddish*
JOY/*mohel.*
moelle de bœuf, *French*
DFT.
mœurs, *French*
DFT.
mofette, *French*
GG.
Mogen David, *Yiddish*
HFY; JOY.
Mogen Dovid, *Hebrew*
DFWPN.
möglich, *German*
OCM.
Moharram, *Arabic*
DFT.
moharrie, *Spanish*
DSTE/*mujer.*
mohel, *Yiddish*
JOY.
moi, *French*
DFT.
moichel, *Yiddish*
JOY.
moins, *French*
OCM.
moiré, *French*
DFWPB; DFWPN; LP.
moire antique, *French*
DFWPB.
Moishe Kapoyr, *Yiddish*
HFY; JOY.
moisson, *French*
DFT.
moitié, *French*
OCM.
moji, *Japanese*
JLE.

mokko, *Japanese*
JLE.

mokum, *Japanese*
JLE.

molasse, *French*
GG.

mole, *Spanish*
DFT; DSTE.

moll, *German*
ICMM/*minor*; ICMM; OCM.

molla, *Turkish*
DFT.

mollah, *Turkish*
DFT/*molla*.

molle, *Italian*
OCM.

mollemente, *Italian*
DFT; OCM/*molle*.

molotov, *Russian*
DFWPN.

molto, *Italian*
DFPCQ; DFT; DFWPN; ICMM;
OCM.

molto allegro, *Italian*
DFT.

moment musical, *French*
OCM.

momme, *Japanese*
JLE.

mompei, *Japanese*
JLE.

momzer, *Yiddish*
DFT; DFWPN; HFY; JOY.

mon, *Japanese*
JLE.

mon ami, *French*
DEP; DFT.

mon cher, *French*
DEP; DFPA; DFT.

monde, *French*
DFT; DFWPN.

Mon Dieu, *French*
DFPA; DFT; DFWPN.

Mondmilch, *Swiss German*
GG.

mondo, *Japanese*
JLE.

monferrina, *Italian*
ICMM.

monocoque, *French*
DFWPB.

monocorde, *French*
ICMM/*monocordo*.

monocordo, *Italian*
ICMM.

Monodrama, *German*
ICMM.

monologue intérieur, *French*
DFWPB; DFWPN.

mono sabio, *Spanish*
DSTE/*237*.

monseigneur, *French*
DFT; DFWPN.

monsieur, *French*
DFT; DFWPN.

monsignore, *Italian*
DFWPN.

monsignore, *pl.* monsignori, *Italian*
DFWPB.

monstrum, *Latin*
DFWPN.

mons veneris, *Latin*
DFWPN.

montage, *French*
DFWPN; LP.

montant, *French*
DA.

monter, *French*
LB; OCM.

montera, *Spanish*
DSTE/*237*.

monticule, *French*
GG.

montre, *French*
ICMM; OCM.

monumentum aere perennius, *Latin*
DFPCQ; DFWPN.

moolah, *Arabic*
DFWPN.

moose, *Japanese*
JLE.

moqueur, *French*
OCM.

moraine, *French*
GG.

morbidezza, *Italian*
DFT; OCM/*morbido.*

morbido, *Italian*
OCM.

morceau, *French*
DFPCQ; DFT; ICMM; ICMM/
piece; OCM.

mordant, *French*
DFWPN.

Mordent, *German*
ICMM/*mordent.*

mordente, *Italian*
DFPCQ; ICMM/*mordent.*

more, *Latin*
DFT.

more Anglico, *Latin*
DFT/*more.*

more Hibernico, *Latin*
DFT/*more.*

more maiorum, *Latin*
DFPCQ.

more majorum, *Latin*
DEP; DFPA; DFT/*more.*

more meo, *Latin*
DFT/*more.*

morendo, *Italian*
DFPCQ; DFT; ICMM; OCM.

mores, *Latin*
DFT; DFWPN.

moresca, *Spanish*
OCM.

Moresco, *Italian*
DFPCQ.

moresco, *Spanish*
OCM/*moresca.*

more Socratico, *Latin*
DFT/*more.*

more solito, *Latin*
DFT/*more.*

more suo, *Latin*
DFT/*more.*

Morgen, *German*
DFWPN.

Morgenblätter, *German*
OCM.

Morgenlied, *German*
OCM.

morisca, *Spanish*
OCM.

morisco, *Spanish*
OCM/*morisca*; OCM/*moresca.*

morisque, *French*
OCM.

morituri salutamus, *Latin*
DFWPN.

morituri te salutamus, *Latin*
DFT.

morituri te salutant, *Latin*
DFWPB.

mormorando, *Italian*
DFT; OCM.

mormorante, *Italian*
OCM/*mormorando.*

mormorevole, *Italian*
OCM/*mormorando.*

mormoroso, *Italian*
OCM/*mormorando.*

morne, *French*
DFT.

morra, *Italian*
DFWPN.

morral, *Spanish*
DSTE.

morro, *Spanish*
GG.

mortifié, *French*
DFT.

morue, *French*
DFT.

mosaique, *French*
DA.

mos majorum, *Latin*
DFPA; DFWPB.

mosquito, *Spanish*
DSTE.

mosso, *Italian*
DFPCQ; DFT; ICMM; OCM.

mot, *French*
DFT; DFWPB; DFWPN.

mot à mot, *French*
DFT/*mot.*

mot d'écrit, *French*
DFT/*mot.*

mot de guet, *French*
DFPA; DFWPN.

mot de l'énigme, *French*
DFT/*mot.*

mot de passe, *French*
DFT/*mot.*

mot de ralliement, *French*
DFT/*mot.*

mot d'ordre, *French*
DFT/*mot*; DFWPN.

mot du guet, *French*
DFT/*mot.*

mot d'usage, *French*
DFT/*mot.*

motetto, *Italian*
DFPCQ.

motif, *French*
DA; DFT; DFWPN; LP; OCM.

motif conducteur, *French*
OCM/*leading motif.*

Motiv, *German*
OCM/*motif.*

motivaguida, *Italian*
OCM/*leading motif.*

motivo, *Italian*
DFPCQ; OCM/*motif.*

mot juste, *French*
DFT/*mot*; DFWPN.

(le) mot juste, *French*
DFWPB.

moto, *Italian*
DFPCQ; DFT; OCM.

moto perpetuo, *Italian*
OCM.

moto precedente, *Italian*
OCM.

mot pour mot, *French*
DFT/*mot.*

mot pour rire, *French*
DFT/*mot.*

mot propre, *French*
DFWPN.

mots de terroir, *French*
DFPA.

mots d'usage, *French*
DFPA; DFPCQ.

motte, *French*
DFT.

motteggiando, *Italian*
OCM.

motu proprio, *Latin*
DFPA; OCM.

motzi, *Yiddish*
JOY.

mouflon, *French*
DFT.

moule, *French*
DFT.

moulin, *French*
GG.

moulinage, *French*
DFT.

mousmee, *Japanese*
JLE.

moussaka, *Modern Greek*
DFWPB.

mousse, *French*
DFT; DFWPB; DFWPN.

mousseline, *French*
DFT.

mousseline-de-laine, *French*
DFT/*mousseline.*

mousseline de soie, *French*
DFWPN.

mousseline-de-soie, *French*
DFT/*mousseline.*

mousseux, *French*
DFT; DFWPB.

moutarde, *French*
DFT.

mouton, *French*
DFT; DFWPN.

moutonnée, *French*
GG.

mouvement, *French*
OCM.

mouvementé, *French*
OCM.

movente, *Italian*
OCM.

movimento, *Italian*
OCM.

moxa, *Japanese*
JLE.

Moyen Age, *French*
DFT; DFWPN; LP.

moyl, *Yiddish*
HFY.

mozo, *Spanish*
DSTE.

mozzetta, *Italian*
DFT.

mridunga, *Hindi*
ICMM.

muchacha, *Spanish*
DFT; DFWPN.

muchacho, *Spanish*
DFT; DFWPN; DSTE.

müde, *German*
OCM.

mufti, *Arabic*
DFWPB; DFWPN.

mühelos, *German*
OCM.

muiñeira, *Spanish*
OCM.

muisetanden, *Dutch*
DA.

mujer, *Spanish*
DSTE.

mulada, *Spanish*
DSTE.

mulatto, *Spanish*
DFT.

muleta, *Spanish*
DSTE/*237.*

mullah, *Arabic*
DFT; DFWPN.

mullah, *Hindi*
DFWPB.

multum in parvo, *Latin*
DEP; DFPA; DFT.

mumbo jumbo, *Mandingo*
DFT.

mume, *Japanese*
JLE.

Mundharmonika, *German*
OCM.

munter, *German*
OCM.

mûr, *French*
DFT.

mura, *Japanese*
JLE.

muraji, *Japanese*
JLE.

murciana, *Spanish*
ICMM; OCM.

mûre, *French*
DFT.

murmelnd, *German*
OCM.

murmurando, *Italian*
OCM/*murmelnd.*

muscae volitantes, *Latin*
DFPA.

muscal, *Spanish*
DSTE/*mezcal.*

musetta, *Italian*
OCM.

musette, *French*
OCM/*musetta.*

mushi disease, *Japanese*
JLE.

mushrebbeyeh, *Arabic*
DA.

musica alla turca, *Italian*
OCM.

musica colorata, *Italian*
OCM.

musica di camera, *Italian*
DFWPN.

musica falsa, *Italian*
OCM.

musica falsa, *Latin*
ICMM.

musica ficta, *Latin*
DFWPB; ICMM; OCM.

musica figurata, *Italian*
ICMM; OCM.

musica mensurata, *Italian*
ICMM.

musica parlante, *Italian*
OCM.

musica reservata, *Latin*
ICMM; OCM.

musique à la turque, *French*
OCM.

musique concrète, *French*
DFWPB; OCM.

musjid, *Arabic*
DFT.

musqueto, *Spanish*
DSTE/*mesquite.*

musquit, *Spanish*
DSTE/*mesquite.*

musquito, *Spanish*
DSTE/*mesquite.*

mussaca, *Russian*
DFWPN.

must, *Anglo-Indian*
DFT.

mustizo, *Spanish*
DFWPN.

mut, *German*
OCM.

muta, *Italian*
ICMM; OCM.

mutano, *Italian*
OCM.

mutatis mutandis, *Latin*
DFPA; DFPCQ; DFT; DFWPB;
DFWPN.

mutato nomine, *Latin*
DFPCQ.

mutche, *Yiddish*
JOY.

mutig, *German*
OCM/*mut.*

Mütterchen, *German*
DFT.

muwashshah, *Arabic*
ICMM.

muy, *Spanish*
DFWPN.

muzh, *Russian*
DFT.

muzhik, *Russian*
DFT; MRWEW/*17.*

Mynheer, *Dutch*
DFT.

mysteriös, *German*
OCM.

mythos, *Greek*
DFWPN.

N

naar, *Yiddish*
JOY/*narr.*

naarishkeit, *Yiddish*
JOY/*narrishkeit.*

Nabeshimayaka, *Japanese*
JLE.

Nabis, Les, *French*
LP.

nabla, *Hebrew*
ICMM.

nacaires, *French*
OCM.

nacchera, *Italian*
ICMM.

naccherone, *Italian*
ICMM.

nach, *German*
OCM.

nachalstvo, *Russian*
MRWEW/*19.*

Nachdruck, *German*
DFT; OCM.

naches, *Yiddish*
JOY.

Nachfolge, *German*
ICMM.

nachgehend, *German*
OCM.

nachlassend, *German*
OCM.

Nachschlag, *German*
ICMM; OCM.

nachsingen, *German*
ICMM.

Nachspiel, *German*
DFT; ICMM; OCM.

Nacht, *German*
DFT.

Nachtanz, *German*
ICMM; OCM.

Nachthorn, *German*
OCM.

Nachtmusik, *German*
DFT; DFWPN; ICMM; OCM.

Nachtstück, *German*
OCM.

nach und nach, *German*
OCM.

nach wie vor, *German*
OCM.

nada, *Spanish*
DFWPN.

nadan, *Yiddish*
JOY.

naenia, *Latin*
OCM.

nafish, *Yiddish*
JOY/*nayfish.*

nafka, *Yiddish*
JOY.

nagarah, *Arabic*
ICMM.

nagasaki, *Japanese*
JLE.

Nagoya, *Japanese*
JLE.

nahe, *German*
OCM.

naï, *Arabic*
ICMM.

naïf, *French*
OCM.

naiv, *German*
OCM/*naïf.*

naïve, *French*
OCM/*naïf.*

naïvement, *French*
OCM/*naïf.*

naïveté, *French*
DFPCQ; DFWPB; DFWPN.

nakhes, *Yiddish*
JOY/*naches.*

nakodo, *Japanese*
JLE.

namban, *Japanese*
JLE.

nämlich, *German*
OCM.

nanako, *Japanese*
JLE.

Nandina, *Japanese*
JLE.

Nanga, *Japanese*
JLE.

nanook, *Eskimo*
DFT.

napoleon, *French*
DFT.

Napoléon, *French*
DFWPN.

napolitaine, *French*
OCM/*napolitana.*

napolitana, *Italian*
OCM.

nappe, *French*
GG.

Nara, *Japanese*
JLE.

nari, *Arabic*
GG.

narikin, *Japanese*
JLE.

narod, *Russian*
MRWEW/*20.*

narodnik, *Russian*
MRWEW/*18.*

narr, *Yiddish*
HFY; JOY.

narrante, *Italian*
OCM.

narrishkeit, *Yiddish*
JOY.

nasetto, *Italian*
OCM/*naso.*

Nashiji, *Japanese*
JLE.

naso, *Italian*
OCM.

natura abhorret vacuum, *Latin*
DFPA.

naturale, *Italian*
OCM.

naturel, *French*
DFT.

nature morte, *French*
LP.

natürlich, *German*
OCM.

Naturtöne, *German*
OCM.

navarin, *French*
DFT; DFWPN.

navarraise, *Spanish*
OCM.

navet, *French*
DFT.

Navidad, *Spanish*
DFWPN.

nay, *Arabic*
ICMM.

nayfish, *Yiddish*
HFY; JOY.

Nazi, *German*
DFPA.

ne, *French*
OCM.

né, *French*
DFPCQ.

nebbech, *Yiddish*
JOY/*nebech.*

nebbish, *Yiddish*
JOY/*nebech.*

nebech, *Yiddish*
DFT; HFY; JOY.

nebechel, *Yiddish*
JOY.

nebechl, *Yiddish*
JOY.

neben, *German*
OCM.

nebish, *Yiddish*
JOY/*nebech.*

neble, *Hebrew*
ICMM.

nebst, *German*
OCM.

nebulae, *Latin*
DFPCQ.

nécessaire, *French*
DFT.

nechtiger tog, a, *Yiddish*
JOY.

née, *French*
DEP; DFPCQ; DFT; DFWPN.

née *fem., French*
DFWPB.

nefasti dies, *Latin*
DFPA; DFPCQ.

nefish, *Yiddish*
JOY/*nayfish.*

negli, *Italian*
OCM.

negligé [*sic*], *French*
DFT.

négligé, *French*
DEP; DFPCQ.

negligé(e) [*sic*], *French*
DFWPN.

negligente, *Italian*
OCM.

negligentemente, *Italian*
DFT; OCM/*negligente.*

nehmen, *German*
OCM.

Nehrung, *German*
GG.

nei, *Arabic*
ICMM/*nay.*

nei, *Italian*
OCM.

Neiderstrich, *German*
OCM.

nein, *German*
DFWPN.

nek, *Afrikaans*
GG.

nekulturny, *Russian*
MRWEW/*20.*

nel, *Italian*
OCM.

Nembutsu, *Japanese*
JLE.

nemine contradicente, *Latin*
DFPA.

nemine discrepante, *Latin*
DFPA.

nemine dissentiente, *Latin*
DFPA.

nenia, *Italian*
OCM.

nenia, *Latin*
ICMM.

ne nimium, *Latin*
DFPCQ; DFT.

neoterici, *Latin*
DFWPN.

ne . . . pas, *French*
OCM.

ne plus ultra, *Latin*
DEP; DFPA; DFPCQ; DFT;
DFWPB; DFWPN.

ne quid nimis, *Latin*
DFPA.

nera, *Italian*
OCM.

nero-antico, *Italian*
DFT.

nerveux, *French*
OCM.

neshoma, *Yiddish*
JOY.

neshuma, *Yiddish*
JOY.

n'est-ce pas, *French*
DFPA; DFT; DFWPN.

net, *French*
OCM.

netsuke, *Japanese*
ACD; DFT; DFWPN; JLE.

netsuké, *Japanese*
DFWPB.

netta, *Italian*
OCM/*netto.*

nette, *French*
OCM/*net.*

netto, *Italian*
OCM.

Neturey Karta, *Yiddish*
HFY.

Neue Sachlichkeit, *German*
LP.

neuf, *French*
OCM.

neuma, *Latin*
OCM.

neumae, *Latin*
OCM/*neuma.*

neun, *German*
OCM.

neuvième, *French*
OCM.

névé, *French*
GG.

nichevo, *Russian*
DFT.

Nichiren, *Japanese*
JLE.

nicht, *German*
OCM.

-nick, *Yiddish*
JOY/*-nik.*

nieder, *German*
OCM.

Niederschlag, *German*
OCM.

niellatori, *Italian*
DFWPN.

niello, *Italian*
DFWPN.

niello, *pl.* nielli, *Italian*
DFWPB.

nien hao, *Chinese*
ACD.

niente, *Italian*
OCM.

nihil, *Latin*
DFT.

nihil ad me attinet, *Latin*
DFPCQ.

nihil ad rem, *Latin*
DFPA; DFPCQ; DFT/*nihil.*

nihil dicit, *Latin*
DFPA.

nihil ex nihilo, *Latin*
DFT/*nihil*; DFWPN.

nihil obstat, *Latin*
DFPA; DFT/*nihil*; DFWPB.

nihil sub sole novi, *Latin*
DFPCQ.

Nihon, *Japanese*
JLE.

Niigata, *Japanese*
JLE.

-nik, *Yiddish*
HFY; JOY.

nikko, *Japanese*
JLE.

niku-bori, *Japanese*
JLE.

nil, *Latin*
DFPCQ.

nil admirari, *Latin*
DFPA; DFT; DFWPN.

nilas, *Russian*
GG.

nil debet, *Latin*
DFPA.

nil sine Deo, *Latin*
DFPCQ.

n'importe, *French*
DEP.

ninfali, *Italian*
OCM.

ninna-nanna, *Italian*
OCM.

ninnarella, *Italian*
OCM/*ninna-nanna.*

niño, *Spanish*
DFT.

Nip, *Japanese*
JLE.

Nippon, *Japanese*
JLE.

nirvana, *Sanskrit*
DFT; DFWPB; DFWPN.

nisei, *Japanese*
DFWPN; JLE.

nisi prius, *Latin*
DFPA.

nitor in adversum, *Latin*
DFPCQ.

No, *Japanese*
JLE.

nobile, *Italian*
OCM.

noblesse, *French*
DFT.

noblesse de robe, *French*
DFPA.

noblesse oblige, *French*
DEP; DFPA; DFPCQ; DFT/
noblesse; DFWPB; DFWPN.

noblezza, *Italian*
OCM.

noch, *German*
OCM.

noch, *Yiddish*
JOY.

noche, *Spanish*
OCM.

noche triste, *Spanish*
DSTE.

nocte (*or* **noctu**), *Latin*
DFPCQ.

nocte silenti, *Latin*
DFPCQ.

nocturne, *French*
DFWPB; OCM.

Noël, *French*
DFT; OCM/*Nowell;* OCM.

nogada, *American Spanish*
DFT.

nogaku, *Japanese*
JLE.

noh, *Japanese*
JLE.

noh/nō, *Japanese*
DFWPB.

noir, *French*
DFT; DFWPB.

noire, *French*
ICMM/*crotchet;* ICMM; OCM.

noisette, *French*
DFT; DFWPB; DFWPN.

noix, *French*
DFT.

noix de muscade, *French*
DFWPN.

nokh, *Yiddish*
HFY.

nolens volens, *Latin*
DEP; DFPA; DFT; DFWPB;
DFWPN.

nolle prosequi, *Latin*
DEP; DFPA; DFPCQ; DFT;
DFWPB; DFWPN.

nolo contendere, *Latin*
DFPA; DFT; DFWPN.

nom, *French*
DFT.

nom de guerre, *French*
DFPA; DFPCQ; DFT/*nom*;
DFWPB; DFWPN.

nom de plume, *French*
DEP; DFPA; DFPCQ; DFT/
nom; DFWPN.

nom de plume, *Pseudo-French*
DFWPB.

nom de théâtre, *French*
DFPA; DFT/*nom*; DFWPB.

nom emprunté, *French*
DFT.

nomen, *Latin*
DFT; DFWPN.

nomen atque omen, *Latin*
DFT/*nomen*.

nomina, *Latin*
DFWPN/*nomen*.

nomos, *Greek*
ICMM.

non, *French*
OCM.

non assumpsi, *Latin*
DFPA.

non compos (mentis), *Latin*
DFT; DFWPB.

non compos mentis, *Latin*
DEP; DFPA; DFPCQ; DFWPN.

non concessit, *Latin*
DFPA.

non constat, *Latin*
DEP; DFPA.

non culpabilis, *Latin*
DFPA.

non ens, *Latin*
DFT.

non esse, *Latin*
DFT.

non est, *Latin*
DFWPN.

non est inventus, *Latin*
DFPA.

Nonett, *German*
ICMM; OCM/*nonet.*

nonette, *French*
OCM/*nonet.*

nonetto, *Italian*
DFPCQ; DFT; ICMM; OCM/
nonet.

non libet, *Latin*
DFPA.

non licet, *Latin*
DFPA; DFPCQ.

non liquet, *Latin*
DFPA; DFPCQ; DFT; DFWPN.

non mi ricordo, *Italian*
DFPCQ.

Nonnengeige, *German*
OCM.

non obstante, *Latin*
DFPCQ.

non obstante veredicto, *Latin*
DFPA.

non olet, *Latin*
DFPA; DFT.

non omnia possumus omnes, *Latin*
DFPCQ.

non omnis moriar, *Latin*
DFPCQ.

non placet, *Latin*
DFPA; DFT; DFWPB; DFWPN.

non plus ultra, *Latin*
DFWPN.

non possumus, *Latin*
DFPA; DFPCQ.

non prosequitur, *Latin*
DFPA; DFT.

non sequitur, *Latin*
DEP; DFPA; DFPCQ; DFT;
DFWPB; DFWPN.

non sum dignus, *Latin*
DFPCQ.

non tanto allegro, *Italian*
ICMM.

non troppo, *Italian*
ICMM.

non troppo presto, *Italian*
DFPA.

non vult contendere, *Latin*
DFPA.

noo-ooo, *Yiddish*
JOY/*nu.*

noques, *French*
DFWPN.

nori, *Japanese*
JLE.

noria, *Spanish*
DSTE.

norimon, *Japanese*
JLE.

norito, *Japanese*
JLE.

Normalton, *German*
ICMM.

norte, *Spanish*
DSTE.

nosce te ipsum, *Latin*
DFPA.

nosce te ipsum (*or* teipsum), *Latin*
DFT.

nosce teipsum, *Latin*
DFPCQ.

nosce tempus, *Latin*
DFPA.

noscitur a sociis, *Latin*
DFPCQ.

nosh, *Yiddish*
HFY; JOY.

noshen, *Yiddish*
JOY/*nosh.*

nosher, *Yiddish*
JOY/*nosh.*

noshi, *Japanese*
JLE.

nota, *Italian*
DFT.

nota bene, *Latin*
DFPA; DFT; DFWPB; DFWPN.

nota bene (N. B.), *Latin*
DEP; DFPCQ.

nota buona, *Italian*
DFT/*nota.*

nota cattiva, *Italian*
DFT/*nota.*

notan, *Japanese*
JLE.

nota sensibile, *Italian*
DFT/*nota.*

nota sostenuta, *Italian*
DFT/*nota.*

notturnino, *Italian*
OCM.

notturno, *Italian*
DFPCQ; DFT; OCM; OCM/
nocturne.

nouilles, *French*
DFWPN.

noumenon, *Greek*
DFWPN.

nous, *Greek*
DFPCQ; DFWPN.

nous pathetikos, *Greek*
DFPA.

nous poietikos, *Greek*
DFPA.

nous verrons, *French*
DEP.

nouveau riche, *French*
DFPA; DFT.

nouveau riche, *fem.* **nouvelle riche,**
pl. **nouveaux riches,** *French*
DFWPB.

nouvelle, *French*
DFWPN.

nouvellette, *French*
DEP.

nouvelle vague, *French*
DFT; DFWPB.

nove, *Italian*
OCM.

novela picaresca, *Spanish*
DFWPN.

novella, *Italian*
DFT; DFWPN.

novia, *Spanish*
DSTE.

novus homo, *Latin*
DFPA; DFPCQ; DFT; DFWPN.

novus homo, *pl.* **novi homines,** *Latin*
DFWPB.

nu, *Yiddish*
HFY; JOY.

nuance, *French*
DFPCQ; LP.

nuances, *French*
ICMM.

nuces relinquere, *Latin*
DFPCQ.

nuchshlepper, *Yiddish*
JOY.

nuda veritas, *Latin*
DFPA.

nudis verbis, *Latin*
DFPA.

nudj, *Yiddish*
DFT.

nudnick, *Yiddish*
JOY/*nudnik.*

nudnik, *Yiddish*
HFY; JOY.

nudum pactum, *Latin*
DFPA.

nudzh, *Yiddish*
HFY; JOY.

nudzhedik, *Yiddish*
JOY/*nudzh.*

nudzheh, *Yiddish*
JOY/*nudzh.*

nudzhik, *Yiddish*
JOY/*nudzh.*

nuée ardente, *French*
GG.

nugae, *Latin*
DFT.

nugae canorae, *Latin*
DFPA.

nugae literariae, *Latin*
DFPA.

nulla bona, *Latin*
DFPCQ.

nullah, *Hindi*
GG.

nulli secundus, *Latin*
DEP; DFPCQ.

nullius filius, *Latin*
DFPCQ.

nullo modo, *Latin*
DFPCQ.

nunakol, *Eskimo*
GG.

nunatak, *Eskimo*
GG.

nunc est bibendum, *Latin*
DFPA; DFT; DFWPB.

nunchakus, *Japanese*
JLE.

nuncio, *Italian*
DFWPN.

nuncio/nuntio, *Obsolete Italian*
DFWPB.

nunc pro tunc, *Latin*
DFPA.

nu-nu?, *Yiddish*
JOY/*nu.*

nuoc nam, *Vietnamese*
DFT.

nuova, *Italian*
OCM/*nuovo.*

nuove musiche, *Italian*
OCM.

nuovo, *Italian*
OCM.

nur, *German*
  OCM.
nutrendo, *Italian*
  OCM.
nutrito, *Italian*
  OCM/*nutrendo.*

nyckel harpa, *Swedish*
  ICMM.
nyet, *Russian*
  DFWPN; MRWEW/*18.*

O

o, *Italian*
OCM.

oban, *Japanese*
JLE.

obang, *Japanese*
JLE.

obbligato, *Italian*
DFPCQ; DFT; DFWPN; ICMM;
OCM.

obbligato/obligato, *Italian*
DFWPB.

obe, *Japanese*
JLE.

oben, *German*
OCM.

ober, *German*
OCM.

Oberwerk, *German*
OCM.

obi, *Japanese*
JLE.

obiit, *Latin*
DFPA; DFT; DFWPN.

obiit sine prole, *Latin*
DFPA.

obiter, *Latin*
DFT.

obiter dicta, *Latin*
DFWPN/*obiter dictum.*

obiter dictum, *Latin*
DFPA; DFPCQ; DFT/*obiter;*
DFWPN.

obiter dictum, *pl.* **obiter dicta,** *Latin*
DFWPB.

obiter scriptum, *Latin*
DFPA; DFT/*obiter.*

objet d'art, *French*
DFPA; DFT.

objet d'art, *pl.* **objets d'art,** *French*
DFWPB.

objet de piété, *pl.* **objets de piété,**
French
DFWPB.

objet de vertu, *pl.* **objets de vertu,**
Pseudo-French
DFWPB.

objet d'occasion, *French*
DFT.

objets d'art, *French*
ACD.

objet trouvé, *French*
LP.

objet trouvé, *pl.* **objets trouvés,**
French
DFWPB.

oblast, *Russian*
DFT; MRWEW/*18.*

obligat, *German*
OCM/*obligato.*

obligé, *French*
OCM/*obligato.*

oboe, basset, *French*
OCM.

oboe d'amore, *French*
OCM.

oboe d'amore, *Italian*
OCM/*amore, amour.*

oboe de caccia, *Italian*
OCM.

obrigado, *Portuguese*
DFT.

obscurum per obscurius, *Latin*
DFPA; DFPCQ; DFT.

observanda, *Latin*
DFPCQ.

observandum, *Latin*
DFT.

occasionem cognosce, *Latin*
DFPCQ.

octandre, *French*
OCM.

octava alta, *Italian*
DFPCQ.

octaves aiguës, *French*
OCM/*octaves graves.*

octaves graves, *French*
OCM.

octavin, *French*
OCM.

octavina, *Italian*
OCM/*octavin.*

octet, *French*
OCM.

octuor, *French*
ICMM/*octet.*

oculus, *Latin*
DFWPN.

od, *Italian*
OCM/*o*; OCM.

o-daiko, *Japanese*
ICMM.

Odeon, *German*
ICMM.

oder, *German*
OCM.

oderint dum metuant, *Latin*
DFPCQ.

odeum, *Latin*
ICMM.

odi et amo, *Latin*
DFPA.

odi profanum vulgus, *Latin*
DFPA; DFPCQ.

odium, *Latin*
DFT.

odium aestheticum, *Latin*
DFT/*odium.*

odium generis humani, *Latin*
DFPA.

odium literarium, *Latin*
DFPA.

odium medicum, *Latin*
DFT/*odium.*

odium musicum, *Latin*
DFT/*odium.*

odium theologicum, *Latin*
DFPA; DFT/*odium.*

odori, *Japanese*
JLE.

odor lucri, *Latin*
DFT.

œil, *French*
DFT.

œil-de-bœuf, *French*
DA; DFPA.

oeuf, *French*
DFWPN.

œuf, *French*
DFT.

oeufs à la coque, *French*
DFWPN.

œufs à la coque, *French*
DFT/*œuf.*

œufs à la neige, *French*
DFT/*œuf.*

œufs à l'indienne, *French*
DFT/*œuf.*

261 omen faustum

oeufs brouillés, *French*
DFWPN.

œufs brouillés, *French*
DFT/*œuf.*

œufs frais, *French*
DFT/*œuf.*

œufs pochés, *French*
DFT/*œuf.*

oeufs sur le plat, *French*
DFWPN.

oeuvre, *French*
DFWPB; DFWPN; LP.

œuvre, *French*
DFT; OCM.

œuvres complètes, *French*
DFPA.

offen, *German*
OCM.

offertoire, *French*
ICMM/*offertorium*; OCM/*offertory.*

offertorium, *Latin*
DFWPN; ICMM; OCM/*offertory.*

officium, *Latin*
ICMM.

officium vesperarum, *Latin*
ICMM/*vespers.*

öffnen, *German*
OCM.

oficleide, *Italian*
OCM.

ofuro, *Japanese*
JLE.

ogni, *Italian*
OCM.

o-goshi, *Japanese*
JLE.

ohne, *German*
OCM.

ohteki, *Japanese*
ICMM.

oiran, *Japanese*
JLE.

ojime, *Japanese*
JLE.

ojo, *Spanish*
DFT; GG.

Okayama, *Japanese*
JLE.

Okazaki, *Japanese*
JLE.

Okazaki (fragment), *Japanese*
JLE.

okimono, *Japanese*
JLE.

Oktave, *German*
OCM.

oktavin, *German*
OCM/*octavin.*

Oktett, *German*
ICMM/*octet.*

Oktyabryata, *Russian*
MRWEW/*20.*

ole, *Spanish*
OCM.

olé, *Spanish*
DFT; ICMM.

olim, *Latin*
DFPCQ.

olim meminisse juvabit, *Latin*
DFPCQ.

olio, *Spanish*
DFWPN.

olla, *Spanish*
DSTE.

olla podrida, *Spanish*
DFPA; DFPCQ; DFWPB; DFWPN; DSTE.

oloroso, *Spanish*
DFWPB.

ombré, *French*
DFWPB.

ombres chinoises *pl.*, *French*
DFWPB.

omen faustum, *Latin*
DEP.

omeyn, *Yiddish*
HFY.

omi, *Japanese*
JLE.

omnes, *Latin*
DFPCQ.

omne vivum ex ovo, *Latin*
DFT.

omne vivum ex vivo, *Latin*
DFPA; DFWPN.

omnia ad Dei gloriam, *Latin*
DFPCQ.

omnia bona bonis, *Latin*
DFPCQ.

omnia mors aequat, *Latin*
DFPA.

omnia opera, *Latin*
DFPA.

omnia vincit amor, *Latin*
DEP; DFPCQ; DFT; DFWPN.

omnia vincit labor, *Latin*
DFPCQ; DFT.

omnium, *Latin*
ACD.

omnium gatherum, *Pseudo-Latin*
DFPA; DFPCQ; DFWPN.

omuramba, *Bantu*
GG.

Omuta, *Japanese*
JLE.

on, *Japanese*
JLE.

ondé, *French*
DFWPB.

ondeggiamento, *Italian*
OCM/*ondeggiando.*

ondeggiando, *Italian*
ICMM; OCM.

ondeggiante, *Italian*
OCM/*ondeggiando.*

on dit, *French*
DEP.

ondulé, *French*
OCM.

ongarese, *Italian*
OCM.

ongepatshket, *Yiddish*
HFY.

ongepotchket, *Yiddish*
JOY.

onnagata, *Japanese*
JLE.

on parle français, *French*
DFT.

onson, *Japanese*
JLE.

onus, *Latin*
DFPCQ.

onus probandi, *Latin*
DFPA; DFPCQ; DFT; DFWPB; DFWPN.

op(ere) cit(ato), *Latin*
DFWPB.

Oper, *German*
OCM.

opera, *Latin*
DFWPN.

opéra bouffe, *French*
DFT; DFWPB; OCM/*opera buffa.*

opéra-bouffe, *French*
DFWPN.

opera buffa, *Italian*
DFPA; DFPCQ; DFWPB; DFWPN; OCM.

opéra comique, *French*
DFT; DFWPB.

opéra-comique, *French*
OCM.

opera del duomo, *Italian*
DA.

opera omnia, *Latin*
DFWPB.

opera seria, *Italian*
DFPCQ; DFWPB; OCM.

operatta, *Italian*
DFPCQ.

opere citato, *Latin*
DFT.

Opferkessel, *German*
GG.
opgeflikt, *Yiddish*
HFY.
opposition, *French*
LB.
oppure, *Italian*
ICMM/*ossia.*
optimates, *Latin*
DFPCQ; DFT.
optimates *pl.*, *Latin*
DFWPB.
opus, *Latin*
DFT; DFWPN; OCM.
opus Alexandrinum, *Latin*
DFWPB; DFWPN.
opus anglicanum, *Latin*
DFWPB.
opusculum, *Latin*
DFPCQ; DFWPN.
opus incertum, *Latin*
DFWPN.
opus isodomum, *Latin*
DFWPN.
opus postumum, *Latin*
DFPA.
opus reticulatum, *Latin*
DFWPN.
opus spicatum, *Latin*
DFWPN.
ora et labora, *Latin*
DEP.
orageuse, *French*
OCM/*orageux.*
orageux, *French*
OCM.
ora pro nobis, *Latin*
DEP; DFPA; DFPCQ; DFT;
DFWPN.
orate fratres, *Latin*
DFT.
oratio vespertina, *Latin*
ICMM/*vespers.*

oratorio, *Italian*
DFPCQ; DFWPB; DFWPN.
orbis terrarum, *Latin*
DFPA.
orchestre de genre, *French*
OCM.
ordinaire, *French*
OCM.
ordinario, *Italian*
DFPCQ; OCM.
ordinarium missae, *Latin*
ICMM.
ordo exsequiarum, *Latin*
OCM.
ordonnance, *French*
DA.
ordre, *French*
ICMM.
orégano, *Spanish*
DFT.
orejones, *Spanish*
DFT.
oremus, *Latin*
DFPA.
organo, *Italian*
OCM.
organo espressivo, *Italian*
OCM/*O.E..*
organum, *Latin*
DFWPB.
orge, *French*
DFT.
Orgel, *German*
DFWPN; OCM; ICMM.
Orgelpunkt, *German*
ICMM/*organ-point*; ICMM/*pedal-point.*
orgia, *Italian*
OCM.
orgue, *French*
DFWPN; OCM.
orgue de barbarie, *French*
OCM.

orgue de salon, *French*
ICMM.

orgue en table, *French*
OCM.

orgue expressif, *French*
OCM.

orgue plein, *French*
OCM.

orgue positif, *French*
OCM.

orido, *Italian*
GG.

origami, *Japanese*
DFWPB; JLE.

origine contrôlée, *French*
DFWPN.

orihon, *Japanese*
JLE.

ormolu, *French*
ACD.

or moulu, *French*
ACD.

ornamenti, *Italian*
DFT.

ornatamente, *Italian*
DFT.

orné, *French*
DFT.

orthose, *French*
GG.

os, *Latin*
DFT; DFT.

osaekomi waza, *Japanese*
JLE.

Osaka, *Japanese*
JLE.

oseille, *French*
DFT.

oshana, *Afrikaans*
GG.

oshibori (towel), *Japanese*
JLE.

O-soto-gari, *Japanese*
JLE.

osservanza, *Italian*
OCM.

osservato, stile, *Italian*
ICMM.

ossia, *Italian*
ICMM; OCM.

ostinato, *Italian*
DFT; OCM.

ostinato, *pl.* ostinati, *Italian*
DFWPB.

Otaru, *Japanese*
JLE.

o tempora! o mores!, *Latin*
DEP; DFPCQ.

O tempora O mores, *Latin*
DFPA; DFT.

ôter, *French*
OCM.

otium cum dignitate, *Latin*
DEP.

ottava, *Italian*
DFT; ICMM; OCM.

ottava alta, *Italian*
ICMM.

ottava rima, *Italian*
DFPA; DFPCQ; DFT; DFWPB;
DFWPN.

ottavina, *Italian*
DFWPN.

ottetto, *Italian*
DFPCQ; ICMM/*octet.*

otto, *Italian*
OCM.

ottone, *Italian*
OCM.

ou, *French*
OCM.

où, *French*
OCM/*ou.*

ouden pragma, *Greek*
DFPCQ.

oued, *French*
GG.

ouklip, *Afrikaans*
  GG.
oule, *Spanish*
  GG.
outré, *French*
  DFPCQ; DFT; DFWPB;
  DFWPN; LP.
ouvert, *French*
  LB; OCM.
ouverte, *French*
  LB/*ouvert*; OCM/*ouvert*.
ouverture, *French*
  DFT; OCM.
ouverture de jambe, *French*
  LB.
ouvrage, *French*
  DFPCQ.
ouvrir, *French*
  OCM.
ouzo, *Modern Greek*
  DFWPB.
ovolo, *Italian*
  ACD.
ovvero, *Italian*
  ICMM/*ossia*; OCM.
Oxoniensis, *Latin*
  DFPA/*Oxon.*.
oy, *Yiddish*
  DFWPN; HFY; JOY.

oy!, *Yiddish*
  JOY/*oy*.
oyama, *Japanese*
  JLE.
oyez, *Anglo-French*
  DFPA.
oyez, *Old French*
  DFWPB; DFWPN.
oy oy, *Yiddish*
  JOY/*oy*.
oy-oy-oy, *Yiddish*
  JOY/*oy*.
oyrech, *Yiddish*
  JOY.
oys-, *Yiddish*
  HFY.
oysgematert, *Yiddish*
  JOY.
oysvorf, *Yiddish*
  JOY.
oytser, *Yiddish*
  JOY.
ozee, *Burmese*
  ICMM.
ozeki, *Japanese*
  JLE.

P

paar, *Hebrew*
GG.

Paar, *German*
OCM.

pacatamente, *Italian*
OCM/*pacato.*

pacato, *Italian*
OCM.

pace, *Latin*
DFPCQ; DFT; DFWPB.

pace et bello, *Latin*
DFPCQ.

pace in terra, *Italian*
DFPA.

Pacem in Maribus, *Latin*
DFPA.

pace tanti nominis, *Latin*
DFPA.

pace tanti viri, *Latin*
DFPA.

pace tua, *Latin*
DFPA; DFT/*pace.*

pace tuâ, *Latin*
DEP.

pachinko, *Japanese*
JLE.

padiglione, *Italian*
OCM.

padmaragaya, *Singhalese*
GG.

padre, *Italian*
DFT; DFWPB; DFWPN.

padre, *Portuguese*
DFT.

padre, *Spanish*
DFT; DSTE.

padrino, *Spanish*
DSTE.

padrone, *Italian*
DEP; DFT; DFWPN.

padron mio, *Italian*
DFPCQ.

paella, *Spanish*
DFT; DFWPB; DFWPN.

paesano, *Italian*
DFWPN.

pahoehoe, *Hawaiian*
GG.

paideia, *Greek*
DFWPN.

p'ai hsiao, *Chinese*
ICMM.

pailles de parmesan, *French*
DFT.

paillette, *French*
DFWPB.

pain, *French*
DFT; DFWPN.

pair, *French*
DFWPB; OCM.

paisano, *Spanish*
DFT; DSTE.

pai ting, *Chinese*
ACD.

pai tun tzu, *Chinese*
ACD.

pai-tun-tzu, *Chinese*
ACD/*porcelain.*

pai tzu, *Chinese*
ACD.

paix, *French*
DFWPN.

pakihi, *Maori*
GG.

pakka, *Anglo-Indian*
DFT/*pucka.*

paktong, *Chinese*
ACD.

palabra, *Spanish*
OCM.

palaestra, *Latin*
DFPCQ.

palang, *Hindi*
DFT.

palazzo, *Italian*
DA; DFT; DFWPN.

palazzo, *pl.* **palazzi,** *Italian*
DFWPB.

palcoscenico, *Italian*
OCM.

paléographie musicale, *French*
OCM.

paléophone, *French*
OCM.

Palestrina, alla, *Italian*
OCM.

palladium, *Latin*
DFPCQ.

palotache, *Hungarian*
OCM.

palo verde, *Spanish*
DSTE.

palsa, *Swedish*
GG.

pampa, *Spanish*
DSTE.

pampas, *Spanish*
DFWPB; DFWPN.

pampre, *French*
DA.

p'an, *Chinese*
ACD.

panache, *French*
DFT; DFWPN.

panaché, *French*
DFT.

panade, *French*
DFWPN.

panais, *French*
DFT.

panatella, *Italian*
DFWPB.

Pandectae, *Latin*
DFPCQ.

panee, *Anglo-Hindi*
DFT.

panee, *Anglo-Indian*
DFT.

panem et circenses, *Latin*
DFPA; DFT; DFWPB; DFWPN.

paner, *French*
DFT.

pange, lingua, *Latin*
DFWPN.

pani, *Hindi*
DFT.

panier, *French*
DA.

panné, *French*
DFWPN.

pannier, *French*
DA.

Pantalone, *Italian*
DFWPN.

panta rei (rhei), *Greek*
DFPA.

panta rhei, *Greek*
DFWPB.

pantomimer, *French*
LB.

pantoum, *Malay*
ICMM.

pañuelo, *Spanish*
DFT.

panure, *French*
DFT.

Panzer, *German*
DFT; DFWPB; DFWPN.

paon, *French*
DFWPN.

papa, *Polynesian*
GG.

papier maché, *French*
ACD; DFPCQ.

papier mâché, *French*
DFPA; DFWPB; DFWPN.

papier-mâché, *French*
DFT.

papiers collés, *French*
LP.

papiers collés *pl.,* *French*
DFWPB.

papiers déchirés *pl.,* *French*
DFWPB.

papiers découpés *pl.,* *French*
DFWPB.

papillon, *French*
DFWPN.

papillote, *French*
DFT.

Parallelkanter, *German*
GG.

par avion, *French*
DFPA; DFT.

pardessus de viole, *French*
OCM.

pardonnez-moi, *French*
DFPA; DFPCQ; DFT.

parech, *Yiddish*
JOY.

par' emoi, *Greek*
DFPCQ.

parendo imperat, *Latin*
DFPCQ.

pareve, *Yiddish*
HFY.

pareveh, *Yiddish*
JOY.

par example [*sic*]**,** *French*
DEP.

par excellence, *French*
DEP; DFPA; DFPCQ; DFT;
DFWPB; DFWPN; LP.

par exemple, *French*
DFPA; DFPCQ; DFT/*exemple.*

parfait, *French*
DFWPB; DFWPN.

parfum, *French*
DFWPB.

par' heautou, *Greek*
DFPCQ.

pari mutuel, *French*
DFT.

pari mütuel [*sic*]**,** *French*
DFPA.

pari passu, *Latin*
DEP; DFPA; DFPCQ; DFT;
DFWPB; DFWPN.

parlando, *Italian*
DFPCQ; DFT; DFWPB;
DFWPN; OCM.

parlante, *Italian*
DFPCQ; DFT/*parlando;*
DFWPB; OCM/*parlando.*

parlato, *Italian*
OCM.

parmentier, *French*
DFWPN.

parmigiana, *Italian*
DFWPN.

parmigiano, *Italian*
DFWPN.

parole, *French*
DFPCQ; DFWPN.

parole d'honneur, *French*
DFPA; DFWPN.

pars pro toto, *Latin*
DFPCQ.

pars rationabilis, *Latin*
DFPA.

Part, *German*
OCM/*part.*

parte, *Italian*
DFPCQ; OCM; OCM/*part.*

par terre, *French*
LB.

Parthie, *German*
OCM.

Parthien, *German*
OCM/*Parthie.*

parti, *French*
DA; DFT.

parti, *Italian*
OCM/*parte*; OCM.

Partialtöne, *German*
ICMM/*partials.*

particeps criminis, *Latin*
DEP; DFPA.

partida, *Spanish*
DSTE.

partie, *French*
DFT; OCM/*part*; OCM/*partita.*

Partie, *German*
ICMM/*partita.*

partim, *Latin*
DFT.

partimenti, *Italian*
ICMM.

parti pris, *French*
DFPA; DFT/*parti*; DFWPB;
DFWPN.

partita, *Italian*
ICMM; OCM.

partition, *French*
ICMM/*score*; OCM.

partito, *Italian*
OCM.

Partitur, *German*
DFT; DFWPN; ICMM/*score*;
OCM/*partition.*

partitura, *Italian*
DFPCQ; ICMM/*score*; OCM/
partition.

partizione, *Italian*
OCM/*partition.*

parure, *French*
DFT.

parva componere magnis, *Latin*
DEP.

parvenu, *French*
DFPCQ; DFT; DFWPN.

parvenu, *fem.* **parvenue,** *French*
DFWPB.

pas, *French*
DFT; DFWPN; ICMM; LB;
OCM.

Pasach, *Hebrew*
DFWPN.

pas battus, *French*
DFWPN.

pas couru, *French*
LB.

pas d'action, *French*
DFWPB; LB.

pas de basque, *French*
DFWPN; LB; OCM.

pas de basque en tournant, *French*
LB/*pas de basque.*

pas de basque en tournant, grand,
French
LB/*pas de basque.*

pas de basque glissé en avant,
French
LB/*pas de basque.*

pas de basque, grand, *French*
LB/*pas de basque.*

pas de basque sauté en avant, *French*
LB/*pas de basque.*

pas de bourrée, *French*
DFWPB; DFWPN; LB.

pas de bourrée changé, *French*
LB/*pas de bourrée.*

**pas de bourrée changé sur les
pointes,** *French*
LB/*pas de bourrée.*

pas de bourrée couru, *French*
LB/*pas de bourrée.*

pas de bourrée derrière, *French*
LB/*pas de bourrée.*

pas de bourrée dessous, *French*
LB/*pas de bourrée.*

pas de bourrée dessus, *French*
LB/*pas de bourrée.*

pas de bourrée détourné, *French*
LB/*pas de bourrée.*

pas de bourrée devant, *French*
LB/*pas de bourrée.*

pas de bourrée en arrière, *French*
LB/*pas de bourrée.*

pas de bourrée en avant, *French*
LB/*pas de bourrée.*

pas de bourrée en tournant, *French*
LB/*pas de bourrée.*

pas de bourrée en tournant en
dedans, *French*
LB/*pas de bourrée.*

pas de bourrée en tournant en
dehors, *French*
LB/*pas de bourrée.*

pas de bourrée fondu, *French*
LB/*pas de bourrée.*

pas de bourrée piqué, *French*
LB/*pas de bourrée.*

pas de bourrée renversé, *French*
LB/*pas de bourrée.*

pas de chat, *French*
DFWPB; DFWPN; LB.

pas de chat jeté, *French*
LB/*pas de chat.*

pas de chat russe, *French*
LB/*pas de chat.*

pas de chat russe, grand, *French*
LB/*pas de chat.*

pas de cheval, *French*
DFWPN; LB.

pas de ciseaux, *French*
LB.

pas de deux, *French*
DFPA; DFT/*pas*; DFWPB;
DFWPN; LB; OCM.

pas de deux, grand, *French*
LB/*pas de deux.*

pas de poisson, *French*
LB.

pas de quatre, *French*
DFWPB; LB; OCM.

pas des écharpes, *French*
DFWPN.

pas-de-souris, *French*
DA.

pas de trois, *French*
DFWPB; LB.

pas de valse, *French*
LB.

pas du tout, *French*
DFPA.

pasear, *Spanish*
DSTE.

paseo, *Spanish*
DFT; DSTE.

paseo de las cuadrillas, *Spanish*
DSTE/*237.*

pas glissant, *French*
DFT/*pas.*

pas glissé, *French*
DFWPN; LB; OCM.

pasha, *Turkish*
DFT; DFWPB; DFWPN.

paskudnak, *Yiddish*
HFY; JOY/*paskudnyak.*

paskudne, *Yiddish*
JOY.

paskudneh, *Yiddish*
JOY.

paskudnyak, *Yiddish*
JOY.

paskustva, *Yiddish*
JOY.

pas marché, *French*
LB.

paso doble, *Spanish*
DFPA; DFT; OCM.

paso fino, *Spanish*
DFPA.

pasquinade, *French*
DFWPN.

passacaglia, *Italian*
OCM; OCM/*chaconne.*

passacaglia, *Spanish*
ICMM.

passacaille, *French*
OCM/*passacaglia.*

passamezzo, *Italian*
ICMM; OCM.

passe, *French*
DFWPB.

passé, *French*
DFPCQ; DFT; DFWPN; LB;
LP.

passé, *fem.* **passée,** *French*
DFWPB.

passecaille, *French*
OCM; OCM/*passacaglia.*

passemezzo, *Italian*
OCM/*passamezzo.*

passend, *German*
OCM.

passe-partout, *French*
DFPCQ; DFT; DFWPB;
DFWPN.

passe-pied, *French*
LB.

passepied, *French*
DFWPB; ICMM; OCM.

passerelle, *French*
DA.

pas seul, *French*
DFPA; DFT/*pas*; DFWPB; LB;
OCM.

passim, *Latin*
DFPA; DFPCQ; DFT; DFWPN.

passionatemente, *Italian*
OCM/*passionato.*

passionato, *Italian*
DFT; OCM.

passione, *Italian*
OCM.

Passionis Domini nostri Jesu Christi,
Latin
ICMM/*passion music.*

pasta, *Italian*
DFT; DFWPN.

pasta asciutta, *Italian*
DFWPN.

pastèque, *French*
DFT.

pasticcio, *Italian*
DA; DFPCQ; DFT; DFWPB;
DFWPN; ICMM; OCM.

pastiche, *French*
DA; DFT; DFWPN; LP; OCM.

pasticheur, *French*
LP.

pastille, *French*
DFT.

pas tombé, *French*
LB.

pastorale, *French*
OCM/*pastoral.*

pastorale, *Italian*
DFPCQ; DFT.

pastorelle, *French*
DFWPN.

pastose, *Italian*
LP.

pastoso, *Italian*
OCM.

pastourelle, *Italian*
OCM/*pastoral.*

pat, *Sindhi*
GG.

patch, *Yiddish*
JOY/*potch*; JOY.

pâte, *French*
DFT.

pâté, *French*
DFT; DFWPB; DFWPN.

paté de foie gras, *French*
DEP.

pâté de foie gras, *French*
DFPA; DFT/*pâté*; DFWPB;
DFWPN.

pâte-de-verre, *French*
ACD; DFWPB.

pâte dure, *French*
ACD; DFT/*pâte*; DFWPB.

pâte feuilletée, *French*
DFT/*pâte*.

patera, *Latin*
ACD.

pater familias, *Latin*
DFPA.

paterfamilias, *Latin*
DEP; DFPCQ; DFT; DFWPB;
DFWPN.

Pater noster, *Latin*
DFPA; DFWPN; DEP; DFPCQ.

pater noster/paternoster, *Latin*
DFWPB.

pater patriae, *Latin*
DFPA; DFPCQ; DFT; DFWPN.

pater patriae, *pl.* **patres patriae,** *Latin*
DFWPB.

pâte sur pâte, *French*
DFT/*pâte*.

pâte-sur-pâte, *French*
ACD; DFWPB.

pâte tendre, *French*
ACD; DFT/*pâte*; DFWPB.

patetico, *Italian*
DFT; OCM.

pathétique, *French*
DFT; ICMM; OCM.

pathetisch, *German*
OCM.

patimento, *Italian*
OCM.

patina, *Italian*
GG.

patio, *Spanish*
DSTE.

pâtisserie, *French*
DFT; DFWPB; DFWPN.

pâtissier, *French*
DFT.

patois, *French*
DFPCQ; DFWPB; DFWPN.

patrem omnipotentem, *Latin*
OCM.

patres conscripti, *Latin*
DFPCQ; DFT.

patria potestas, *Latin*
DFPA.

patris est filius, *Latin*
DFPCQ.

patron, *French*
DA.

patron, *Spanish*
DSTE.

patshke, *Yiddish*
HFY.

pau, *Hawaiian*
DFT.

paucas pallabris, *Latin*
DFPA.

pauca verba, *Latin*
DFPA.

paucis verbis, *Latin*
DFPA; DFPCQ.

Pauken, *German*
ICMM; OCM.

pausa, *Italian*
OCM.

pause, *French*
OCM.

Pause, *German*
OCM.

pavé, *French*
DFT.

paventato, *Italian*
OCM.

paventoso, *Italian*
OCM/*paventato*.

pavillon, *French*
ICMM; OCM.

pavillon chinois, *French*
ICMM.

Pax, *Latin*
DFT; DFWPN.

Pax Britannica, *Latin*
DFPA.

Pax Dei, *Latin*
DFT/*Pax*.

Pax Ecclesiae, *Latin*
DFT/*Pax*.

pax in bello, *Latin*
DEP.

Pax Romana, *Latin*
DFPA; DFT/*Pax*.

pax tecum, *Latin*
DFPA.

pax vobiscum, *Latin*
DFPA; DFPCQ; DFT/*Pax*;
DFWPN.

payess, *Yiddish*
JOY.

paysage, *French*
DFT.

pays de cocagne, *French*
DFPCQ.

peau, *French*
OCM.

peau de soie, *French*
DFWPN.

peau-de-soie, *French*
DFWPB.

peccavi, *Latin*
DEP; DFPA; DFPCQ; SPICE.

pêche, *French*
DFT; DFWPN.

péché mortel, *French*
ACD; DFWPB.

peckel, *Yiddish*
JOY/*pekl*.

pecunia non olet, *Latin*
DFPA.

Pedalcoppel, *German*
OCM.

pedale, *Italian*
DFPCQ; OCM.

pédale, *French*
ICMM/*organ-point*.

Pedalflügel, *German*
OCM.

Pedalgebrauch, *German*
OCM.

pedaliera, *Italian*
OCM.

Pedalklavier, *German*
OCM.

Pedalpauken, *German*
OCM.

pedregal, *Spanish*
DSTE.

pedrigal, *Spanish*
DSTE/*pedregal*.

peignoir, *French*
DFT; DFWPN.

peinture, *French*
DFWPB; DFWPN.

peinture à la colle, *French*
DFWPB.

peinture à l'essence, *French*
LP.

peinture claire, *French*
LP.

pekel, *Yiddish*
JOY/*pekl*.

pekl, *Yiddish*
JOY.

pelado, *Spanish*
DSTE.

pelota, *Spanish*
DFT; DFWPN.

pelure, *French*
DFT.

peña, *Spanish*
GG.

peñasco, *Spanish*
GG.

Penates, *Latin*
DFPCQ.

penché, penchée, *French*
LB.

penco, *Spanish*
DSTE/*237*.

pendant, *French*
OCM.

pendente lite, *Latin*
DFPA; DFPCQ; DFT.

penetralia, *Latin*
DFPCQ.

penetralia mentis, *Latin*
DFPCQ.

pénétrant, *French*
OCM.

penitent, *French*
GG.

peñon, *Spanish*
GG.

pensée, *French*
DFPCQ; DFWPN.

penseur, *French*
DFWPN.

pensieroso, *Italian*
DFPCQ; DFT.

pension, *French*
DFT; DFWPB.

Pentatonon, *German*
ICMM.

pentimento, *Italian*
LP.

pentimento, *pl.* **pentimenti,** *Italian*
DFWPB.

peon, *Spanish*
DSTE.

per, *Italian*
OCM.

per accidens, *Latin*
DFPA; DFT; DFWPN.

per ambages, *Latin*
DFPA.

per angusta ad augusta, *Latin*
DFPCQ.

per annum, *Latin*
DEP; DFPA; DFPCQ; DFT;
DFWPB; DFWPN.

per ardua ad astra, *Latin*
DFWPN.

per aspera ad astra, *Latin*
DEP; DFT.

per capita, *Latin*
DEP; DFPA; DFPCQ; DFT;
DFWPB; DFWPN.

per cent(um), *Latin*
DFWPB; DFWPN.

per centum, *Latin*
DEP; DFPCQ; DFT.

per consequens, *Latin*
DFPA.

per contra, *Latin*
DEP; DFPA; DFPCQ; DFT;
DFWPB.

percossa, *Italian*
OCM.

per curiam, *Latin*
DFPA.

perdendo, *Italian*
DFT; OCM.

perdendo le forze, *Italian*
ICMM.

perdendosi, *Italian*
DFPCQ; DFT/*perdendo*; OCM/
perdendo.

per diem, *Latin*
DEP; DFPA; DFPCQ; DFT;
DFWPB; DFWPN.

perdreaux, *French*
DFWPN.

perdrix, *French*
DFT.

perdu, *French*
DEP.

perdu(e), *French*
DFWPN.

père, *French*
DFT; DFWPN.

pereletok, *Russian*
GG.

per favore, *Italian*
DFWPN.

périgourdine, *French*
OCM.

perito, *pl.* **periti,** *Italian*
DFWPB.

però, *Italian*
OCM.

perpetuo, *Italian*
OCM.

perpetuum mobile, *Latin*
DFPA; DFWPB; DFWPN; OCM.

per procurationem, *Latin*
DFPA.

per procuratorem, *Latin*
DFPA.

per saltum, *Latin*
DEP; DFT.

per se, *Latin*
DEP; DFPA; DFPCQ; DFT;
DFWPB; DFWPN.

persiflage, *French*
DFPCQ; DFT; DFWPB;
DFWPN.

persifleur, *French*
DFT.

persil, *French*
DFT.

persona, *Latin*
DFT.

persona ficta, *Latin*
DFT/*persona.*

persona grata, *Latin*
DFT/*persona;* DFWPN.

persona gratissima, *Latin*
DFT/*persona.*

persona ingrata, *Latin*
DFWPN.

persona muta, *Latin*
DFT/*persona.*

persona non grata, *Latin*
DFPA; DFT/*persona;* DFWPN.

persona non grata, *pl.* **personae non
gratae,** *Latin*
DFWPB.

perspectif cavalière, *French*
DA.

per totam curiam, *Latin*
DFPA.

pes, *Latin*
OCM.

Pesach, *Hebrew*
DFWPN.

Pesach, *Yiddish*
JOY.

pesant, *French*
OCM.

pesante, *Italian*
DFPCQ; DFT; ICMM; OCM/
pesant.

pesce, *Italian*
DFWPN.

peso, *Spanish*
DFT; DFWPN.

peso duro, *Spanish*
DFT/*peso.*

petate, *Spanish*
DSTE.

petenera, *Spanish*
ICMM.

petimtse, *Chinese*
DFWPN.

petit, *French*
DEP; DFT; LB; OCM.

petit beurre, *French*
DFWPB.

petit bourgeois, *French*
DFPA; DFPCQ; DFT/*petit;*
DFWPN.

petit bugle, *French*
OCM/*bugle.*

petit caporal, *French*
DFT/*petit.*

petit dejeuner, *French*
DFT/*déjeuner.*

petit détaché, *French*
OCM.

petite, *French*
LB/*petit;* OCM/*petit.*

petite flûte, *French*
OCM.

petite flûte octave, *French*
OCM/*petite flûte.*

petite marmite, *French*
DFWPN.

petite pedale, *French*
ICMM/*una corda.*

petite pièce, *French*
DFPA.

petites gens, *French*
DFPA.

petites morales, *French*
DFPA.

petit four, *French*
DFWPB.

petitio principii, *Latin*
DEP; DFPA; DFPCQ; DFT.

petit-lait, *French*
DFT.

petit mal, *French*
DFPA; DFT/*petit.*

petit point, *French*
DFT/*petit*; DFWPB; DFWPN.

petits-chevaux, *French*
DFT.

petits droits, *French*
OCM.

petits fours, *French*
DFWPN.

petits jeux, *French*
DFPA.

petit souper, *French*
DFPA; DFT/*petit.*

petits pois, *French*
DFT; DFWPN.

petits tours, *French*
LB.

petit sujet, *French*
DFWPN.

petit verre, *French*
DFT/*petit*; DFWPN.

petra dura, *Italian*
DFT.

petto, *Italian*
OCM.

petuntse, *Chinese*
ACD; ACD/*porcelain.*

peu, *French*
DFPCQ; OCM.

peut-être, *French*
DFT.

peyes, *Yiddish*
HFY.

peyote, *Spanish*
DSTE.

pezzo, *Italian*
DFT; ICMM/*piece*; OCM.

Pfeife, *German*
ICMM; OCM.

pfiffig, *German*
OCM.

Phantasie, *German*
OCM.

Phantasiebild, *German*
OCM/*Phantasie.*

Phantasien, *German*
OCM/*Phantasie.*

Phantasiestück, *German*
ICMM/*fantasia*; OCM/*Phantasie.*

photinx, *Greek*
ICMM.

piacere, *Italian*
OCM.

piacere, a, *Italian*
ICMM.

piacevole, *Italian*
DFPCQ; DFT; ICMM; OCM.

pia mater, *Latin*
DFWPN.

pianamente, *Italian*
OCM.

piangendo, *Italian*
DFPCQ; DFT; ICMM; OCM.

piangente, *Italian*
OCM/*piangendo.*

piangevole, *Italian*
OCM.

piangevolmente, *Italian*
OCM/*piangevole.*

pianissimo, *Italian*
DFPCQ; DFT; DFWPB;
DFWPN; ICMM; OCM.

piano, *Italian*
DFPCQ; DFT; DFWPB; ICMM;
OCM.

piano à queue, *French*
OCM.

pianoforte, *Italian*
ACD; DFWPN.

piano-mécanique, *French*
ICMM.

piano nobile, *Italian*
DA.

pianto, *Italian*
OCM.

piatti, *Italian*
ICMM; OCM.

piazza, *Italian*
DA; DFT.

piazza, *pl.* **piazze,** *Italian*
DFWPB.

pibcorn, *Welsh*
OCM.

pibgorn, *Welsh*
OCM/*pibcorn.*

picador, *Spanish*
DFT; DFWPN; DSTE/*237.*

picaro, *Spanish*
DFWPN.

picchettato, *Italian*
OCM.

picchiettando, *Italian*
OCM/*picchettato.*

picchiettato, *Italian*
OCM/*picchettato.*

piccola, *Italian*
OCM/*piccolo.*

piccolo, *Italian*
DFPCQ; OCM.

Pickleföte, *German*
OCM.

picot, *French*
DFT.

pièce, *French*
DFT; DFWPN; ICMM/*piece.*

pièce à thèse, *French*
DFPA.

pièce bien faite, *French*
DFWPN.

pièce de circonstance, *French*
DFT/*pièce.*

pièce de resistance, *the, French*
SPICE.

pièce de résistance, *French*
DFPA; DFPCQ; DFT/*pièce*;
DFWPB; DFWPN.

pièce de spectacle, *French*
DFWPB.

pièce de théâtre, *French*
DFT/*pièce.*

pièce d'occasion, *French*
DFPA; DFT/*pièce*; DFWPB.

pièce montée, *French*
DFWPB.

pièce noire, *French*
DFWPB.

pièce rose, *French*
DFWPB.

pied, *French*
DFT; OCM.

pied, être de, *French*
LB.

pied à demi, *French*
LB.

pied à quart, *French*
LB.

pied à terre, *French*
LB.

pied-à-terre, *French*
DFT; DFWPB.

pied à trois quarts, *French*
LB.

pied de biche, *French*
ACD.

pied en l'air, *French*
OCM.

piedroit, *French*
DA.

pieds, cinq positions des, *French*
LB.

piena, *Italian*
OCM/*pieno.*

pien ch'ing, *Chinese*
ICMM/*pien k'ing.*

pien chung, *Chinese*
ICMM.

pien k'ing, *Chinese*
ICMM.

pieno, *Italian*
ICMM; OCM.

pien yao, *Chinese*
ACD.

Pietà, *Italian*
DFT; DFWPB; DFWPN; LP;
OCM.

piétiner, *French*
LB.

pietosamente, *Italian*
OCM/*pietà.*

pietoso, *Italian*
ICMM; OCM/*pietà.*

pifferari, *Italian*
ICMM.

piffero, *Italian*
DFT; ICMM.

pikieren, *German*
OCM.

pilaff, *Persian*
DFWPN.

pilar, *Spanish*
GG.

pilau, *Persian*
DFT.

pilav/pilaf, *Turkish*
DFWPB.

pilaw, *Persian*
DFT/*pilau.*

pilon, *Spanish*
DFT; DSTE.

piloncillo, *Spanish*
DSTE.

pilpul, *Yiddish*
HFY; JOY.

pimiento, *Spanish*
DFT.

piña, *Spanish*
DFT.

piñata, *Spanish*
DSTE.

pincé, *French*
DFWPB; ICMM; ICMM/*mor-
dent*; OCM.

pince-nez, *French*
DFT; DFWPB.

pingo, *Eskimo*
GG.

pinole, *Spanish*
DFT; DSTE.

piñon, *Spanish*
DSTE.

pinto, *Spanish*
DSTE.

pinxit, *Latin*
DFPA; DFT; LP.

pio, *Italian*
OCM.

piote, *Spanish*
DSTE/*peyote.*

p'i p'a, *Chinese*
ICMM.

piperno, *Italian*
GG.

pipkrake, *Swedish*
GG.

piquante, *French*
DFWPN.

piqué, *French*
DFWPB; DFWPN; LB; OCM.

piqué à terre, *French*
LB.

piqué détourné, *French*
LB.

piqué enveloppé, *French*
LB.

piquer la pointe, *French*
LB.

piquet, *French*
DFWPB.

piqué tour, *French*
DFWPN; LB.

piqué tour en dedans, *French*
LB/*piqué tour.*

piqué tour en dehors, *French*
LB/*piqué tour.*

piquiren, *German*
OCM.

pirogen, *Russian*
DFWPN.

pirogi, *Russian*
DFT.

pirouette, *French*
DFWPB; DFWPN; LB; OCM.

pirouette, grande, *French*
LB/*pirouette.*

pirouette renversée, *French*
LB/*pirouette.*

pis aller, *French*
DFPCQ; DFT; DFWPB;
DFWPN.

pis-aller, *French*
DFPA.

pis aller, *a,* *French*
SPICE.

pisco, *Spanish*
DFT.

pisé, *French*
DFT.

pisher, *Yiddish*
JOY.

pisherkeh, *Yiddish*
JOY.

pishke, *Yiddish*
JOY; JOY/*pushke.*

pishkeh, *Yiddish*
JOY.

pisk, *Yiddish*
JOY.

pistolet, *French*
LB.

piston, *French*
OCM.

pistone, *Italian*
OCM.

pistoni, *Italian*
OCM/*pistone.*

pistons, bugle à, *French*
OCM.

pistons, trombone à, *French*
OCM.

pita, *Spanish*
DSTE.

pithecanthropus erectus, *New Latin*
DFPA.

piton, *French*
DFT; GG.

pitsel, *Yiddish*
JOY.

pitseleh, *Yiddish*
JOY.

Pittura Metafisica, *Italian*
LP.

piu, *Italian*
OCM.

più, *Italian*
DFPCQ; DFT; ICMM.

più allegro, *Italian*
DFT/*più.*

più lento, *Italian*
DFPCQ; DFT/*più;* DFWPN.

più mosso, *Italian*
DFT/*mosso;* DFT/*più.*

piuttosto, *Italian*
OCM.

piva, *Italian*
ICMM; OCM.

pizzicato, *Italian*
DFPCQ; DFT; DFWPB;
DFWPN; ICMM; OCM.

placé, *French*
LB.

placebo, *Latin*
DFPCQ; DFT; ICMM.

placer, *Spanish*
DSTE.

place, sur, *French*
LB.

placet, *Latin*
DFPA; DFPCQ; DFWPB;
DFWPN.

placidezza, *Italian*
OCM/*placido.*

placido, *Italian*
OCM.

placito, *Italian*
OCM.

plage, *French*
GG.

plainte, *French*
ICMM.

plaisant, *French*
OCM.

planaas, *Danish*
GG.

planchette ronflante, *French*
OCM/*thunder stick*; OCM.

plané, *French*
LB.

planèze, *French*
GG.

plaqué, *French*
OCM.

plat, *French*
DFT.

plata, *Spanish*
DSTE.

plat du jour, *French*
DFPA.

plateau, *French*
DFPCQ; OCM.

plateaux, *French*
OCM/*plateau.*

plate carrée projection, *French*
GG.

platke-macher, *Yiddish*
HFY; JOY.

Platte, *German*
GG.

platz, *Yiddish*
JOY/*plotz.*

plaudernd, *German*
OCM.

playa, *Spanish*
DFT; DSTE; GG.

playera, *Spanish*
ICMM; OCM.

plaza, *Spanish*
GG.

plaza de toros, *Spanish*
DFPA; DSTE/*237.*

plebs, *Latin*
DFPCQ.

plein, *French*
OCM.

plein air, *French*
DFT; DFWPB; DFWPN; LP.

pleine, *French*
OCM/*plein.*

plein jeu, *French*
ICMM; OCM.

pleno, *Italian*
ICMM/*pieno*; OCM.

pleno jure, *Latin*
DFPA.

plenum, *Latin*
DFPCQ.

pletsl, *Yiddish*
HFY; JOY.

plica, *Latin*
ICMM.

plié, *French*
DFWPB; LB.

plié, grand, *French*
LB/*plié.*

plier, *French*
DFWPN.

plique à jour, *French*
ACD/*enamel*; ACD.

pliqué à jour, *French*
DFWPB.

plissé, *French*
DFT; DFWPN.

plosher, *Yiddish*
HFY; JOY.

plotst, *Yiddish*
JOY/*plotz*.

plotz, *Yiddish*
HFY; JOY.

plötzlich, *German*
OCM.

plus, *French*
OCM.

pneuma, *Greek*
OCM.

pobrecito, *Spanish*
DSTE.

pochade, *French*
LP.

poché, *French*
DA; DFWPN.

pochette, *French*
OCM.

pochettino, *Italian*
OCM/*pochetto*.

pochetto, *Italian*
OCM.

pochissimo, *Italian*
OCM.

poco, *Italian*
DFPCQ; DFT; ICMM; OCM.

poco, *Spanish*
DFWPN; DSTE.

poco allegro, *Italian*
DFT/*poco*.

poco a poco, *Italian*
DFT/*poco*.

poco à poco [*sic*], *Italian*
DFPCQ.

poco curante, *Italian*
DFPCQ.

poco curante, *pl.* **poco curanti,**
Italian
DFWPB.

pococurante, *Italian*
DFT.

poco forte, *Italian*
DFT/*poco*.

poco più lento, *Italian*
DFT/*poco*.

poêle, *French*
DFWPN.

poelée, *French*
DFWPN.

poema sinfonico, *Italian*
OCM/*symphonic poem*; OCM/
poème symphonique.

poème symphonique, *French*
ICMM/*symphonic poem*; OCM/
symphonic poem; OCM.

poggiato, *Italian*
OCM.

pogrom, *Russian*
DFT; DFWPB; DFWPN.

pogrom, *Yiddish*
HFY.

poids, *French*
OCM.

point, *French*
DFWPN.

point d'Angleterre, *French*
DFWPN.

point d'appui, *French*
DFPA.

point de France, *French*
DFWPN.

point de repère, *French*
DFPA.

point d'esprit, *French*
DFWPN.

point d'orgue, *French*
ICMM/*organ-point*; ICMM/*pedal-
point*; ICMM; ICMM/*pause*;
OCM.

pointé, *French*
OCM.

pointe, *French*
DFWPB; OCM.

pointes, sur les, *French*
LB.

pointes, temps de, *French*
LB.

pointe tendue, *French*
LB.

pointe tendue à terre, *French*
LB/*pointe tendue.*

pointillisme, *French*
DFWPB.

pointilliste, *French*
DFWPB.

poire, *French*
DFWPN.

poireau, *French*
DFT.

pois, *French*
DFWPN.

poisson, *French*
DFT; DFWPN.

poitrine, *French*
DFT.

poitrine d'agneau, *French*
DFT/*poitrine.*

poivrade, *French*
DFT.

poivre, *French*
DFT.

polacca, *Italian*
ICMM; OCM/*polonaise.*

polder, *Old Flemish*
GG.

polenta, *Italian*
DFPCQ; DFT; DFWPN.

politesse, *French*
DFT.

politico, *Italian*
DFT.

politico, *Spanish*
DFT.

politikon zoon, *Greek*
DFWPN.

polje, *Serbo-Croatian*
GG/*Croatian.*

pollice presso, *Latin*
DFWPN.

pollice verso, *Latin*
DFPA; DFT; DFWPN.

pollo, *Italian*
DFWPN.

pollo, *Spanish*
DFT.

polnisch, *German*
OCM.

polo, *Spanish*
ICMM; OCM.

polonaise, *French*
DFWPN; ICMM.

Polonäse, *German*
OCM.

polska, *Polish*
OCM.

polska, *Swedish*
ICMM.

Polster, *German*
GG.

Polstertanz, *German*
OCM.

Poltergeist, *pl.* **Poltergeister,** *German*
DFWPB.

polynya, *Russian*
GG.

pomme, *French*
DFWPN.

pomme de terre, *French*
DFPA; DFWPN.

pommes frites, *French*
DFWPN.

pomodoro, *Italian*
DFWPN.

pompadour, *French*
DFT.

pompeuse, *French*
OCM/*pompeux.*

pompeux, *French*
OCM.

pomposo, *Italian*
DFPCQ; DFT; ICMM; OCM.

poncho, *Spanish*
DSTE.

ponderoso, *Italian*
OCM.

pondoroso, *Italian*
OCM/*ponderoso.*

pongo, *Quechua*
GG.

ponor, *Serbo-Croatian*
GG/*Croatian.*

pons asinorum, *Latin*
DEP; DFPA; DFPCQ; DFT/
pons; DFWPB; DFWPN.

ponticello, *Italian*
DFT; DFWPN; ICMM; OCM.

poort, *Afrikaans*
GG.

porc, *French*
DFT.

porcellanite, *Italian*
GG.

pordon dantza, *Basque*
OCM.

por favor, *Spanish*
DFPA; DFT.

port à beul, *Scottish*
OCM.

portamento, *Italian*
DFT; DFWPB; DFWPN;
ICMM; OCM.

portando, *Italian*
OCM.

portato, *Italian*
DFT; OCM/*portando.*

port de bras, *French*
DFWPB; LB.

port de voix, *French*
ICMM; OCM.

porté, *French*
LB; OCM.

portée, *French*
ICMM/*stave*; OCM/*porté.*

porte-monnaie, *French*
DFPCQ.

porter la voix, *French*
OCM.

portico, *Italian*
DFWPN.

portière, *French*
DFT.

Portunal, *German*
OCM.

Portunalflöte, *German*
OCM/*Portunal.*

pos, *French*
OCM.

posada, *Spanish*
DSTE.

Posaune, *German*
ICMM; OCM.

pose, *French*
DFPCQ.

posé, *French*
DFWPB; LB.

posément, *French*
OCM.

poser, *French*
LB.

positif, *French*
OCM.

positif-récit, *French*
OCM/*p.r..*

position, *French*
OCM/*pos.*

position fermée, *French*
LB.

position naturelle, *French*
OCM/*pos. nat..*

position ouverte, *French*
LB.

positions soulevées, *French*
LB.

posizione, *Italian*
OCM; OCM/*pos.*

posse comitatus, *Latin*
DFPA; DFPCQ; DFT; DFWPN.

possibile, *Italian*
OCM.

post, *Latin*
DFPCQ.

post bellum auxilium, *Latin*
DFPCQ.

post cibum, *Latin*
DFT.

post diem, *Latin*
DFT.

post facto, *Latin*
DFWPN.

post-facto, *Latin*
DFWPB.

post hoc, ergo propter hoc, *Latin*
DFPCQ; DFT; DFWPB;
DFWPN.

postiche, *French*
DFT.

post judicium, *Latin*
DFPA.

post litem motam, *Latin*
DFPA.

post meridiem, *Latin*
DFPA; DFT; DFWPB.

post meridiem (P.M.), *Latin*
DFPCQ.

post mortem, *Latin*
DEP; DFPA; DFPCQ; DFT;
DFWPB; DFWPN.

post nubila Phoebus, *Latin*
DEP.

post obitum, *Latin*
DEP.

post partum, *Latin*
DFPA.

post scriptum (P.S.), *Latin*
DFPCQ.

post scriptum, *pl.* **post scripta,** *Latin*
DFWPB.

post terminum, *Latin*
DFT.

postulatum, *pl.* **postulata,** *Latin*
DFPCQ.

potage, *French*
DFT; DFWPN.

potage à la queue de bœuf, *French*
DFT/*potage.*

potage au gras, *French*
DFPA; DFT/*potage.*

potage de printanier, *French*
DFT/*potage.*

potage du jour, *French*
DFWPN.

pot au feu, *French*
DFWPB.

pot-au-feu, *French*
DFT; DFWPN.

potch, *Yiddish*
JOY.

potchkee, *Yiddish*
JOY/*potchkeh.*

potchkeh, *Yiddish*
JOY.

potiche, *French*
DFT.

potiron, *French*
DFT.

pot pourri, *French*
DFT; DFWPB.

pot-pourri, *French*
OCM.

potpourri, *French*
DFWPN.

potro, *Spanish*
DSTE.

pouce, *French*
OCM.

pouding, *French*
DFT.

poularde, *French*
DFT; DFWPN.

poulet, *French*
DFT; DFWPN.

poulet roti, *French*
DFT/*poulet.*

poult-de-soie, *French*
DFWPN.

pour, *French*
OCM.

pour passer le temps, *French*
DEP.

pourquoi, *French*
DFT.

poussé, *French*
DFT; ICMM; OCM.

pousse-cafe, *French*
DFT.

pousse-café, *French*
DFWPB.

poussin, *French*
DFT.

pou stō, *Greek*
DFPCQ.

pow wow, *Algonquin*
DFT.

pozo, *Spanish*
DFT.

prächtig, *German*
OCM.

prachtvoll, *German*
OCM/*paächtig.*

präcis, *German*
OCM.

Prado, *Spanish*
DFT.

praeludium, *Latin*
ICMM/*prelude.*

praemissis praemittendis, *Latin*
DFPA.

praenomen, *Latin*
DFPCQ; DFWPN.

praesertim, *Latin*
DFPCQ.

praeteriti anni, *Latin*
DFPCQ.

praline, *French*
DFWPN.

praliné, *French*
DFWPB.

Pralltriller, *German*
ICMM; OCM.

Präludium, *German*
OCM.

prana, *Sanskrit*
DFWPN.

pranzo, *Italian*
DFT.

Pravda, *Russian*
DFWPN.

praya, *Portuguese*
GG.

précédemment, *French*
OCM.

preces, *Latin*
OCM.

précieux, *French*
DFWPN.

préciosité, *French*
DFWPN.

precipitando, *Italian*
DFPCQ; DFT; OCM/*precipitato.*

precipitandosi, *Italian*
OCM/*precipitato.*

precipitato, *Italian*
OCM.

précipité, *French*
LB; OCM.

precipitosamente, *Italian*
OCM/*precipitato.*

precipitoso, *Italian*
OCM/*precipitato.*

précis, *French*
DFPCQ; DFT; DFWPB;
DFWPN.

precisione, *Italian*
OCM/*preciso.*

preciso, *Italian*
DFT; OCM.

pregando, *Italian*
OCM.

preghiera, *Italian*
OCM.

prego, *Italian*
DFT.

prélude, *French*
ICMM/*prelude.*

préluder, *French*
OCM.

preludio, *Italian*
DFPCQ; ICMM/*prelude*; OCM.

premier, *French*
LB; OCM.

premier coup, *French*
DFWPN.

premier cru, *French*
DFWPB.

premier danseur, *fem.* **première
danseuse,** *French*
DFWPB.

premier danseur étoile, *fem.* **première
danseuse étoile,** *French*
DFWPB.

première, *French*
DFT; DFWPB; DFWPN; LB/
premier; OCM/*premier.*

première danseuse, *French*
DFT; DFWPN.

première, en, *French*
LB.

première position, *French*
LB/*pieds, cinq positions des*; LB/
bras, positions de.

prendre, *French*
OCM.

préparation, *French*
LB.

près, *French*
OCM.

presa, *Italian*
DFT; ICMM.

pré-salé, *French*
DFT.

présalé, *French*
DFWPB.

presidente, *Spanish*
DSTE.

presidio, *Spanish*
DFT; DSTE.

presque, *French*
OCM.

pressando, *Italian*
OCM.

pressant, *French*
OCM/*pressando.*

pressante, *Italian*
OCM/*pressando.*

pressez, *French*
OCM.

pressieren, *German*
OCM/*pressez.*

prestige, *French*
DFPCQ.

prestissimo, *Italian*
DFPCQ; DFT; ICMM.

presto, *Italian*
DFPCQ; DFT; DFWPB;
DFWPN; ICMM; OCM.

prêt(e), *French*
DFWPN.

prie-dieu, *French*
ACD.

prière, *French*
OCM.

prima, *Italian*
DFT; OCM.

prima ballerina, *French*
LB/*ballerina.*

prima ballerina assoluta, *Italian*
DFWPB.

prima buffa, *Italian*
DFT/*prima.*

prima donna, *Italian*
DFPA; DFPCQ; DFT/*prima*;
DFWPB; DFWPN; ICMM;
OCM.

prima facie, *Latin*
DEP; DFPA; DFPCQ; DFT;
DFWPB; DFWPN.

prima inter pares, *Latin*
DFT.

Primärrumpf, *German*
GG.

prima volta, *Italian*
DFPCQ; DFT/*volta*; DFT/*prima*.

primo, *Italian*
DFT; ICMM.

primo, *Latin*
DFPCQ; DFT.

primo basso, *Italian*
DFT/*primo*.

prim'-omo, *Italian*
DFT/*primo*.

primo nomo, *Italian*
DFWPN.

primo tempo, *Italian*
DFPCQ.

primo tenore, *Italian*
DFT/*primo*.

primo uomo, *Italian*
DFT/*primo*; ICMM.

primum mobile, *Latin*
DFPA; DFPCQ; DFT; DFWPN.

primus inter omnes, *Latin*
DFPCQ.

primus inter pares, *Latin*
DEP; DFPA; DFPCQ; DFT;
DFWPB; DFWPN.

primus motor, *Latin*
DFPA.

principale, *Italian*
OCM.

principia, *Latin*
DFPCQ.

printanier, *French*
DFT.

printanière, *French*
DFWPN.

Prinzipale, *German*
OCM.

prise, *French*
DFT.

privato consensu, *Latin*
DFPCQ.

prix, *French*
DA; DFT.

Prix de Rome, *French*
LP.

prix fixe, *French*
DFPA; DFT/*prix*; DFWPB.

probatum est, *Latin*
DFPCQ.

pro bono publico, *Latin*
DEP; DFPA; DFPCQ; DFT;
DFWPB; DFWPN.

procès-verbal, *French*
DFPA.

pro confesso, *Latin*
DFPA.

pro et con, *Latin*
DFPA.

pro et con (*for*** contra),** *Latin*
DFPCQ.

pro et con(tra), *Latin*
DFWPN.

pro et contra, *Latin*
DFPA; DFT.

profanum vulgus, *Latin*
DFPA; DFPCQ; DFT; DFWPN.

profil perdu, *French*
LP.

profondo, *Italian*
OCM.

pro forma, *Latin*
DFPA; DFPCQ; DFT; DFWPB;
DFWPN.

progressivamente, *Italian*
OCM/*progressivo*.

progressivo, *Italian*
OCM.

pro hac vice, *Latin*
DFPA.

pro hâc vice, *Latin*
DEP.

projet, *French*
DA.

prolegomena, *Greek*
DFPCQ; DFWPN/*prolegomenon*.

prolegomenon, *Greek*
DFWPN.

prolétaire, *French*
DFPCQ.

promenade, en, *French*
LB.

promotor fidei, *Latin*
DFPA.

promptement, *French*
OCM.

pronto, *Italian*
DFT; OCM.

pronto, *Spanish*
DFT; DFWPB; DSTE.

pronunciamiento, *Spanish*
DFPCQ; DSTE.

prooemium, *Latin*
DFPCQ.

pro patria, *Latin*
DFPCQ; DFT.

Proportz, *German*
ICMM/*Nachtanz*.

proposta, *Italian*
ICMM.

proprietas, *Latin*
ICMM.

propriété littéraire, *French*
DFPCQ.

proprio motu, *Latin*
DFPA.

proprium missae, *Latin*
ICMM.

propter affectum, *Latin*
DFPA.

propter delictum, *Latin*
DFPA.

propter falsos testes, *Latin*
DFPA.

propter hoc, *Latin*
DFT.

pro rata, *Latin*
DFPA; DFPCQ; DFT; DFWPB;
DFWPN.

pro ratâ, *Latin*
DEP.

pro re nata, *Latin*
DFPA; DFPCQ; DFT; DFWPB.

prosa, *Latin*
ICMM/*sequence.*

prosciutto, *Italian*
DFWPB; DFWPN.

proshchái, *Russian*
DFT.

proshcháite, *Russian*
DFT/*proshchái.*

prosit, *German*
DFPCQ; DFT.

prosit, *Latin*
DFPA; DFT; DFWPB; DFWPN.

proslambanomenos, *Greek*
ICMM.

prost, *Yiddish*
JOY.

pro tanto, *Latin*
DFPCQ.

protégé, *French*
DEP; DFPCQ; DFT; DFWPN.

protégé, *fem.* protégée, *French*
DFWPB.

pro tem, *Latin*
DFWPN; SPICE.

pro tem(pore), *Latin*
DFWPB.

pro tempore, *Latin*
DEP; DFPA; DFPCQ; DFT;
DFWPN.

Provençal, *French*
DFWPN.

provençale, *French*
OCM.

proviso, *Latin*
DFPCQ.

pruneau, *French*
DFT.

Psalter, *German*
ICMM/*psaltery.*

psaltérion, *French*
ICMM/*psaltery.*

psalterium, *Latin*
ICMM/*psaltery.*

psaume, *French*
OCM.

pteroma, *Greek*
DA.

publici juris, *Latin*
DFPA.

publico consilio, *Latin*
DFPCQ.

pucka, *Anglo-Indian*
DFT.

pudenda, *Latin*
DFWPN.

pueblito, *American Spanish*
DFT.

pueblo, *Spanish*
DFT; DFWPN.

puerto, *Spanish*
GG.

pug, *Anglo-Indian*
DFT.

puggree, *Anglo-Indian*
DFT.

pugi, *Anglo-Indian*
DFT.

pugnis et calcibus, *Latin*
DFPCQ.

pukka, *Anglo-Indian*
DFT/*pucka.*

Pulcinella, *Italian*
DFWPN.

pulque, *Mexican Spanish*
DFT.

pulque, *Spanish*
DFWPN; DSTE.

pulqueria, *Spanish*
DSTE.

Pult, *German*
OCM.

Pulte, *German*
OCM/*Pult.*

puma, *Spanish*
DSTE.

punctum contrapunctum, *Latin*
DFWPN.

punctus, *Latin*
ICMM.

Punica fides, *Latin*
DFPCQ; DFT.

punta, *Italian*
OCM.

puntilla, *Spanish*
DFT; DSTE/*237.*

punto coronato, *Italian*
OCM.

punto d'organo, *Italian*
ICMM/*organ-point*; OCM/*punto coronato.*

pupik, *Yiddish*
HFY; JOY.

pupitre, *French*
OCM.

pupule, *Hawaiian*
DFT.

purdah, *Hindi*
DFWPN.

purdonium, *Latin*
ACD.

purée, *French*
DFT; DFWPB; DFWPN.

purée de pois, *French*
DFT/*purée.*

purée d'oignons, *French*
DFT/*purée.*

Purim, *Hebrew*
DFWPN.

Purim, *Yiddish*
JOY.

purpureus pannus, *Latin*
DFPA.

pushke, *Yiddish*
HFY; JOY.

Putsch, *German*
DFT; DFWPN.

utsch, *Swiss German*
  DFWPB.
utti, *Italian*
  DFT.
utto, *Italian*
  LP.

putto, *pl.* **putti,** *Italian*
  DFWPB.
putz, *Yiddish*
  HFY; JOY.
pyote, *Spanish*
  DSTE/*peyote.*

Q

qanat, *Arabic*
GG.

qua, *Latin*
DFPA.

Quadrat, *German*
OCM.

quadratista, *pl.* quadratisti, *Italian*
DFWPB.

quadratum, B, *Latin*
ICMM.

quadrille, *French*
ICMM; LB.

quadrivium, *Latin*
DFWPB; DFWPN; ICMM.

quadroon, *Spanish*
DSTE.

quadruple-croche, *French*
OCM.

quaere, *Latin*
DFPCQ; DFT.

quae vide, *Latin*
DFPA; DFT.

quaich, *Scottish*
ACD.

Qual, *German*
OCM.

quanto, *Italian*
OCM.

quantum, *Latin*
DFPCQ; DFT.

quantum libet, *Latin*
DEP; DFPCQ; DFT/*quantum.*

quantum meruit, *Latin*
DFPCQ.

quantum placet, *Latin*
DFT/*quantum.*

quantum sufficit, *Latin*
DEP; DFPCQ; DFT/*quantum.*

quarré, en, *French*
LB.

quart, *French*
LB.

quarte, *French*
DFT.

quartes, *French*
ICMM.

Quartett, *German*
OCM.

quartetto, *Italian*
ACD; DFPCQ; DFWPB; OCM.

quart-fagotto, *Italian*
ICMM.

Quartflöte, *German*
ICMM.

Quartgeige, *German*
ICMM.

quartier, *French*
DFT.

Quartier Latin, *French*
DFWPN.

quarto, *Italian*
OCM.

quartus cantus, *Latin*
OCM.

quasi, *Italian*
ICMM; OCM.

quasi, *Latin*
DEP; DFPCQ.

quatre, *French*
LB; OCM.

quatrefoil, *French*
ACD.

quatrième, *French*
LB.

quatrième derrière, à la, *French*
LB.

quatrième derrière, grande, *French*
LB.

quatrième devant, à la, *French*
LB.

quatrième devant, grande, *French*
LB.

quatrième en avant, *French*
LB/*bras, positions de.*

quatrième en haut, *French*
LB/*bras, positions de.*

quatrième position, *French*
LB/*pieds, cinq positions des.*

quattro, *Italian*
OCM.

quattrocento, *Italian*
DA; DFPA; DFT; LP.

quatuor, *French*
ICMM; OCM.

que, *French*
OCM.

quebrada, *Spanish*
DFT; GG.

que dice, *Spanish*
DSTE.

que hubo le, *Spanish*
DSTE.

quel dommage, *French*
DFPA.

quelque, *French*
OCM.

quelque chose, *French*
DFPCQ; DFT; DFWPN.

quelques, *French*
OCM/*quelque.*

quelqu'un, *French*
DFT.

quem quaeritis, *Latin*
DFWPN.

quenelle, *French*
DFT; DFWPB.

quenelles, *French*
DFWPN.

qué pasa, *Spanish*
DFT.

Querflöte, *German*
ICMM; OCM.

querida, *Spanish*
DSTE.

querido, *Spanish*
DFT.

Querpfeife, *German*
ICMM.

Querstand, *German*
ICMM.

que será será, *Spanish*
DFPA.

questa, *Italian*
OCM/*questo.*

qu'est-ce que c'est, *French*
DFT; DFWPN.

questo, *Italian*
OCM.

qué'tal, *Spanish*
DFT.

que tal, *Spanish*
DFPA; DSTE.

queue, *French*
ICMM; OCM.

quid nunc?, *Latin*
DEP; DFPCQ.

qui docet, discit, *Latin*
DFPCQ.

quid pro quo, *Latin*
  DEP; DFPA; DFPCQ; DFT;
  DFWPB; DFWPN.

quid pro quo, a, *Latin*
  SPICE.

quien sabe, *Spanish*
  DSTE.

quien savvy, *Spanish*
  DSTE/*quien sabe.*

quieto, *Italian*
  OCM.

quietus, *Latin*
  DFPCQ.

quilisma, *Latin*
  ICMM.

quincunx, *Latin*
  DFWPN.

quinquennium, *Latin*
  DFPCQ.

quinta, *Italian*
  OCM/*quinto.*

quinta falsa, *Italian*
  ICMM.

quinte de viole, *French*
  ICMM.

Quintett, *German*
  ICMM; OCM/*quintet.*

quintette, *French*
  ICMM; OCM/*quintet.*

quintetto, *Italian*
  DFPCQ; ICMM; OCM/*quintet.*

quinto, *Italian*
  OCM.

quintoyer, *French*
  ICMM.

Quintsaite, *German*
  OCM.

quintuor, *French*
  OCM/*quintet*; OCM.

quintus, *Latin*
  ICMM.

quiproquo, *Latin*
  DFPCQ.

quirt, *Spanish*
  DSTE.

qui tollis, *Latin*
  OCM.

quitter, *French*
  OCM.

qui vive, *French*
  DFPA; DFT; DFWPB; DFWPN.

qui vive?, *French*
  DEP; DFPCQ.

qui vive, on the, *French + English*
  SPICE.

quo?, *Latin*
  DFPCQ.

quo animo, *Latin*
  DFPA.

quo animo?, *Latin*
  DFPCQ.

quod erat demonstrandum, *Latin*
  DEP; DFPA; DFT; DFWPB;
  DFWPN.

quod erat demonstrandum (Q.E.D.),
Latin
  DFPCQ.

quod erat faciendum, *Latin*
  DFT.

quod erat faciendum (Q.E.F.), *Latin*
  DFPCQ.

quod est, *Latin*
  DFT.

quodlibet, *Latin*
  DFPCQ; DFT; DFWPN; ICMM;
  OCM.

quod vide, *Latin*
  DFPA; DFT.

quod vide (Q.V.), *Latin*
  DFPCQ.

quod vide, *pl.* **quae vide,** *Latin*
  DFWPB.

quoique, *French*
  OCM.

quo iure, *Latin*
  DFPCQ.

quondam, *Latin*
DFPCQ; DFT; DFWPB;
DFWPN.

quoniam, *Latin*
OCM.

quo pacto?, *Latin*
DFPCQ.

quot homines, tot sententiae, *Latin*
DFPCQ.

quotidie, *Latin*
DFPCQ.

quousque tandem, *Latin*
DFT.

quo vadis, *Latin*
DFPA; DFT; DFWPB; DFWPN.

quo warranto, *Anglo-Latin*
DFPA.

R

rabbia, *Italian*
OCM.

râble, *French*
DFT.

râble de lièvre rôti, *French*
DFT/*râble*.

raccourci, *French*
LB.

rachmones, *Yiddish*
JOY.

raconteur, *French*
DFPCQ; DFT.

raconteur, *fem.* raconteuse, *French*
DFWPB.

raddolcendo, *Italian*
DFT; OCM.

raddolcente, *Italian*
OCM/*raddolcendo*.

raddoppiamento, *Italian*
ICMM.

raddoppiare, *Italian*
OCM.

raffiné, *French*
DFT.

raffrenando, *Italian*
OCM.

rafraîchissements, *French*
DFT.

rageur, *French*
OCM.

raggioni, *Italian*
GG.

ragoke, *Russian*
ICMM.

ragout [*sic*], *French*
DFWPN.

ragoût, *French*
DFPCQ; DFWPB.

raifort, *French*
DFT.

raison, *French*
DFT.

raison d'état, *French*
DFPA; DFT/*raison*.

raison d'état, *pl.* raisons d'état,
French
DFWPB.

raison d'être, *French*
DFPA; DFPCQ; DFT/*raison*;
DFWPB; DFWPN; LP.

raisonné, *French*
LP.

raisonneur, *French*
DFWPN.

raja, *Hindi*
DFT/*rajah*.

rajah, *Hindi*
DFT; DFWPB; DFWPN.

raku, *Japanese*
JLE.

râle, *French*
DFT.

râle de la mort, *French*
DFT/*râle.*

ralentir, *French*
OCM.

rallentando, *Italian*
DFPCQ; DFT; DFWPB;
DFWPN; ICMM; OCM/*ral-
lentare.*

rallentare, *Italian*
OCM.

rallentato, *Italian*
OCM/*rallentare.*

ramada, *Spanish*
DSTE.

Ramadan, *Arabic*
DFT.

ramal, *Spanish*
DSTE.

ramassé, *French*
LB.

rana, *Hindi*
DFT.

raña, *Spanish*
GG.

rance, *French*
GG.

rancheria, *Spanish*
DFT.

ranchero, *Spanish*
DFT; DFWPB; DSTE.

rancho, *Spanish*
DFT; DFWPN; DSTE.

Randkluft, *German*
GG.

randori, *Japanese*
JLE.

randori, *verb, Japanese*
JLE.

ranee, *Hindi*
DFT/*rani*; DFWPB.

rani, *Hindi*
DFT.

ranz des vaches, *French*
OCM.

ranz des vaches, *Swiss French*
OCM.

rapakivi, *Finnish*
GG.

rape, *Italian*
DFWPN.

rapidamente, *Italian*
ICMM; OCM/*rapido.*

rapidità, *Italian*
OCM/*rapido.*

rapido, *Italian*
OCM.

rapport, *French*
DFT.

rappresentativo, stile, *Italian*
ICMM.

rapprochement, *French*
DFPCQ; DFT; DFWPB;
DFWPN.

rapprocher, *French*
OCM.

rapsodia, *Italian*
OCM.

rara avis, *Latin*
DEP; DFPCQ; DFT; DFWPN
SPICE.

rara avis, *pl.* **rarae aves,** *Latin*
DFWPB.

ras, *Arabic*
GG.

rasch, *German*
OCM.

rascher, *German*
OCM/*rasch.*

Rassenkreis, *German*
GG.

ratatiné, *French*
DFWPN.

Rathaus, *German*
DA.

Rathskeller, *German*
DA.

Ratsche, *German*
OCM.

Ratskeller, *German*
DFWPN.

rattenendo, *Italian*
OCM/*rattenere.*

rattenere, *Italian*
OCM.

rattenuto, *Italian*
OCM/*rattenere.*

rauh, *German*
OCM.

rauschend, *German*
OCM.

ravigote, *French*
DFT.

ravinement, *French*
GG.

raviolo, *Italian*
DFWPN.

ravissant, *French*
DFT.

ravvivando, *Italian*
OCM.

ravvivato, *Italian*
OCM/*ravvivando.*

rayonnant, *French*
DA.

re, *French*
ICMM.

re, *Italian*
ICMM; OCM.

re, *Latin*
DFPA; DFT; DFWPN.

real, *Spanish*
DFWPN; DSTE.

Realpolitik, *German*
DFT; DFWPB; DFWPN.

reata, *Spanish*
DSTE.

Reb, *Yiddish*
HFY; JOY; JOY.

rebbe, *Yiddish*
JOY.

rebbetsen, *Yiddish*
JOY/*rebbitsin.*

rebbitsin, *Yiddish*
JOY.

re bémol, *French*
ICMM.

rebosa, *Spanish*
DSTE/*reboso.*

reboso, *Spanish*
DSTE.

rebozo, *Spanish*
DFT; DSTE/*reboso.*

rebute, *French*
OCM.

Reb Yankel, *Yiddish*
HFY.

réchauffé, *French*
DFPCQ; DFT; DFWPB;
DFWPN.

recherche, *French*
ICMM.

recherché, *French*
DFPCQ; DFT; DFWPB;
DFWPN.

recherches, *French*
DFWPN.

recht, *German*
OCM.

rechte, *German*
OCM/*recht.*

récit, *French*
OCM; OCM/*r..*

recita, *Italian*
ICMM.

recitando, *Italian*
DFT; OCM.

recitante, *Italian*
OCM/*recitando.*

récitatif, *French*
ICMM/*recitative.*

Recitativ, *German*
ICMM/*recitative.*

recitativo, *Italian*
DFPCQ; DFT; DFWPN;
ICMM/*recitative*; OCM/*recitative.*

recitativo

recitativo, *pl.* recitativi, *Italian*
DFWPB.

recitativo accompagnato, *Italian*
DFT/*recitativo.*

recitativo parlando, *Italian*
DFT/*recitativo.*

recitativo secco, *Italian*
DFT/*recitativo*; DFWPB;
DFWPN.

recitativo stromentato, *Italian*
DFT/*recitativo*; DFWPN.

récittant, *French*
OCM/*recitando.*

reconnaissance, *French*
DFPCQ.

recoupé, *French*
DFT.

recto, *Latin*
DFT; DFWPN; LP.

rectus in curiâ, *Latin*
DEP.

recueil, *French*
DFT; DFWPN.

recueil choisi, *French*
DFT/*recueil.*

recueilli, *French*
OCM.

reculant, en, *French*
LB.

redan, *French*
DA.

redend, *German*
OCM.

redingote, *French*
DFT.

redoublement, *French*
OCM/*redoubler.*

redoubler, *French*
OCM.

redoute, *French*
ICMM; OCM.

Redoutensaal, *German*
OCM/*redoute.*

Redoutentänze, *German*
OCM/*redoute.*

red tai, *Japanese*
JLE.

reduciren, *German*
ICMM.

reductio ad absurdum, *Latin*
DEP; DFPA; DFPCQ; DFT;
DFWPB; DFWPN.

reductio ad impossibile, *Latin*
DFPA; DFT; DFWPN.

réduire, *French*
OCM.

reduzieren, *German*
OCM/*réduire.*

reflet, *French*
DFT.

reflet métallique, *French*
DFT/*reflet.*

reflet nacré, *French*
DFT/*reflet.*

refrapper, *French*
OCM.

reg, *Hamitic*
GG.

regale, *Italian*
OCM.

régale, *French*
OCM/*regale.*

régale à percussion, *French*
OCM.

régale à vent, *French*
OCM/*regale.*

regalia, *Latin*
DFPCQ.

Regalwerke, *German*
OCM.

Régence, *French*
ACD.

régime, *French*
DFPCQ; DFWPN.

regina, *Latin*
DFPCQ.

regina coeli, *Latin*
ICMM.
regina scientiarum, *Latin*
DFPA.
registrieren, *German*
OCM.
Registrierung, *German*
OCM/*registrieren.*
registro, *Italian*
OCM.
Regius Professor, *Latin*
DFWPN.
Regur, *Hindi*
GG.
Reibungsbreccia, *German*
GG.
Reich, *German*
DFPCQ; DFT; DFWPB;
DFWPN.
Reichstag, *German*
DFPCQ; DFT; DFWPN.
rein, *German*
OCM.
rejouissance, *French*
ICMM.
réjouissance, *French*
OCM.
relâche, *French*
DFT.
relâché, *French*
OCM.
relevé, *French*
DA; DFT; DFWPB; DFWPN;
LB.
relevé, temps, *French*
LB.
relevé de potage, *French*
DFWPN.
relevé derrière, *French*
LB/*relevé.*
relevé devant, *French*
LB/*relevé.*
relevé passé, *French*
LB/*relevé.*

relievo, *Italian*
DFT.
religieuse, *French*
OCM/*religieux.*
religieux, *French*
OCM.
religio loci, *Latin*
DFPA.
religiosamente, *Italian*
DFT; OCM/*religioso.*
religioso, *Italian*
DFT; OCM.
rem acu tetigisti, *Latin*
DEP.
remanet, *Latin*
DFPA.
remanié, *French*
GG.
remanié assemblage, *French*
GG.
remettre, *French*
OCM.
rémolade, *French*
DFT.
remonta, *Spanish*
DFT.
remontant, en, *French*
LB.
remoulade, *French*
DFWPN.
rémoulade, *French*
DFT/*rémolade.*
remplissage, *French*
DFT; ICMM.
remuda, *Spanish*
DSTE.
renaissance, *French*
DEP; DFPCQ.
rendez-vous, *French*
DFT.
rendezvous, *French*
DFPCQ.
rendu, *French*
DA.

renforcer, *French*
OCM.

renga, *Japanese*
JLE.

rentrée, *French*
OCM.

renversé, *French*
DFWPN; LB.

renversée, *French*
LB/*renversé.*

renvoi, *French*
OCM.

reol, *Danish*
ICMM.

repartimiento, *Spanish*
DFT.

repas maigre, *French*
DFT; DFT/*maigre.*

repente, *Latin*
DFPCQ.

repertoire, *French*
ICMM.

répéter, *French*
LB.

répétiteur, *French*
OCM.

répétition, *French*
ICMM; LB.

Repetitor, *German*
OCM/*répétiteur.*

repetitore, *Italian*
ICMM; OCM/*répétiteur.*

repi, *Modern Greek*
GG.

replat, *French*
GG.

replica, *Italian*
DFPCQ; OCM.

replicato, *Italian*
DFT; OCM.

répondez s'il vous plait [*sic*], *French*
DFPA.

répondez, s'il vous plaît, *French*
DFWPB; DFWPN; DFT.

repos, *French*
OCM.

repoussage, *French*
DFT.

repoussé, *French*
ACD; DA; DFT; DFWPB;
DFWPN.

repoussoir, *French*
DFWPB; LP.

reprendre, *French*
OCM.

reprise, *French*
DFT; ICMM/*repeat*; OCM.

requiem, *Latin*
DFPCQ.

requiescant in pace, *Latin*
DFWPN.

requiescat in pace, *Latin*
DEP; DFPA; DFT; DFWPN.

requiescat in pace (R.I.P.), *Latin*
DFPCQ.

requiescat in pace, *pl.* **requiescant in
pace,** *Latin*
DFWPB.

requiescit in pace, *Latin*
DFT.

res, *Latin*
DFT; DFWPN.

res adjudicata, *Latin*
DFPA; DFT/*res.*

res alienae, *Latin*
DFPA; DFT/*res.*

res angusta domi, *Latin*
DEP.

réseau, *French*
DFT.

res facta, *Latin*
ICMM.

res gestae, *Latin*
DFPA; DFT/*res*; DFWPN.

residuum, *Latin*
DFPCQ.

res integra, *Latin*
DFPA.

res ipsa loquitur, *Latin*
DFPA.

(la) Résistance, *French*
DFWPB.

res judicata, *Latin*
DFPA; DFPCQ; DFT/*res.*

res nullius, *Latin*
DFPA.

résolument, *French*
OCM.

resoluto, *Italian*
OCM.

resoluzione, *Italian*
OCM.

respice finem, *Latin*
DFPA; DFPCQ; DFT.

responsorium, *Latin*
ICMM.

res publica, *Latin*
DFPCQ.

ressaut, *French*
DA.

ressortir, *French*
OCM.

restaurateur, *French*
DFT; DFWPB.

restez, *French*
OCM.

Reststrahlen, *German*
GG.

résumé, *French*
DFPCQ; DFT; DFWPB;
DFWPN.

retardando, *Italian*
OCM.

retenant, *French*
OCM.

retenu, *French*
OCM/*retenant.*

retiré, *French*
DFWPB.

retiré, battement, *French*
LB/*retiré, temps.*

retiré, temps, *French*
LB.

retirer, *French*
OCM.

retiré sauté, *French*
LB/*retiré, temps.*

retroussage, *French*
DFWPB.

retroussé, *French*
DFT.

retrouvez, *French*
OCM.

retsina/retzina, *Modern Greek*
DFWPB.

réunis, *French*
OCM.

reus, *Latin*
DFWPN.

réveil, *French*
DFPCQ; OCM/*reveille.*

revenir, *French*
OCM.

re vera, *Latin*
DFT.

revera, *Latin*
DFPCQ; DFT/*re vera.*

révérence, *French*
LB.

rêverie, *French*
DFWPB.

rêveur, *French*
OCM.

revidiert, *German*
OCM.

rex, *Latin*
DFPCQ.

rex bibendi, *Latin*
DFPA.

rex iudaecorum (*or* Judaeorum),
Latin
DFWPN.

rez-de-chausée, *French*
DA.

Rezitativ, *German*
OCM.

rhythmé, *French*
OCM.

rhythmique, *French*
OCM/*rhythmé.*

rhythmisch, *German*
OCM.

Rhythmus, *German*
OCM.

ri, *Japanese*
JLE.

ria, *Spanish*
GG.

rialto, *Italian*
DFPCQ.

ribattuta, *Italian*
ICMM.

Riboyne Shel O'lem, *Yiddish*
JOY.

ributhe, *Scottish*
OCM.

ric-à-ric, *French*
DFT.

ricercare, *Italian*
DFWPB.

richettato, *Italian*
OCM.

richtig, *German*
OCM.

ricksha, *Japanese*
JLE.

rickshaw, *Japanese*
JLE.

ricotte, *Italian*
DFWPN.

rideau, *French*
GG; OCM.

ridotto, *Italian*
DFT; ICMM/*redoute*; OCM.

riduzione, *Italian*
OCM.

Riegel, *German*
GG.

rien, *French*
DFWPN.

rien ne va plus, *French*
DFWPB.

rifacimento, *Italian*
DFPCQ; DFT.

riffioramenti, *Italian*
DFPCQ.

rigolet, *French*
GG.

rigore, *Italian*
OCM.

rigor mortis, *Latin*
DFPA; DFT; DFWPB; DFWPN.

rigoroso, *Italian*
OCM/*rigore.*

rigueur, *French*
DFPCQ.

rijsttafel, *Dutch*
DFWPB.

rikisha, *Japanese*
JLE.

rikka, *Japanese*
JLE.

rilasciando, *Italian*
OCM.

rilasciante, *Italian*
OCM/*rilasciando.*

rilievo, *Italian*
DFT.

Rillenkarren, *German*
GG.

Rillenstein, *German*
GG.

rillettes, *French*
DFWPN.

rima chiusa, *Italian*
DFWPB.

rimettendo, *Italian*
OCM.

rimettendosi, *Italian*
OCM/*rimettendo.*

rin, *Japanese*
JLE.

rinceau, *French*
DFWPB.
rincon, *Spanish*
DSTE; GG.
rinforzando, *Italian*
DFPCQ; DFT; DFWPN; ICMM;
OCM.
rinforzato, *Italian*
OCM/*rinforzando.*
Rinnenkarren, *German*
GG.
Rinnental, *German*
GG.
rinzaffato, *Italian*
DFWPB.
rio, *Italian*
DFT.
rio, *Portuguese*
DFT.
rio, *Spanish*
DFWPN; GG.
riobitsu, *Japanese*
JLE.
rioyo, *Japanese*
JLE.
ripetizione, *Italian*
OCM.
ripieno, *Italian*
DFPCQ; DFT; DFWPB; ICMM;
OCM.
ripopée, *French*
DFT.
riposatamente, *Italian*
DFT.
riposato, *Italian*
OCM/*riposo.*
riposo, *Italian*
OCM.
riprendere, *Italian*
OCM.
ripresa, *Italian*
ICMM; OCM.
riscaldano, *Italian*
OCM.

ris de veau, *French*
DFPA; DFT; DFWPN.
riso, *Italian*
DFWPN.
risolutamente, *Italian*
OCM/*risoluto.*
risoluto, *Italian*
DFPCQ; OCM/*resoluto*; OCM.
Risorgimento, *Italian*
DFT.
risotto, *Italian*
DFT; DFWPB; DFWPN.
rispetto, *Italian*
OCM.
risposta, *Italian*
ICMM.
risqué, *French*
DFT; DFWPN.
rissolé, *French*
DFT; DFWPN.
ristringendo, *Italian*
OCM.
risus sardonicus, *Latin*
DFWPB.
risvegliato, *Italian*
DFT; ICMM; OCM.
ritardando, *Italian*
DFPA; DFPCQ; DFT; DFWPN;
ICMM; ICMM; OCM/*ritardare.*
ritardare, *Italian*
OCM.
ritardato, *Italian*
OCM/*ritardare.*
ritardo, *Italian*
OCM.
rite de passage, *pl.* **rites de passage,**
French
DFWPB.
ritenendo, *Italian*
OCM.
ritenente, *Italian*
OCM/*ritenendo.*
ritenuto, *Italian*
DFT; DFWPB; DFWPN;
ICMM; OCM.

ritmico, *Italian*
OCM.

ritmo, *Italian*
OCM.

ritmo di tre battute, *Italian*
OCM.

Ritornell, *German*
OCM/*ritornel.*

ritornello, *Italian*
DFPCQ; DFT; ICMM; OCM/
ritornel.

ritornello, *pl.* **ritornelli,** *Italian*
DFWPB.

ritorno, *Italian*
OCM.

ritournelle, *French*
ICMM; OCM/*ritornel.*

ritsu, *Japanese*
JLE.

ritterlich, *German*
OCM.

rive gauche, *French*
DFWPB.

riverso, al, *Italian*
OCM.

rivière, *French*
DFT.

rivolgimento, *Italian*
ICMM.

riz, *French*
DFT.

río, *Spanish*
DFT.

robe de chambre, *French*
DEP; DFT; DFWPB.

robe de cour, *French*
DFT.

robe de nuit, *French*
DFT.

robe de style, *French*
DFWPN.

robezo, *Spanish*
DSTE/*reboso.*

robusto, *Italian*
DFWPB.

rocaille, *French*
ACD; DFWPB; DFWPN.

roche moutonnée, *French*
GG.

roco, *Italian*
OCM.

rodeo, *Spanish*
DFWPN; DSTE.

Rogenstein, *German*
GG.

rognon, *French*
DFT.

roh, *German*
OCM.

Rohr, *German*
OCM.

roisin dub, *Irish*
DFPA.

Rōjū, *Japanese*
JLE.

rôle, *French*
DFPCQ; DFWPB.

rôle de l'équipage, *French*
DFPA.

Rollschweller, *German*
OCM.

Rolltrommel, *German*
OCM.

rolpens, *Dutch*
DFT.

romaika, *Modern Greek*
ICMM.

Romaji, *Japanese*
JLE.

romal, *Spanish*
DSTE/*ramal.*

romalis, *Spanish*
OCM.

roman, *French*
DFWPN.

roman à clef, *French*
DFPA; DFT; DFWPB; DFWPN.

roman à thèse, *French*
DFPA; DFWPB.
roman bourgeois, *French*
DFWPN.
romance, *French*
OCM.
romance, *Spanish*
OCM.
romance sans paroles, *French*
OCM.
romanesca, *Italian*
ICMM; OCM.
romanesque, *French*
OCM/*romanesca.*
roman expérimental, *French*
DFWPB.
roman-fleuve, *French*
DFWPB.
roman poétique, *French*
DFWPB.
roman policier, *French*
DFPA; DFWPB.
romanza, *Italian*
DFPCQ; DFT; OCM.
Romazi, *Japanese*
JLE.
rombando, *Italian*
OCM.
romer, *German*
ACD.
rond, *French*
LB.
rond, en, *French*
LB.
ronda, *Spanish*
OCM.
rondalla, *Spanish*
OCM/*ronda.*
rond de jambe, *French*
DFWPB; DFWPN; LB.
rond de jambe à terre, *French*
LB/*rond de jambe.*

rond de jambe à terre, demi-grand,
French
LB/*rond de jambe.*
rond de jambe à terre, grand, *French*
LB/*rond de jambe.*
rond de jambe en l'air, *French*
LB/*rond de jambe.*
rond de jambe en l'air, demi-grand,
French
LB/*rond de jambe.*
rond de jambe en l'air, grand, *French*
LB/*rond de jambe.*
rond de jambe en l'air sauté, *French*
LB/*rond de jambe.*
rond de jambe fermé, *French*
LB/*rond de jambe.*
rond de jambe jeté en l'air, *French*
LB/*rond de jambe.*
rond de jambe ouvert, *French*
LB/*rond de jambe.*
rond de jambe piqué, *French*
LB/*rond de jambe.*
ronde, *French*
ICMM/*semibreve;* OCM.
rondeau, *French*
DFWPN; ICMM/*rondo.*
rondeña, *Spanish*
OCM.
rondena, *Spanish*
ICMM.
rondino, *Italian*
DFPCQ.
rondo, *French*
ICMM.
rondo, *Italian*
DFPCQ; DFWPN.
rondoletto, *Italian*
DFPCQ; DFT.
ronds de bras, *French*
LB.
ronds de jambe balancé, *French*
LB/*rond de jambe.*
ronds de jambe en l'air entournant,
French
LB/*rond de jambe.*

ronin, *Japanese*
JLE.

rontondo, *Italian*
DA.

ropak, *Russian*
GG.

Roquefort, *French*
DFWPN.

rosalia, *Italian*
DFT.

rosbif, *French*
DFT.

rosé, *French*
DFWPB.

rose du Barry, *French*
ACD; DFT.

Rosh Hashanah, *Hebrew*
DFPA; DFWPN.

Rosh Hashanah, *Yiddish*
JOY.

Rosh Hashona, *Yiddish*
JOY/*Rosh Hashanah.*

Rosh Hashonah, *Yiddish*
JOY/*Rosh Hashanah.*

Rosh Hoshanah, *Yiddish*
JOY/*Rosh Hashanah.*

Roshi, *Japanese*
JLE.

rosso antico, *Italian*
DFWPB; DFWPN.

rostra, *Latin*
DFPCQ.

rota, *Latin*
OCM.

rotation, *French*
LB.

rôti, *French*
DFT; DFWPN.

rôtisserie, *French*
DFT; DFWPB; DFWPN.

rôtissoire, *French*
DFWPN.

Rotliegende, *German*
GG.

rotondo, *Italian*
OCM.

rotunda, *Italian*
DA.

roué, *French*
DFPCQ; DFT; DFWPB;
DFWPN.

rouelle de veau, *French*
DFT.

rouge, *French*
DFPCQ; DFWPB; DFWPN.

rouge et noir, *French*
DFPCQ; DFT; DFWPN.

rouge-et-noir, *French*
DFWPB.

rouge-et-noire, *French*
DFPA.

roulade, *French*
DFT; DFWPB; DFWPN;
ICMM; OCM.

roulant, *French*
OCM.

roulante, *French*
OCM/*roulant.*

rouleau, *French*
DFT.

roulette, *French*
DFPCQ; DFWPN.

roux, *French*
DFT; DFWPB; DFWPN.

rov, *Yiddish*
JOY.

rovescio, al, *Italian*
ICMM; OCM.

royale, *French*
LB.

royale double, *French*
LB.

royale double fermé, *French*
LB/*royale double.*

royale double ouvert, *French*
LB/*royale double.*

rubato, *Italian*
DFPCQ; DFT; DFWPB;
DFWPN; ICMM.

Rucksack, *German*
DFWPN.

rudement, *French*
OCM.

rue, *French*
DFT.

rueda, *Spanish*
OCM.

ruggiero, *Italian*
ICMM.

Ruhe, *German*
OCM.

Ruhepunkt, *German*
OCM.

Ruhezeichen, *German*
OCM/*Ruhepunkt*.

Rühne, *German*
ICMM/*scena*.

Rührtrommel, *German*
OCM.

Rührung, *German*
OCM.

ruiné, *French*
DFT.

rumaki, *Japanese*
JLE.

Rumpffläche, *German*
GG.

rupee, *Hindi*
DFWPB.

rurales, *Spanish*
DSTE.

ruse de guerre, *French*
DEP.

rus in urbe, *Latin*
DFPA.

russa, *Italian*
OCM/*russo*; OCM.

russo, *Italian*
OCM.

Rute, *German*
OCM.

Ruthe, *German*
OCM/*Rute*.

ruvido, *Italian*
OCM.

rynok, *Russian*
MRWEW/*20*.

ryo, *Japanese*
JLE.

Ryobu (Shinto), *Japanese*
JLE.

ryokan, *Japanese*
JLE.

ryot, *Anglo-Indian*
DFT.

rythme, *French*
OCM.

rythmique, *French*
OCM/*rythme*.

Ryukyu, *Japanese*
JLE.

Ryukyuan, *Japanese*
JLE.

S

Sabbati Zvi, *Yiddish*
JOY.

sabe, *Spanish*
DSTE.

sabi, *Japanese*
JLE.

sabkha, *Arabic*
GG.

sabot, *French*
DFWPN.

sacate, *Spanish*
DSTE/*zacate*.

sacaton, *Spanish*
DSTE/*zacaton*.

saccadé, *French*
OCM.

sachel, *Yiddish*
JOY.

Sackgeige, *German*
ICMM.

Sackpfeife, *German*
ICMM; OCM.

sacré, *French*
DFT.

sacre bleu, *French*
DFPA.

sacré bleu, *French*
DFT.

sacre rappresentazioni, *Italian*
OCM.

saeta, *Spanish*
ICMM; OCM.

safari, *Arabic*
DFT.

saguaro, *Spanish*
DSTE.

saheb, *Arabic*
DFT/*sahib*.

saheb, *Hindi*
DFT/*sahib*.

sahib, *Arabic*
DFT; DFWPN.

sahib, *Hindi*
DFT; DFWPB.

sahibah, *Arabic*
DFT.

sahibah, *Hindi*
DFT.

saignant, *French*
DFT.

sainete, *Spanish*
OCM.

Saite, *German*
ICMM; OCM.

Saiten-instrument, *German*
ICMM.

Saitenspiel, *German*
ICMM.

sakai, *Japanese*
JLE.

sakaki, *Japanese*
JLE.

sake, *Japanese*
DFT; JLE.

sakura, *Japanese*
JLE.

sal, *Latin*
DFT.

sala, *Spanish*
DSTE.

salaam, *Arabic*
DFT; DFWPN.

salaam, *Hindi*
DFWPB.

salaam aleikum, *Arabic*
DFPA; DFT/*salaam.*

salada, *Spanish*
GG.

salam, *Arabic*
DFT/*salaam.*

salar, *Spanish*
GG.

Sal Atticum, *Latin*
DFPA; DFPCQ; DFT/*sal*;
DFWPN.

Salband, *German*
GG.

salé, *French*
DFT.

salina, *Spanish*
GG.

salle, *French*
DEP; DFT.

salle, au tour de la, *French*
LB.

salle à manger, *French*
DFPA; DFT/*salle.*

salle d'armes, *French*
DFT/*salle.*

salle d'attente, *French*
DFPA.

salle de danse, *French*
DFT/*salle.*

salle de jeu, *French*
DFPA.

salle privée, *French*
DFWPB.

salmagundi, *French*
DFWPN.

salmi, *French*
DFWPB; DFWPN.

salmis, *French*
DFT; DFWPN.

salmo, *Italian*
OCM.

salon, *French*
DFT; DFWPN.

Salon d'Automne, *French*
LP.

Salon des Indépendants, *French*
LP.

Salon des Refusés, *French*
LP.

saloperie, *French*
DFT.

salpicon, *French*
DFWPB.

salpinx, *Greek*
ICMM.

saltando, *Italian*
ICMM/*sautillé*; OCM.

saltarello, *Italian*
DFT; DFWPB; ICMM.

saltarello, *Spanish*
ICMM.

saltato, *Italian*
ICMM/*sautillé*; OCM/*saltando.*

salterio, *Italian*
ICMM/*psaltery.*

saltierra, *Spanish*
GG.

salud, *Spanish*
DFT; DFWPN.

saludos, *Spanish*
DFT.

salut, *French*
DFT.

salute, *Italian*
DFT.

salve!, *Latin*
DFPCQ.

salve, *Latin*
DFPA.

salve regina, *Latin*
ICMM.

salvo conducto, *Spanish*
DSTE.

sama, *Japanese*
DFT.

samadh, *Hindi*
DFT.

samadhi, *Hindi*
DFT.

samba, *Spanish*
DFWPN.

sambuque, *Hebrew*
ICMM.

samisen, *Japanese*
ICMM; JLE.

samizdat, *Russian*
DFT; MRWEW/17.

samo, *Japanese*
DFT.

samo-tori, *Japanese*
DFT/*samo.*

samovar, *Russian*
DFT; DFWPN.

sampan, *Chinese*
DFT.

samsien, *Japanese*
JLE.

sämtlich, *German*
OCM.

samurai, *Japanese*
DFT; DFWPN; JLE.

samurai, *pl.* **samurai,** *Japanese*
DFWPB.

san, *Japanese*
DFT; JLE.

sanatorium, *Latin*
DFPCQ.

sanbenito, *Spanish*
DFWPB.

sanctum, *Latin*
DFPCQ.

sanctum (sanctorum), *Latin*
DFWPB.

sanctum sanctorum, *Latin*
DFPA; DFPCQ; DFT; DFWPN.

sanctus, *Latin*
DFWPB; ICMM; OCM.

sandhi, *Sanskrit*
DFWPN.

sandia, *Spanish*
GG.

sandur, *Icelandic*
GG.

sanft, *German*
DFT; OCM.

sang-de-boeuf, *French*
DFT.

sang-froid, *French*
DFPA; DFPCQ; DFT.

sangfroid, *French*
DFWPN.

sanglier, *French*
DFT.

sanglot, *French*
ICMM.

sangría, *Spanish*
DFT.

sanhedrin, *Yiddish*
JOY.

san hsien, *Chinese*
ICMM.

sanpaku, *Japanese*
JLE.

Sanron, *Japanese*
JLE.

sans, *French*
DFPCQ; DFT; DFWPN; OCM.

sans-culotte, *French*
DFT.

sansculotte, *French*
DFWPB.

sans culottes, *French*
DFPA.

sans Dieu, rien, *French*
DFPCQ.

sans doute, *French*
DFPCQ; DFT/*sans.*

sansei, *Japanese*
JLE.

sans mélange, *French*
DFT/*sans.*

sans pareil, *French*
DFPA; DFT/*sans.*

sans peur et sans reproche, *French*
DEP.

sans souci, *French*
DFPA; DFPCQ; DFT/*sans;*
DFWPN.

santé, *French*
DFPCQ; DFT.

san tsai, *Chinese*
ACD.

Sapporo, *Japanese*
JLE.

saraband, *French*
DFWPN.

sarabande, *French*
ICMM.

sarape, *Spanish*
DSTE/*zarape.*

sardana, *Spanish*
ICMM.

sarepe, *Spanish*
DSTE/*zarape.*

sari, *Hindi*
DFWPB; DFWPN.

sarode, *Hindi*
ICMM.

Sartor Resartus, *Latin*
DFT; DEP; DFPCQ.

Sasankwa, *Japanese*
JLE.

sasanqua, *Japanese*
JLE.

Sasebo, *Japanese*
JLE.

sashimi, *Japanese*
JLE.

sassofono, *Italian*
OCM.

sassophone, *Italian*
ICMM.

sat-bhai, *Hindi*
DFT.

sate, *Malay*
DFT.

satis accipere, *Latin*
DFPCQ.

satis, superque, *Latin*
DFPCQ.

satori, *Japanese*
JLE.

satsuma, *Japanese*
JLE.

Sattel, *German*
ICMM.

Saturnalia, *Latin*
DFWPN.

Saturno rege, *Latin*
DFPCQ.

Satz, *German*
ICMM; OCM.

sauce à la menthe, *French*
DFT/*sauce.*

sauce au beurre, *French*
DFT/*sauce.*

sauce aux câpres, *French*
DFT/*sauce.*

sauce béarnaise, *French*
DFT/*sauce.*

sauce blanche, *French*
DFT/*sauce;* DFWPN.

sauce financière, *French*
DFT/*sauce.*

sauce hollandaise, *French*
DFT/*sauce.*

sauce meunière, *French*
DFT/*sauce.*

sauce piquante, *French*
DFT/*sauce*; DFWPN.

sauce relevée, *French*
DFT/*sauce*.

sauce verte, *French*
DFT/*sauce*.

saucisse, *French*
DFT.

saucisson, *French*
DFT/*saucisse*; DFWPN.

saudades, *Portuguese*
OCM.

Sauerbraten, *German*
DFT; DFWPN.

Sauerkraut, *German*
DFPCQ; DFWPN.

saumon, *French*
DFT.

sauna, *Finnish*
DFWPB.

saut de basque, *French*
LB.

saut de chat, *French*
LB.

saut de flèche, *French*
LB.

sauté, *French*
DFT; DFWPB; DFWPN; LB.

sautillé, *French*
ICMM; OCM.

sauvage, *French*
DFT.

sauve qui peut, *French*
DFPCQ.

savannah, *Spanish*
DFWPN.

savant, *French*
DFPCQ; DFT; DFT; DFWPB.

savate, *French*
DFT.

savez, *Spanish*
DSTE/*sabe*.

savoir faire, *French*
DFPCQ; DFWPB; DFWPN.

savoir-faire, *French*
DFPA; DFT.

savoir vivre, *French*
DFPA; DFPCQ; DFWPB;
DFWPN.

savoir-vivre, *French*
DFT.

Saxofon, *German*
OCM/*saxofonia*.

saxofonia, *Italian*
OCM.

saxofono, *Italian*
OCM/*saxofonia*.

saynète, *French*
OCM/*sainete*.

sayonara, *Japanese*
DFT; JLE.

sbalzato, *Italian*
OCM/*sbalz.* .

scacciapensieri, *Italian*
OCM.

scaglia, *Italian*
GG.

scagliola, *Italian*
ACD.

scala, *Italian*
ICMM/*scale*.

scala enigmatica, *Italian*
ICMM.

scala enigmatica, *New Latin*
OCM.

scalpellino, *pl.* scalpellini, *Italian*
DFWPB.

scampanata, *Italian*
OCM.

scampanio, *Italian*
ICMM.

scampi, *Italian*
DFT.

scampi *pl.*, *Italian*
DFWPB.

scandalum magnatum, *Latin*
DEP.

scannello 316

scannello, *Italian*
ICMM.

scannetto, *Italian*
ICMM.

Scaramouche, *Italian*
DFWPN.

scemando, *Italian*
OCM.

scena, *Italian*
DFPCQ; DFT; ICMM.

scenario, *Italian*
ICMM.

Scenarium, *German*
OCM.

scène, *French*
ICMM/*scena*; LB.

scène à faire, *French*
DFWPN.

scène d'action, *French*
LB.

Schablone, *German*
ICMM.

Schadenfreude, *German*
DFWPB.

Schale, *German*
OCM.

Schalen, *German*
OCM/*Schale*.

schalkhaft, *German*
OCM.

Schall-becken, *German*
ICMM.

Schallbecken, *German*
OCM.

Schalmei, *German*
ICMM.

Schalmey, *German*
ICMM.

Schalmuse, *German*
ICMM.

Schalstein, *German*
GG.

scharf, *German*
OCM.

schärfe, *German*
OCM.

schatchen, *Yiddish*
DFT; JOY.

schauerig, *German*
OCM/*schaurig*.

schauerlich, *German*
OCM/*schaurig*.

schaurig, *German*
OCM.

schaygetz, *Yiddish*
DFWPN.

Schelle, *German*
OCM.

Schellen, *German*
ICMM; OCM/*Schelle*.

Schellenbaum, *German*
OCM.

Schellengeläute, *German*
OCM.

Schellentrommel, *German*
ICMM; OCM.

schelmisch, *German*
OCM.

schema, *Latin*
LP.

Scherz, *German*
OCM.

scherzando, *Italian*
DFPCQ; DFT; DFWPB;
DFWPN; ICMM; OCM.

scherzante, *Italian*
OCM/*scherzando*.

scherzare, *Italian*
OCM.

scherzetto, *Italian*
OCM.

scherzevole, *Italian*
OCM/*scherzando*.

scherzevolmente, *Italian*
OCM/*scherzando*.

scherzi, *Italian*
OCM/*scherzo*.

scherzino, *Italian*
OCM/*scherzetto.*

scherzo, *Italian*
DFPCQ; DFT; DFWPB;
DFWPN; ICMM; OCM.

scherzosamente, *Italian*
OCM/*scherzoso.*

scherzoso, *Italian*
DFPCQ; ICMM; OCM.

schiacciato rilievo, *Italian*
DFWPB.

schicker, *Yiddish*
DFWPN.

Schiefer, *German*
GG.

schiefrig, *German*
GG.

schietto, *Italian*
OCM.

schiksa, *Yiddish*
DFWPN.

Schiller, *German*
GG.

schisma, *Greek*
ICMM.

schizzo, *Italian*
ICMM/*sketch.*

Schlacht, *German*
OCM.

schlack, *Yiddish*
JOY/*shlock*; JOY.

Schlag, *German*
OCM.

schlag, *Yiddish*
JOY.

Schlägel, *German*
OCM.

schlagen, *German*
OCM.

Schlaginstrumente, *German*
ICMM; OCM.

Schlagobers, *German*
DFT.

Schlagwort, *German*
DFT.

Schlagzither, *German*
ICMM; OCM.

Schlangenrohr, *German*
ICMM; OCM.

Schlegel, *German*
OCM.

Schleifer, *German*
OCM/*slide.*

schlemiehl, *Yiddish*
JOY.

schlemiel, *Yiddish*
DFT; JOY/*shlemiel*; JOY.

schlemiel/schlemihl, *Yiddish*
DFWPB.

schlemihl, *Yiddish*
DFWPN; JOY.

schlemozzle/schemozzle/shemozzle,
Yiddish
DFWPB.

schlep, *Yiddish*
JOY.

schleppend, *German*
DFT; OCM.

schleppen, nicht, *German*
ICMM.

Schlieren, *German*
GG.

schlimazel, *Yiddish*
JOY/*shlimazl.*

schlock, *Yiddish*
JOY/*shlock.*

schlok, *Yiddish*
JOY.

schloomp, *Yiddish*
JOY.

Schlummerlied, *German*
OCM.

schlump, *Yiddish*
JOY.

Schluss, *German*
OCM.

Schlüssel, *German*
  ICMM; OCM.

Schlusszeichen, *German*
  OCM.

schmachtend, *German*
  OCM.

schmaltz, *Yiddish*
  DFT; DFWPB; JOY; JOY/
  shmaltz.

Schmalz, *German*
  OCM.

schmalz, *Yiddish*
  DFWPN.

schmeichelnd, *German*
  OCM.

schmelzend, *German*
  OCM.

Schmerz, *German*
  OCM.

schmetternd, *German*
  OCM.

schmo, *Yiddish*
  JOY.

schmuck, *Yiddish*
  DFWPB; JOY.

Schnabel, *German*
  ICMM.

Schnabelflöte, *German*
  ICMM; OCM.

Schnapps, *German*
  DFWPN.

schnaps, *Yiddish*
  JOY/*shnaps.*

Schnarre, *German*
  OCM.

schneidend, *German*
  OCM.

schneider, *Yiddish*
  JOY.

schnell, *German*
  DFT; DFWPN.

Schneller, *German*
  ICMM.

Schnitzel, *German*
  DFWPN.

schnook, *Yiddish*
  JOY.

schnorrer, *Yiddish*
  DFWPB; JOY/*shnorrer.*

schola cantorum, *Latin*
  DFPA.

scholium, *Latin*
  DFPCQ.

schorre, *Dutch*
  GG.

Schottisch, *German*
  OCM/*schottische.*

Schottische, *German*
  ICMM.

Schrammkapelle, *German*
  OCM.

schrittmässig, *German*
  OCM.

schrittweise, *German*
  OCM/*schrittmässig.*

Schrund, *German*
  GG.

schüchtern, *German*
  OCM.

Schuhplattler, *German*
  ICMM.

Schulflöte, *German*
  OCM.

Schuppenstruktur, *German*
  GG/*schuppen* structure.

Schuss, *German*
  DFWPB.

schütteln, *German*
  OCM.

schwach, *German*
  OCM.

schwächer, *German*
  OCM/*schwach.*

schwankend, *German*
  OCM.

Schwebung, *German*
  OCM.

Schweigen, *German*
OCM.

Schweinehund, *German*
DFT.

schwellen, *German*
OCM.

schwer, *German*
OCM.

schwermütig, *German*
OCM.

schwermutsvoll, *German*
OCM/*schwermütig.*

schwindend, *German*
OCM.

Schwirrholz, *German*
OCM/*thunder stick*; OCM.

Schwung, *German*
OCM.

scialumo, *Italian*
ICMM.

scil(icet), *Latin*
DFWPB.

scilicet, *Latin*
DFPA; DFPCQ; DFWPN.

scintilla, *Latin*
DFPCQ.

scintillante, *Italian*
DFT; OCM.

scioltamente, *Italian*
OCM/*sciolto.*

sciolto, *Italian*
DFPCQ; DFT; OCM.

sciolto, con scioltezza, *Italian*
ICMM.

scire facias, *Latin*
DFPA; DFPCQ; DFT.

scivolando, *Italian*
OCM.

scordato, *Italian*
DFT; OCM.

scordatura, *Italian*
DFT; ICMM; OCM.

scorrendo, *Italian*
DFT; ICMM; OCM.

scorrevole, *Italian*
ICMM; OCM/*scorrendo.*

scozzese, *Italian*
DFPCQ; OCM.

scripsit, *Latin*
DFT.

scriptor classicus, *Latin*
DFWPN.

scriptor proletarius, *Latin*
DFWPN.

scrittura, *Italian*
ICMM.

scrutoire, *French*
ACD.

scucito, *Italian*
OCM.

sculpsit, *Latin*
DFPA; DFT.

scusa, *Italian*
DFWPN.

scusate, *Italian*
DFT/*scusi.*

scusatemi, *Italian*
DFT/*scusi.*

scusi, *Italian*
DFT.

sdegno, *Italian*
OCM.

sdegnoso, *Italian*
DFT.

sdrucciolando, *Italian*
OCM.

se, *Italian*
OCM.

sê, *Chinese*
ICMM.

séance, *French*
DFPCQ; DFT; DFWPB;
DFWPN.

séance d'essais, *French*
DFWPB.

sec, *French*
DFWPB; DFWPN; OCM.

secco, *Italian*
DFWPB; DFWPN; LP; OCM.

sèche, *French*
OCM/*sec.*

sechs, *German*
OCM.

Sechzehntel, *German*
ICMM/*semiquaver*; OCM.

Sechzehntelnote, *German*
OCM/*Sechzehntel.*

second, *French*
LB.

seconda, *Italian*
OCM/*secondo.*

secondando, *Italian*
OCM.

seconda volta, *Italian*
DFT; DFT/*volta.*

seconde, *French*
LB/*second.*

seconde, à la, *French*
LB.

seconde, en, *French*
LB.

seconde, grande, *French*
LB.

seconde position, *French*
LB/*pieds, cinq positions des.*

secondo, *Italian*
OCM.

secrétaire, *French*
DFT; DFWPB.

secrétaire à abattant, *French*
DFWPB.

Section d'Or, La, *French*
LP.

Secundarius, *German*
OCM.

secundum artem, *Latin*
DEP; DFPCQ.

secundum legem, *Latin*
DFPA.

secundum naturam, *Latin*
DFPCQ.

secundum usum, *Latin*
DFPA.

se defendendo, *Latin*
DFPCQ.

Seder, *Yiddish*
JOY.

sedilia *pl.*, *Latin*
DFWPB.

Seele, *German*
OCM.

Sefer Torah, *Yiddish*
JOY.

Sefirah, *Yiddish*
JOY.

Sefiras Haomer, *Yiddish*
JOY.

segarrito, *Spanish*
DSTE/*cigarrito.*

segno, *Italian*
DFPCQ; DFT; ICMM; OCM.

segue, *Italian*
DFPCQ; DFT; ICMM; OCM.

seguendo, *Italian*
OCM/*seguente.*

seguente, *Italian*
OCM.

seguidilla, *Spanish*
DFT; ICMM; OCM.

seguro, *Spanish*
DSTE.

sêh, *Chinese*
ICMM/*sê.*

se habla español, *Spanish*
DFT.

Sehnsucht, *German*
OCM.

sehr, *German*
OCM.

sei, *Italian*
OCM.

seicento, *Italian*
LP.

seiche, *French*
GG.

seif, *Arabic*
GG.

seigneur, *French*
DFT.

Seite, *German*
OCM.

sel, *French*
DFT.

selle, *French*
DFT.

selle de mouton, *French*
DFT/*selle.*

semibiscroma, *Italian*
OCM.

semicroma, *Italian*
ICMM/*semiquaver*; ICMM;
OCM.

semiditas, *Latin*
ICMM.

semifusa, *Italian*
OCM.

semifusa, *Latin*
ICMM.

semiminima, *Latin*
ICMM/*crotchet*; OCM.

semiseria, *Italian*
ICMM.

semolino, *Italian*
DFWPN.

semper, *Latin*
DFT.

semper et ubique, *Latin*
DFT/*semper.*

semper felix, *Latin*
DFPCQ.

semper fidelis, *Latin*
DFPCQ; DFT/*semper*; DFWPN.

semper fidelis, *pl.* **semper fideles,**
Latin
DFWPB.

semper idem, *Latin*
DEP.

semper idem (*fem.*** eadem),** *Latin*
DFPCQ.

semper paratus, *Latin*
DEP; DFPCQ; DFT/*semper*;
DFWPN.

semplice, *Italian*
DFPCQ; DFT; ICMM; OCM.

semplicità, *Italian*
OCM/*semplice.*

sempre, *Italian*
DFPCQ; DFT; ICMM; OCM.

sen, *Japanese*
JLE.

senatus consultum, *Latin*
DFPCQ.

sendai, *Japanese*
JLE.

Sendai (virus), *Japanese*
JLE.

sendero, *Spanish*
DSTE.

senhor, *Portuguese*
DFT.

senhora, *Portuguese*
DFT/*senhor.*

senhorita, *Portuguese*
DFT/*senhor.*

señor, *Spanish*
DFT; DFWPN; DSTE.

señora, *Spanish*
DFT; DFWPN.

Señor Don, *Spanish*
DFT/*señor.*

señorita, *Spanish*
DFT; DFWPN; DSTE.

señorito, *Spanish*
DFT.

sensibile, *Italian*
OCM.

sensibilità, *Italian*
OCM/*sensibile.*

sensorium, *Latin*
DFPCQ.

sensu bono, *Latin*
DFPA.

sensu lato, *Latin*
DFPA.

sensu malo, *Latin*
DFPA.

sensu proprio, *Latin*
DFPA.

sentito, *Italian*
OCM.

sentoku, *Japanese*
JLE.

senza, *Italian*
DFT; ICMM; OCM.

senza accompagnamento, *Italian*
OCM.

senza organe, *Italian*
DFPCQ.

senza organo, *Italian*
DFT/*senza.*

senza replica, *Italian*
DFPCQ; DFT/*senza.*

senza sordini, *Italian*
DFT/*senza*; OCM/*senza ordino.*

senza sordino, *Italian*
OCM.

senza stromenti, *Italian*
DFT/*senza.*

senza tempo, *Italian*
DFT/*senza.*

separatio a mensa et toro, *Latin*
DFPCQ.

séparé, *French*
OCM.

Sephardi, *Yiddish*
HFY; JOY.

Sephardic, *Yiddish*
JOY.

Sephardim, *Hebrew*
DFWPN.

Sephardim, *Yiddish*
JOY.

sepoy, *Anglo-Indian*
DFT.

seppa, *Japanese*
JLE.

seppa dai, *Japanese*
JLE.

seppia, *Italian*
DFT.

seppuku, *Japanese*
DFT; JLE.

sept, *French*
LB; OCM.

Septett, *German*
ICMM/*septet.*

septetto, *Italian*
DFPCQ; DFT; ICMM/*septet.*

septième, *French*
OCM.

septum, *Latin*
DFPCQ.

septuor, *French*
ICMM/*septet.*

sequentia, *Latin*
ICMM/*sequence.*

sequentiae, *Latin*
DFWPN.

sequitur, *Latin*
DFT.

sérac, *Swiss French*
DFT.

serai, *Hindi*
DFT.

serai, *Persian*
DFT.

serape, *Spanish*
DFT; DSTE/*zarape.*

serdab, *Arabic*
DFT.

serena, *Italian*
ICMM.

serenade, *French*
OCM.

sérénade, *French*
ICMM/*serenade.*

serenata, *Italian*
DFPCQ; DFWPB; ICMM/
serenade; ICMM.

serenatella, *Italian*
OCM.

serenitá, *Italian*
OCM/*sereno.*

sereno, *Italian*
OCM.

seria, *Italian*
OCM/*serio*; OCM.

seriamente, *Italian*
OCM.

seriatim, *Latin*
DFPCQ.

seriatim, *New Latin*
DFT.

sérieuse, *French*
OCM/*sérieux.*

sérieux, *French*
OCM.

sérieux, *fem.* **sérieuse,** *French*
DFWPB.

serinette, *French*
DFWPB; OCM.

serio, *Italian*
OCM.

seriosa, *Italian*
OCM/*serio.*

seriosamente, *Italian*
OCM.

serioso, *Italian*
OCM/*serio.*

serpentone, *Italian*
ICMM; OCM.

serrando, *Italian*
OCM.

serrant, *French*
OCM/*serrando.*

serrato, *Italian*
OCM/*serrando.*

serré, *French*
LB; OCM/*serrando.*

serrer les reins, *French*
LB.

serus in cælum redeas, *Latin*

serviette, *French*
DFWPN.

Servus Servorum Dei, *Latin*
DFT/*servus.*

sesqui, *Latin*
DFPCQ.

sesquialtera, *Latin*
ICMM.

sesquipedalia verba, *Latin*
DFPA; DFPCQ; DFT.

sesquitone, *Latin*
ICMM.

sesshin, *Japanese*
JLE.

sesterce, *Latin*
DFWPN.

sestetto, *Italian*
DFPCQ; DFT; ICMM/*sextet*;
OCM/*sextet.*

sestina, *Italian*
ICMM/*sextolet.*

sestuor, *French*
OCM/*sextet.*

seter, *Norwegian*
GG.

se tirer d'affaire, *French*
DFPCQ.

sette, *Italian*
OCM.

seufzend, *German*
OCM.

seul, *French*
OCM.

seule, *French*
OCM/*seul.*

seules, *French*
OCM/*seul.*

seuls, *French*
OCM/*seul.*

severamente, *Italian*
OCM/*severo.*

severo, *Italian*
OCM.

sevillana, *Spanish*
ICMM; OCM.

sext, *Latin*
ICMM.

Sextett, *German*
ICMM/*sextet*; OCM/*sextet*.

sextette, *French*
OCM/*sextet*.

Sextole, *German*
ICMM/*sextolet*.

sextolet, *French*
ICMM.

sextuor, *French*
ICMM/*sextet*.

sextus, *Latin*
ICMM.

sfogato, *Italian*
ICMM; OCM.

sfoggiando, *Italian*
OCM.

sforzando, *Italian*
DFPCQ; DFT; DFWPB;
DFWPN; ICMM; OCM.

sforzato, *Italian*
DFPCQ; DFT/*sforzando*; ICMM;
OCM/*sforzando*.

sfregazzi, *Italian*
DFWPN.

sfumatezza, *Italian*
DFWPB.

sfumato, *Italian*
DFT; DFWPB; DFWPN; LP.

sgambato, *Italian*
OCM.

sgraffiato, *Italian*
ACD.

sgraffito, *Italian*
ACD; DFT; DFWPN; LP.

sgraffito, *pl.* **sgraffiti,** *Italian*
DFWPB.

sh-, *Yiddish*
HFY; JOY.

Shabbatsi Zvi, *Yiddish*
JOY/*Sabbati Zvi*.

Shabbes, *Yiddish*
JOY.

Shabbes goy, *Yiddish*
JOY.

shabbos, *Hebrew*
DFWPN.

shabka, *Arabic*
GG.

Shabtsitvainik, *Yiddish*
JOY.

Shabtsi Zvi, *Yiddish*
JOY/*Sabbati Zvi*.

Shabuot, *Yiddish*
JOY/*Shevuoth*.

shachris, *Yiddish*
JOY.

shadchen, *Yiddish*
DFT; DFWPN; JOY.

Shah, *Yiddish*
HFY; JOY.

shaku, *Japanese*
JLE.

shaku bioshi, *Japanese*
ICMM.

shakudo, *Japanese*
JLE.

shakuhachi, *Japanese*
ICMM; JLE.

shalom, *Hebrew*
DFT.

Shalom, *Yiddish*
HFY; JOY; JOY/*sholem*.

shalom aleichem, *Hebrew*
DFWPN.

shalom alekhem, *Hebrew*
DFPA.

shaman, *Russian*
DFT.

shammes, *Yiddish*
DFT; JOY.

shammus, *Yiddish*
JOY/*shammes*.

shamus, *Yiddish*
HFY; JOY/*shammes*.

shashlik, *Russian*
DFWPB.

shaygets, *Yiddish*
JOY.

shayner Yid, *Yiddish*
JOY.

shaytl, *Yiddish*
JOY.

Shechinah, *Yiddish*
JOY.

sheeny, *Yiddish*
JOY.

Shehecheyanu, *Yiddish*
JOY.

sheik, *Arabic*
DFT.

sheikh, *Arabic*
DFWPB.

sheitel, *Yiddish*
JOY/*shaytl.*

shekel, *Yiddish*
JOY.

Shekhinah, *Yiddish*
JOY/*Shechinah.*

Shema, *Yiddish*
JOY.

Shema Yisrael, *Yiddish*
JOY.

Shemona Esray, *Yiddish*
JOY.

shemozzl, *Yiddish*
JOY.

shêng, *Chinese*
ICMM.

shereef, *Arabic*
DFT.

sherif, *Arabic*
DFT/*shereef.*

sherpa, *Tibetan*
DFWPB.

Shevuoth, *Yiddish*
JOY.

sheygets, *Yiddish*
HFY.

shiah, *Arabic*
DFWPN.

shiatsu, *Japanese*
JLE.

shibuichi, *Japanese*
JLE.

shibuichi-doshi, *Japanese*
JLE.

shiddach, *Yiddish*
JOY.

Shiga (bacillus), *Japanese*
JLE.

shikii, *Japanese*
JLE.

Shikimi, *Japanese*
JLE.

shikken, *Japanese*
JLE.

shikker, *Yiddish*
DFT; HFY; JOY.

shiksa, *Yiddish*
DFT; DFWPB; JOY.

shikse, *Yiddish*
HFY.

shikseh, *Yiddish*
JOY.

shimonoseki, *Japanese*
JLE.

shimose (powder), *Japanese*
JLE.

Shin, *Japanese*
JLE.

Shingen tsuba, *Japanese*
JLE.

Shingon, *Japanese*
JLE.

shinkansen, *Japanese*
JLE.

Shin-shu, *Japanese*
JLE.

shintai, *Japanese*
JLE.

Shinto, *Japanese*
JLE; JLE.

shippo (ware), *Japanese*
JLE.

shirakashi, *Japanese*
JLE.

shish kebab, *Arabic*
DFWPN.

shish kebab, *Turkish*
DFWPB.

shitogi tsuba, *Japanese*
JLE.

shivah, *Yiddish*
JOY.

shizoku, *Japanese*
JLE.

Shizuoka, *Japanese*
JLE.

shlemazl, *Yiddish*
HFY.

shlemiehl, *Yiddish*
JOY/*shlemiel.*

shlemiel, *Yiddish*
HFY; JOY.

shlemihl, *Yiddish*
JOY/*shlemiel.*

shlemozzl, *Yiddish*
JOY/*shemozzl.*

shlep, *Yiddish*
DFT; HFY; JOY.

shlepper, *Yiddish*
JOY.

shlimazl, *Yiddish*
JOY.

shlock, *Yiddish*
DFT; HFY; JOY.

shloomp, *Yiddish*
JOY.

shlub, *Yiddish*
JOY.

shlump, *Yiddish*
DFT; HFY; JOY.

shm-, *Yiddish*
HFY/*sh-*; JOY.

Shma, *Yiddish*
JOY/*Shema.*

shmaltz, *Yiddish*
DFT; DFT/*schmaltz*; HFY; JOY.

shmatte, *Yiddish*
HFY; JOY.

Shma Yisrael, *Yiddish*
JOY/*Shema Yisrael.*

shmeck tabac, *Yiddish*
JOY.

shmeer, *Yiddish*
HFY; JOY.

shmegegge, *Yiddish*
HFY; JOY.

shmei, *Yiddish*
HFY.

shmeikel, *Yiddish*
HFY.

shmeker, *Yiddish*
HFY.

shmendrick, *Yiddish*
JOY.

shmendrik, *Yiddish*
DFT.

Shmerl Narr, *Yiddish*
HFY.

shmo, *Yiddish*
HFY.

shmontses, *Yiddish*
HFY.

shmoos, *Yiddish*
HFY; JOY/*shmooz.*

shmooz, *Yiddish*
DFT; JOY.

shmooze, *Yiddish*
JOY/*shmooz.*

shmotte, *Yiddish*
JOY/*shmatte.*

shmuck, *Yiddish*
HFY; JOY.

shmues, *Yiddish*
JOY/*shmooz.*

shmulky, *Yiddish*
HFY.

shnaps, *Yiddish*
HFY; JOY.

Shnippishok, *Yiddish*
JOY.

shnir, *Yiddish*
JOY/*shnur*.

shnook, *Yiddish*
HFY; JOY.

shnorer, *Yiddish*
HFY; JOY/*shnorrer*.

shnorren, *Yiddish*
JOY/*shnorrer*.

shnorrer, *Yiddish*
JOY.

shnoz, *Yiddish*
HFY; JOY.

shnozzle, *Yiddish*
JOY.

shnuk, *Yiddish*
JOY; JOY/*shnook*.

shnur, *Yiddish*
JOY.

shochet, *Yiddish*
HFY; JOY.

shofar, *Hebrew*
ICMM.

shofar, *Yiddish*
HFY; JOY.

shogaol, *Japanese*
JLE.

shogi, *Japanese*
JLE.

shogun, *Japanese*
DFWPB; DFWPN; JLE.

shoji, *Japanese*
DFT; JLE.

sholem, *Yiddish*
JOY.

Sholem aleichem, *Yiddish*
HFY; JOY.

sholom, *Hebrew*
DFWPN.

sholom, *Yiddish*
JOY/*sholem*.

sholom aleicham, *Hebrew*
DFWPN.

sholom aleichem, *Yiddish*
JOY/*sholem aleichem*.

shomio, *Japanese*
JLE.

shool, *Yiddish*
DFWPN.

shott, *Arabic*
GG.

Showa, *Japanese*
JLE.

shoya, *Japanese*
JLE.

shoyu, *Japanese*
JLE.

shpilkes, *Yiddish*
HFY.

shtarker, *Yiddish*
HFY.

shtchav, *Yiddish*
JOY.

shteiger, *Yiddish*
JOY.

shtetl, *Yiddish*
HFY; JOY.

shtik, *Yiddish*
DFT; JOY.

shtikeleh, *Yiddish*
JOY/*shtik*.

shtikl, *Yiddish*
JOY/*shtik*.

shtiklech, *Yiddish*
JOY/*shtik*.

shtoop, *Yiddish*
JOY/*shtup*.

shtreimel, *Yiddish*
JOY.

shtunk, *Yiddish*
HFY; JOY.

shtup, *Yiddish*
HFY; JOY.

shtus, *Yiddish*
HFY.

shtuss, *Yiddish*
JOY.

shubunkin

328

shubunkin, *Japanese*
JLE.
Shuha, *Japanese*
JLE.
shul, *Yiddish*
JOY.
shvartz, *Yiddish*
HFY; JOY.
shvartzeh, *Yiddish*
JOY; JOY/*shvartz*.
shvartzer, *Yiddish*
JOY/*shvartz*; JOY.
shviger, *Yiddish*
JOY.
shvitzbad, *Yiddish*
JOY/*shvitzbud*.
shvitzbud, *Yiddish*
JOY.
shvitzer, *Yiddish*
JOY.
si, *French*
DFWPN; ICMM.
si, *Italian*
OCM.
si, *Spanish*
DSTE.
sì, *Italian*
DFWPN.
si bémol, *French*
ICMM.
sic, *Latin*
DFPA; DFPCQ; DFT; DFWPB.
Siccatif de Courtrai, *French*
LP/*drier*.
Siccatif de Haarlem, *French*
LP/*drier*.
sich, *German*
OCM.
siciliana, *Italian*
DFPCQ; OCM/*siciliano*.
siciliano, *Italian*
ICMM; OCM; OCM.
sicilienne, *French*
OCM/*siciliano*.

sic itur ad astra, *Latin*
DEP; DFPCQ.
sic jubeo, *Latin*
DFPCQ.
sic passim, *Latin*
DFPA; DFPCQ; DFT; DFWPB.
sic semper tyrannis, *Latin*
DEP; DFWPB; DFWPN.
sic transit gloria mundi, *Latin*
DFPCQ; DFT; DFWPB;
DFWPN.
sicut ante, *Latin*
DFPA.
Siddur, *Yiddish*
JOY.
si dièse, *French*
ICMM.
sieben, *German*
OCM.
siècle, *French*
DFT.
siècle d'or, *French*
DFPA; DFT/*siècle*.
Sieg Heil, *German*
DFPA.
Siegheil, *German*
DFWPN.
Sierozem, *Russian*
GG.
sierra, *Spanish*
DFPCQ; DFT; DFWPB; GG.
siesta, *Spanish*
DFPCQ; DFWPB; DFWPN;
DSTE.
Sifflöte, *German*
OCM.
si fortuna iuvat, *Latin*
DFPCQ.
siglo de oro, *Spanish*
DFPA.
Signalhorn, *German*
OCM/*bugle*.
signor, *Italian*
DFT; DFWPN.

signora, *Italian*
DFT; DFWPN.

signore, *Italian*
DFT.

signorina, *Italian*
DFT; DFWPN.

signorino, *Italian*
DFT.

sika, *Japanese*
JLE.

sikussak, *Eskimo*
GG.

silenzio, *Italian*
OCM.

s'il vous plaît, *French*
DFPA; DFT; DFWPN.

si majeur, *French*
ICMM.

simba, *Swahili*
DFT.

simcha, *Yiddish*
JOY.

Simchath Torah, *Yiddish*
JOY.

simche, *Yiddish*
JOY/*simcha*.

Simhat Torah, *Yiddish*
JOY/*Simchath Torah*.

simile, *Italian*
OCM.

simili, *Italian*
OCM/*simile*.

simpatico, *Italian*
DFPCQ; DFT.

simpatico, *fem.* simpatica, *Italian*
DFWPB.

simpático, *Spanish*
DFWPN.

simpkin, *Anglo-Indian*
DFT.

simple, *French*
LB.

simplement, *French*
OCM.

simplex munditiis, *Latin*
DFPCQ; DFWPN.

sin', *Italian*
OCM; OCM/*sino*.

sine, *Latin*
DFT.

sine anno, *Latin*
DFT/*sine*.

sine cura, *Latin*
DFPCQ.

sine die, *Latin*
DEP; DFPA; DFPCQ; DFT/*sine*;
DFWPB.

sine dubio, *Latin*
DFPA; DFPCQ; DFT/*sine*.

sine ira et studio, *Latin*
DFPA; DFT/*sine*.

sine legitima prole, *Latin*
DFPA.

sine loco, anno, vel nomine, *Latin*
DFT/*sine*.

sine loco et anno, *Latin*
DFT/*sine*.

sine mascula prole, *Latin*
DFPA.

sine prole superstite, *Latin*
DFPA.

sine qua non, *Latin*
DEP; DFPA; DFPCQ; DFT/*sine*;
DFWPB; DFWPN.

sine qua non, a, *Latin*
SPICE.

sinfonia, *Italian*
DFPCQ; DFT.

sinfonia concertante, *Italian*
DFWPB.

sinfonica, *Italian*
OCM/*sinfonico*.

sinfonico, *Italian*
OCM.

sinfonietta, *Italian*
OCM.

Sinfonische Dichtung, *German*
OCM/*symphonic poem*.

singbar, *German*
OCM.

singe, *French*
DFT.

singend, *German*
OCM.

singerie, *French*
DFWPB.

singhiozzando, *Italian*
OCM.

singlemon, *Yiddish*
JOY.

Singspiel, *German*
DFT; ICMM.

sinistra, *Italian*
OCM.

Sinn Fein, *Irish*
DFWPB.

sino, *Italian*
DFT; ICMM; OCM.

sino al segno, *Italian*
DFT/*sino.*

sinopia, *Italian*
DFWPB.

Siomio, *Japanese*
JLE.

si parla italiano, *Italian*
DFT.

sirocco, *Italian*
DFT; DFWPN.

sirocco/scirocco, *Italian*
DFWPB.

sisol, *French*
LB.

sissonne, *French*
DFWPB.

sissonne, pas, *French*
LB.

sissonne battue, *French*
LB/*sissonne, pas.*

sissonne changée, *French*
LB/*sissonne, pas.*

sissonne doublée, *French*
LB/*sissonne, pas.*

sissonne fermée, *French*
LB/*sissonne, pas.*

sissonne fondue, *French*
LB/*sissonne, pas.*

sissonne ouverte, *French*
LB/*sissonne, pas.*

sissonne ouverte en tournant, *French*
LB/*sissonne, pas.*

sissonne retombée, *French*
LB/*sissonne, pas.*

sissonne simple, *French*
LB/*sissonne, pas.*

sissonne simple détournée, *French*
LB/*sissonne, pas.*

sissonne simple en tournant, *French*
LB/*sissonne, pas.*

sissonne soubresaut, *French*
LB/*sissonne, pas.*

sissonne tombée, *French*
LB/*sissonne, pas.*

sistema, *Italian*
ICMM/*stave.*

siste viator, *Latin*
DFPCQ.

sitar, *Hindi*
ICMM.

Sitzkrieg, *German*
DFWPN.

sivigliana, *Italian*
OCM/*sivigliano.*

sivigliano, *Italian*
OCM.

six, *French*
LB; OCM.

skål, *Norwegian*
DFWPB.

skärtråg, *Swedish*
GG.

skavl, *Norwegian*
GG.

skibby, *Japanese*
JLE.

skimmia, *Japanese*
JLE.

Skizze, *German*
ICMM/*sketch*; OCM.

Skizzen, *German*
OCM/*Skizze.*

skolien, *Swedish*
ICMM.

slàinte, *Gaelic*
DFT.

slalom, *Norwegian*
DFWPB.

slancio, *Italian*
OCM.

slargando, *Italian*
OCM.

slargandosi, *Italian*
OCM/*slargando.*

slegato, *Italian*
OCM.

slentando, *Italian*
DFPCQ; DFT; ICMM; OCM.

sluit, *Afrikaans*
GG.

smalto, *pl.* **smalti,** *Italian*
DFWPB.

smania, *Italian*
OCM.

smaniante, *Italian*
DFT.

smanicare, *Italian*
ICMM.

smanioso, *Italian*
ICMM.

sminuendo, *Italian*
OCM.

sminuito, *Italian*
OCM/*sminuendo.*

smorendo, *Italian*
OCM.

smorfioso, *Italian*
OCM.

smorgasbord, *Swedish*
DFWPN.

smorzando, *Italian*
DFPCQ; DFT; ICMM; OCM.

smorzanto, *Italian*
DFT/*smorzando.*

snellamente, *Italian*
OCM/*snello.*

snello, *Italian*
OCM.

so, *German*
OCM.

soave, *Italian*
DFPCQ; DFT; ICMM; OCM.

soavemente, *Italian*
DFT/*soave.*

soavità, *Italian*
OCM/*soave.*

soba, *Japanese*
JLE.

sobald, *German*
OCM.

sobriquet, *French*
DFPCQ; DFT; DFWPB.

Société des Vingt, *French*
LP.

société en commandite, *French*
DFT/*commandite.*

sodoku, *Japanese*
JLE.

soeben, *German*
OCM.

soffione, *Italian*
GG.

sofort, *German*
OCM.

soga, *Spanish*
DSTE.

soggetto, *Italian*
DFPCQ; DFT; ICMM/*subject*; ICMM; OCM.

sogleich, *German*
OCM.

soi-disant, *French*
DFPA; DFPCQ; DFT; DFWPB; DFWPN; LP.

soie, *French*
DFWPN.

soigné, *French*
DFT.

soigné, *fem.* **soignée,** *French*
DFWPB.

soirée, *French*
DFPCQ; DFWPB; DFWPN.

Soka Gakkai, *Japanese*
JLE.

sol, *French*
OCM.

sol, *Italian*
OCM.

sola, *Italian*
OCM.

Soldatenzug, *German*
OCM.

sol dièse, *French*
ICMM.

soleá, *Spanish*
OCM.

solemnis, *Latin*
OCM/*solennis*; OCM.

solenne, *Italian*
OCM.

solennel, *French*
OCM.

solennelle, *French*
OCM/*solennel.*

solennemente, *Italian*
OCM/*solenne.*

solennis, *Latin*
OCM; OCM/*solemnis.*

solennità, *Italian*
OCM/*solenne.*

sol-fa, *Italian*
OCM.

solfège, *French*
ICMM; OCM/*solfeggio.*

solfeggio, *Italian*
DFPCQ; DFT; OCM.

soli, *Italian*
ICMM; OCM.

solidarité, *French*
DFPCQ.

solito, *Italian*
OCM.

sollecitando, *Italian*
OCM.

sollecito, *Italian*
OCM.

solo, *Italian*
ICMM; OCM.

solo, *Spanish*
DSTE.

Soloklavier, *German*
OCM.

solo, *pl.* **soli,** *Italian*
DFWPB.

soltanto, *Italian*
OCM.

solus, *Latin*
DFT.

sombre, *French*
OCM.

sombrée, *French*
ICMM.

sombrero, *Spanish*
DFWPB; DFWPN; DSTE.

somma, *Italian*
OCM/*sommo.*

sommeils, *French*
ICMM.

sommelier, *French*
DFWPB.

sommesso, *Italian*
OCM.

sommo, *Italian*
OCM.

son, *French*
OCM.

so na, *Chinese*
ICMM.

sonare, *Italian*
OCM.

sonata, *Italian*
DFPCQ; DFWPB.

sonata a tre, *Italian*
OCM.

sonata da camera, *Italian*
OCM.

sonata da chiesa, *Italian*
OCM.

sonate, *French*
OCM.

Sonate, *German*
OCM.

Sonaten, *German*
OCM/*sonate.*

sonates, *French*
OCM/*sonate.*

sonatina, *Italian*
DFPCQ; DFT.

sonatine, *French*
OCM.

sonevole, *Italian*
OCM.

sonnerie, *French*
OCM.

sonore, *French*
OCM.

sonoro, *Italian*
OCM/*sonore.*

sons, *French*
OCM/*son.*

sons bouchés, *French*
OCM.

sons partiels, *French*
ICMM/*partials.*

sons résultants, *French*
ICMM/*resultant tones.*

sopra, *Italian*
DFT; OCM.

sopra bianco, *Italian*
DFWPN.

Sopran, *German*
OCM.

soprana, *Italian*
OCM.

soprano, *Italian*
DFPCQ; ICMM.

soprano acuto, *Italian*
ICMM.

soprano leggiero, *Italian*
ICMM.

soprano, *pl.* **soprani,** *Italian*
DFWPB.

soprano sfogato, *Italian*
ICMM.

sorda, *Italian*
OCM/*sordo;* OCM.

sordamente, *Italian*
DFT; OCM/*sorda.*

sordina, *Italian*
OCM.

sordine, *Italian*
ICMM.

sordini, *Italian*
DFPCQ; OCM/*sordino.*

sordino, *Italian*
DFT; ICMM; OCM.

sordo, *Italian*
DFT; OCM.

Sordun, *German*
OCM.

Sorgfalt, *German*
OCM.

Sortes Vergilianae, *Latin*
DFPA; DFT.

sortie, *French*
DFPCQ; DFWPN; OCM.

sortita, *Italian*
ICMM.

sospirando, *Italian*
DFPCQ; DFT; OCM.

sospirante, *Italian*
DFT/*sospirando;* OCM/*sospirando.*

sospirevole, *Italian*
OCM/*sospirando.*

sospiroso, *Italian*
DFT; OCM/*sospirando.*

sostenendo, *Italian*
OCM.

sostenente, *Italian*
OCM/*sostenendo.*

sostenuto, *Italian*
DFPCQ; DFT; DFWPB; ICMM;
OCM.

sótano, *Spanish*
GG.

sotol, *Mexican*
DFT.

sotol, *Spanish*
DSTE.

sotto in su, *Italian*
DFWPB.

sotto portico, *Italian*
DA.

sotto voce, *Italian*
DFPA; DFPCQ; DFT; DFWPB;
DFWPN; ICMM; OCM.

sou, *French*
DFWPB; DFWPN.

soubasse, *French*
OCM.

soubresaut, *French*
DFWPB; LB.

soubresaut, grand, *French*
LB/*soubresaut.*

soubrette, *French*
DFT; ICMM; OCM.

soubriquet, *French*
DFWPN.

soudainement, *French*
OCM.

soufflé, *French*
DFWPB; DFWPN.

soufflée, *French*
DFT.

souffleur, *French*
DFT.

souling, *Javanese*
ICMM.

soupçon, *French*
DFPCQ; DFT; DFWPB;
DFWPN.

soupe, *French*
DFT.

soupe de l'Inde, *French*
DFT/*soupe.*

soupe grasse, *French*
DFT/*soupe*; DFT/*gras.*

soupe maigre, *French*
DFT/*maigre*; DFT/*soupe.*

souper, *French*
DFT.

soupir, *French*
DFT; ICMM.

soupirant, *French*
OCM.

souple, *French*
OCM.

sourd, *French*
OCM.

sourde, *French*
OCM/*sourd.*

sourdine, *French*
ICMM; OCM.

sous, *French*
OCM.

soussus, *French*
LB.

soutenu, *French*
LB; OCM.

soutenu en tournant, *French*
LB.

sovkhoz, *Russian*
MRWEW/*18.*

sowar, *Anglo-Indian*
DFT.

spagnicoletta, *Italian*
OCM/*spagnoletto.*

spagniletta, *Italian*
OCM/*spagnoletto.*

spagnoletta, *Italian*
OCM/*spagnoletto.*

spagnoletto, *Italian*
OCM.

spandendo, *Italian*
OCM.

sparsim, *Latin*
DFPCQ.

sparta, *Italian*
OCM.

335

Spartieren, *German*
ICMM/*spartire*.

spartire, *Italian*
ICMM.

spartita, *Italian*
OCM/*sparta*.

spartito, *Italian*
OCM/*sparta*.

sparto, *Italian*
OCM/*sparta*.

spasibo, *Russian*
DFT.

Spass, *German*
OCM.

spassapensiere, *Italian*
ICMM.

spassapensieri, *Italian*
OCM.

spasshaft, *German*
OCM.

später, *German*
OCM.

spécialité de la maison, *French*
DFWPB.

spediendo, *Italian*
OCM.

sperdendosi, *Italian*
OCM.

spero meliora, *Latin*
DFPCQ.

spes, *Latin*
DFT.

Sphärophon, *German*
OCM.

spianato, *Italian*
DFT; DFWPN; ICMM; OCM.

spiccato, *Italian*
DFPCQ; DFT; DFWPN; ICMM;
OCM.

spicilegium, *Latin*
DFPCQ.

spiegando, *Italian*
OCM.

Spiel, *German*
OCM.

spielen, *German*
OCM/*spiel*.

Spinnen des Tons, *German*
OCM.

Spinnerlied, *German*
OCM.

Spinnlied, *German*
OCM.

spirante, *Italian*
OCM.

spirito, *Italian*
DFPCQ; DFT; DFWPN; OCM.

spiritoso, *Italian*
DFPCQ; DFT; ICMM.

spirituel, *French*
DFT.

spiritus, *Latin*
DFT.

spiritus asper, *Latin*
DFT/*spiritus*.

spiritus frumenti, *Latin*
DFPA.

spiritus lenis, *Latin*
DFT/*spiritus*.

spitskop, *Afrikaans*
GG.

Spitze, *German*
OCM.

Spitzflöte, *German*
OCM.

spitzig, *German*
OCM.

Spitzkarren, *German*
GG.

spolia opima, *Latin*
DFPA; DFPCQ; DFT.

sponte sua, *Latin*
DFPA; DFPCQ; DFT; DFWPB;
DFWPN.

sponte suâ, *Latin*
DEP.

spöttisch, *German*
OCM.

Sprachgefühl, *German*
DFWPB.

Sprechchor, *German*
OCM.

sprechend, *German*
OCM.

Sprechen sie Deutsch?, *German*
DFPCQ.

Sprechgesang, *German*
DFWPB.

Sprechstimme, *German*
DFWPB.

sprezzatura, *Italian*
DFWPB.

springar, *Norwegian*
OCM.

springdans, *Norwegian*
OCM.

springend, *German*
OCM.

Spruchsprecher, *German*
OCM.

spruit, *Afrikaans*
GG.

spugna, bacchetta di, *Italian*
OCM.

spumone, *Italian*
DFWPN.

sputnik, *Russian*
DFT; DFWPB; MRWEW/*17*.

squillante, *Italian*
OCM.

squillanti, *Italian*
OCM/*squillante*.

Staatskapelle, *German*
OCM.

Stäbchen, *German*
OCM.

stabile, *Italian*
OCM.

staccato, *Italian*
DFPCQ; DFT; DFWPB;
DFWPN; ICMM; OCM.

stagione, *Italian*
ICMM.

Stahlharmonika, *German*
OCM.

Stalag, *German*
DFWPN.

stampita, *Italian*
OCM.

stamukha, *Russian*
GG.

Ständchen, *German*
ICMM/*serenade*; ICMM; OCM.

standhaft, *German*
OCM.

Standhaftigkeit, *German*
OCM/*standhaft*.

stanghetta, *Italian*
ICMM.

stark, *German*
OCM.

statt, *German*
OCM.

statu quo, *Latin*
DFPCQ.

statu quo ante bellum, *Latin*
DEP.

status belli, *Latin*
DFPA.

status in quo, *Latin*
DFT/*status quo*.

status quaestionis, *Latin*
DFPA.

status quo, *Latin*
DEP; DFPA; DFT; DFWPB;
DFWPN.

status quo ante, *Latin*
DFWPB; DFWPN.

status quo ante bellum, *Latin*
DFPA.

stecco, *Italian*
ACD.

Steg, *German*
ICMM; OCM.

Steilwand, *German*
GG.

Steinharmonika, *German*
OCM.

Steinkern, *German*
GG.

Stelle, *German*
OCM.

Stellen, *German*
OCM/*Stelle.*

stendendo, *Italian*
OCM.

Stengel Gneiss, *German*
GG.

stentare, *Italian*
OCM.

stentato, *Italian*
ICMM.

stentorg, *Swedish*
GG.

steppe, *Russian*
DFWPB; DFWPN.

sterbend, *German*
OCM.

steso, *Italian*
OCM.

stessa, *Italian*
OCM/*stesso.*

stesso, *Italian*
DFPCQ; DFT; OCM.

stet, *Latin*
DEP; DFPA; DFPCQ; DFWPN.

stet processus, *Latin*
DFPA.

stets, *German*
OCM.

stiacciato, *Italian*
DFT.

sticcado, *Italian*
ICMM.

sticcato, *Italian*
ICMM.

sticciato, *Italian*
DFWPN.

stichomythia, *Greek*
DFWPN.

Stierhorn, *German*
OCM.

(De) Stijl, *Dutch*
DFWPB.

Stijl, De, *Dutch*
LP.

stilecht, *German*
ICMM.

stile rappresentativo, *Italian*
OCM.

still, *German*
OCM.

Stimmbogen, *German*
OCM.

Stimmbücher, *German*
ICMM/*part books.*

Stimme, *German*
ICMM; OCM/*part*; OCM.

Stimmführung, *German*
ICMM.

Stimmung, *German*
LP.

stinguendo, *Italian*
DFT; OCM.

Stinkstein, *German*
GG.

stiracchiando, *Italian*
OCM/*stirando.*

stiracchiato, *Italian*
OCM/*stirando.*

stirando, *Italian*
OCM.

stirato, *Italian*
OCM/*stirando.*

stockend, *German*
OCM.

Stockflöte, *German*
OCM.

Stollen, *German*
DFWPN.

GG.
stornello, *Italian*
ICMM; OCM.
Stoss, *German*
GG.
straat, *Afrikaans*
GG.
stracciacalando, *Italian*
OCM.
straccinato, *Italian*
OCM.
strada, *Italian*
DFT.
straff, *German*
OCM.
straffando, *Italian*
OCM.
straffato, *Italian*
OCM/*straffando.*
straffer, *German*
OCM/*straff.*
strambotto, *Italian*
ICMM; OCM.
strascicando, *Italian*
OCM.
strascinando, *Italian*
ICMM; OCM.
strascinando l'arco, *Italian*
ICMM.
strascinato, *Italian*
OCM/*strascinando.*
Strasse, *German*
DFPCQ; DFT.
straticule, *French*
GG.
stravagante, *Italian*
OCM.
straziante, *Italian*
OCM.
Streich, *German*
OCM.
Streichquartett, *German*
OCM/*Streich.*

Streichstimmen, *German*
OCM/*Streich.*
Streichzither, *German*
ICMM.
streng, *German*
OCM.
strepito, *Italian*
DFPCQ; OCM.
strepitosamente, *Italian*
OCM/*strepito.*
strepitoso, *Italian*
DFT; ICMM; OCM/*strepito.*
stretto, *Italian*
DFPCQ; DFT; DFWPB;
DFWPN; ICMM; OCM.
striae, *Latin*
DFPCQ.
Strich, *German*
ICMM; OCM.
stricto sensu, *Latin*
DFT.
strimpellata, *Italian*
OCM.
stringendo, *Italian*
DFPCQ; DFT; ICMM; OCM.
strisciando, *Italian*
ICMM; OCM.
strisciato, *Italian*
OCM/*strisciando.*
Strohfiedel, *German*
ICMM; OCM.
stromenti, *Italian*
DFPCQ; DFT; OCM/*stromento.*
stromenti da arco, *Italian*
DFT/*stromenti.*
stromenti da fiato, *Italian*
DFT/*stromenti.*
stromenti da percossa, *Italian*
DFT/*stromenti.*
stromenti da tasto, *Italian*
DFT/*stromenti.*
stromenti di corda, *Italian*
DFT/*stromenti.*

stromenti di lengo, *Italian*
DFT/*stromenti.*

stromento, *Italian*
OCM.

Strudel, *German*
DFWPN.

Strukturboden, *German*
GG.

strumenti, *Italian*
OCM/*strumento.*

strumento, *Italian*
OCM.

stucco lustro, *Italian*
DFWPB.

Stück, *German*
ICMM; ICMM/*piece*; OCM;
DFT.

stückchen, *German*
DFT.

stukach, *Russian*
MRWEW/*20.*

stupor mundi, *Latin*
DFPA.

stürmend, *German*
OCM.

stürmisch, *German*
OCM/*stürmend.*

Sturm und Drang, *German*
DFPA; DFPCQ; DFT; DFWPB;
DFWPN.

(le) style, c'est l'homme, *French*
DFWPB.

style champêtre, *French*
DFWPB.

style de perruque, *French*
OCM.

style galant, *French*
OCM.

style mécanique, *French*
DFWPB.

su, *Italian*
OCM.

sua sponte, *Latin*
DFWPN.

suave, *French*
DFPCQ.

suave, *Italian*
OCM.

suavità, *Italian*
OCM/*suave.*

subahdar, *Hindi*
DFT.

subahdar, *Persian*
DFT.

sub anno, *Latin*
DFWPB.

subbotnik, *Russian*
MRWEW/*18.*

sub condicione, *Latin*
DFPA/*sub conditione.*

sub conditione, *Latin*
DFPA.

subida, *Spanish*
GG.

sub Iove, *Latin*
DFPCQ.

subitamente, *Italian*
DFT.

subito, *Italian*
DFPCQ; DFT; ICMM; OCM.

subito, *Latin*
DFPCQ.

Subjekt, *German*
ICMM/*subject.*

sub judice, *Latin*
DEP; DFPA; DFPCQ; DFT;
DFWPB; DFWPN.

sub modo, *Latin*
DFPA.

sub plumbo, *Latin*
DFPA.

sub poena, *Latin*
DFPA; DFPCQ; DFT; DFWPN.

subpoena, *Latin*
DFWPB.

sub rosa, *Latin*
DFPA; DFPCQ; DFT; DFWPB;
DFWPN.

sub rosâ, *Latin*
DEP.

sub sigillo, *Latin*
DFPA; DFT.

sub silentio, *Latin*
DFPA.

sub specie, *Latin*
DFPA; DFT.

substratum, *Latin*
DFPCQ.

subsultim, *Latin*
DFPCQ.

sub verbo, *Latin*
DFPA; DFT/*sub voce*.

sub vi, *Latin*
DFPA.

sub voce, *Latin*
DEP; DFPA; DFT; DFWPB;
DFWPN.

succah, *Yiddish*
JOY.

succentor, *Latin*
ICMM.

succès de mouchoir, *French*
DFPA.

succès de ridicule, *French*
DFWPB.

succès de scandale, *French*
DFPA; DFWPB; DFWPN; LP.

succès de snobisme, *French*
DFWPB.

succès d'estime, *French*
DFPA; DFT; DFWPB; DFWPN;
LP.

succès fou, *French*
DFPA; DFWPB; DFWPN.

Succoth, *Yiddish*
JOY.

succubus, *pl.* succubi, *Latin*
DFWPB.

sucre, *French*
DFT.

sucre en morceaux, *French*
DFT/*sucre*.

sudadero, *Spanish*
DFT.

suerte, *Spanish*
DFT; DSTE/*237*.

sugi, *Japanese*
JLE.

sugli, *Italian*
OCM; OCM/*sul*.

sui, *Italian*
OCM/*sul*; OCM/*slugi*.

sui compos, *Latin*
DFPA.

sui generis, *Latin*
DEP: DFPA; DFPCQ; DFT;
DFWPB; DFWPN.

sui juris, *Latin*
DFPA.

suiseki, *Japanese*
JLE.

suite, *French*
DFPCQ.

suite, de, *French*
LB.

suivez, *French*
DFT; ICMM; OCM.

sujet, *French*
ICMM/*subject*; LB.

sukiyaki, *Japanese*
JLE.

sul, *Italian*
OCM.

sul G, *Italian*
OCM.

sul IV, *Italian*
OCM/*sul G*.

sull, *Italian*
OCM/*sul*.

sulla, *Italian*
OCM/*sul*.

sulla tastiera, *Italian*
ICMM; OCM.

sulle, *Italian*
OCM/*sul*.

sul ponticello, *Italian*
DFWPB; DFWPN; ICMM;
OCM.

sul tasto, *Italian*
OCM.

sumi, *Japanese*
JLE.

sumi-e, *Japanese*
JLE.

summa cum laude, *Latin*
DFPA; DFT; DFWPB; DFWPN.

summend, *German*
OCM.

summum bonum, *Latin*
DEP; DFPA; DFPCQ; DFT;
DFWPN.

summum jus, summa injuria, *Latin*
DEP.

sumo, *Japanese*
JLE.

sumotori, *Japanese*
JLE.

sunyasi, *Anglo-Indian*
DFT.

suo, *Italian*
OCM.

suo loco, *Latin*
DFPA.

suo motu, *Latin*
DFPCQ.

suonare, *Italian*
OCM.

suoni, *Italian*
OCM/*suono.*

suono, *Italian*
OCM.

suo nomine, *Latin*
DFWPN.

suo periculo, *Latin*
DFPA.

superba, *Italian*
OCM/*superbo.*

superbo, *Italian*
OCM.

supercherie, *French*
DFT.

suppliant, *French*
OCM.

supplicando, *Italian*
OCM.

supplichevole, *Italian*
OCM.

supplichevolmente, *Italian*
OCM/*supplichevole.*

suppressio veri, suggestio falsi, *Latin*
DEP.

supprimez, *French*
OCM.

supra, *Latin*
DFPCQ; DFT; DFWPB.

suprême, *French*
DFWPN.

sur, *French*
LB; OCM.

sura, *Arabic*
DFT.

surah, *Arabic*
DFT/*sura.*

surbahar, *Hindi*
ICMM.

sur canapé, *French*
DFWPN.

Sûreté, *French*
DFWPB.

sur fond réservé, *French*
DFWPB.

sur la touche, *French*
OCM.

sur le chevalet, *French*
OCM.

sur le cou du pied, *French*
DFWPB.

sur les pointes, *French*
DFWPN.

sur le vif, *French*
DFWPB.

surnai, *Hindi*
ICMM.

sursum corda, *Latin*
OCM.

surtout, *French*
DFT; OCM.

sushi, *Japanese*
DFT; JLE.

süss, *German*
OCM.

Süsschen, *German*
DFT.

susurando [*sic*], *Italian*
DFT.

susurrando, *Italian*
OCM.

susurrante, *Italian*
DFT/*susurando*; OCM/*susurrando*.

suum cuique, *Latin*
DEP; DFPA; DFPCQ; DFT;
DFWPN.

suum cuique pulcrum, *Latin*
DFPCQ.

suus cuique mos, *Latin*
DFPCQ.

suzerain, *French*
DFPCQ.

svegliando, *Italian*
OCM.

svegliato, *Italian*
DFT; OCM/*svegliando*.

svelte, *French*
DFT.

svelto, *Italian*
OCM.

svolgimento, *Italian*
OCM; OCM/*development*.

swami, *Hindi*
DFWPB.

Swami, *Sanskrit*
DFT.

sympathique, *French*
DFWPB.

symphoneta, *Greek*
ICMM.

symphonique, *French*
OCM.

symphonisch, *German*
OCM/*symphonique*.

Symphonische Dichtung, *German*
ICMM/*symphonic poem*.

symposium, *Latin*
DFPCQ.

syrinx, *Greek*
ICMM.

System, *German*
ICMM/*stave*.

système D, *French*
DFWPB.

T

tabac, *French*
DFT.

tabac à fumer, *French*
DFT/*tabac.*

tabatière, *French*
DFT.

tabatière á musique, *French*
OCM.

tabi, *Japanese*
DFT; JLE.

tablature, *French*
OCM/*tablature.*

table, *French*
DFT.

table à manger, *French*
DFT/*table.*

tableau, *French*
DFPCQ; LB.

tableau (vivant), *pl.* **tableaux (vivants),** *French*
DFWPB.

tableau vivant, *French*
DEP; DFT.

table d'hôte, *French*
DFPA; DFPCQ; DFT/*table*;
DFWPB; DFWPN.

table d'instrument, *French*
ICMM.

tablier, *French*
DFT.

tabouret, *French*
ACD.

tabourin, *French*
ICMM.

tabula rasa, *Latin*
DFPA; DFPCQ; DFT; DFWPB;
DFWPN.

Tabulatur, *German*
ICMM/*tablature*; OCM/*tablature.*

tacere, *Italian*
OCM.

tacet, *Latin*
DFT; DFWPB; ICMM.

tachi, *Japanese*
JLE.

tachisme, *French*
DFWPB; LP.

tachiste, *French*
LP.

tachlis, *Yiddish*
JOY.

taci, *Italian*
ICMM.

taciasi, *Italian*
ICMM.

Tact, *German*
ICMM.

Tact-linie, *German*
ICMM.

Tactmesser, *German*
ICMM.

Tact-pause, *German*
ICMM.

Tact-schläger, *German*
ICMM.

Tact-strich, *German*
ICMM.

tactus, *Latin*
ICMM/*time*; ICMM.

taedium vitae, *Latin*
DFPA; DFT.

tafelberg, *Afrikaans*
GG.

Tafelklavier, *German*
OCM.

tafelkop, *Afrikaans*
GG.

Tafel-musik, *German*
ICMM.

Tafelmusik, *German*
OCM.

tagliato, *Italian*
ICMM.

Tago-Sato-Kosaka, *Japanese*
JLE.

tai, *Japanese*
JLE.

T'ai Chi, *Chinese*
DFWPN; DFWPN.

tai chi chuan, *Chinese*
DFT.

taiga, *Russian*
GG; MRWEW/*18.*

taiko, *Japanese*
ICMM.

taille, *French*
ICMM; OCM.

taille de basson, *French*
ICMM.

taille d'épargne, *French*
DFWPB.

taille de violon, *French*
ICMM.

taille douce, *French*
DFWPB.

tailleur, *French*
DFT.

Taisho, *Japanese*
JLE.

tajo, *Spanish*
DFT.

taka-makiye, *Japanese*
DFT.

Takamatsu, *Japanese*
JLE.

Takaoka, *Japanese*
JLE.

takir, *Russian*
GG.

Takt, *German*
ICMM; ICMM/*time*; ICMM;
OCM.

Taktmesser, *German*
OCM/*metronome.*

tala, *Mongolian*
GG.

talik, *Russian*
GG.

talis, *Yiddish*
HFY.

talith, *Yiddish*
JOY/*tallis.*

tallis, *Yiddish*
JOY.

tallit, *Yiddish*
JOY/*tallis.*

talmid chachem, *Yiddish*
JOY.

talmouse, *French*
DFT.

Talmud, *Hebrew*
DFWPN.

Talmud, *Yiddish*
JOY.

Talmud Torah, *Yiddish*
JOY.

talon, *French*
ICMM; OCM.

talpatate, *American Spanish*
GG.

talus, *French*
GG.

Talweg, *German*
GG.

tamal, *Mexican Spanish*
DFT/*tamale.*

tamal, *Spanish*
DSTE.

tamale, *Mexican Spanish*
DFT.

tamale, *Spanish*
DFWPN; DSTE/*tamal.*

tamaule, *Spanish*
DSTE/*tamal.*

tambour, *French*
ICMM; OCM.

tambour de Basque, *French*
OCM; ICMM.

tambour de Provence, *French*
OCM.

tambouret, *French*
ICMM.

tambourin, *French*
ICMM; OCM.

tambour militaire, *French*
OCM.

Tamburin, *German*
OCM.

tamburino, *Italian*
ICMM; OCM/*tamburin.*

tamburo, *Italian*
ICMM.

tamburo basco, *Italian*
OCM.

tamburo grande, *Italian*
OCM.

tamburo grosso, *Italian*
OCM/*tamburo grande.*

tamburo militare, *Italian*
OCM.

tamburone, *Italian*
OCM.

tamburo piccolo, *Italian*
OCM.

tamburo rullante, *Italian*
OCM.

tamo, *Japanese*
JLE.

tampon, *French*
OCM.

tan, *Japanese*
JLE.

Tändelei, *German*
OCM.

tändelnd, *German*
ICMM; OCM.

tangi, *Persian*
GG.

tangiwai, *Maori*
GG.

tango, *Spanish*
DFWPN.

tanka, *Japanese*
JLE.

Tannenbaum, *German*
DFT.

tant, *French*
OCM.

tanto, *Italian*
DFT; ICMM; OCM.

tanto, *Japanese*
JLE.

tant soit peu, *French*
OCM.

Tantum Ergo, *Latin*
DFWPB.

tantum ergo sacramentum, *Latin*
OCM.

Tanz, *German*
OCM.

Tänze, *German*
OCM/*Tanz.*

Tao, *Chinese*
DFWPN; DFT.

tapadero, *Spanish*
DSTE.

tapaojos, *Spanish*
DSTE.

tapotement, *French*
DFT.

taqueté, *French*
LB.

tarantella, *Italian*
DFT; DFWPB; DFWPN;
ICMM; OCM.

tarantelle, *French*
OCM/*tarantella.*

tararam, *Yiddish*
HFY.

tarda, *Italian*
OCM/*tardo.*

tardamente, *Italian*
DFT; ICMM.

tardando, *Italian*
DFT; ICMM.

tardo, *Italian*
OCM.

tarn, *Icelandic*
GG.

tarogato, *Hungarian*
OCM.

tarole, *French*
OCM.

tarole grégoire, *French*
OCM/*tarole.*

tarrarom, *Yiddish*
JOY.

tarsia, *Italian*
ACD/*intarsia.*

tartilloes, *Spanish*
DSTE/*tortilla.*

tartine, *French*
DFT.

Taste, *German*
OCM.

Tasten, *German*
OCM/*taste.*

Tasten-brett, *German*
ICMM.

tasti, *Italian*
OCM/*tasto.*

tastiera, *Italian*
OCM.

tasto, *Italian*
OCM.

tata, *Yiddish*
HFY; JOY.

tata-mama, *Yiddish*
HFY.

tatami, *Japanese*
JLE.

tateleh, *Yiddish*
JOY.

tatto, *Italian*
ICMM/*time.*

tauromaquia, *Spanish*
DSTE//*237.*

taus, *Hindi*
ICMM.

tazza, *Italian*
ACD; DA; DFT; DFWPB.

tchardache, *Hungarian*
OCM/*Czardas.*

tcheppeh, *Yiddish*
JOY.

tchotchke, *Yiddish*
JOY; JOY/*tsatske.*

tchotchkeleh, *Yiddish*
JOY/*tsatske.*

teatrino, *Italian*
ICMM.

tedesca, *Italian*
ICMM; OCM.

tedesca, alla, *Italian*
ICMM.

tedesco, *Italian*
DFT; ICMM/*tedesca.*

Te Deum, *Latin*
DFPCQ; DFWPB.

Te Deum laudamus, *Latin*
DFWPN; OCM.

tefillin, *Yiddish*
JOY.

tegua, *Spanish*
DSTE.

Teil, *German*
OCM.

Teilzone, *German*
GG.

teimpanetto, *Italian*
ICMM.

Teitch-Chumesh, *Yiddish*
JOY/*Teitsh-Chumash.*

Teitsh-Chumash, *Yiddish*
JOY.

teivel, *Yiddish*
JOY.

tejano, *Spanish*
DSTE.

tejon, *Spanish*
GG.

te judice, *Latin*
DEP; DFPA; DFPCQ; DFT.

tele, *Norwegian*
GG.

Teller, *German*
OCM.

tel quel, *French*
DFPA.

tema, *Italian*
DFPCQ; ICMM; ICMM/*subject*;
ICMM/*theme*; OCM.

tema con variazioni, *Italian*
DFWPN.

tema fondamentale, *Italian*
OCM/*leading motif.*

temblor, *Spanish*
GG.

temmoku, *Japanese*
ACD.

tempestosamente, *Italian*
OCM/*tempestoso.*

tempestoso, *Italian*
OCM.

tempête, *French*
ICMM.

tempo, *Italian*
DFPCQ; DFT; ICMM/*time.*

tempo, *Japanese*
JLE.

tempo alla breve, *Italian*
ICMM; OCM.

tempo a piacere, *Italian*
ICMM.

tempo commodo, *Italian*
DFT/*tempo*; OCM/*tempo comodo.*

tempo comodo, *Italian*
DFT/*tempo*; ICMM; OCM.

tempo di ballo, *Italian*
DFT/*tempo*; ICMM; OCM;
OCM/*ballo.*

tempo di cappella, *Italian*
ICMM.

tempo di gavotta, *Italian*
ICMM.

tempo di marcia, *Italian*
DFT/*tempo.*

tempo di menuetto, *Italian*
DFT/*tempo*; ICMM.

tempo di minuetto, *Italian*
OCM.

tempo di polacca, *Italian*
ICMM.

tempo di prima parte, *Italian*
DFT/*tempo.*

tempo di valse, *Italian*
ICMM.

tempo frettevole, *Italian*
ICMM.

tempo fretto-losó, *Italian*
ICMM/*tempo frettevole.*

tempo giusto, *Italian*
DFPCQ; DFT/*tempo*; DFWPB;
ICMM; OCM.

tempo maggiore, *Italian*
OCM.

tempo minore, *Italian*
OCM.

tempo ordinario, *Italian*
ICMM; OCM.

tempo perduto, *Italian*
ICMM.

tempo, *pl.* **tempi,** *Italian*
DFWPB.

tempo primo, *Italian*
DFT/*tempo*; ICMM; OCM.

tempo reggiato, *Italian*
ICMM.

tempo rubato, *Italian*
DFT/*tempo*; DFT/*rubato*;
DFWPB; ICMM; OCM.

Tempo wie vorher, *German*
ICMM; OCM.

temps, *French*
LB; OCM.

temps, tems, *French*
ICMM.

temps de cou-de-pied, *French*
LB.

temps de cuisse, *French*
LB.

temps de flèche, *French*
LB.

temps de l'ange, *French*
LB.

temps d'élévation, *French*
LB.

temps de pointes, *French*
LB.

temps de poisson, *French*
LB.

temps frappé, *French*
ICMM.

temps levé, *French*
DFWPB; ICMM; LB.

temps lié, *French*
LB.

temps plané, *French*
LB.

tempura, *Japanese*
DFT; JLE.

tempus, *Latin*
DFT; ICMM; ICMM/*time.*

tempus edax rerum, *Latin*
DFPCQ.

tempus fugit, *Latin*
DEP; DFPA; DFPCQ; DFT/
tempus; DFWPB; DFWPN.

tempus omnia revelat, *Latin*
DFPCQ.

Tendai, *Japanese*
JLE.

tendre, *French*
OCM.

tendrement, *French*
OCM/*tendre.*

tendu, *French*
LB.

tendue, *French*
LB/*tendu.*

tenebrae, *Latin*
ICMM.

tenebrosi, *Italian*
DFWPN.

tenebroso, *Italian*
OCM.

tenendo, *Italian*
OCM.

tenendo il canto, *Italian*
ICMM.

teneramente, *Italian*
DFPCQ; DFT.

teneramente, con tenerezza, *Italian*
ICMM.

tenerezza, *Italian*
DFT.

tenero, *Italian*
ICMM; OCM.

tenete, *Italian*
OCM.

tenno, *Japanese*
JLE.

ténor, *French*
OCM.

Tenor, *German*
OCM/*ténor.*

tenore, *Italian*
DFPCQ; DFT; OCM.

tenor ebuffo, *Italian*
DFT/*tenore.*

tenore buffo, *Italian*
ICMM.

tenore di grazia, *Italian*
DFWPN.

tenore leggiero, *Italian*
DFT/*tenore*; OCM.

tenore primo, *Italian*
ICMM.

tenore ripieno, *Italian*
ICMM.

tenore robusto, *Italian*
DFT/*tenore*; DFWPN; OCM.

Tenor Flügelhorn, *German*
OCM.

Tenorgeige, *German*
OCM.

tenorista, *Italian*
ICMM.

Tenor-posaune, *German*
ICMM.

Tenorposaune, *German*
OCM.

Tenor-schlüssel, *German*
ICMM.

Tenorstimme, *German*
OCM.

tenu, *French*
OCM.

tenue, *French*
OCM/*tenu.*

tenuta, *Italian*
OCM.

tenute, tenuto, *Italian*
ICMM.

tenuto, *Italian*
DFPCQ; DFT; DFWPN; OCM.

tepee, *Dakota*
DFT.

tepidamente, *Italian*
ICMM.

tepido, *Italian*
OCM.

teppe, *Persian*
GG.

tequila, *Spanish*
DFT; DSTE.

tera, *Japanese*
DFT.

terce, *Latin*
ICMM.

tercet, *French*
ICMM.

terceto, *Spanish*
ICMM.

teriyaki, *Japanese*
JLE.

terminé, *French*
LB.

terminus, *Latin*
DFPCQ.

terminus ad quem, *Latin*
DEP; DFPA; DFT; DFWPB.

terminus ante quem, *Latin*
DFPA.

terminus a quo, *Latin*
DEP; DFPA; DFT; DFWPB.

ternario tempo, *Italian*
ICMM.

terra, *Latin*
DFT.

terra alba, *Latin*
LP.

terra cotta, *Italian*
DEP; DFPCQ; DFWPB;
DFWPN.

terra-cotta, *Italian*
GG.

terracotta, *Italian*
ACD.

terra es, terram ibis, *Latin*
DFPCQ.

terra firma, *Latin*
DEP; DFPA; DFPCQ; DFT/
terra; DFWPB; DFWPN.

terra incognita, *Latin*
DEP; DFPA; DFPCQ; DFT/
terra.

terra incognita, *pl.* **terrae incognitae,**
Latin
DFWPB.

terra irredenta, *Italian*
DFPA.

terrarom, *Yiddish*
JOY/*tarrarom*.

terra rossa, *Italian*
GG.

terra verde, *Italian*
GG.

terra verte, *Latin*
LP.

terrazzo, *Italian*
DFWPB.

terre, à, *French*
LB.

terre, par, *French*
LB.

terre à terre, *French*
DFWPB; LB.

terre de pipe, *French*
ACD; DFWPB.

terre pisée, *French*
DFWPB.

terre verte, *French*
DFWPB; GG.

terribilità, *Italian*
DFWPB.

terrine de foie gras, *French*
DFT.

ter sanctus, *Latin*
OCM.

tertium quid, *Latin*
DEP.

terza maggiore, *Italian*
ICMM.

terza minore, *Italian*
ICMM.

terza rima, *Italian*
DFPA; DFT; DFWPB; DFWPN.

Terzen, *German*
ICMM.

terzet, *German*
OCM.

terzetto, *Italian*
DFPCQ; DFT; ICMM; OCM/
terzet.

Terz Flöte, *German*
ICMM.

terzina, *Italian*
ICMM/*triplet*; ICMM.

terzi tuoni, *Italian*
OCM.

Teshu Lama, *Tibetan*
DFWPN.

tesserae, *Latin*
LP.

tessitura, *Italian*
DFT; ICMM; OCM.

testa, *Italian*
OCM.

testo, *Italian*
OCM.

tête, *French*
DFT; LB.

tête à tête, *French*
DFWPN.

tête-à-tête, *French*
DFPA; DFPCQ; DFT; DFWPB;
SPICE.

tête-bêche, *French*
DFWPB.

tête de veau, *French*
DFPA; DFT/*tête*.

teufel, *Yiddish*
JOY/*teivel*.

Teutsch, *German*
ICMM.

teuvel, *Yiddish*
JOY/*teivel*.

textus receptus, *Latin*
DFPA.

t'fillin, *Yiddish*
JOY / *tefillin*.

Thalweg, *German*
GG.

Theater, *German*
OCM.

thé dansant, *French*
DFT; DFWPB; DFWPN.

Theil, *German*
OCM / *Teil*.

Theile, *German*
ICMM.

thema, *Italian*
DFPCQ.

Thema, *German*
ICMM / *subject*; ICMM / *theme*.

thême, *French*
ICMM / *theme*.

thé musical, *pl.* **thés musicaux,**
French
DFWPB.

Theorbe, *German*
ICMM.

Thesis, *German*
OCM.

thon, *French*
DFT.

threnodia, *Latin*
ICMM.

threnodie, *Greek*
ICMM.

thufa, *Icelandic*
GG.

tibia utricularis, *Latin*
OCM.

tief, *German*
OCM.

tiefgespannt, *German*
OCM.

Tief Kammerton, *German*
OCM.

tieftönend, *German*
ICMM.

tiempo, *Spanish*
DSTE.

tiento, *Spanish*
ICMM.

tierce, *French*
ICMM; OCM.

tierce de picardie, *French*
ICMM; OCM.

tierce picarde, *French*
OCM / *tierce de picardie*.

tiercet, *French*
ICMM.

tierra blanca, *Spanish*
GG.

tiers état, *French*
DFPA; DFT; DFWPB.

tiers-état, *French*
DFPCQ.

timbale, *French*
DFT; DFWPN; ICMM.

timballo, *Italian*
ICMM.

timbre, *French*
DFT; ICMM.

timbre-poste, *French*
DFPCQ.

timbrer, *French*
OCM.

timidezza, *Italian*
OCM / *timido*.

timidezza, con, *Italian*
ICMM.

timido, *Italian*
OCM.

timore, *Italian*
OCM.

timorosamente, *Italian*
ICMM.

timoroso, *Italian*
DFT; ICMM.

timpanetto, *Italian*
ICMM.

timpani, *Italian*
DFPCQ; DFT; ICMM; OCM.

timpani *pl., Italian*
DFWPB.

timpani coperti, *Italian*
DFT/*timpani*; OCM.

timpani sordi, *Italian*
ICMM.

timpanista, *Italian*
ICMM.

timtum, *Yiddish*
JOY.

tinaja, *Spanish*
DFT; DSTE; GG.

tinajita, *Spanish*
GG.

ting, *Chinese*
ACD.

tintement, *French*
OCM/*tinter*.

tinter, *French*
OCM.

tintinnabulum, *Latin*
ICMM.

tintinnare, *Italian*
OCM.

tinto, *Italian*
OCM.

tiorba, *Italian*
ICMM.

tiorba, *Spanish*
ICMM.

tirana, *Spanish*
OCM.

tirando, *Italian*
OCM/*tirare*.

tirare, *Italian*
OCM.

tirasse, *French*
DFT; ICMM; OCM.

tirato, *Italian*
ICMM; OCM/*tirare*.

tira tutto, *Italian*
ICMM.

tiré, *French*
ICMM; OCM/*tirer*.

tire-bouchon, en, *French*
LB.

tirer, *French*
OCM.

tirolese, *Italian*
OCM.

tisane, *French*
DFT.

tisane de champagne, *French*
DFT/*tisane*.

Tisha B'ab, *Yiddish*
JOY/*Tisha Bov*.

Tisha B'av, *Yiddish*
JOY/*Tisha Bov*.

Tisha Bov, *Yiddish*
JOY.

ti tzŭ, *Chinese*
ICMM.

tjaele, *Swedish*
GG.

tobend, *German*
ICMM.

tobira, *Japanese*
JLE.

toccata, *Italian*
DFT; DFWPB; ICMM; OCM.

toccatella, *Italian*
DFT.

toccatina, *Italian*
DFT/*toccatella*.

toches, *Yiddish*
DFT; HFY.

tochis, *Yiddish*
JOY.

Todesgesang, *German*
ICMM.

Todeslied, *German*
ICMM.

todt, *German*
OCM.

Todtentanz, *German*
DFWPN.

tofu, *Japanese*
JLE.

toga virilis, *Latin*
DFPCQ; DFT.

togli, *Italian*
OCM.

toile, *French*
DFWPB; OCM.

to kalon, *Greek*
DFPA; DFPCQ.

tokonoma, *Japanese*
DFWPB; JLE.

tokus, *Yiddish*
DFT/*toches.*

Tokushima, *Japanese*
JLE.

tokyo, *Japanese*
JLE.

tolkach, *Russian*
MRWEW/*20.*

tombant, *French*
LB.

tombé, *French*
LB.

tombeau, *French*
OCM.

tombée, *French*
LB/*tombé.*

tombolo, *Italian*
GG.

tome, *French*
DFPCQ; OCM.

ton, *French*
OCM; DFT; ICMM.

Ton, *German*
OCM.

Tonabstand, *German*
ICMM; OCM.

tonada, *Spanish*
ICMM; OCM.

tonadilla, *Spanish*
ICMM; OCM.

tonante, *Italian*
OCM.

Tonart, *German*
DFT; ICMM; OCM.

Ton-ausweichung, *German*
ICMM.

Tonbild, *German*
DFT; OCM.

Tonbühne, *German*
OCM/*Tonbild.*

Tondichter, *German*
DFT; ICMM; OCM/*Tonbild.*

Tondichtung, *German*
ICMM; OCM; OCM/*symphonic poem.*

tondo, *Italian*
LP; OCM.

tondo, *pl.* **tondi,** *Italian*
DFWPB.

ton doux, *French*
ICMM.

Töne, *German*
OCM.

Tonfall, *German*
ICMM.

Tonfarbe, *German*
ICMM; OCM.

Tonfolge, *German*
ICMM; OCM/*Tonfarbe.*

Tonführung, *German*
ICMM.

Tonfülle, *German*
OCM/*Tonfarbe.*

Tongang, *German*
ICMM.

Tongattung, *German*
ICMM.

ton-generateur, *French*
ICMM.

Tongeschlecht, *German*
ICMM/*Tongattung;* OCM.

Tonhöhe, *German*
OCM.

tonica, *German*
ICMM/*tonic.*

tonica, *Italian*
ICMM/*tonic.*

Tonika-do, *German*
OCM.

tonique, *French*
ICMM/*tonic.*

tonitruone, *Italian*
OCM.

Tonkunst, *German*
ICMM; OCM.

Tonkünstler, *German*
ICMM; OCM/*Tonkunst.*

Tonlage, *German*
OCM.

Tonlehre, *German*
OCM.

Tonleiter, *German*
ICMM/*scale;* ICMM; OCM.

tonlos, *German*
OCM.

ton majeur, *French*
ICMM.

Tonmalerei, *German*
OCM.

Tonmass, *German*
ICMM.

Tonmesser, *German*
ICMM.

ton mineur, *French*
ICMM.

tonnelet, *French*
LB.

tonnerre, *French*
OCM.

tono, *Italian*
ICMM/*ton;* OCM/*tuono;* OCM.

tono, *Spanish*
OCM.

Tonreihe, *German*
OCM; OCM/*note-row.*

Tonsatz, *German*
ICMM.

Tonschluss, *German*
ICMM.

Tonschlüssel, *German*
ICMM; OCM.

Tonschrift, *German*
ICMM.

tons de l'église, *French*
ICMM.

Tonsetzer, *German*
ICMM; OCM.

Tonsetzung, *German*
ICMM.

Tonstein, *German*
GG.

Tonstück, *German*
ICMM.

Tonsystem, *German*
ICMM.

tonto, *Spanish*
DSTE.

tonus, *Greek*
ICMM.

tonus, *Latin*
OCM.

Tonveränderung, *German*
ICMM.

Tonwerk, *German*
ICMM.

Tonwissenschaft, *German*
ICMM.

tope, *Anglo-Indian*
DFT.

toph, *Hebrew*
ICMM.

topos, *Greek*
DFWPB.

to prepon, *Greek*
DFPCQ.

Torah, *Yiddish*
HFY; JOY.

torchère, *French*
ACD.

tordion, *French*
OCM/*tourdion.*

toreador, *Spanish*
DFWPB; DFWPN.

toreo, *Spanish*
DFT.

torero, *Spanish*
DFT; DFWPB; DFWPN; DSTE/ 237.

torii, *Japanese*
JLE.

toril, *Spanish*
DSTE/237.

tornada, *Spanish*
DSTE/*tornado*; OCM.

tornadeo, *Spanish*
DSTE/*tornado.*

tornando, *Italian*
OCM/*tornare.*

tornare, *Italian*
OCM.

toro, *Spanish*
DFT; DFWPN; DSTE.

torreon, *Spanish*
DSTE.

torsk, *Danish*
DFT.

torta, *Italian*
DFT.

torta, *Spanish*
DFT.

Torte, *German*
DFT; DFWPN.

tortilla, *Spanish*
DFT; DFWPB; DSTE.

tortillia, *Spanish*
DSTE/*tortilla.*

tortillon, *French*
DFWPB; LP.

tortue, *French*
DFT.

tortue claire, *French*
DFT/*tortue.*

torü, *Japanese*
DFT.

torvo, *Italian*
OCM.

tosca, *Spanish*
GG.

tostamente, *Italian*
ICMM/*tosto.*

tostissimamente, tostissimo, *Italian*
ICMM.

tosto, *Italian*
DFT; ICMM.

toston, *Spanish*
DSTE.

totem, *Ojibway*
DFWPN.

Totenglöckchen, *German*
ICMM.

Totenlied, *German*
ICMM.

Toten Marsch, *German*
ICMM.

Toten Musik, *German*
ICMM.

Totentanz, *German*
OCM.

tot homines, quot sententiae, *Latin*
DFPCQ.

totidem verbis, *Latin*
DEP; DFPCQ.

toties quoties, *Latin*
DFPA; DFPCQ.

toto caelo, *Latin*
DFPA.

toto cœlo, *Latin*
DEP.

totum, *Latin*
DFPCQ.

totum in eo est, *Latin*
DFPCQ.

touché, *French*
DFWPB; DFWPN.

touche, *French*
OCM.

toujours, *French*
DFPCQ; OCM.

toujours l'amour, *French*
DFPA.

toupet, *French*
DFWPN.

tour, *French*
DFT; DFWPB; LB.

tour de basque, *French*
LB.

tour de force, *French*
DFPA; DFPCQ; DFT/*tour*;
DFWPB; DFWPN; LB; LP.

tour de gosier, *French*
ICMM.

tour de main, *French*
DFT/*tour*.

tour de reins, *French*
LB.

tourdion, *French*
OCM.

tour en l'air, *French*
DFWPB; LB.

tour jeté, *French*
LB.

tournant, en, *French*
LB.

tourné d'adage, *French*
LB.

tournedos, *French*
DFT; DFWPB.

tourner, *French*
LB.

tours, chaînés, *French*
LB.

tours, petits, *French*
LB.

tours de force, *French*
ICMM.

tourte, *French*
DFT.

tous, *French*
OCM/*tout*.

tout, *French*
OCM.

tout à coup, *French*
OCM.

tout à fait, *French*
DFPA; DFT; DFWPN; OCM.

tout-à-fait, *French*
DFPCQ.

tout court, *French*
DFPA; DFT; DFWPB; DFWPN.

tout de suite, *French*
DFPA; DFT; DFWPB; DFWPN;
OCM.

toute, *French*
OCM/*tout*.

tout ensemble, *French*
DEP; DFT; DFT/*ensemble*;
DFWPB; DFWPN; OCM.

toutes, *French*
OCM/*tout*.

tout le monde, *French*
DFPA; DFPCQ; DFT; DFWPN.

tovarish, *Russian*
DFT.

tovarishch, *Russian*
DFWPN.

Toyama, *Japanese*
JLE.

toyo, *Japanese*
JLE.

Toyohashi, *Japanese*
JLE.

. . . toyten bankes, *Yiddish*
JOY.

trabajo, *Spanish*
DFT.

trabattere, *Italian*
ICMM.

tracto, *Spanish*
ICMM.

tractulus, *Latin*
ICMM.

tractus, *Latin*
ICMM.

tradolce, *Italian*
ICMM.

tradotto, *Italian*
OCM.

traduction, *French*
OCM/*traduzione*.

traduit, *French*
OCM/*tradotto.*

traduzione, *Italian*
OCM.

tragédienne, *French*
DFT.

trainé, *French*
ICMM; OCM.

trait, *French*
ICMM.

trait de chant, *French*
ICMM.

trait d'harmonie, *French*
ICMM.

trällern, *German*
ICMM.

tranche de vie, *French*
DFPA.

traînée, *French*
ICMM.

tranquillamente, *Italian*
DFT; ICMM.

tranquillezza, tranquillità, tranquillo,
Italian
ICMM.

tranquillo, *Italian*
DFWPN; OCM.

trap, *Swedish*
GG.

trascinando, *Italian*
ICMM; OCM.

trascrizione, *Italian*
OCM.

trasognata, *Italian*
ICMM.

trattenuto, *Italian*
ICMM; OCM.

tratto, *Italian*
OCM.

trattoria, *Italian*
DFT.

trattoria, *pl.* **trattorie,** *Italian*
DFWPB.

Trauergesang, *German*
ICMM.

Trauermarsch, *German*
ICMM.

Trauermusik, *German*
ICMM.

Traum, *German*
OCM.

traurig, *German*
ICMM; OCM.

Trautonium, *German*
OCM.

Trautwein, *German*
OCM/*Trautonium.*

traversa, *Italian*
OCM.

Traversflöte, *German*
OCM/*traversa.*

traversière, *French*
OCM/*traversa.*

traverso, *Italian*
OCM/*traversa.*

travertine, *Italian*
GG.

travesti, en, *French*
LB.

trayf, *Yiddish*
DFT; JOY.

tre, *Italian*
DFWPN.

trecento, *Italian*
DFT.

tre corde, *French*
OCM.

tre corde, *Italian*
DFT; DFWPB; ICMM.

treibend, *German*
OCM.

tremando, *Italian*
DFPCQ; DFT; OCM.

tremante, *Italian*
OCM/*tremando.*

tremblant, *French*
OCM; OCM/*shake.*

tremblement, *French*
ICMM.

tremendo, *Italian*
OCM.

tremolando, *Italian*
DFT/*tremando*; OCM; OCM/
tremando.

tremolante, *Italian*
OCM.

tremolo, *Italian*
DFPCQ; DFT; DFWPN; ICMM.

trenodia, *Italian*
OCM.

trente et quarante, *French*
DFT.

trente-et-quarante, *French*
DFPA; DFWPB.

treppverter, *Yiddish*
HFY.

très, *French*
OCM.

très animé, *French*
ICMM.

très bien, *French*
DFPA; DFPCQ; DFT/*bien*.

tresca, *Italian*
ICMM.

trescone, *Italian*
OCM.

très fort, *French*
ICMM.

très lentement, *French*
ICMM.

très piano, *French*
ICMM.

très vif, *French*
ICMM.

très vite, *French*
ICMM.

Treter, *German*
ICMM.

treyf, *Yiddish*
HFY.

treyfener, *Yiddish*
HFY.

treyfnyak, *Yiddish*
HFY.

Triangel, *German*
ICMM; OCM.

triangolo, *Italian*
ICMM; OCM.

trias, *Latin*
ICMM.

tricinium, *Latin*
ICMM.

tricot, *French*
DFT; DFWPN.

trillando, *Italian*
ICMM.

trillare, *Italian*
ICMM.

trille, *French*
ICMM; OCM/*shake*.

Triller, *German*
ICMM; OCM/*shake*.

Trillerkette, *German*
ICMM.

trillern, *German*
ICMM.

trilletta, *Italian*
ICMM/*trillette*.

trillette, *French*
ICMM.

trilletto, *Italian*
ICMM/*trillette*.

trilli, *Italian*
ICMM.

trillo, *Italian*
DFPCQ; ICMM; OCM/*shake*.

trilogia, *Italian*
OCM/*trilogy*.

trilogie, *French*
OCM/*trilogy*.

trilogie, *German*
OCM/*trilogy*.

Trinkgesang, *German*
ICMM.

Trinklied, *German*
ICMM; OCM.

trino, *Spanish*
ICMM.

trio, *Italian*
DFWPB; ICMM.

triole, *Italian*
DFPCQ.

Triole, *German*
ICMM/*triplet.*

triolet, *French*
ICMM/*triplet.*

trionfale, *Italian*
OCM.

trionfante, *Italian*
OCM/*trionfale.*

tripas, *Spanish*
DSTE.

Tripelconcert, *German*
OCM/*Tripelkonzert.*

Tripelkonzert, *German*
OCM.

Tripeltakt, *German*
ICMM/*triple time.*

triple croche, *French*
ICMM.

triple-croche, *French*
OCM.

triplice, *Italian*
ICMM.

triplum, *Latin*
ICMM.

triptyque, *French*
OCM/*triptych.*

trisagion, *Greek*
ICMM.

trisagium, *Latin*
ICMM.

triste, *French*
DFPCQ; DFWPN; OCM.

triste, *Spanish*
DSTE.

tristesse, *French*
DFPCQ; OCM.

tristezza, *Italian*
DFT; OCM/*tristesse.*

tristèzza, *Italian*
ICMM.

tristo, *Italian*
OCM/*triste.*

triton, *French*
ICMM.

tritono, *Italian*
ICMM.

tritonus, *Latin*
ICMM.

trittico, *Italian*
OCM.

Trittkarren, *German*
GG.

trivium, *Latin*
DFWPB; DFWPN.

trochaeus chorius, *Latin*
ICMM.

trochäisch, *German*
ICMM.

trochäus, *German*
ICMM.

Trogschluss, *German*
GG.

troika, *Russian*
DFT; DFWPB; MRWEW/*17.*

trois, *French*
LB; OCM.

troisième, *French*
LB; OCM.

troisième en avant, *French*
LB/*bras, positions de.*

troisième en haut, *French*
LB/*bras, positions de.*

troisième position, *French*
LB/*pieds, cinq positions des.*

trois-quarts, *French*
LB.

tromba, *Italian*
DFPCQ; DFT; ICMM; OCM.

tromba a macchina, *Italian*
OCM.

tromba bassa, *Italian*
OCM.

tromba clarino, *Italian*
ICMM.

tromba cromatica, *Italian*
OCM.

tromba da tirarsi, *Italian*
OCM.

tromba di basso, *Italian*
ICMM.

tromba di tirarsi, *Italian*
ICMM.

tromba marina, *Italian*
OCM.

tromba sorde, *Italian*
ICMM.

tromba spezzata, *Italian*
ICMM; OCM.

tromba ventile, *Italian*
OCM.

trombenik, *Yiddish*
HFY; JOY.

trombenyik, *Yiddish*
JOY.

trombetta, *Italian*
ICMM.

tromboni, *Italian*
ICMM.

trombonino, *Italian*
OCM.

Trommel, *German*
ICMM; OCM.

Trommel, Grosse, *German*
ICMM.

Trommel, Kleine, *German*
ICMM.

Trommelboden, *German*
ICMM.

Trommelflöte, *German*
OCM.

Trommelkasten, *German*
ICMM.

Trommelklöpfel, *German*
ICMM.

Trommelschlägel, *German*
ICMM/*Trommelklöpfel.*

tromp, *French*
OCM.

trompa, *Latin*
ICMM.

trompe, *French*
ICMM/*trompa*; OCM/*tromp.*

trompe de béarn, *French*
ICMM; OCM/*tromp.*

trompe de berne, *French*
OCM/*tromp.*

trompe de laquais, *French*
OCM/*tromp.*

trompe l'oeil, *French*
ACD; LP.

trompe-l'oeil, *French*
DFPA; DFWPB; DFWPN.

trompes de chasse, *French*
ICMM.

Trompete, *German*
ICMM; OCM.

Trompetengeige, *German*
OCM.

Trompeten-register, *German*
ICMM.

Trompetenzug, *German*
ICMM/*Trompeten-register.*

trompette, *French*
ICMM; OCM.

trompette à coulisse, *French*
OCM.

trompette à pistons, *French*
ICMM; OCM.

trompette basse, *French*
OCM.

trompette chromatique, *French*
OCM.

trompette d'harmonie, *French*
OCM.

trompette harmonique, *French*
ICMM.

trompette marine, *French*
OCM.

trompette parlante, *French*
ICMM.

tronco, *Italian*
ICMM.

trop, *French*
OCM.

troppo, *Italian*
DFT; ICMM; OCM.

tropus, *Latin*
ICMM/*trope.*

trottoir, *French*
GG.

trouvères, *French*
OCM.

trüb, *German*
ICMM; OCM.

trübe, *German*
OCM/*trüb.*

truffe, *French*
DFT.

truffes, *French*
DFWPN.

Trugschluss, *German*
ICMM.

truité, *French*
DFT.

truite, *French*
DFT.

truite au bleu, *French*
DFT/*truite.*

truite de lac, *French*
DFT/*truite.*

truites, *French*
DFWPN.

truite saumonée, *French*
DFT/*truite.*

Trumbscheit, *German*
OCM.

Trummscheidt, *German*
ICMM.

Trumscheit, *German*
OCM.

tryphone, *French*
OCM.

tsadaka, *Yiddish*
JOY/*tzedaka.*

tsatske, *Yiddish*
HFY; JOY.

tsatskeleh, *Yiddish*
JOY/*tsatske.*

tsedoodelt, *Yiddish*
JOY.

tsedoodelteh, *Yiddish*
JOY/*tsedoodelt.*

tsedoodelter, *Yiddish*
JOY/*tsedoodelt.*

tsedraydelt, *Yiddish*
JOY/*tsedrayt.*

tsedrayt, *Yiddish*
JOY.

tsedrayteh, *Yiddish*
JOY/*tsedrayt.*

tsedrayter, *Yiddish*
JOY/*tsedrayt.*

tsedreyt, *Yiddish*
HFY.

tsedudlt, *Yiddish*
HFY.

tsetumlt, *Yiddish*
HFY.

tsetummelt, *Yiddish*
JOY.

tsetummelteh, *Yiddish*
JOY/*tsetummelt.*

tsetummelter, *Yiddish*
JOY/*tsetummelt.*

tsigane, *French*
OCM/*tzigane;* OCM.

tsimmes, *Yiddish*
HFY; JOY.

tsimmis, *Yiddish*
DFT.

tsitser, *Yiddish*
JOY.

tsores, *Yiddish*
HFY.

tsoriss, *Yiddish*
JOY/*tsuris.*

tsouris, *Yiddish*
JOY/*tsuris.*

tsuba, *Japanese*
ACD; JLE.

tsubo, *Japanese*
JLE.

Tsuga, *Japanese*
JLE.

tsugaresinol, *Japanese*
JLE.

tsunami, *Japanese*
DFT; GG; JLE.

tsuris, *Yiddish*
JOY.

tsuriss, *Yiddish*
JOY/*tsuris.*

tsurugi, *Japanese*
JLE.

tsutcheppenish, *Yiddish*
JOY.

tsutsugamushi (disease, mite), *Japanese*
JLE.

tsutsumu, *Japanese*
JLE.

tuba mirabilis, *Latin*
ICMM.

tubo di ricambio, *Italian*
OCM.

tuches, *Yiddish*
DFWPN.

tuchis, *Yiddish*
JOY/*tochis.*

tuebor, *Latin*
DFPCQ.

tufa, *Italian*
DFWPB; GG.

tulare, *Spanish*
GG.

tulle, *French*
DFWPN.

tulwar, *Anglo-Indian*
DFT.

tummel, *Yiddish*
JOY.

tummler, *Yiddish*
JOY.

tumultuoso, *Italian*
ICMM.

tunneldal, *Danish*
GG.

tuoni ecclesiastici, *Italian*
ICMM.

tuono, *Italian*
ICMM; OCM.

tuono mezzo, *Italian*
ICMM.

tu quoque, *Latin*
DFPCQ; DFT; DFWPB.

tu quoque, Brute!, *Latin*
DEP.

turbae, *Latin*
ICMM.

turca, *Italian*
OCM/*turco.*

turca, alla, *Italian*
ICMM; OCM.

turca, turchesco, turco, *Italian*
ICMM.

turco, *Italian*
OCM.

türkisch, *German*
OCM.

Türmermeister, *German*
OCM/*Turm-musik.*

Turm-musik, *German*
OCM.

Turmsonaten, *German*
OCM/*Turm-musik.*

turque, *French*
OCM.

Turquerie, *French*
ACD; DFWPB.

Tusch, *German*
OCM.

tush, *Yiddish*
HFY.

tushy (tush), *Yiddish*
HFY.

tutenag, *Marathi*
ACD.

Tuthorn, *German*
ICMM.

tutta, *Italian*
DFT; ICMM; OCM; OCM/*tutto.*

tutta forza, *Italian*
DFT/*tutta*; ICMM.

tutta la forza, *Italian*
ICMM/*tutta forza.*

tutte, *Italian*
ICMM; OCM/*tutta.*

tutte le corde, *Italian*
OCM.

tutti, *Italian*
DFPCQ; DFT; DFWPB; ICMM;
OCM.

tutti frutti, *Italian*
DFWPB.

tutti-frutti, *Italian*
DFWPN.

tutti unisoni, *Italian*
ICMM.

tutto, *Italian*
ICMM/*tutta*; OCM.

tutto arco, *Italian*
ICMM.

tutu, *French*
DFWPB; LB.

tuum est, *Latin*
DFPCQ.

tympanon, *French*
ICMM.

typophone, *French*
ICMM.

tyrolienne, *French*
ICMM.

tzaddik, *Yiddish*
JOY.

tzedaka, *Yiddish*
JOY.

tzigane, *French*
OCM/*tsigane*; OCM.

tzitzit, *Yiddish*
JOY.

Tziyon, *Yiddish*
JOY/*Zion.*

U

ubac, *French*
GG.

über, *German*
OCM.

Übereinstimmung, *German*
ICMM.

Übergang, *German*
DFT; ICMM.

Überleitung, *German*
DFT.

übermassig [*sic*], *German*
DFT.

übermässig, *German*
ICMM.

Übermensch, *German*
DFT; DFWPB.

uberrima fides, *Latin*
DFWPB.

Überschlagen, *German*
DFT.

ubi libertas, ibi patria, *Latin*
DFPCQ.

ubique, *Latin*
DFPCQ; DFT.

ubi sunt, *Latin*
DFT; DFWPN.

ubi supra, *Latin*
DFPCQ; DFT.

Übung, *German*
DFT; OCM.

udo, *Japanese*
JLE.

Uebung, *German*
OCM/*Übung*.

ugestüm, *German*
OCM.

uguale, *Italian*
ICMM; OCM.

uguali, *Italian*
OCM/*uguale*.

uisge beatha, *Irish*
DFPA.

uji, *Japanese*
JLE.

ukase, *Russian*
DFWPB; DFWPN.

ukelele, *Hawaiian*
DFWPB.

ukiyo-e, *Japanese*
JLE.

ultima, *Italian*
OCM/*ultimo*.

ultima ratio, *Latin*
DFPCQ.

ultima ratio mundi, *Latin*
DFPA.

ultima ratio regum, *Latin*
DEP; DFPCQ.

ultima Thule, *Latin*
DEP; DFPA; DFPCQ; DFT;
DFWPB; DFWPN.

ultimatum, *Latin*
DEP; DFPCQ.

ultimo, *Italian*
OCM.

ultimo (ult.), *Latin*
DFPCQ.

ultimus Romanorum, *Latin*
DFPA.

ultra, *Latin*
DFPCQ.

umana, *Italian*
ICMM; OCM/*umano.*

umano, *Italian*
ICMM; OCM.

umbilicus, *Latin*
DFPCQ.

ume, *Japanese*
JLE.

Umfang, *German*
DFT; ICMM.

Umkehrung, *German*
ICMM; OCM.

Umlaut, *German*
DFWPB.

umore, *Italian*
DFT; OCM.

umstimmen, *German*
OCM.

Umstimmung, *German*
DFT.

un, *French*
OCM/*un'.*

un', *Italian*
OCM/*uno*; OCM.

una, *Italian*
OCM/*uno*; OCM/*un'.*

una corda, *Italian*
DFPCQ; DFT; DFWPB; ICMM.

una corda, *Latin*
OCM.

una voce, *Latin*
DFPCQ.

una volta, *Italian*
DFT; DFT/*volta.*

unbezogen, *German*
ICMM.

und, *German*
DFT; OCM.

unda maris, *French*
OCM.

unda maris, *Latin*
ICMM.

Undezime, *German*
ICMM.

undulazione, *Italian*
ICMM.

une, *French*
OCM/*un'.*

ungar, *German*
OCM.

ungebunden, *German*
OCM.

Ungeduld, *German*
OCM.

ungefähr, *German*
OCM.

ungepotchket, *Yiddish*
JOY.

ungerade Taktart, *German*
ICMM.

Ungestüm, *German*
ICMM.

ungezwungen, *German*
ICMM; OCM.

ungherese, *Italian*
OCM.

unheimlich, *German*
OCM.

uni, *French*
OCM.

uniment, *French*
OCM.

unisono, aria all', *Italian*
OCM.

uniti, *Italian*
OCM.

Universitaet, *German*
DFPCQ.

unmerklich, *German*
OCM.

uno, *Italian*
OCM/*un'*; OCM.

uno animo, *Latin*
DFPCQ.

un peu, *French*
OCM.

un poco, *Italian*
OCM.

un poète manqué, *French*
DFT.

unrein, *German*
DFT.

Unruhe, *German*
OCM.

unruhig, *German*
OCM.

unschuldig, *German*
OCM.

unsingbar, *German*
ICMM.

unten, *German*
OCM.

unter, *German*
OCM.

Unterbass, *German*
ICMM.

Unterbrechung, *German*
ICMM.

Unterhaltungs-Stück, *German*
ICMM.

Untersatz, *German*
OCM.

Unterseeboot, *German*
DFT.

Unterstaz, *German*
ICMM.

Untertasten, *German*
ICMM.

Unterwerk, *German*
OCM.

un, une, *French*
LB.

uomo universale, *Italian*
DFPA.

urheen, *Chinese*
ICMM.

Ursprache, *German*
DFT.

ursprünglich, *German*
OCM.

Urtext, *German*
OCM.

urushi, *Japanese*
JLE.

urushiye, *Japanese*
JLE.

usque ad nauseam, *Latin*
DEP; DFPA; DFPCQ; DFWPN.

usus loquendi, *Latin*
DEP; DFPA; DFPCQ; DFT.

usus promptum reddit, *Latin*
DFPCQ.

ut, *Latin*
OCM.

ut bémol, *French*
ICMM.

ut dièse mineur, *French*
ICMM.

ut infra, *Latin*
DFPA; DFPCQ; DFT; DFWPB;
DFWPN.

ut mineur, *French*
ICMM.

ut saepe, *Latin*
DFWPN.

ut supra, *Latin*
DFPA; DFPCQ; DFT; DFWPB;
DFWPN; ICMM.

utz, *Yiddish*
HFY; JOY.

uvala, *Serbo-Croatian*
GG/*Croatian*.

uxor, *Latin*
  DFWPN.
uyezd, *Russian*
  DFT.

úzhin, *Russian*
  DFT.

V

va, *Italian*
ICMM; OCM.

vaca, *Spanish*
DFT.

vache, *French*
DFT.

vache à lait, *French*
DFT/*vache.*

vacherie, *French*
DFT.

vacillando, *Italian*
ICMM; OCM/*vacillant.*

vacillant, *French*
OCM.

vacquero, *Spanish*
DSTE/*vaquero.*

vacuo, *Latin*
DFT.

vacuum, *Latin*
DFPCQ.

vade mecum, *Latin*
DEP; DFPA; DFPCQ; DFWPB;
DFWPN.

vae victis, *Latin*
DFPCQ; DFWPN.

vagans, *Latin*
ICMM.

vago, *Italian*
OCM.

val, *French*
GG.

vale, *Latin*
DFPA; DFPCQ.

valeas!, *Latin*
DFPCQ.

valenki, *Russian*
MRWEW/*20.*

valet de chambre, *French*
DEP; DFT; DFWPB.

valet de pied, *French*
DFT.

valet de place, *French*
DFT.

valete, *Latin*
DFPA.

valete ac plaudite, *Latin*
DFPCQ.

valeur, *French*
OCM.

valgame dios, *Spanish*
DSTE.

valleuse, *French*
GG.

vallon, *French*
GG.

valore, *Italian*
OCM.

valse, *French*
ICMM; OCM/*waltz.*

valse à deux temps, *French*
ICMM.

vámonos, *Spanish*
DFWPN.

vamoos, *Spanish*
DSTE/*vamos.*

vamoose, *Spanish*
DFWPN; DSTE/*vamos.*

vamos, *Spanish*
DSTE.

vamose, *Spanish*
DSTE/*vamos.*

vaporeuse, *French*
OCM/*vaporeux.*

vaporeux, *French*
OCM.

vaquero, *Spanish*
DFT; DSTE.

variae lectiones, *Latin*
DFWPN/*varia lectio.*

varia lectio, *Latin*
DFPA; DFWPN.

variamente, *Italian*
ICMM.

variamento, *Italian*
ICMM/*variamente.*

variante, *French, Italian*
OCM.

Variante, *German*
ICMM/*variant.*

variata, *Italian*
OCM/*variato.*

variation, *French*
DFWPB; LB.

variato, *Italian*
OCM.

variazione, *Italian*
OCM.

variazioni, *Italian*
DFPCQ; DFT; OCM/*variazione.*

varié, *French*
OCM.

variorum, *Latin*
DFWPB; DFWPN.

variorum notae, *Latin*
DFPA; DFT.

varsoviana, *Italian*
ICMM.

varve, *Swedish*
GG.

varzea, *Portuguese*
GG.

vas, *Latin*
DFT.

vas deferens, *Latin*
DFT/*vas.*

vase, *French*
GG.

Vaterland, *German*
DFPCQ; DFT.

vaterländisch, *German*
OCM.

Vater Unser, *German*
OCM.

vates, *Latin*
DFWPN.

vates sacer, *Latin*
DFPCQ; DFWPN.

vaudeville, *French*
ICMM.

vaya con Dios, *Spanish*
DFPA; DFT.

veau, *French*
DFT; DFWPN.

Veda, *Sanskrit*
DFWPN.

veduta, *pl.* vedute, *Italian*
DFWPB.

veemente, *Italian*
OCM.

velata, *Italian*
ICMM; OCM/*velato.*

velato, *Italian*
OCM.

veldt, *Dutch*
DFWPN.

velis et remis, *Latin*
DFPCQ.

vellutata, *Italian*
ICMM.

vellutato, *Italian*
ICMM/*vellutata*.

veloce, *Italian*
DFPCQ; DFT; ICMM; OCM.

velocemente, *Italian*
OCM/*veloce*.

velours, *French*
DFWPN.

velouté, *French*
DFT; DFWPB; DFWPN; OCM.

vena, *Latin*
DFT.

vena cava, *Latin*
DFT/*vena*.

venaison, *French*
DFT.

vendetta, *Italian*
DFWPB.

venire (facias), *Latin*
DFT.

veni sancte spiritus, *Latin*
ICMM.

veni, vidi, vici, *Latin*
DEP; DFPA; DFPCQ; DFT;
DFWPB; DFWPN.

vent, *French*
OCM.

venta, *Spanish*
DSTE.

Ventil, *German*
ICMM; OCM.

ventile, *Italian*
OCM.

ventile, corno, *Italian*
OCM.

ventile, trombone, *Italian*
OCM.

Ventilhorn, *German*
OCM.

Ventilposaune, *German*
OCM.

Ventiltrompete, *German*
OCM.

ventis remis, *Latin*
DFPCQ.

ventis secundis, *Latin*
DFPA; DFPCQ.

venusto, *Italian*
OCM.

vera da pozzo, *Italian*
DA.

verbatim et literatim, *Latin*
DEP; DFPCQ.

Verbi Dei Minister, *Latin*
DFT.

verboten, *German*
DFT; DFWPN.

verbum sat sapienti, *Latin*
DEP; DFPCQ.

verde antico, *Italian*
DFWPB; DFWPN.

verdigris, *French*
DFWPN; LP.

verdoppeln, *German*
OCM.

verdura, *Italian*
DFWPN.

verdure, *French*
DFWPB.

Verein, *German*
OCM.

vergette, *Italian*
ICMM.

verghetta, *Italian*
ICMM/*vergette*.

verglas, *French*
GG.

vergnügt, *German*
OCM.

verhallen, *German*
ICMM.

verhallend, *German*
ICMM; OCM.

verismo, *Italian*
DFWPN; ICMM; OCM.

vérité, *French*
DFPCQ; DFWPB.

verklärt, *German*
OCM.

Verlag, *German*
DFWPN.

Verlauf, *German*
OCM.

verliebt, *German*
OCM.

verlierend, *German*
OCM.

verlöschend, *German*
OCM.

vermeil, *French*
ACD.

vermicelli, *Italian*
DFPCQ; DFWPN.

vermindert, *German*
ICMM.

vernaccia, *Italian*
DFT.

vernehmbar, *German*
OCM.

vernis Martin, *French*
ACD.

vernissage, *French*
DFWPB; LP.

Vernunft, *German*
DFWPN.

verre, *French*
DFT.

verre églomise, *French*
ACD.

verroterie cloisonné, *French*
ACD.

Verschiebung, *German*
OCM; ICMM.

verschieden, *German*
OCM.

verschwindend, *German*
OCM.

vers de société, *French*
DFPA; DFT; DFWPN.

vers de société *pl.*, *French*
DFWPB.

Versetten, *German*
ICMM.

Versetzung, *German*
ICMM; OCM.

Versetzungs-zeichen, *German*
ICMM.

versiculum, *Latin*
ICMM/*versicle.*

vers libre, *French*
DFPA; DFT; DFWPB; DFWPN.

Versmass, *German*
ICMM.

verso, *Latin*
DFT; DFWPN; LP.

verso pollice, *Latin*
DFPA.

Verspätung, *German*
ICMM.

verst, *Russian*
DFWPN.

Verstand, *German*
DFWPN.

verstärken, *German*
OCM.

verstärkt, *German*
OCM.

verstimmt, *German*
DFT; ICMM.

versus, *Latin*
DEP; DFPCQ.

verte, *Latin*
DFT.

Verte, *German*
OCM.

verteilt, *German*
OCM.

vert émeraude, *French*
LP.

verte subito, *Latin*
ICMM.

vertheilt, *German*
OCM/*verteilt.*

vertönen, *German*
ICMM.

vert Paul Véronèse, *French*
LP.

vertu, *French*
DFPCQ.

verwandt, *German*
ICMM.

Verwechselung, *German*
ICMM.

verweilend, *German*
ICMM; OCM.

verziert, *German*
ICMM.

Verzierungen, *German*
ICMM/*ornaments.*

Verzögerung, *German*
ICMM.

verzweiflungsvoll, *German*
ICMM.

vesperae, *Latin*
ICMM/*vespers.*

vespéral, *French*
OCM.

vespérale, *French*
OCM/*vespéral.*

vesperale, *Latin*
ICMM.

Vesperbrot, *German*
DFT.

vestigia, *Latin*
DFPCQ.

vestigia nulla retrorsum, *Latin*
DEP.

vetro di trina, *Italian*
ACD.

Vetter Michel, *German*
OCM.

vexata quaestio, *Latin*
DFPCQ.

vezzosamente, *Italian*
ICMM.

via, *Italian*
OCM.

viâ, *Latin*
DEP.

via, *Latin*
DFPCQ.

via dolorosa, *Latin*
DFWPB; DFWPN.

via media, *Latin*
DEP; DFPA; DFPCQ.

viaticum, *Latin*
DFPCQ.

vibrante, *Italian*
ICMM.

vibrato, *Italian*
DFPCQ; DFT; DFWPB;
DFWPN; ICMM.

vibrer, *French*
OCM.

vice, *Latin*
DEP; DFPCQ; DFWPB.

vicendevole, *Italian*
ICMM.

vicendevolemente, *Italian*
ICMM/*vicendevole.*

vice versa, *Latin*
DEP; DFPA; DFPCQ; DFT;
DFWPB; DFWPN.

vicino, *Italian*
OCM.

vicuña, *Spanish*
DFWPB; DFWPN; DSTE.

vide, *French*
DFT; ICMM; OCM.

vide, *Latin*
DFPCQ; DFT; DFWPB;
DFWPN.

vide ante, *Latin*
DFT/*vide*; DFWPN.

vide et crede, *Latin*
DEP.

vide infra, *Latin*
DFT/*vide*; DFWPN.

videlicet, *Latin*
DFT; DFWPB; DFWPN.

videlicet (viz.), *Latin*
DFPCQ.

vide post, *Latin*
DFT/*vide*; DFWPN.

vide supra, *Latin*
DFPA; DFT/*vide*; DFWPN.

vide ut supra, *Latin*
DFPCQ; DFT/*vide*.

vie de Bohème, *French*
LP.

viel, *German*
OCM.

vielle, *French*
DFT; ICMM; OCM.

vier, *German*
OCM.

vierfach, *German*
OCM.

vierhändig, *German*
DFT; OCM.

vierstimmig, *German*
DFT.

Viertelnote, *German*
ICMM/*crotchet*.

Viertelton, *German*
ICMM.

Vierundsechzigstel, *German*
OCM.

Vierundsechzigstelnote, *German*
OCM/*Vierundsechzigstel*.

vi et armis, *Latin*
DEP.

vieux, *French*
DFT.

vif, *French*
ICMM; OCM.

vigneron, *French*
DFT.

vignette, *French*
DFWPB; DFWPN; LP.

vigore, *Italian*
OCM/*vigueur*.

vigorosamente, *Italian*
OCM/*vigueur*.

vigoroso, *Italian*
DFPCQ; DFT; OCM/*vigueur*.

vigoureusement, *French*
OCM/*vigueur*.

vigoureux, *French*
OCM/*vigueur*.

vigueur, *French*
OCM.

vihuela, *Spanish*
ICMM.

villancico, *Spanish*
ICMM; OCM.

villanella, *Italian*
ICMM; OCM.

villanelle, *French*
ICMM.

villanesca, *Spanish*
OCM.

villota, *Italian*
ICMM; OCM.

villotta, *Italian*
OCM/*villota*.

vin, *French*
DFT; DFWPN.

viña, *Spanish*
DFT.

vinaigre, *French*
DFT.

vinaigre de toilette, *French*
DFT/*vinaigre*.

vinaigrette, *French*
ACD; DFWPB; DFWPN.

vin blanc, *French*
DFWPB.

vincit amor patriae, *Latin*
DFPCQ.

vin coupé, *French*
DFT/*vin*.

vinctus invictus, *Latin*
DFPCQ.

vinculum matrimonii, *Latin*
DEP.

vin de paille, *French*
DFT/*vin*.

vin de table, *French*
DFWPB.

vin d'honneur, *French*
DFPA; DFT/*vin.*

vin du pays, *French*
DFPA; DFT/*vin;* DFWPB.

Vingt, Les, *French*
LP.

vingt et un, *French*
DFT.

vingt-et-un, *French*
DFWPB.

vingt-un, *French*
DFT/*vingt et un.*

vin léger, *French*
DFWPN.

vin mousseux, *French*
DFWPB; DFWPN.

vino, *Italian*
DFWPN.

vin ordinaire, *French*
DFT/*vin;* DFWPB; DFWPN.

vino veritas, in, *Latin*
SPICE.

vin pur, *French*
DFT/*vin.*

vin rosé, *French*
DFWPB.

vin rouge, *French*
DFWPB.

viola alta, *Italian*
ICMM.

viola bastarda, *Italian*
ICMM; OCM.

viola da braccio, *Italian*
DFPA; ICMM; OCM.

viola da gamba, *Italian*
DFPA; DFT; DFWPN; ICMM;
OCM.

viola d'amore, *Italian*
DFT; ICMM; OCM; OCM/
amore, amour.

viola da spalla, *Italian*
ICMM.

viola di bordone, *Italian*
ICMM; OCM.

viola di fagotto, *Italian*
ICMM.

viola paradon, *Italian*
OCM.

viola pomposa, *Italian*
ICMM; OCM.

viol da gamba, *Italian*
DFWPN.

viol d'amore, *Italian*
DFWPN.

viol d'orchestre, *French*
ICMM.

viole, *French*
OCM.

viole, *Italian*
OCM.

viole d'amour, *French*
OCM.

Violen, *German*
OCM.

violentamente, *Italian*
OCM/*violento.*

violento, *Italian*
OCM.

violenza, *Italian*
OCM.

violetta, *Italian*
ICMM.

violetta piccola, *Italian*
ICMM.

Violinbogen, *German*
ICMM.

Violine, *German*
ICMM.

violini, *Italian*
OCM/*violino.*

violini unisoni, *Italian*
ICMM.

violino, *Italian*
DFT; ICMM; OCM.

violino piccolo, *Italian*
ICMM.

violino principale, *Italian*
ICMM.

Violin-steg, *German*
ICMM.

violon, *French*
ICMM; OCM.

Violoncell, *German*
ICMM.

violoncelle, *French*
ICMM; OCM.

violoncello, *Italian*
OCM.

violoncello piccolo, *Italian*
ICMM.

violon d'amour, *French*
ICMM.

violone, *Italian*
DFPCQ; DFT; ICMM; OCM.

violotta, *Italian*
ICMM.

Virgo, *Latin*
DFPCQ.

virtù, *Italian*
DFWPB.

virtuoso, *Italian*
DFWPN; LP.

virtuoso, *pl.* **virtuosi,** *Italian*
DFWPB.

virtus, *Latin*
DFT.

virtute officii, *Latin*
DFPCQ.

vis, *Latin*
DFT.

vis à vis, *French*
DEP.

vis-à-vis, *French*
DFPA; DFPCQ; DFT; DFWPB;
DFWPN; LP.

vis comica, *Latin*
DFPCQ; DFT/*vis.*

vis inertiae, *Latin*
DFPA; DFT/*vis.*

vis major, *Latin*
DFPA; DFT/*vis.*

vis mortua, *Latin*
DFT/*vis.*

vis poetica, *Latin*
DFPCQ; DFT/*vis.*

vis vitae, *Latin*
DFPCQ; DFT/*vis.*

vis viva, *Latin*
DFT/*vis.*

vita brevis, ars longa, *Latin*
DFPCQ; DFWPN.

vite, *French*
DFT; ICMM; OCM.

vitello, *Italian*
DFWPN.

vitement, *French*
OCM/*vite.*

vito, *Spanish*
OCM.

vitrail, *French*
DA.

vitrine, *French*
ACD.

vitz, *Yiddish*
JOY.

viva, *Italian*
DFPCQ; DFT; DFWPN.

viva, *Spanish*
DSTE.

vivace, *Italian*
DFPCQ; DFT; DFWPN; ICMM;
OCM.

vivace ma non troppo, *Italian*
ICMM/*vivace.*

vivacissimo, *Italian*
ICMM/*vivace.*

viva il papa, *Italian*
DFPA.

vivamente, *Italian*
OCM.

vivat, *French*
DFT/*vive.*

vivat regina, *Latin*
DEP; DFPA; DFPCQ.

vivat respublica, *Latin*
DEP; DFPCQ.

vivat rex, *Latin*
DEP; DFPA; DFPCQ.

viva voce, *Latin*
DFPA; DFPCQ; DFT; DFWPB;
DFWPN.

vivâ voce, *Latin*
DEP.

vive, *French*
DFT; OCM/*vif*; OCM.

vive la différence, *French*
DFPA.

vive la république, *French*
DEP.

vive l'empereur, *French*
DEP.

vive le roi, *French*
DEP.

vive, vale, *Latin*
DEP; DFPCQ.

vivezza, *Italian*
OCM.

vivido, *Italian*
OCM.

vivo, *Italian*
DA; DFT; ICMM; OCM.

vlei, *Dutch*
GG.

vloer, *Afrikaans*
GG.

vocalise, *French*
ICMM; OCM.

vocalizzo, *Italian*
ICMM/*vocalise*; OCM.

voce, *Italian*
DFPCQ; DFT; OCM; OCM/*part*.

voce bianca, *Italian*
DFT/*voce*.

voce di gola, *Italian*
ICMM.

voce di petto, *Italian*
DFPCQ; DFT/*petto*; DFT/*voce*;
DFWPN; ICMM/*voice chest*;
ICMM; OCM.

voce di testa, *Italian*
DFPA; DFPCQ; DFT/*voce*;
DFWPN; ICMM; OCM/*voce di
petto*.

voce granita, *Italian*
DFT/*voce*.

voce mista, *Italian*
DFT/*voce*.

voce pastosa, *Italian*
DFT/*voce*.

voces aequales, *Latin*
ICMM/*equal voices*; OCM/*equal
voices*; OCM.

voce spiccata, *Italian*
DFT/*voce*.

voce velata, *Italian*
DFT/*voce*; ICMM/*veiled voice*.

voci, *Italian*
OCM/*voce*.

voci eguali, *Italian*
OCM/*voces aequales*.

voci equali, *Italian*
OCM/*equal voices*.

voci pari, *Italian*
ICMM/*equal voices*.

Vogelflöte, *German*
ICMM.

Vogelgesang, *German*
ICMM.

Vogelpfeife, *German*
ICMM.

voglia, *Italian*
OCM.

voilà, *French*
DEP; DFPA; DFPCQ; DFT;
DFWPN.

voile, *French*
DFT; DFWPN; OCM.

voix, *French*
DFT; ICMM; OCM/*part*; OCM.

voix aiguë, *French*
ICMM.

voix argentine, *French*
ICMM.

voix blanche, *French*
DFWPN.

voix céleste, *French*
DFT/*voix*; OCM/*celesta*; OCM.

voix de poitrine, *French*
ICMM.

voix de tête, *French*
ICMM.

voix humaine, *French*
OCM.

voix mixte, *French*
ICMM.

Vokal, *German*
DFT.

volador, *Spanish*
DFT.

volaille, *French*
DFT; DFWPN.

volant, *French*
DFT.

volante, *Italian*
DFT; ICMM; OCM.

volata, *Italian*
DFPCQ; DFT; ICMM.

vol au vent, *French*
DFWPN.

vol-au-vent, *French*
DFPA; DFT; DFWPB.

volcanello, *Italian*
GG.

volé, *French*
LB.

volée, *French*
LB/*volé.*

volée, de, *French*
LB.

Volksgesang, *German*
ICMM.

Volkskammer, *German*
DFT.

Volkslied, *German*
ICMM; OCM.

Volkston, *German*
OCM.

Volkstümliches Lied, *German*
ICMM.

voll, *German*
ICMM; OCM.

Volles Werk, *German*
OCM.

völlig, *German*
OCM.

vollstimmig, *German*
DFT; ICMM.

volltönend, *German*
OCM/*volltönig.*

volltönig, *German*
OCM.

volonté, *French*
ICMM; OCM.

volost, *Russian*
DFT.

volta, *Italian*
DFPCQ; DFT; ICMM; OCM.

volte, *French*
ICMM.

volte, *Italian*
OCM/*volta.*

volte-face, *French*
DFPA; DFT; DFWPB; DFWPN.

volteggiando, *Italian*
DFT; ICMM.

volti, *Italian*
DFPCQ; DFT; ICMM; OCM.

volti subito, *Italian*
DFPCQ; DFT/*volti.*

volubile, *Italian*
OCM.

volubilmente, *Italian*
OCM/*volubile.*

vom, *German*
OCM.

von, *German*
OCM.

von hier, *German*
OCM.

vor, *German*
OCM.

voraus, *German*
OCM.

vorbereiten, *German*
OCM.

Vorhalt, *German*
ICMM; OCM.

vorhanden, *German*
OCM.

vorher, *German*
ICMM; OCM.

vorherig, *German*
OCM/*vorher.*

vorig, *German*
OCM.

vornehm, *German*
OCM.

Vorsänger, *German*
ICMM.

Vorschlag, *German*
ICMM; OCM.

Vorspiel, *German*
DFT; ICMM/*prelude*; ICMM;
OCM.

Vorspieler, *German*
ICMM.

Vortrag, *German*
ICMM; OCM.

vortragen, *German*
OCM.

Vortragsstück, *German*
ICMM.

vorwärts, *German*
OCM/*vortragen.*

Vorzeichnung, *German*
ICMM.

vorzutragen, *German*
OCM/*vortragen.*

vospitanie, *Russian*
MRWEW/*20.*

vox, *Latin*
DFT; ICMM.

vox acuta, *Latin*
ICMM.

vox angelica, *Latin*
DFT/*vox*; DFWPB.

vox barbara, *Latin*
DFT/*vox.*

vox faucibus haesit, *Latin*
DFPCQ.

vox humana, *Latin*
DFPA; DFT/*vox*; DFWPB;
DFWPN; ICMM.

vox populi, *Latin*
DFT/*vox*; DFWPB; DFWPN.

vox populi, vox Dei, *Latin*
DFPCQ; DEP.

voyagé, *French*
LB.

voyagée, *French*
LB/*voyagé.*

voyeur, *French*
DFWPB.

voyez, *French*
DFT.

vraisemblance, *French*
DFPCQ; DFWPB; DFWPN.

vuden, *Yiddish*
HFY.

vulgata editio, *Latin*
DFPA.

vulgo, *Latin*
DFPCQ; DFWPN.

vulneratus, non victus, *Latin*
DFPCQ.

vuota, *Italian*
OCM/*vuoto.*

vuota, *Latin*
ICMM.

vuoto, *Italian*
OCM/*vortragen.*

W

wacadash, *Japanese*
JLE.

wachsend, *German*
OCM.

Wachtel, *German*
OCM.

Wacke, *German*
GG.

wadi, *Arabic*
DFWPB; GG.

wahine, *Hawaiian*
DFT.

während, *German*
OCM.

waka, *Japanese*
JLE.

Wakayama, *Japanese*
JLE.

wakizashi, *Japanese*
JLE.

Waldflöte, *German*
ICMM; OCM.

Waldglas, *German*
ACD.

Waldhorn, *German*
ICMM.

walla, *Anglo-Indian*
DFT.

wallah, *Anglo-Indian*
DFT/*walla*.

Walzer, *German*
ICMM/*waltz*; OCM/*waltz*.

Walzertempo, *German* + *Italian*
OCM.

Wanderjahre, *German*
DFPCQ; DFT; DFWPN.

Wanderlust, *German*
DFT; DFWPB; DFWPN.

wankend, *German*
OCM.

warabi, *Japanese*
JLE.

Wärme, *German*
OCM.

wasabi, *Japanese*
JLE.

Wasser, *German*
DFT.

Wasserorgel, *German*
ICMM.

Watt, *German*
GG.

Wattenschlick, *German*
GG.

Wechselgesang, *German*
ICMM.

wechseln, *German*
OCM.

Wechselnoten, *German*
ICMM.

wedeln, *German*
DFWPB.

Weg, *German*
OCM.

Wehmut, *German*
OCM.

Wehmuth, *German*
OCM/*Wehmut.*

Wehrmacht, *German*
DFWPN.

weich, *German*
OCM.

Weihnachten, *German*
DFT.

Weihnachtslieder, *German*
OCM.

weinend, *German*
OCM.

Weinlied, *German*
OCM.

Weinstube, *German*
DFT.

Weite Harmonie, *German*
ICMM.

Weltanschauung, *German*
DFPA; DFT; DFWPN.

Weltanschauung, *pl.* **Weltanschauungen,** *German*
DFWPB.

Weltansicht, *German*
DFT.

Weltgeschichte, *German*
DFT.

Weltkrieg, *German*
DFT.

Weltpolitik, *German*
DFT.

Weltschmerz, *German*
DFT; DFWPB; DFWPN.

Weltweisheit, *German*
DFT.

wenig, *German*
OCM.

werden, *German*
OCM.

Werk, *German*
DFT.

Wesentliche Septime, *German*
ICMM.

Wetterharfe, *German*
OCM.

Wettgessang, *German*
ICMM.

wie, *German*
OCM.

wieder, *German*
OCM.

Wiederanfangen, *German*
ICMM.

Wiederholung, *German*
ICMM/*repeat*; ICMM.

Wiederholungszeichen, *German*
ICMM/*Wiederholung.*

wie geht's, *German*
DFPA; DFT.

Wiegenlied, *German*
DFT; OCM.

wienerisch, *German*
OCM.

Wiener Schnitzel, *German*
DFWPB; DFWPN.

Wildflysch, *German*
GG.

Windharfe, *German*
OCM.

Wirbel, *German*
ICMM/*peg*; OCM.

Wirbeltrommel, *German*
OCM.

wohlgefällig, *German*
OCM.

wuchtig, *German*
OCM.

wunderbar, *German*
DFWPB.

Wunderkind, *pl.* **Wunderkinder,** *German*
   DFWPB.
Wunsch, *German*
   OCM.
Würde, *German*
   OCM.
Wurst, *German*
   DFT.

Wut, *German*
   OCM.
Wuth, *German*
   OCM/ *Wut.*
wu ts'ai, *Chinese*
   ACD.

xabo, *Spanish*
   OCM.

xacara, *Spanish*
   OCM.

xaleo, *Spanish*
   OCM.

xota, *Spanish*
   OCM.

xylophon, *French*
   ICMM.

Y

yachna, *Yiddish*
  JOY/*yachne.*
yachne, *Yiddish*
  JOY.
yagi, *Japanese*
  JLE.
yahrtzeit, *Yiddish*
  JOY.
Yahveh, *Hebrew*
  DFWPN.
Yahveh, *Yiddish*
  HFY; JOY.
yakitori, *Japanese*
  JLE.
yakuza, *Japanese*
  JLE.
yali, *Turkish*
  DA.
Yamaguchigumi, *Japanese*
  JLE.
yamamai, *Japanese*
  JLE.
Yamato-e, *Japanese*
  JLE.
yamoto, *Japanese*
  JLE.
yamun, *Chinese*
  DA.
yang, *Chinese*
  DFWPN.

yang ch'in, *Chinese*
  ICMM.
yang-ts'ai, *Chinese*
  ACD.
Yankel, *Yiddish*
  HFY/*Chaim Yankel.*
yao, *Chinese*
  ACD.
yardang, *Turkish*
  GG.
yarmulkah, *Yiddish*
  JOY.
yarmulke, *Yiddish*
  DFT; JOY/*yarmulkah.*
yashmak, *Turkish*
  DFT.
Yawata, *Japanese*
  JLE.
yayoi, *Japanese*
  JLE.
Yekke, *Yiddish*
  JOY.
yekl, *Yiddish*
  JOY.
yen, *Chinese, Japanese*
  DFWPN.
yen, *Japanese*
  JLE.
yenbond, *Japanese*
  JLE.

yenta, *Yiddish*
DFT; JOY.

yente, *Yiddish*
HFY; JOY/*yenta.*

yents, *Yiddish*
HFY.

yentz, *Yiddish*
JOY.

yentzer, *Yiddish*
JOY.

yerba, *Spanish*
DSTE.

yerba (maté), *Spanish*
DFWPB.

yeshiba, *Yiddish*
JOY/*yeshiva.*

yeshiva, *Yiddish*
JOY.

yeshiva bokher, *Yiddish*
HFY.

yeshiva bucher, *Yiddish*
JOY.

yeti, *Tibetan*
DFWPB.

YHVH, *Yiddish*
HFY; JOY.

yiches, *Yiddish*
JOY.

yichus, *Yiddish*
JOY/*yiches.*

Yid, *Yiddish*
JOY.

yideneh, *Yiddish*
JOY.

yihus, *Yiddish*
JOY/*yiches.*

yingatsh, *Yiddish*
HFY.

yin yang, *Chinese*
DFWPN.

Yisrael, *Yiddish*
JOY/*Yisroel.*

Yisroel, *Yiddish*
JOY.

Yizkor, *Yiddish*
JOY.

Yodel, *German*
ICMM/*Jodel.*

yoga, *Hindi*
DFWPB.

yoga, *Sanskrit*
DFT; DFWPN.

yogi, *Hindi*
DFT; DFWPB.

yok, *Yiddish*
HFY.

Yokkaichi, *Japanese*
JLE.

Yokohama, *Japanese*
JLE.

Yokosuka, *Japanese*
JLE.

yokozuna, *Japanese*
JLE.

yold, *Yiddish*
HFY; JOY.

Yom Kippur, *Hebrew*
DFPA; DFWPB; DFWPN.

Yom Kippur, *Yiddish*
JOY.

yom tov, *Yiddish*
JOY/*yontif.*

yontif, *Yiddish*
HFY.

yontifdig, *Yiddish*
JOY/*yontif.*

yontifdik, *Yiddish*
JOY/*yontif.*

yontiff, *Yiddish*
JOY/*yontif.*

yontik, *Yiddish*
JOY.

Yortsayt, *Yiddish*
HFY.

Yortzeit, *Yiddish*
JOY.

yu, *Chinese*
ACD.

yucca, *Spanish*
   DSTE.
yün lo, *Chinese*
   ICMM.

yusho, *Japanese*
   JLE.
yveh ch'in, *Chinese*
   ICMM.

Z

za, *French*
ICMM.

zabaglione, *pl.* **zabaglioni,** *Italian*
DFWPB.

zabaione, *Italian*
DFWPN.

zacate, *Spanish*
DSTE.

zacaton, *Spanish*
DSTE.

zaddik, *Yiddish*
JOY.

zaftig, *Yiddish*
DFT; JOY.

zaftik, *Yiddish*
HFY.

Zählzeit, *German*
OCM.

zaibatsu, *Japanese*
JLE.

zaikai, *Japanese*
JLE.

zamacuca, *Spanish*
ICMM.

zamar, *Hindi*
ICMM.

zambacuca, *Spanish*
ICMM.

zambra, *Spanish*
OCM.

zampogino, *Italian*
ICMM.

zampogna, *Italian*
DFT; ICMM; OCM.

zampognare, *Italian*
ICMM.

zampoña, *Spanish*
OCM/*zampogna*.

zampouna, *Greek*
OCM/*zampogna*.

zanjón, *Spanish*
GG.

zapateado, *Spanish*
ICMM; OCM.

Zapfenstreich, *German*
ICMM.

zarape, *Spanish*
DSTE.

Zarge, *German*
ICMM.

zart, *German*
DFT; ICMM; OCM.

Zartestimmen, *German*
ICMM.

Zartflöte, *German*
ICMM.

zarzuela, *Spanish*
ICMM; OCM.

Zauberflöte, *German*
OCM.

zavtrak, *Russian*
DFT.

zayde, *Yiddish*
JOY.

zazen, *Japanese*
JLE.

zchuss, *Yiddish*
JOY.

zdrávstvui, *Russian*
DFT.

zdrávstvuite, *Russian*
DFT/*zdrávstvui.*

zecca, *Italian*
DA.

zeffiroso, *Italian*
ICMM.

zehn, *German*
OCM.

Zeichen, *German*
OCM.

Zeichen, alt, *German*
ICMM.

Zeilenbau, *German*
DA.

Zeitgeist, *German*
DFT; DFWPB; DFWPN; LP.

Zeitmass, *German*
OCM.

Zeitung, *German*
DFPCQ.

zelo, *Italian*
OCM.

zelosamente, *Italian*
DFT; OCM/*zelo.*

zeloso, *Italian*
DFT; OCM/*zelo.*

Zen, *Japanese*
DFT; JLE.

zendo, *Japanese*
JLE.

zequia, *Spanish*
DSTE/*acequia.*

zetz, *Yiddish*
JOY.

Zeuge, *German*
GG.

Zeugenberg, *German*
GG.

zeyde, *Yiddish*
HFY; JOY/*zayde.*

zhená, *Russian*
DFT.

zhlob, *Yiddish*
JOY/*zhlub.*

zhlub, *Yiddish*
HFY; JOY.

ziehen, *German*
OCM.

Ziehharmonika, *German*
OCM.

ziemlich, *German*
DFT; OCM.

zierlich, *German*
OCM.

Zigeuner, *German*
OCM.

zilafone, *Italian*
ICMM.

zimbalon, *Hungarian*
OCM.

Zinck, *German*
OCM/*Zink.*

zingara, *Italian*
OCM/*zingaro.*

zingaresa, *Italian*
ICMM.

zingaro, *Italian*
OCM.

Zink, *German*
OCM.

Zinke, *German*
ICMM; OCM/*Zink.*

ziogoon, *Japanese*
JLE.

Zion, *Yiddish*
JOY.

Zither, *German*
OCM.

zitternd, *German*
OCM.

zogan, *Japanese*
JLE.

zögernd, *German*
DFT; OCM.

Zohar, *Yiddish*
JOY.

zombie, *West African*
DFWPB.

zonam solvere, *Latin*
DFPCQ.

Zopf, *German*
ICMM; OCM.

Zopfstil, *German*
OCM.

zoppa, alla, *Italian*
ICMM; OCM.

zori, *Japanese*
JLE.

zortziko, *Basque*
ICMM.

zortziko, *Spanish*
OCM.

zourna, *Russian*
ICMM.

zu, *German*
OCM.

zuerst, *German*
OCM.

zufolo, *Italian*
DFT.

Zug, *German*
ICMM; OCM.

zugeeignet, *German*
OCM.

zugehen, *German*
OCM.

zum, *German*
OCM.

Zunge, *German*
OCM.

zur, *German*
OCM.

zurück, *German*
OCM.

zusammen, *German*
OCM.

zutraulich, *German*
OCM.

zuvor, *German*
OCM.

zwei, *German*
OCM.

Zweikanter, *German*
GG.

zweimal, *German*
OCM.

zweite, *German*
OCM.

zweites, *German*
OCM/*zweite.*

Zweiunddreissigstel, *German*
OCM.

Zweiunddreissigstelnote, *German*
OCM/*Zweiunddreissigstel.*

Zwieback, *German*
DFWPB; DFWPN.

Zwinger, *German*
DA.

zwischen, *German*
OCM.

Zwischengebirge, *German*
GG.

Zwischenmusik, *German*
DFT.

Zwischenspiel, *German*
DFT; OCM.

Zwischenstück, *German*
DFT.

zwo, *German*
OCM.

zwölf, *German*
OCM.

Index of Words and Phrases
by Language

N.B.: *The policy of the editors has been to list words and phrases as they were found in the sources; hence, pecularities in spelling, diacritical marking, syntax, capitalization (especially of German nouns), and language identification, as well as other typographic details have been reproduced exactly as they appeared originally.*

African

hoodoo

Afrikaans

apartheid	laagte	poort	straat
dorbank	nek	sluit	tafelberg
kloof	oshana	spitskop	tafelkop
koppie	ouklip	spruit	vloer
krantz			

Algonquin

pow wow

American Spanish

berrendo	cañon	guarapo	nogada
bisagre	central	legadero	pueblito
caliche	chamisal	mescal	talpatate

Anglo-French

oyez

Anglo-Hindi

charpoy   panee

Anglo-Indian

buksheesh	must	pugi	sunyasi
bukshish	pakka	pukka	tope
charpoy	panee	ryot	tulwar
ghee	pucka	sepoy	walla
ghi	pug	simpkin	wallah
memsahib	puggree	sowar	

Anglo-Latin

quo warranto

Arabic

alcázar	goz	jehad	moolah
Allah	hadj	jihad	mufti
Allah akbar	Hadji	kaffiyeh	mullah
allahu akbar	haj	kafir	mushrebbeyeh
amir	haji	keffiyeh	musjid
bahr	hammada	kess-kess	muwashshah
caliph	hegira	kheneg	nagarah
couscous	hookah	khor	naï
emir	howdah	Koran	nari
fatihah	imam	Mahdi	nay
fulji	iman	masjid	nei
gassi	jebel	Moharram	qanat

Arabic, continued

Ramadan	sahibah	shabka	shish kebab
ras	salaam	sheik	shott
sabkha	salaam aleikum	sheikh	sura
safari	salam	shereef	surah
saheb	seif	sherif	wadi
sahib	serdab	shiah	

Baluchi

karez

Bantu

dambo	omuramba

Basque

jai alai	jai-alai	pordon dantza	zortziko

Bengali

bhil	khal	khari

Berber

agouni	asif	irhzer

Bohemian

furiant

Bulgarian

guzla

Burmese

ozee

Canadian French

coteau

Catalan

contrapás

Celtic

clàrsach

Chinese

an hua	fu	kuan hua	nien hao
cha	hao t'ung	kuei	p'ai hsiao
cheng	hsiao	kung fu	pai ting
chiao-tou	hu ch'in	la pa	pai tun tzu
ch'in	kan pei	lei	pai-tun-tzu
chow fan	kao-lin	li	pai tzu
chüeh	kaolin	ling lung	paktong
êrh hsien	kaolin(e)	mahjong	p'an
fei ts'ui	k'in	mao tai	petimtse
fêng ling	ku	mei ping	petuntse

Chinese, continued

pien ch'ing	sê	ting	yang-ts'ai
pien chung	sêh	ti tzŭ	yao
pien k'ing	shêng	urheen	yen
pien yao	so na	wu ts'ai	yin yang
p'i p'a	T'ai Chi	yamun	yu
sampan	tai chi chuan	yang	yün lo
san hsien	Tao	yang ch'in	yveh ch'in
san tsai			

Choctaw
bayou

Czech
baborácka   baborák

Dakota
tepee

Danish

fōhrde	krone	reol	torsk
fōrde	lur	storis	tunneldal
isblink	planaas		

Dutch

aanhangsel	berm	loessoïde	rolpens
aanleidinge	binnacle	matelotte	schorre
aanmerking	colk	mijnheer	(De) Stijl
aard	de	muisetanden	Stijl, De
Afrikaans	groente	Mynheer	veldt
berg	kopje	rijsttafel	vlei

Eskimo

nanook	nunatak	pingo	sikussak
nunakol			

Finnish
kantele   rapakivi   sauna

French

a	abatis de dinde	abat-voix	à bras ouverts
à	abat-jour	à bientôt	abrégé
abaissé	abat-sons	à bon compte	abreuvoir
abandonné	abattis	à bon droit	abricot
à bas	abattoir	à bon marché	abricot-pêche
abatis	abat-vent	à bonne raison	absence d'esprit

French, continued

acajou
acariâtre
accentué
accolade
accord
accord à l'ouvert
accorder
accouchement
accouplement
accoupler
accusé
accusée
à chacun son goût
à coeur ouvert
à compte
à contre cœur
à contre coeur
à couvert
âcre
adage
à demi
a demi jeu
a demi voix
à dessein
à deux
a deux
à deux cordes
à deux mains
a deux mains
a deux temps
adieu
à discrétion
adoucir
adret
à droite
affaiblissant
affaire
affaire d'amour
affaire (de coeur)
affaire de cœur
affaire de coeur
affaire d'honneur
affaire du cœur
affaire du coeur
affaire flambée
affaires

affleuré
à fond
à gauche
agent provocateur
agilement
agilité
agité
agneau
agneau du
   printemps
à gogo
agraffé
à grand choeur
à grand orchestre
agréable
agréation
agréé
agrégation
agrégé
agrémens
agrément
agréments
agreste
à haute voix
à huis clos
aide (de camp)
aide de camp
aide-de-camp
aide mémoire
aide-mémoire
aigre-doux
aigrette
aigu
aiguë
aiguière
aiguille
aiguillette
ailes de pigeons
aimable
aîné (*masc.*), ainée
   (*fem.*)
air
air à boire
air de caractère
air détaché
air écossais

air, en l'
air irlandais
airs russes
air varié
aise
à jour
ajouter
ajutage
à l'
à la
à la belle étoile
à la bonne heure
à la bordelaise
à la bourgeoise
à l'abri
à la broche
à la campagnarde
à la campagne
à la carte
à la chinoise
à la compagne
à la corde
à la diable
à la fin
à la Française
à la française
à la grecque
à la hollandaise
à la jardinière
à la main
à la maison
à la maître
   d'hôtel
à la marengo
à l'américaine
à la militaire
à la mode
a la mode
à la napolitaine
à l'ancienne
à l'Anglaise
à la parisienne
à la pointe
   d'archet
à la provençale
à la rigueur

à la russe
a la rústica
à la sourdine
à la suédoise
à la viennoise
à la villageoise
à l'espagnole
à l'estragon
alexandrin
à l'extérieur
à l'extrémité
à l'huile
à l'impromptu
à l'improviste
à l'intérieur
à l'irlandaise
à l'italienne
allant
alléchant
allée
allége
allégrement
allemand
allemande
allez
allonge
allongée
allonger
allons
allure
almain
alman
almand
à loisir
à l'ordinaire
a l'ordinaire
alouette
aloyau
altiste
alto
alto moderne
à main armée
amande
amateur
ambiance
ambulant

French, continued

French, continued

au jus
au lait
au miroir
au naturel
au pair
au pied de la
  lettre
au pis aller
au point
au premier
au premier coup
au revoir
au sérieux
au soleil
aussi
autre
autrefois
autres
aux choux
aux confitures
aux cressons
aux morilles
aux oignons
aux petits pois
avant
avant-coureur
avant, en
avant-garde
avant la lettre
avant propos
avant-propos
avant-scène
avec
avec les pieds
aven
à voix forte
à volonté
à votre santé
a votre santé
à vue
à vue d'oeil
axe
baba
baba au rhum
baccara(t)
baccarat

bacchanale
badinage
badinerie
bagasse
bagatelle
baguette
baguettes de bois
baguettes
  d'éponge
baignoire
bain-marie
baisser
balancement
balancé, pas
balançoire, en
ballabile
ballet
ballet blanc
ballet chanté
ballet classique
ballet d'action
ballet romantique
Ballet Russe
ballon
ballon d'essai
ballonné
ballonné à trois
  temps, pas
ballonné composé,
  pas
ballonné, pas
ballotté
ballotté, pas
banco
banquette
bar
barbarie, orgue de
barbeau
barbotine
barbouillage
barcarolle
barége
barège
bariolage
baroque
baroquerie

barrage
barre
baryton-Martin
bas
bas bleu
bas-dessus
bas, en
basques
bas relief
bas-relief
basse
basse chantante
basse chiffrée
basse continue
basse cour
basse danse
basse de flandres
basse de viole
  d'armour
basse d'harmonie
basse taille
basse-taille
basson
basson quinte
basson russe
bastide
bastile
Bastille
batiste
Bâton
battement
battement arrondi
battement
  arrondi, grand
battement battu
battement dégagé
battement
  développé
battement fini pi-
  qué, grand
battement fondu
battement fouetté
battement frappé
battement glissé
battement, grand

battement jeté,
  grand
battement jeté
  pointé, grand
battement ouvert,
  grand
battement, petit
battement piqué
battement
  raccourci, grand
battement relevé
battement retiré
battements battus,
  petits
battements en
  balançoire
battements en
  cloche
battements en
  cloche, grands
battement soutenu
battements serrés
battements sur le
  cou-de-pied,
  petits
battement tendu
battement tendu
  jeté
battement tendu
  relevé
batterie
batterie de cuisine
batterie, grande
batterie, petite
battre
battre les cartes
battu
batture
bavardage
bavarois
bavaroise
béarnaise
beau
beaucoup
beaufait
beau geste

French, continued

beau idéal
beau monde
Beaune
beauté du diable
Beauvais
beaux arts
beaux-arts
beaux esprits
bébé
bec
bécarre
bécassine
becfigue
béchamel
bêche-de-mer
beignet
beignets de pom-
  mes
bel esprit
bel étage
bel-étage
belle
belle âme
Belle Epoque, La
belle époque, la
belle indifférence
belle peinture
belles lettres
belles-lettres
bémol
bercement
berceuse
béret
beret
bergamasque
bergère
bergerette
bergerie
besant
besoin
bête
bête noire
béton
betterave
beurré
beurre

beurre fondu
beurre noir
bibelot
bibliothèque
bidet
bien
bien aimée
bien cuit
bien entendu
bienvenue
bière
bifteck
bijou
bijouterie
billet
billet doux
billet-doux
biniou
bis
bise
bisque
bistro
blanc de blancs
blanc-de-chine
blanc-de-Chine
blanc fixe
blanchailles
blanche
blanchir
blanc mange
blanquette
blasé
blocage
blonde de veau
bluette
bobèche
bocage
bocal
bocanne
boche
boeuf
boeuf à la mode
Bohême
bohémien
bohémienne
bois

boisson
boîte
bombardon
bombé
bombe
bombe glacée
bombe panachée
bombe surprise
bon
bon ami
bonbon
bonbonnière
bonbonnières
bon goût
bon gré, mal gré
bonheur-du-jour
bonhomie
bon jour
bonjour
bon marché
bon mot
bonne
bonne amie
bonne année
bonne bouche
bonne chance
bonne nuit
bonne santé
bonnet de nuit
bon soir
bonsoir
bon temps de la
  mesure
bon ton
bon vivant
bon viveur
bon voyage
bore
borry
bosquet
bouche
bouche bée
bouchée
bouchée aux
  huîtres
bouche fermée

bouche fermée, à
bouchés, sons
bouclé
boudin
boudinage
boudin de lièvre
boudiné
boudin noir
boudin ordinaire
boudoir
bouffant
bouffe
bouffes parisiens
bouffonistes
bouffons
bouffons, guerre
  des
bouillabaisse
bouilli
bouillie
bouillon
boulanger
boulangerie
boule
boulette
boulettes de
  hachis
bouquet d'herbes
bouquet garni
bouquin, cornet à
bourdon
bourdon de
  l'orgue
bourdon de mu-
  sette
bourgeois
bourgeois(e)
Bourgeois
  Gentilhomme
bourgeoisie
Bourgogne
bourrée
bout
boutade
bouteille
boutique

French, continued

French, continued

chalumeau
chambranle
chambré
champêtre
champignon
champlevé
Champville
changement battu
changement de
  pieds
changer de pied
changer, sans
changez
chanson
chanson de geste
chanson des rues
chansonnette
chansonnier
chanson sans pa-
  roles
chansons de geste
chansons de toile
chantant
chanterelle
chanterres
chant funèbre
chantre
chant sacré
chapeau chinois
chapeau de fer
chapelle
chapelle, maître
  de
chapon
chaque
charbonnier
charcuterie
charcutier
chargé d'affaires
chargé(e)
charger, se
charivari
charlatan
charmante
charrette
Chartreuse

chassé
chasse
chasse-café
chasse, cor de
chasse-cousins
chassé croisé
chassé-croisé
chassée
chassé en
  tournant
chassé, pas
chassé passé en
  avant
chassis
château
châteaubriant
château d'eau
chatelaine
chatoyance
chatoyant
chaud-froid
chaudière
chaudron
chef d'attaque
chef de bataillon
chef de cabinet
chef de cuisine
chef d'oeuvre
chef-d'œuvre
chef-d'oeuvre
chef d'orchestre
cheneau
chenier
cher
cherchez la femme
chère amie
chéri
chérie
cheval
chevalet
chevalier
chevaux
chevet
cheville
chevrette
chevreuil

chevrotement
chez
chic
chicane
chiffonier
chiffonière
chiffonnier
chiffré
chifonie
Chinoiserie
chœur
choregraphe
choregraphie
chose
chou
choucroute
chou-fleur
choufleur
chou marin
choux de Brux-
  elles
chromatique
chromophonie
chronique
  scandaleuse
chute
ci-devant
ciment fondu
cinéaste
cinéma-vérité
cinq
cinque-pas
cinquième
cinquième en
  avant
cinquième en bas
cinquième en haut
cinquième
  position
ciré
cire perdue
cirque
cirque niveau
ciseaux
ciseaux, pas de
ciselé

cistre
civet
civet de chevreuil
claire, caisse
clair-obscur
clairon
claque
claquebois
clarinette alto
clarinette basse
clarinette
  contrabasse
clarion
  harmonique
clavecin
clavecin oculaire
claveoline
clavier de récit
clavier des
  bombardes
cliché
clique
cloche, en
cloches
clochette
cloisonné
cloisonnisme
clou
cluse
cochon
cochon de lait
code civil
Code Napoléon
coeur
cognac
coif
coiffeur
coiffure
Cointreau
col
collage
collé
colombage
colophane
combien
Comblanchien

French, continued

comédie de moeurs
Comédie Française
comédie humaine
comédie larmoyante
comique
commandite
comme
comme ci comme ça
comme ci, comme ça
comme il faut
comment allez-vous
comment ça va
commère
commissionnaire
commode
communiqué
compagnon de voyage
comparses
compère
Compiègne
complainte
composé
composé, pas
compositeur
compote
compris
compter
compte rendu
comte
comtesse
concert d'orgue
concerts du conservatoire
concierge
concièrge
conciergerie
concombre
concours
confidante

confiserie
confiseur
confit
confiture
confitures
confrère
confrérie de la passion
connaisseur
conservatoire
conserver
consistoire
consommé
consommé de tête de veau
conte
conté crayon
conteur
contre basse
contrebasse
contrebasson
contrecoup
contredanse
contretemps
convenance
coq
coq au vin
coq de bruyère
coq de combat
coq d'Inde
coquetterie
coquillage
coquille
coquilles de moules
cor
cor anglais
cor à pistons
cor chromatique
corde
corde à jour
corde à vide
cor de basset
cor de chasse
corde fausse
cordelle

cor de nuit
cor de postillon
cor des alpes
cor de vaches
cor d'harmonie
cordon bleu
cordon militaire
cordon rouge
cordon sanitaire
cor mixte
cornemuse
cornet à bouquin
cornet d'harmonie
corps
corps de ballet
corps de garde
corps de rechange
corps de voix
corps diplomatique
corsage
cor simple
cortège
coryphée
cosaque
costumier
côte
Côte d'Azur
côté, de
Côte d' Ivoire
Côte d'Or
côtelette
côtelette de filet
côtelette en papillote
côtelettes
coterie
côtes de bœuf
couac
cou-de-pied
cou-de-pied, sur le
coulamment
coulé
coulée
coulee
couleur de rose

coulisse
couloir
coup
coup d'archet
coup de bourse
coup d'éclat
coup de dès
coup de fond
coup de foudre
coup de glotte
coup de grâce
coup de main
coup de maître
coup d'épée
coup de plume
coup de soleil
coup d'essai
coup d'état
coup de tête
coup de théâtre
coup d'œil
coup d'oeil
coupé
coupé ballotté
coupé brisé
coupé chassé en tournant
coupé dessous
coupé dessus
coupé en tournant
coupé fouetté raccourci
coupé jeté en tournant
coup en passant
coupé, pas
coupure
courante
courge
courge à la moelle
couronne, en
courroie
court-bouillon
couru
couture
couturier

French, continued

couturière
couvert
couverte
crabe
cracovienne
cramignon
craquelé
craquelure
crécelle
crèche
crème
crème
crème à la glace
crème brûlèe
crème de la crême
crème de la crême
crème de menthe
crème de menthe
crème fouettée
crème glacée
créole
crêpe
crêpe de Chine
crêpe lisse
crêpes suzette
crépon
cresson
crêt
crevasse
crève-cœur
crevette
cri de coeur
cri du coeur
crime passionel
crime passionnel
critique
croche
crochet
croisé
croisé derrière
croisé devant
croisée
croisé en arrière
croisé en avant
croiser
croissant

croix botonée
Croix de Guerre
croix, en
croix fourchée
croix pattée
croix pommée
croix sonore
cromorne
croquante
croque-en-bouche
croquembouche
croquette
croquis
crotales
croupier
croustade
croûte
croute calcaire
croûton
croutons
cru
crudités
crystallo ceramie
cuisine
cuisine bourgeoise
cuisinier
cuisse
cuissot
cuit à point
cuivré
cuivre
cul-de-four
cul-de-lampe
cul-de-sac
culotte
curé
curettage
curette
cuvée
cymbales
cythare
d'
d'abord
d'accord
dallage
dame

dance du ventre
dansant
danse
danse comique
danse de caractère
danse d'école
danse de demi-
  caractère
danse de vertige
danse du ventre
Danse Macabre
danse noble
danseur
danseur noble
danseur, premier
danseuse
danseuse,
  première
dariole
darne
daube
Dauphin
de
débâcle
débile
déboîté, pas
debouchment
debouchure
déboulés
débris
début
débutant
décalage
déchant
décidé
decime
déclassé
décollement
décolletage
décolleté
décolletée
décor
décoration
découpage
découpler
dedans, en

de droit
de fait
défaut
défense de fumer
dégagé
dégagé en
  tournant
dégagé, pas
dégager
déhanchement
dehors
dehors, en
déjà vécu
déjà vu
déjeuner
déjeûner
de la
délicatesse
délié
de luxe
démancher
démarche
demi
demi-
demi-bras
demi-caractère
demi-contretemps
demi-détourné
demie-tasse
demi-hauteur
demi-jeu
demi-mondaine
demimondaine
demi-monde
demimonde
demi-pause
demi-plié
demi-pointe
demi-pointes, sur
  les
demi-position
demi-rond de
  jambe
demi-rond de
  jambe à terre

French, continued

demi-seconde
position
demi-tasse
demi-ton
demi-tour
demi-voix
démodé
demoiselle
dénouement
de nouveau
département
de pied en cap
dépôt
dépucellage
de race
de règle
de rigueur
dernier
dernier cri
dernier cri, le
dernier ressort
déroulé
derrière
des
descendant, en
déshabillé
dessin
dessous
dessous des cartes
dessus
dessus de table
dessus de viole
de suite
détaché
détente
détiré, temps
détonner
détour
détourné
détourné d'adage
de trop
deux
deuxième
deux temps
deux-temps
devant

développé
développé en
fondu
développement
développé passé
développé, temps
diable
diablerie
diagonale
diagonale, en
dialogue intérieur
diamanté
diapason à
bouche
diapason à
branches
diapason normal
dièse
diésis
Dieu
Dieu et mon droit
Dieu vous garde
difficile
dinde
dinde en daube
dindon
dindonneaux
dîner
diner
Directoire
discothèque
distingué
distrait
dit
dithyrambe
divertissement
divisés
dix
doigt
doit
doivent
donnée
d'orsay
dos à dos
dos-à-dos
dos au public

dossier
douane
douanier
doublé
double
double bémol
doublé cadence
double corde
double croche
double-croche
double dièse
double entendre
double entente
doublette 2
doublure
douce
doucement
douceur
doucine
douleur
doux
doyen
drame lyrique
drapeau tricolore
draperie mouillée
dressage
droit
droit du seigneur
droite
droite, à
du
duchesse
du jour
duo
dur
dureté
duvet
eau
eau de Cologne
eau de vie
eau forte
eau rougie
eau sucrée
ébéniste
ébénisterie
écarté

échappé
échappé battu
échappé changé
échappée de
lumière
échappé royale
échappé sans
changer
échappé sauté,
grand
échappé sauté,
petit
échappé sur les
pointes
échappé, temps
écharpe
échelette
échelle
echelle
échelle
chromatique
échelle diatonique
échelon
echelon
éclair
éclat
éclatant
école
ecole militaire
école normale
ecole
polytechnique
école primaire
écorché
écossaise
écoulement
écrasement
écraseur
écrevisse
écritoire
écru
écuelle
effacé
effacé derrière
effacé devant
effacée

French, continued

French, continued

esquisse-esquisse
essence, l'
estaminet
estampida
estampie
estompé
esturgeon
et
étage
étagère
étang
état
Etats Unis
éteindre
étendre
étendue
étoile
étoile de mer
étouffé
étouffer
être
étude
etude de concert
études
étudiant
étui
étuvée
évasé
éveillé
exactement
exercices à la
  barre
exercices au mi-
  lieu
explication de
  texte
exposé
expressif
extension
extrêmement
fabliau
façade
face, de
face, en
facettes
facile

facilement
façon de parler
façonné
fa dièse
faible
faience
faience anglais
faience Japonnée
faience parlante
faience populaire
faience porcelaine
faillé
faille
failli, pas
faire
faire le salon
faisan
fait
fait accompli
faites
faites vos jeux
falaise
famille jaune
famille noire
famille rose
famille verte
fantaisie
fantasque
farandole
farce
farci
fatrasie
fausset
fausse tortue
fauteuil
(Les) Fauves
fauvisme
faux
faux ami
faux amis
fauxbourdon
faux pas
fedora
femme
femme couverte

femme de cham-
  bre
femme fatale
fendu
fenêtre
fenouil
ferme
fermé(e)
fermer
fête
fête champêtre
feu de joie
feuille d'album
feuilletage
feuilleton
fève
fève de marais
fiancée
ficelles
fier
fière
figurant
figure
figuré
filer
filer la voix
filer le son
filet
filet mignon
fille
fille de joie
fils
filtre
fin
financière
fin de siècle
fine (champagne)
fine champagne
fines herbes
fin gourmet
flacon
flacon d'odeur
flageolet
flageolet notes
flageolet tones
flambé

flânerie
flatté
flattément
flatter
flautendo
flèche
flèche d'amour
fléchir
fleur
fleur de lis
fleur-de-lis
fleur de lys
fleuret
fleuron
flic-flac
flic-flac en
  tournant
flottant
flotter
flûté
flûte
flûte à bec
flûte à cheminée
flûte allemande
flûte alto
flûte à pavillon
flûte d'amour
flûte d'angleterre
flûte douce
foie
foie de veau
foie gras
foies gras
fois
folie de grandeur
fondant
fondé(e)
fonds d'orgue
fondu
fondue
fonte
force de frappe
force majeure
forlane
format de poche
formes libres

French, continued

fort
forte
fou
fouetté
fouetté, demi
fouetté, grand
fouetté, petit
fouetté en l'air
fouetté en
    tournant, petit
fouetté raccourci
fouetté rond de
    jambe en
    tournant
fougueuse
fougueux
four
fourchette
fourragère
foyer
fracas
fraîche
frais
fraise
framboise
franc
français
française
franchise
frangipane
frappé
frapper
fredon
fredonner
frère
friandise
fricassé
fricassée
frit
friture
froid
fromage
fronton
frottage
fugue
fumage

funèbre
furieusement
furieux
fusain
fusée
fuyant
gaffe
gai
gaiement
gaillard
gaillarde
galamment
galant
galanteries
galantine
galbe
galimathias
galliard
galop
galoubet
gamine
gamme
garbure
garçon
garde du corps
garde mobile
garder
gardez la foi
gare
gargouillade
garni
garniture de
    cheminée
gastronome
gâteau
gâte-sauce
gauche
gauche, à
gaucherie
gaufrette
gavage
gavotte
gelée
gelée de groseille
gendarme
gendarmerie

gendarmes
génépi
genou
genre
gens d'armes
gens de condition
gens d'église
gens de guerre
gens de lettres
gens de loi
gens de peu
gens de robe
gens du bien
gens du monde
gentil
gentilhomme
gentille
gibelotte
gibier
gibier à plume
gibier de potence
gigot
gigue
gilet
girandole
gisement
glace
glacé
glacière
glacier remanié
glissade
glissade changée
glissade derrière
glissade devant
glissade en arrière
glissade en avant
glissade précipitée
glissade sur les
    pointes
glissant
glissé
glisser
godiveau
gommeux
gorge de pigeon
gorge-de-pigeon

gouache
gouffre
gour
gourmand
gourmandise
gourmet
goût
goût de chant
goûter
goût raffiné
goutte
goutte à goutte
gracieuse
gracieux
gradin
gradine
graduellement
grand
grand bourdon
grand bugle
grand chœur
grand choeur
grand cru
grand détaché
grande
grande dame
grande flûte
grande parure
grand jeu
grand mal
grand orchestre
grand orgue
grand-positif-récit
Grand Prix
grand prix de
    Rome
Grand-Récit
grand seigneur
gras
grasseyé
gratin
gratinée
gravement
grelots
grenouille
grillé

French, continued

griotte
grippe
grisaille
gros
gros-bois
groseille
groseille à ma-
    quereau
groseille verte
grosgrain
gros point
gros poisson
grosse
grosse caisse
gros tambour
groupe
Guéridon
guerre
guerre à
    l'outrance
guerre à mort
guerre à outrance
guerre des bouf-
    fons
guilloche
guillotine
guimbarde
guimpe
guingette
guipure
guitare
guitare d'amour
habitant
hachis
hanaise
hardi
hardiment
hareng
hareng frais
hareng fumé
hareng pec
haricot
haricot
    de mouton
haricots verts

harmonie
harmonie, basse
    d'
harmonie,
    cor d'
harmonie, cornet
    d'
harmonie,
    trompette d'
harmonique
harpchorde
harpe à crochets
hasardé
haut
haut, en
hautbois
hautbois d'amour
hautboy
haute
haute bourgeoisie
haute coiffure
haute couture
haute cuisine
haute danse
hauteur
haut goût
haut-relief
haut ton
havanaise
hectare
héroïque
hocket
hollandais
hollandaise
homard
homme
homme d'affaires
homme de bien
homme de guerre
homme de lettres
homme de paille
homme d'épée
homme d'esprit
homme d'état
homme de théâtre

homme du monde
homme du peuple
homme moyen
    sensuel
honnête homme
hon(n)i soit qui
    mal y pense
hoquet
hors concours
hors d'affaire
hors de combat
hors de commerce
hors de concours
hors de propos
hors de saison
hors d'œuvre
hors d'oeuvre
hors d'oeuvres
hors la loi
hôtel
Hôtel de Ville
hôtel Dieu
hôtel garni
hôtel meublé
huchet
huit
huitain
huître
huîtres en coquille
humoresque
ibérien
ibérienne
ici
ici on parle
    français
idée fixe
idée maîtresse
idée mère
idées reçues
il
il faut
il n'y a pas de
    quoi
il y a
impair
impétueux

imprimé
impromptu
incliné
inclinée
inconnu
inconnu(e)
inégales, notes
ingenue
ingénue
inquiet
insouciance
insouciant
instrument à
    cordes
instrument à vent
intermède
intime
intimiste
j'accuse
Jacquerie
Jacques
    Bonhomme
jalousie
jambe
jambon
japonaiseries
jardin
jardinière
je m'en fous
je ne sais quoi
je-ne-sais-quoi
je suis prêt
jet d'eau
jeté
jeté, grand
jeté, pas
jeté, petit
jeté bateau
jeté battu
jeté de côté
jeté dessous
jeté dessus
jetée
jeté en arrière,
    grand

French, continued

jeté en arrière,
  petit
jeté en attitude
jeté en avant,
  grand
jeté en avant,
  petit
jeté en tournant
jeté en tournant
  entrelacé, grand
jeté en tournant
  par demi-tours
jeté en tournant
  par terre
jeté entrelacé
jeté enveloppé
jeté fermé
jeté fermé de côté
jeté fouetté, grand
jeté passé
jeté renversé,
  grand
jetés battements
jeté sur les
  pointes
jeté volé de côté
jeu
jeu de clochettes
jeu de hasard
jeu de mots
jeu d'esprit
jeu de théâtre
jeu de timbers
jeu du hasard
jeune fille
jeunesses
  musicales
jeu ordinaire
jeux
jeux d'anches
(les) jeux sont
  faits
Jodel
joie de vivre

joli
joli(e)
jongleur
jouer
jour
jour gras
jour maigre
journal intime
joyeuse
joyeux
Joyeux Noël
jubé
julienne
jumelle
jus
jusqu'à
juste
juste milieu
juste-milieu
j'y suis, j'y reste
kari
kari à l'indienne
koum
krakovienne
l'
la
la belle dame sans
  merci
la belle époque
la bémol
la bonne bouche
lâcher
(la) comédie
  humaine
la comédie
  larmoyante
la condition
  humaine
la douce France
la fortune passe
  partout
La Grande
  Voleuse
lagune
la haute politique

lai
laisser
laisser-aller
laisser faire
laisser-faire
laissez aller
laissez-aller/
  laisser-aller
laissez dire
laissez faire
laissez-faire/
  laisser-faire
laissez passer
lait
laitance
lait coupé
laitue
la majeur
lambrequin
lamé
la mineur
lampons
lamproie
la nation bouti-
  quière
langage
langoureusement
langoureux
langouste
langue
langue de chat
langue-de-chat
langue d'oc
langue d'oïl
langue maternelle
languettes
langueur
langue verte
languissant
la nouvelle cuisine
lapereau
la petite bourgeoi-
  sie
lapin
lapin au kari
la règle du jeu

(la) Résistance
large
largement
l'argent
largeur
larmier
l'art de vivre
L'Art Nouveau
l'art pour l'art
lay
le
le beau monde
le bon genre
leçon
le demi-monde
(le) dernier cri
le dernier cri
le dernier mot
le dessous des
  cartes
le droit des gens
le fin mot
légature
léger
légère
légèrement
Légion d'Honneur
le grand mal
Le Grand Mo-
  narque
le grand monde
le grand prix
le grand siècle
le haut monde
le juste milieu
le juste-milieu
l'élan vital
Le Métro
le monde
le monde savant
(le) mot juste
le mot juste
Le Moyen Age
lent
lentille
l'envoi

French, continued

le petit caporal
le petit coin
le petit monde
le premier pas
le premier venu
le roi est mort,
    vive le roi
le roi le veut
le roi s'avisera
les
les affaires font
    les hommes
le Salon
les amis du vin
le savoir-faire
le savoir-vivre
les convenances
lèse majesté
lèse-majesté
les jeux sont faits
l'esprit de suite
lesquercade
les savants
les scènes à faire
L'état, c'est moi
l'état c'est moi!
le tout ensemble
lettre
lettre de cachet
lettre de change
lettre de créance
lettre de crédit
lettre de récréance
levee
levraut
l'homme
liaison
liberté, égalité,
    fraternité
liberté, egalité,
    fraternité
libre
librement
libret
lié
lieu

lièvre
ligne
limande
limon
liqueur
lisse
lit de justice
littérateur
livre
livre à clef
livres d'heures
locale
logiste
loin
lointain
longe
Louis-d'or
Louis Quatorze
Louis Quinze
Louis Seize
Louis Treize
lourd
lourde
loure
lugubre
lumière
lumineux
lune
l'usage du monde
luth
luthier
lycée
lyre, en
lyrique
macabre
macédoine
ma chère
ma chérie
machine à vent
macle
madeleine
mademoiselle
madère
madrilène
magot
maigre

mailloche
maillot
main
main droite
mains
mairie
mais
maison
maison de jeu
maître
maître de ballet
maître de chapelle
maître de danse
maître d'hôtel
maîtrise
majestueuse
majestueux
majeur
mal
malades
    imaginaires
maladie du pays
maladresse
maladroit
mal à propos
malapropos
mal de mer
mal du pays
malgré lui
malgré moi
malgré nous
malgré soi
malgré tout
mal (maladie) du
    siècle
manche
manécanterie
manége
manège
manège, en
manicorde
mannequin
manqué
maquereau
maquette
maquillage

marabout
marbré
marche
marche aux
    flambeaux
Mardi Gras
mariage
mariage de con-
    science
mariage de conve-
    nance
mariage de la
    main gauche
mariage de poli-
    tique
mariage
    d'inclination
marinade
mariné(e)
marli
marmite
marouflage
marque
marqué
marque de
    fabrique
marquer
marqueterie
marquis
marquise
marron
marron d'inde
marron glacé
marrons glacés
Marseillaise
marteau
martelé
martellement
mascarade
masque
massé
massepain
masseur
masseuse
massier
matassins

French, continued

matelassé
matelote
matelotte
matière
mattachins
mauresque
mauvaise honte
mauvais goût
mauvais ton
mazagran
me
medaille
mélange
mélange de genres
mêlé
mêlée
mélopée
même
mémoire
ménage
ménage à trois
ménestrandie
ménestrel
ménestrel de
  bouche
ménestrel de
  guerre
ménestrier
menthe
mention
menu
menuet
menu gibier
menuisier
menu peuple
merci
merci beaucoup
merde
mer de glace
mère
meringue
merlan
merveilleux
mésalliance
mesdemoiselles
messe des morts

mesure
mesure à trois
  temps
méthode
métier
mètre
métronome
mettre
meubles
meubles
  d'occasion
mi
mi bemol
Midi
mi diese
mignard
mignardise
mignon
mijoter
milieu
milieu, au
militaire
millefleurs
millier
mimer
mineur
mirliton
miroton
mise
mise a la masse
mise en scène
misère
miséricorde
modéré
modestie
modiste
moelle de bœuf
mœurs
mofette
moi
moins
moiré
moire antique
moisson
moitié
molasse

moment musical
mon ami
mon cher
monde
Mon Dieu
monocoque
monocorde
monologue
  intérieur
monseigneur
monsieur
montage
montant
monter
monticule
montre
moqueur
moraine
morceau
mordant
morisque
morne
mortifié
morue
mosaique
mot
mot à mot
mot d'écrit
mot de guet
mot de l'énigme
mot de passe
mot de ralliement
mot d'ordre
mot du guet
mot d'usage
motif
motif conducteur
mot juste
mot pour mot
mot pour rire
mot propre
mots de terroir
mots d'usage
motte
mouflon
moule

moulin
moulinage
mousse
mousseline
mousseline-de-
  laine
mousseline de
  soie
mousseline-de-soie
mousseux
moutarde
mouton
moutonnée
mouvement
mouvementé
Moyen Age
mûr
mûre
musette
musique à la
  turque
musique concrète
Nabis, Les
nacaires
naïf
naïve
naïvement
naïveté
Napoléon
napoleon
napolitaine
nappe
naturel
nature morte
navarin
navet
né
ne
nécessaire
née
negligé
negligé(e)
nerveux
ne . . . pas
n'est-ce pas
net

French, continued

nette
neuf
neuvième
névé
n'importe
noblesse
noblesse de robe
noblesse oblige
nocturne
Noël
noir
noire
noisette
noix
noix de muscade
nom
nom de guerre
nom de plume
nom de théâtre
nom emprunté
non
nonette
noques
nouilles
nous verrons
nouveau riche
nouveaux riches
nouvelle
nouvelle riche
nouvellette
nouvelle vague
nuance
nuances
nuée ardente
objet d'art
objet de piété
objet d'occasion
objets d'art
objet trouvé
obligé
oboe, basset
oboe d'amore
octandre
octaves aiguës
octaves graves
octavin

octet
octuor
œuf
oeuf
œufs à la coque
oeufs à la coque
œufs à la neige
œufs à l'indienne
œufs brouillés
oeufs brouillés
œufs frais
œufs pochés
oeufs sur le plat
œuvre
oeuvre
œuvres complètes
offertoire
ombré
ombres chinoises
ondé
on dit
ondulé
on parle français
opéra bouffe
opéra-bouffe
opéra comique
opéra-comique
opposition
orageuse
orageux
orchestre de genre
ordinaire
ordonnance
ordre
orge
orgue
orgue de barbarie
orgue de salon
orgue en table
orgue expressif
orgue plein
orgue positif
origine contrôlée
ormolu
or moulu
orné

orthose
oseille
ôter
où
ou
oued
outré
ouvert
ouverte
ouverture
ouverture de
  jambe
ouvrage
ouvrir
pailles de parme-
  san
paillette
pain
pair
paix
paléographie
  musicale
paléophone
pampre
panaché
panache
panade
panais
paner
panier
panné
pannier
pantomimer
panure
paon
papier mâché
papier maché
papier-mâché
papiers collés
papiers déchirés
papiers découpés
papillon
papillote
par avion
pardessus de viole
pardonnez-moi

par example
par excellence
par exemple
parfait
parfum
pari mütuel
pari mutuel
parmentier
parole
parole d'honneur
par terre
parti
partie
parti pris
partition
parure
parvenu
pas
pas battus
pas couru
pas d'action
pas de basque
pas de basque en
  tournant
pas de basque en
  tournant, grand
pas de basque
  glissé en avant
pas de basque,
  grand
pas de basque
  sauté en avant
pas de bourrée
pas de bourrée
  changé
pas de bourrée
  changé sur les
  pointes
pas de bourrée
  couru
pas de bourrée
  derrière
pas de bourrée
  dessous
pas de bourrée
  dessus

French, continued

Language Index

pas de bourrée détourné
pas de bourrée devant
pas de bourrée en arrière
pas de bourrée en avant
pas de bourrée en tournant
pas de bourrée en tournant en de- dans
pas de bourrée en tournant en dehors
pas de bourrée fondu
pas de bourrée piqué
pas de bourrée renversé
pas de chat
pas de chat jeté
pas de chat russe
pas de chat russe, grand
pas de cheval
pas de ciseaux
pas de deux
pas de deux, grand
pas de poisson
pas de quatre
pas des écharpes
pas-de-souris
pas de trois
pas de valse
pas du tout
pas glissant
pas glissé
pas marché
pasquinade
passacaille
passé
passe

passecaille
passe-partout
passe-pied
passepied
passerelle
pas seul
pastèque
pastiche
pasticheur
pastille
pas tombé
pastorale
pastorelle
pâté
pâte
pâté de foie gras
paté de foie gras
pâte-de-verre
pâte dure
pâte feuilletée
pâte sur pâte
pâte-sur-pâte
pâte tendre
pathétique
pâtisserie
pâtissier
patois
patron
pause
pavé
pavillon
pavillon chinois
paysage
pays de cocagne
peau
peau de soie
peau-de-soie
pêche
péché mortel
pédale
peignoir
peinture
peinture à la colle
peinture à l'essence
peinture claire

pelure
penché, penchée
pendant
pénétrant
penitent
pensée
penseur
pension
perdreaux
perdrix
perdu
perdu(e)
père
périgourdine
persiflage
persifleur
persil
perspectif cavalière
pesant
petit
petit beurre
petit bourgeois
petit bugle
petit caporal
petit dejeuner
petit détaché
petite
petite flûte
petite flûte octave
petite marmite
petite pedale
petite pièce
petites gens
petites morales
petit four
petit-lait
petit mal
petit point
petits-chevaux
petits droits
petits fours
petits jeux
petit souper
petits pois
petits tours

petit sujet
petit verre
peu
peut-être
piano à queue
piano-mécanique
picot
pièce
pièce à thèse
pièce bien faite
pièce de circon- stance
pièce de resis- tance
pièce de résis- tance
pièce de spectacle
pièce de théâtre
pièce d'occasion
pièce montée
pièce noire
pièce rose
pied
pied, être de
pied à demi
pied à quart
pied à terre
pied-à-terre
pied à trois quarts
pied de biche
pied en l'air
piedroit
pieds, cinq posi- tions des
piétiner
pincé
pince-nez
piquante
piqué
piqué à terre
piqué détourné
piqué enveloppé
piquer la pointe
piquet
piqué tour

French, continued

piqué tour en dedans
piqué tour en dehors
pirouette
pirouette, grande
pirouette renversée
pis aller
pis-aller
pisé
pistolet
piston
pistons, bugle à
pistons, trombone à
piton
placé
place, sur
plage
plainte
plaisant
planchette ronflante
plané
planèze
plaqué
plat
plat du jour
plateau
plateaux
plate carrée projection
plein
plein air
pleine
plein jeu
plié
plié, grand
plier
pliqué à jour
plique à jour
plissé
plus
pochade
poché

pochette
poêle
poelée
poème symphonique
poids
point
point d'Angleterre
point d'appui
point de France
point de repère
point d'esprit
point d'orgue
pointé
pointe
pointes, sur les
pointes, temps de
pointe tendue
pointe tendue à terre
pointillisme
pointilliste
poire
poireau
pois
poisson
poitrine
poitrine d'agneau
poivrade
poivre
politesse
polonaise
pomme
pomme de terre
pommes frites
pompadour
pompeuse
pompeux
porc
port de bras
port de voix
porté
portée
porte-monnaie
porter la voix
portière

pos
posé
pose
posément
poser
positif
positif-récit
position
position fermée
position naturelle
position ouverte
positions soulevées
postiche
potage
potage à la queue de bœuf
potage au gras
potage de printanier
potage du jour
pot au feu
pot-au-feu
potiche
potiron
pot pourri
pot-pourri
potpourri
pouce
pouding
poularde
poulet
poulet roti
poult-de-soie
pour
pour passer le temps
pourquoi
poussé
pousse-café
pousse-cafe
poussin
praliné
praline
précédemment
précieux

préciosité
précipité
précis
prélude
préluder
premier
premier coup
premier cru
premier danseur
premier danseur étoile
première
première danseuse
première, en
première position
prendre
préparation
près
pré-salé
présalé
presque
pressant
pressez
prestige
prêt(e)
prie-dieu
prière
prima ballerina
printanier
printanière
prise
prix
Prix de Rome
prix fixe
procès-verbal
profil perdu
projet
prolétaire
promenade, en
promptement
propriété littéraire
protégé
protégée
Provençal
provençale
pruneau

French, continued

French, continued

rien
rien ne va plus
rigolet
rigueur
rillettes
rinceau
ripopée
ris de veau
risqué
rissolé
rite de passage
ritournelle
rive gauche
rivière
riz
robe de chambre
robe de cour
robe de nuit
robe de style
rocaille
roche moutonnée
rognon
rôle
rôle de l'équipage
roman
roman à clef
roman à thèse
roman bourgeois
romance
romance sans pa-
   roles
romanesque
roman
   expérimental
roman-fleuve
roman poétique
roman policier
rond
rond, en
rond de jambe
rond de jambe à
   terre
rond de jambe à
   terre, demi-
   grand

rond de jambe à
   terre, grand
rond de jambe en
   l'air
rond de jambe en
   l'air, demi-
   grand
rond de jambe en
   l'air, grand
rond de jambe en
   l'air sauté
rond de jambe
   fermé
rond de jambe
   jeté en l'air
rond de jambe
   ouvert
rond de jambe
   piqué
ronde
rondeau
rondo
ronds de bras
ronds de jambe
   balancé
ronds de jambe
   en l'air en-
   tournant
Roquefort
rosbif
rosé
rose du Barry
rotation
rôti
rôtisserie
rôtissoire
roué
rouelle de veau
rouge
rouge et noir
rouge-et-noir
rouge-et-noire
roulade
roulant
roulante

rouleau
roulette
roux
royale
royale double
royale double
   fermé
royale double
   ouvert
rudement
rue
ruiné
ruse de guerre
rythme
rythmique
sabot
saccadé
sacré
sacre bleu
sacré bleu
saignant
salé
salle
salle, au tour de
   la
salle à manger
salle d'armes
salle d'attente
salle de danse
salle de jeu
salle privée
salmagundi
salmi
salmis
salon
Salon d'Automne
Salon des In-
   dépendants
Salon des Refusés
saloperie
salpicon
salut
sang-de-boeuf
sang-froid
sangfroid
sanglier

sanglot
sans
sans-culotte
sansculotte
sans culottes
sans Dieu, rien
sans doute
sans mélange
sans pareil
sans peur et sans
   reproche
sans souci
santé
saraband
sarabande
sauce à la menthe
sauce au beurre
sauce aux câpres
sauce béarnaise
sauce blanche
sauce financière
sauce hollandaise
sauce meunière
sauce piquante
sauce relevée
sauce verte
saucisse
saucisson
saumon
saut de basque
saut de chat
saut de flèche
sauté
sautillé
sauvage
sauve qui peut
savant
savate
savoir faire
savoir-faire
savoir vivre
savoir-vivre
saynète
scène
scène à faire
scène d'action

French, continued

scrutoire
séance
séance d'essais
sec
sèche
second
seconde
seconde, à la
seconde, en
seconde, grande
seconde position
secrétaire
secrétaire à abat-
tant
Section d'Or, La
seiche
seigneur
sel
selle
selle de mouton
séparé
sept
septième
septuor
serenade
sérénade
sérieuse
sérieux
serinette
serrant
serré
serrer les reins
serviette
sestuor
se tirer d'affaire
seul
seule
seules
seuls
sextette
sextolet
sextuor
si
si bémol
Siccatif de Cour-
trai

Siccatif de Haar-
lem
sicilienne
si dièse
siècle
siècle d'or
s'il vous plaît
si majeur
simple
simplement
singe
singerie
sisol
sissonne
sissonne, pas
sissonne battue
sissonne changée
sissonne doublée
sissonne fermée
sissonne fondue
sissonne ouverte
sissonne ouverte
en tournant
sissonne retombée
sissonne simple
sissonne simple
détournée
sissonne simple en
tournant
sissonne
soubresaut
sissonne tombée
six
sobriquet
Société des Vingt
société en com-
mandite
soi-disant
soie
soigné
soirée
sol
sol dièse
solennel
solennelle
solfège

solidarité
sombre
sombrée
sommeils
sommelier
son
sonate
sonates
sonatine
sonnerie
sonore
sons
sons bouchés
sons partiels
sons résultants
sortie
sou
soubasse
soubresaut
soubresaut, grand
soubrette
soubriquet
soudainement
soufflé
soufflée
souffleur
soupçon
soupe
soupe de l'Inde
soupe grasse
soupe maigre
souper
soupir
soupirant
souple
sourd
sourde
sourdine
sous
soussus
soutenu
soutenu en
tournant
spécialité de la
maison
spirituel

straticule
(le) style, c'est
l'homme
style champêtre
style de perruque
style galant
style mécanique
suave
succès de
mouchoir
succès de ridicule
succès de scandale
succès de snob-
isme
succès d'estime
succès fou
sucre
sucre en
morceaux
suite
suite, de
suivez
sujet
supercherie
suppliant
supprimez
suprême
sur
sur canapé
Sûreté
sur fond réservé
sur la touche
sur le chevalet
sur le cou du pied
sur les pointes
sur le vif
surtout
suzerain
svelte
sympathique
symphonique
système D
tabac
tabac à fumer
tabatière

French, continued

tabatière á
musique
tablature
table
table à manger
tableau
tableau (vivant)
tableau vivant
table d'hôte
table d'instrument
tablier
tabouret
tabourin
tachisme
tachiste
taille
taille de basson
taille d'épargne
taille de violon
taille douce
tailleur
talmouse
talon
talus
tambour
tambour de
Basque
tambour de Pro-
vence
tambouret
tambourin
tambour militaire
tampon
tant
tant soit peu
tapotement
taqueté
tarantelle
tarole
tarole grégoire
tartine
tel quel
tempête
temps
temps, tems

temps de cou-de-
pied
temps de cuisse
temps de flèche
temps de l'ange
temps d'élévation
temps de pointes
temps de poisson
temps frappé
temps levé
temps lié
temps plané
tendre
tendrement
tendu
tendue
ténor
tenu
tenue
tercet
terminé
terre, à
terre, par
terre à terre
terre de pipe
terre pisée
terre verte
terrine de foie
gras
tête
tête à tête
tête-à-tête
tête de veau
thé dansant
thème
thé musical
thon
tierce
tierce de picardie
tierce picarde
tiercet
tiers état
tiers-état
timbale
timbre
timbre-poste

timbrer
tintement
tinter
tirasse
tiré
tire-bouchon, en
tirer
tisane
tisane de cham-
pagne
toile
tombant
tombé
tombeau
tombée
tome
ton
ton doux
ton-generateur
tonique
ton majeur
ton mineur
tonnelet
tonnerre
tons de l'église
torchère
tordion
tortillon
tortue
tortue claire
touché
touche
toujours
toujours l'amour
toupet
tour
tour de basque
tour de force
tour de gosier
tour de main
tour de reins
tourdion
tour en l'air
tour jeté
tournant, en
tourné d'adage

tournedos
tourner
tours, chaînés
tours, petits
tours de force
tourte
tous
tout
tout à coup
tout à fait
tout-à-fait
tout court
tout de suite
toute
tout ensemble
toutes
tout le monde
traduction
traduit
tragédienne
trainé
traînée
trait
trait de chant
trait d'harmonie
tranche de vie
traversière
travesti, en
tre corde
tremblant
tremblement
trente et quarante
trente-et-quarante
très
très animé
très bien
très fort
très lentement
très piano
très vif
très vite
tricot
trille
trillette
trilogie
triolet

French, continued

triple croche
triple-croche
triptyque
triste
tristesse
triton
trois
troisième
troisième en avant
troisième en haut
troisième position
trois-quarts
tromp
trompe
trompe de béarn
trompe de berne
trompe de laquais
trompe l'oeil
trompe-l'oeil
trompes de chasse
trompette
trompette à cou-
lisse
trompette à pis-
tons
trompette basse
trompette
chromatique
trompette
d'harmonie
trompette
harmonique
trompette marine
trompette parlante
trop
trottoir
trouvères
truffe
truffes
truité
truite
truite au bleu
truite de lac
truites
truite saumonée
tryphone

tsigane
tulle
turque
Turquerie
tutu
tympanon
typophone
tyrolienne
tzigane
ubac
un
unda maris
une
uni
uniment
un peu
un poète manqué
ut bémol
ut dièse mineur
ut mineur
vache
vache à lait
vacherie
vacillant
val
valet de chambre
valet de pied
valet de place
valeur
valleuse
vallon
valse
valse à deux
temps
vaporeuse
vaporeux
variante
variation
varié
vase
vaudeville
veau
velours
velouté
venaison
vent

verdigris
verdure
verglas
vérité
vermeil
vernis Martin
vernissage
verre
verre églomise
verroterie
cloisonné
vers de société
vers libre
vert émeraude
vert Paul Véro-
nèse
vertu
vespéral
vespérale
vibrer
vide
vie de Bohème
vielle
vieux
vif
vigneron
vignette
vigoureusement
vigoureux
vigueur
villanelle
vin
vinaigre
vinaigre de toi-
lette
vinaigrette
vin blanc
vin coupé
vin de paille
vin de table
vin d'honneur
vin du pays
Vingt, Les
vingt et un
vingt-et-un
vingt-un

vin léger
vin mousseux
vin ordinaire
vin pur
vin rosé
vin rouge
viol d'orchestre
viole
viole d'amour
violon
violoncelle
violon d'amour
vis à vis
vis-à-vis
vite
vitement
vitrail
vitrine
vivat
vive
vive la différence
vive la république
vive l'empereur
vive le roi
vocalise
voilà
voile
voix
voix aiguë
voix argentine
voix blanche
voix céleste
voix de poitrine
voix de tête
voix humaine
voix mixte
volaille
volant
vol au vent
vol-au-vent
volé
volée
volée, de
volonté
volte
volte-face

French, continued

voyagé	voyeur	vraisemblance	za
voyagée	voyez	xylophon	

French + English

qui vive, *on the*

French + Norwegian

après-ski

Gaelic

eirēann go brat	Erin go bragh	Feis	slāinte

German

ab	Affekt	am	anstatt
A-B-C Dieren	Affektenlehre	amboss	anstimmen
abdämpfen	agitiert	A moll	Anstrich
Abend	agitirt	an	anwachsend
Abendlied	ähnlich	anblasen	anzublasen
Abendmusiken	Ais	Andacht	äqual
aber	Aisis	Andacht, mit	arabeske
abgestossen	Akkord	andauernd	artig
Ablaut	Aktiengesellschaft	ander	artikuliert
ablösenabneh-	Albumblatt	andere	As
mend	alle	Anfang	AsAs
Absatz	allein	Anfang, vom	Ases
abschwellen	allmählich	Anfangsritornell	Asymphonie
absetzen	allmählig	Angelica	Atempause
abstossen	allmälig	angemessen	auch
Abstufung	Alpenhorn	angenehm	auf
Abtragung	als	angreifen	Aufeis
abwechseln	also	Angst	aufführen
abwechselnd	als ob	ängstlich	Aufführung
abzuwechseln	alt	anhalten	aufgeregt
acht	Alterthum	Anhang	aufgeweckt
Achtel	Altertum	Anklang	aufhalten
Achtelnote	Altertumswissen-	anklingen	Aufklärung
Achtelpause	schaft	anlaufen	Auflage
Achtung	Altflöte	Anmut	auflösen
Adel	Altflügelhorn	Anmuth	Auflösung
Adjuvant	Altgeige	anreissen	Auflösungszeichen
A dur	Althoboe	Ansatz	Aufschlag
aehnlich	Althorn	anschauung	Aufschnitt
aengstlich	Altklarinette	Anschlag	Aufschwung
Aeolsharfe	Altkornett	Anschluss	Aufstrich
aequal	Altposaune	anschmiegend	Auftakt
aeusserst	Altschlüssel	anschwellend	auf Wiedersehen

German, continued

Aufwuchs
Aufzug
Augen
aus
Ausdruck
Ausfüllgeiger
Ausgabe
ausgehalten
ausgelassen
aushalten
Aushaltung
Auslese
ausschlagen
ausser
äusserst
Austausch
Auszug
Autobahn
Bacchuslied
Backfisch
Bad
Bagatelle
Bahnhof
balladenmässig
Band
Bände
Barkarole
Barock
Baryton
Baskische Tänze
Baskische
　Trommel
bass
Bassettflöte
Bassflöte
Bassflügelhorn
bassist
Bass-posaune
Bassposaune
Bass-saite
Basstrompete
Bauer
Bauernleier
Bauernlied
Bauernsuppe
Bauhaus

Bawren Leyer
B dur
Be
bearbeiten
bearbeitet
Bearbeitung
bebend
Bebung
Beck
Becken
bedächtig
Bedarfsfall
bedeutend
bedrohlich
begeistert
begleiten
begleitend
Begleitung
behaglich
behend
behendig
Behendigkeit
beherzt
beide
beinahe
Beispiel
Beisser
beklemmt
beklommen
belebend
belebt
belebter
Belieben
beliebig
belustigend
bequem
bereite vor
bereits
Bergreigen
Bergschrund
Bernstein
beruhigen
Bes
beschleunigen
beseelt
bestimmt

betend
betont
Betonung
Betrübnis
betrübt
beweglich
bewegt
Bewegung
Bezifferter Bass
Bibelorgel
Bibelregal
Bibliothek
Biedermeier
Bier
Bierstube
Bildung
Bildungsroman
Bindung
Bindungszeichen
Birne
bis
bitte
bittend
Blaseinstrument
blasend, stark
Bläser
Blasinstrumente
Blasmusik
Blaue Reiter, Der
Blech
Blechinstrumente
Blechmusik
bleiben
Blende
Blintze
Blitzkrieg
Blockflöte
bloss
Blut und Boden
Blut und Eisen
B moll
Bockbier
Bockfeife
Bodden
Bogen
Bogenstrich

Böschung
Bratsche
bratwurst
Brauhaus
Brautlied
Bravour Arie
breit
Brief
Briefmarke
Brucke, Die
(die) Brücke
Brummeisen
Brummscheit
Brustwerk
Buchhandel
Bügelhorn
Bühnenfestspiel
Bühnenweihfest-
　spiel
Bund
Bundesrat
Bundesrepublik
Bundestag
Bundfrei
Burg
Bürgermeister
cam
Cantate
Capelle
Capellmeister
Capellmeis-
　termusik
Capodaster
Cassation
C dur
Ces
C eses
Charakterstück
Choral
choralmässig
Choral Vorspiel
Chor-amt
Chorbuch
Chormässige
　Stimmung
Chorstimmung

German, continued

Chorton
Chor Zinck
cink
Cis
Ciscis
Cis dur
Cisis
Cis moll
Clarin
Clarina
Clarinblasen
Clausel
Clavier
Clavier-auszug
Clavieren
Clavierübung
componiert
Concertmeister
Concertstück
Coppel
Cornett-ton
Cromatische
　Harmonika
Cyklus
Cymbelstern
Czakane
Dachshund
Dämpfer
danke
danke schön
Danklied
darunter
das
Dasein
Dasia-notierung
dasselbe
Dauer
dauernd
dazu
D dur
Decke
Deckenkarren
dell
dem
demüthig
demütig

den
Denkschrift
dennoch
der
derb
der Führer
derselbe
Des
Des dur
Deses
Des moll
deutlich
Deutsch
Deutsche
Deutsche
　Demokratische
　Republik
Deutscher Tanz
Deutschland über
　alles
diapente
Dichtung
Dichtung und
　Wahrheit
dick
die
die geistige Welt
Die Götterdäm-
　merung
die schöne Welt
dieselbe
diesis
Die Zauberflöte
Dirndl
Dis
Discant Zinck
Disis
Diskant
Dis moll
doch
Dolzflöte
Donner
doppel
Doppel B
Doppel-Be

Doppelchor
Doppelfagott
Doppelflöte
Doppelfuge
Doppelgänger
Doppelhorn
Doppelkreuz
doppeln
Doppelschlag
Doppeltaktnote
doppelt so schnell
drängend
Drang nach Osten
Dreher
Drehleier
drei
Dreikanter
dreinfach
dreinfahren
dreitaktig
dringend
dritte
drohend
Druse
Dudelkasten
Dudelkastensack
Dudelsack
duett
duftig
dulcian
dumpf
dunkel
Dur
durch
durchaus
durchdringend
Durchführung
durchkomponiert
durchweg
düster
ebenfalls
ebenso
Echoklavier
edel
Edelweiss
E dur

Eifer
eifrig
Eile
eilen
eilig
ein
eine
einfach
Einfacher Choral
einige
Einkanter
Einleitung
Einleitungspiel
Einleitungssatz
einlenken
einmal
Einsang
Einschnitt
einstimmig
eintritt
ein wenig
　schneller
einzeln
Eis
Eisen und Blut
Eisis
E moll
Empfindung
emphase
Endrumpf
Engelstimme
enger
Engführung
Englisches Horn
entfernt
Entrückung
entschieden
entschlafen
entschlossen
Entwurf
Epicidion
ergriffen
erhaben
Erhöhungs-zeichen
erleichterung
erlöschend

German, continued

Ermangelung
ermattend
ermattet
erniedrigen
Erniedrigung
Ersatz
erschüttert
erst
erste
ersterbend
erstickt
erweitert
Erzähler
Erziehungsroman
erzürnt
Es
Eses
Es moll
es tut mir leid
etwas
etwas langsamer
Euphonion
ewige Jude, der
Exequien
Fach
Fackeltanz
Fagott
Fahlband
Fahlerz
Fahlore
Fahnen-marsch
fahren
Fall
Falle
Fantasiestück
fantastisch
Farbe
Farbe-ton
Fassung
fast
F dur
feierlich
feldpartita
Feldrohr
Feldton
Feld-trompete

Fenster
fermate
ferne
Fernflöte
Fernwerk
fertig
fertigkeit
Fes
Feses
Fest
festlich
Festschrift
Festspiel
Feuer
Feuerstein
feurig
Fiedel
Figuralmusik
figuriert
Fingerfertigkeit
Fingersatz
firn
Firnspiegel
Fis
Fis, Fisis
Fisis
Fladen
Flageolett
Flageolettöne
Flatterzunge
Fleckschiefer
Fledermaus
flehend
fliessend
Floetz
Flöte
flüchtig
Fluegelhorn
Flügel
Flügelhorn
flüssig
Flysch
F moll
Foehn
Föhn
Folge

folgen
Formkreis
fort
fortfahren
Fortrücken
Fortsetzung
Fossildiagenese
Fraktur
Frau
Frauenchor
Fräulein
frei
freie
Freiekombination
Freude
freudig
frisch
fröhlich
Frosch
Fruchtschiefer
früher
Frühlingslied
fuehrer
führend
Führer
Führer, der
Füllflöte
Fülligstimmen
Füllstimme
fünf
für
Fusshang
Gabelklavier
Galanterien
Galanter Stil
Gambe
ganz
ganze Note
Ganzetaktnote
Garbenschiefer
Gassenhauer
G dur
Gebet
Gebrauch
Gebrauchsmusik
gebunden

gedact
gedämpft
gedeckt
gedehnt
Gedicht
Gefallen
gefällig
Gefühl
gegen
Gegengesang
gehalten
gehaucht
geheimnisvoll
gehend
gehörig
Geige
Geigen
Geigenprinzipal
Geist
Geisterharfe
geistlich
gekneipt
gekoppelt
gelassen
geläufig
Geld
Gellenflöte
gemächlich
gemässigt
gemessen
Gemshorn
gemüt(h)
gemütlich
Gemütlichkeit
genannt
genau
general-bass
Gerader Zinck
Geröllton
gerührt
Ges
Gesamtausgabe
gesangvoll
geschlagen
geschleift
geschlossen

German, continued

Geschmack	graziös	Handharmonika	Hief-horn
geschwind	Grenz	Handregistrierung	hier
Ges dur	Griff	Handtrommel	hinsterbend
Gesellschaft	Griffbrett	Harfe	Hinstrich
Geses	grimmig	Harmoniemusik	Hinterland
gesprochen	grob	Harmonika	Hirt
Gestalt	gross	harmonische Töne	hirtlich
Gestapo	grosse	Hart	His
gesteigert	Grosse Flöte	Harte	H moll
gestopft	Grosses Orchester	Hartschiefer	Hoboe
gestossen	Grosse Trommel	Hasenpfeffer	Hochdruckstim-
Gesundheit	Grossflöte	hastig	men
geteilt	grotesk	Haupt	Hochkammerton
getheilt	Grundstimmen	Hauptstimme	höchst
getragen	Grundthema	Hauptthema	Hochzeitsmarsch
gewichtig	Grus	Hauptwerk	Hochzeitszug
gewidmet	gut	Hausfrau	Hohlflöte
gewöhnlich	Guten Abend	Hausmaler	Holz
gezogen	Gute Nacht	H dur	Holzbläser
Gipfelflur	Guten Morgen	Heckelclarina	Holzblasinstru-
Gis	guten Tag	Heckelklarinette	mente
Gisis	Gymnasium	Heckelphone	Holzflöte
glänzend	Haber-rohr	heftig	Holzharmonika
Glasharmonika	Hackbrett	Heil	Holzschlägel
Glasspiel	Haff	heiss	Holztrompete
Glasstabhar-	hahnebüchen	heiter	Hook
monika	Hahnentrapp	Heldentenor	Hopser
glatt	Hakenharfe	hell	Hörner
gleich	halb	Hellflöte	Hornquinten
Gleiche Stimmen	Halbe	Herabstrich	Hornstein
gleitend	Halbenote	Heraufstrich	Horst
Gletscherschlucht	Halbe-pause	Herbstlied	hübsch
Glimmer	Halbetaktnote	hernach	Humoreske
Glöckchen	Halbprinzipal	heroisch	hüpfend
Glocke	Halbsopran	Herr	hurtig
Glocken	Halbtenor	Herstrich	Hydraulicon
Glockenspiel	Haldenhang	Herunterstimmen	ich
glühend	hälfte	Herunterstrich	Ich dien
Glühwein	hallen	hervorgehoben	ich dien'
Gnomenreigen	Halt	hervorragend	immer
Götterdämmerung	halten	herzhaft	immer schlimmer
Graben	Hammerklavier	herzig	imponierend
Grat	Hanacca	herzlich	im voraus
Graupel	Hanakisch	Hes	innig
Grauwacke	Hand	Hexentanz	Inselberg
Graywacke	Hände	hexerei	inständig

German, continued

German, continued

Liebesoboe	Maskenspiel	mysteriös	ohne
Lieblichflöte	mässig	nach	Oktave
Lieblich Gedact	Maul-trommel	Nachdruck	oktavin
Lied	Maultrommel	Nachfolge	Oktett
Lieder	Meerschaum	nachgehend	Oper
Liederkranz	mehr	nachlassend	Opferkessel
Liederkreis	mehrere	Nachschlag	Orgel
Liederspiel	mein Gott	nachsingen	Orgelpunkt
Liedertafel	Mein Herr	Nachspiel	Paar
Liedertanz	Meistersinger	Nacht	Panzer
Liedform	Melismatisch	Nachtanz	Parallelkanter
Lied ohne Worte	Mengwacke	Nachthorn	Part
Liniensystem	Mensch	Nachtmusik	Parthie
linke Hand	Menuett	Nachtstück	Parthien
Loess	merz	nach und nach	Partialtöne
Loess Kindchen	Messing	nach wie vor	Partie
los	Metrik	nahe	Partitur
Löss	militär	naiv	passend
luftig	Militärtrommel	nämlich	pathetisch
Luftwaffe	minder	natürlich	Pauken
Lust	Minne	Naturtöne	Pause
Lustig	Minnesänger	Nazi	Pedalcoppel
lyra	Minnesingers	neben	Pedalflügel
lyre	mit	nebst	Pedalgebrauch
lyrisch	mitleidig	nehmen	Pedalklavier
Lyrisches Stück	Mittagessen	Nehrung	Pedalpauken
mächtig	Mittagsessen	Neiderstrich	Pentatonon
Mädchen	Mitte	nein	Pfeife
Maigelein	Mitteleuropa	Neue Sachlichkeit	pfiffig
majestätisch	mit Verschiebung	neun	Phantasie
Mal	möglich	nicht	Phantasiebild
Malerisch	moll	nieder	Phantasien
Manier	Monodrama	Niederschlag	Phantasiestück
Manieren	Mordent	noch	Pickleföte
Männer	Morgen	Nonett	pikieren
Männergesangver-	Morgenblätter	Nonnengeige	piquiren
ein	Morgenlied	Normalton	Platte
Manualkoppel	Motiv	nur	plaudernd
Märchen	müde	oben	plötzlich
Märchen	mühelos	ober	polnisch
markiert	Mundharmonika	Oberwerk	Polonäse
markig	munter	obligat	Polster
Marsch	murmelnd	Odeon	Polstertanz
marschmässig	mut	oder	poltergeist
Marzipan	mutig	offen	Portunal
Maschinenpauken	Mütterchen	öffnen	Portunalflöte

German, continued

Posaune
prächtig
prachtvoll
präcis
Pralltriller
Präludium
pressieren
Primärrumpf
Prinzipale
Proportz
prosit
Psalter
Pult
Pulte
Putsch
Quadrat
Qual
Quartett
Quartflöte
Quartgeige
Querflöte
Querpfeife
Querstand
Quintett
Quintsaite
Randkluft
rasch
rascher
Rassenkreis
Rathaus
Rathskeller
Ratsche
Ratskeller
rauh
rauschend
Realpolitik
recht
rechte
Recitativ
redend
Redoutensaal
Redoutentänze
reduciren
reduzieren
Regalwerke
registrieren

Registrierung
Reibungsbreccia
Reich
Reichstag
rein
Repetitor
Reststrahlen
revidiert
Rezitativ
rhythmisch
Rhythmus
richtig
Riegel
Rillenkarren
Rillenstein
Rinnenkarren
Rinnental
Ritornell
ritterlich
Rogenstein
roh
Rohr
Rollschweller
Rolltrommel
romer
Rotliegende
Rucksack
Ruhe
Ruhepunkt
Ruhezeichen
Rühne
Rührtrommel
Rührung
Rumpffläche
Rute
Ruthe
Sackgeige
Sackpfeife
Saite
Saiten-instrument
Saitenspiel
Salband
sämtlich
sanft
Sattel
Satz

Sauerbraten
Sauerkraut
Saxofon
Scenarium
Schablone
Schadenfreude
Schale
Schalen
schalkhaft
Schall-becken
Schallbecken
Schalmei
Schalmey
Schalmuse
Schalstein
scharf
schärfe
schauerig
schauerlich
schaurig
Schelle
Schellen
Schellenbaum
Schellengeläute
Schellentrommel
schelmisch
Scherz
Schiefer
schiefrig
Schiller
Schlacht
Schlag
Schlägel
schlagen
Schlaginstrumente
Schlagobers
Schlagwort
Schlagzither
Schlangenrohr
Schlegel
Schleifer
schleppend
schleppen, nicht
Schlieren
Schlummerlied
Schluss

Schlüssel
Schlusszeichen
schmachtend
Schmalz
schmeichelnd
schmelzend
Schmerz
schmetternd
Schnabel
Schnabelflöte
Schnapps
Schnarre
schneidend
schnell
Schneller
Schnitzel
Schottisch
Schottische
Schrammkapelle
schrittmässig
schrittweise
Schrund
schüchtern
Schuhplattler
Schulflöte
Schuppenstruktur
Schuss
schütteln
schwach
schwächer
schwankend
Schwebung
Schweigen
Schweinehund
schwellen
schwer
schwermütig
schwermutsvoll
schwindend
Schwirrholz
Schwung
sechs
Sechzehntel
Sechzehntelnote
Secundarius
Seele

German, continued

Sehnsucht
sehr
Seite
Septett
seufzend
Sextett
Sextole
sich
sieben
Sieg Heil
Siegheil
Sifflöte
Signalhorn
Sinfonische
  Dichtung
singbar
singend
Singspiel
Sitzkrieg
Skizze
Skizzen
so
sobald
soeben
sofort
sogleich
Soldatenzug
Soloklavier
Sonate
Sonaten
Sopran
Sordun
Sorgfalt
Spartieren
Spass
spasshaft
später
Sphärophon
Spiel
spielen
Spinnen des Tons
Spinnerlied
Spinnlied
Spitze
Spitzflöte
spitzig

Spitzkarren
spöttisch
Sprachgefühl
Sprechchor
sprechend
Sprechen sie
  Deutsch?
Sprechgesang
Sprechstimme
springend
Spruchsprecher
Staatskapelle
Stäbchen
Stahlharmonika
Stalag
Ständchen
standhaft
Standhaftigkeit
stark
statt
Steg
Steilwand
Steinharmonika
Steinkern
Stelle
Stellen
Stengel Gneiss
sterbend
stets
Stierhorn
stilecht
still
Stimmbogen
Stimmbücher
Stimme
Stimmführung
Stimmung
Stinkstein
stockend
Stockflöte
Stollen
Stoss
straff
straffer
Strasse
Streich

Streichquartett
Streichstimmen
Streichzither
streng
Strich
Strohfiedel
Strudel
Strukturboden
Stück
stückchen
stürmend
stürmisch
Sturm und Drang
Subjekt
summend
süss
Süsschen
symphonisch
Symphonische
  Dichtung
System
Tabulatur
Tact
Tact-linie
Tactmesser
Tact-pause
Tact-schläger
Tact-strich
Tafelklavier
Tafel-musik
Tafelmusik
Takt
Taktmesser
Talweg
Tamburin
Tändelei
tändelnd
Tannenbaum
Tanz
Tänze
Taste
Tasten
Tasten-brett
Teil
Teilzone
Teller

Tempo wie vorher
Tenor
Tenor Flügelhorn
Tenorgeige
Tenor-posaune
Tenorposaune
Tenor-schlüssel
Tenorstimme
Terzen
terzet
Terz Flöte
Teutsch
Thalweg
Theater
Theil
Theile
Thema
Theorbe
Thesis
tief
tiefgespannt
Tief Kammerton
tieftönend
tobend
Todesgesang
Todeslied
todt
Todtentanz
Ton
Tonabstand
Tonart
Ton-ausweichung
Tonbild
Tonbühne
Tondichter
Tondichtung
Töne
Tonfall
Tonfarbe
Tonfolge
Tonführung
Tonfülle
Tongang
Tongattung
Tongeschlecht
Tonhöhe

German, continued

tonica	Trinkgesang	Umfang	verdoppeln
Tonika-do	Trinklied	Umkehrung	Verein
Tonkunst	Triole	Umlaut	vergnügt
Tonkünstler	Tripelconcert	umstimmen	verhallen
Tonlage	Tripelkonzert	Umstimmung	verhallend
Tonlehre	Tripeltakt	unbezogen	verklärt
Tonleiter	Trittkarren	und	Verlag
tonlos	trochäisch	Undezime	Verlauf
Tonmalerei	trochäus	ungar	verliebt
Tonmass	Trogschluss	ungebunden	verlierend
Tonmesser	Trommel	ungeduld	verlöschend
Tonreihe	Trommel, Grosse	ungefähr	vermindert
Tonsatz	Trommel, Kleine	ungerade Taktart	vernehmbar
Tonschluss	Trommelboden	Ungestüm	Vernunft
Tonschlüssel	Trommelflöte	ungezwungen	Verschiebung
Tonschrift	Trommelkasten	unheimlich	verschieden
Tonsetzer	Trommelklöpfel	Universitaet	verschwindend
Tonsetzung	Trommelschlägel	unmerklich	Versetten
Tonstein	Trompete	unrein	Versetzung
Tonstück	Trompetengeige	Unruhe	Versetzungs-
Tonsystem	Trompeten-	unruhig	zeichen
Tonveränderung	register	unschuldig	Versmass
Tonwerk	Trompetenzug	unsingbar	Verspätung
Tonwissenschaft	trüb	unten	Verstand
Torte	trübe	unter	verstärken
Totenglöckchen	Trugschluss	Unterbass	verstärkt
Totenlied	Trumbscheit	Unterbrechung	verstimmt
Toten Marsch	Trummscheidt	Unterhaltungs-	Verte
Toten Musik	Trumscheit	Stück	verteilt
Totentanz	türkisch	Untersatz	vertheilt
trällern	Türmermeister	Unterseeboot	vertönen
Trauergesang	Turm-musik	Unterstaz	verwandt
Trauermarsch	Turmsonaten	Untertasten	Verwechselung
Trauermusik	Tusch	Unterwerk	verweilend
Traum	Tuthorn	Ursprache	verziert
traurig	über	ursprünglich	Verzierungen
Trautonium	Ubereinstimmung	Urtext	Verzögerung
Trautwein	Ubergang	Variante	verzweiflungsvoll
Traversflöte	Uberleitung	Vaterland	Vesperbrot
treibend	übermassig	vaterländisch	Vetter Michel
Treter	Ubermässig	Vater Unser	viel
Triangel	Ubermensch	Ventil	vier
Triller	Uberschlagen	Ventilhorn	vierfach
Trillerkette	Ubung	Ventilposaune	vierhändig
trillern	Uebung	Ventiltrompete	vierstimmig
trilogie	ugestüm	verboten	Viertelnote

German, continued

Viertelton
Vierundsechzigstel
Vierundsechzig-
  stelnote
Violen
Violinbogen
Violine
Violin-steg
Violoncell
Vogelflöte
Vogelgesang
Vogelpfeife
Vokal
Volksgesang
Volkskammer
Volkslied
Volkston
Volkstümliches
  Lied
voll
Volles Werk
völlig
vollstimmig
volltönend
volltönig
vom
von
von hier
vor
voraus
vorbereiten
Vorhalt
vorhanden
vorher
vorherig
vorig
vornehm
Vorsänger
Vorschlag
Vorspiel
Vorspieler
Vortrag
vortragen
Vortragsstück

vorwärts
Vorzeichnung
vorzutragen
wachsend
Wachtel
Wacke
während
Waldflöte
Waldglas
Waldhorn
Walzer
Wanderjahre
Wanderlust
wankend
wärme
Wasser
Wasserorgel
Watt
Wattenschlick
Wechselgesang
wechseln
Wechselnoten
wedeln
Weg
Wehmut
Wehmuth
Wehrmacht
weich
Weihnachten
Weihnachtslieder
weinend
Weinlied
Weinstube
Weite Harmonie
Weltanschauung
Weltansicht
Weltgeschichte
Weltkrieg
Weltpolitik
Weltschmerz
Weltweisheit
wenig
werden
Werk

Wesentliche
  Septime
Wetterharfe
Wettgessang
wie
wieder
Wiederanfangen
Wiederholung
Wiederholung-
  szeichen
wie geht's
Wiegenlied
wienerisch
Wiener Schnitzel
Wildflysch
Windharfe
Wirbel
Wirbeltrommel
wohlgefällig
wuchtig
wunderbar
Wunderkind
Wunsch
Würde
Wurst
Wut
Wuth
Yodel
Zählzeit
Zapfenstreich
Zarge
zart
Zartestimmen
Zartflöte
Zauberflöte
zehn
Zeichen
Zeichen, alt
Zeilenbau
Zeitgeist
Zeitmass
Zeitung
Zeuge
Zeugenberg

ziehen
Ziehharmonika
ziemlich
zierlich
Zigeuner
Zinck
Zink
Zinke
Zither
zitternd
zögernd
Zopf
Zopfstil
zu
zuerst
Zug
zugeeignet
zugehen
zum
Zunge
zur
zurück
zusammen
zutraulich
zuvor
zwei
Zweikanter
zweimal
zweite
zweites
Zweiunddreissig-
  stel
Zweiunddreissig-
  stelnote
Zwieback
Zwinger
zwischen
Zwischengebirge
Zwischenmusik
Zwischenspiel
Zwischenstück
zwo
zwölf

German, continued
German + Italian   Walzertempo

Greek

Greek, continued

photinx
pneuma
politikon zoon
pou stō
prolegomena

prolegomenon
proslambanome-
    nos
pteroma
salpinx

schisma
stichomythia
symphoneta
syrinx
threnodie

to kalon
tonus
topos
to prepon
trisagion

Hamitic   reg

Hausa   fadama

Hawaiian

aloha
aloha oe
amau
haole

kamaina
kipuka
lau lau
lei

mahalo
mai a
malahini
pahoehoe

pau
pupule
ukelele
wahine

Hebrew

Adonai
aggadah
Ashkenazim
badchonim
bar-mitzva
bar mitzvah
bar mizvah (mitz-
    vah, mitzwah)
Baruch
bas mitzvah
ben
beth
bnai
B'nai B'rith
chalil
chinor

chutzpah
Elohim
goy
Hadassah
Haggadah
hallelujah
hasid
hasidim
hazzan
hosanna
kasher
keren
kibbutz
kibbutznik
kinnor
knesset

l'chaim
machalath
machol
magrepha
mahhol
mashrogiytha
matze
matzo
Menorah
meshugah
Mogen Dovid
nabla
neble
paar
Pasach
Pesach

Purim
Rosh Hashanah
sambuque
Sephardim
shabbos
shalom
shalom aleichem
shalom alekhem
shofar
sholom
sholom aleicham
Talmud
toph
Yahveh
Yom Kippur

Hindi

achar
ankus
babu
baksheesh
bakshish
banya
bheesty
bhisti

chaori
char
chatri
esraj
fakir
ghat
guru
holi

hoolee
izzat
jalatarang
jheel
jhil
kabab
kankar
khana

khud
khushi
magoridi
maharaja
Maharajah
Maharanee
maharani
mahout

Hindi, continued

mridunga	rana	salaam	subahdar
mullah	ranee	samadh	surbahar
nullah	rani	samadhi	surnai
palang	Regur	sari	swami
pani	rupee	sarode	taus
purdah	saheb	sat-bhai	yoga
raja	sahib	serai	yogi
rajah	sahibah	sitar	zamar

Hungarian

a	csárdás	kos	tarogato
cigány	Czardas	lassú	tchardache
cimbalom	kalamaika	palotache	zimbalon

Icelandic

gja	langleik	long spiel	tarn
jokul	langspil	sandur	thufa
jökulhlaup			

Irish

caoine	Erin go bragh	roisin dub	uisge beatha
céad míle fáilte	fáilte	Sinn Fein	

Italian

a	abbellimenti	acciaio,	a cembalo
a battuta	abbellimento	istrumento d'	a cinque
abbadare	a bene placito	accompagnamento	acuto
abbadia	a beneplacito	accompagnato	ad
abbandonarsi	abilità, aria d'	accompagnatore	ad agio
abbandonata-	abruptio	accoppiare	adagietto
ménte	abruzzese	accoppiato	adagio
abbandone,	a capella	accordamento	adagio assai
abbandono, con	a cappella	accordando	adagissimo
abbandonevol-	a capriccio	accordanza	addio
mente	accademia	accordare	addolcendo
abbandono	accarezzevole	accordata	addolorato
abbassamento	accarezzevolmente	accordate	adiratamente
abbassamento di	accelerando	accordati	adirato
mano	accelerato	accordato	adornamento
abbassamento di	accento	accordatura	a due
voce	accentuare	accordo	a due corde
abbassare	acciaccato	accrescendo	a due cori
abbazzo	acciaccatura	accrescere	a due strumenti

Italian, continued

a due voci
adulatoriamente
aeroforo
affabile
affanato
affannato
affannosamente
affannoso
affettivo
affetto
affetto, con
affettuosa
affettuoso
affetuoso
affezione
afflitto
affrettando
affrettare
affrettatamente
affrettato
affrettoso
affrettuoso
agevole
agevolezza
aggio
aggiornamento
aggiunta, aria
aggiustamente
aggradevole
agiatamente
agilità
agilita
agilmente
agitamento
agitatamente
agitato
agitato allegro
agitato con pas-
 sione
agitazione
aglio
agnellotti
ai
al
alcun'
alcuna

alcuno
al dente
al fine
al fresco
all'
alla
alla breve
alla caccia
alla capella
alla cappella
alla danza tedesca
alla fine
alla milanese
alla prima
allargando
alla vostra salute
alle
allegramente
allegrettino
allegretto
allegrezza
allegro
allegro di molto
allegro furioso
allegro moderato
allegro non tanto
allentamento
allentando
al loco
allora
all' ottava
al piacere
al più
al rovescio
al segno
al solito
alta
al tedesco
alternativo
altezza
altezza sonora
altieramente
altissimo
altista
alto
alto relievo

alto rilievo
alto-rilievo
altra
altra volta
altre
altri
altro
alzati
alzato
amabile
amarevole
amarezza
amarezza, con
amarissimamente
amarissimo
a mezza aria
a mezza di voce
a mezza voce
a mezzo voce
amore
amore, con
a moresco
amoretto
amorevole
amorino
amorosamente
amoroso
ampollosamente
anche
ancia
ancona
ancora
ancora una volta
andamento
andante
andante cantabile
andante maestoso
andante ma non
 troppo
andantino
andare
andno
anelantemente
anglico
angore
angoscia

angosciamento
angosciosissima-
 mente
anima
anima, con
animando
animato
animo
animosamente
animoso
ansia
antica
antico
antipasto
aperto
a piacere
a poco a poco
appassionata
appassionato
appena
appenato
appoggiando
appoggiato
appoggiatura
a prima vista
a punta d'arco
arcata
arcato
archi
archiviola
arciliuto
arciviola
arciviola da
 gamba
arco
ardente
ardentemente
arditamente
arditezza, con
ardito
ardore
argille scagliose
aria
aria aggiunta
aria all'unisono
aria buffa

Italian, continued

Italian, continued

breccia
brecciola
brillante
brindisi
brio
broletto
bruscamente
buccina
buccolico
buffa
buffo
buffone
buffonescamente
buffonesco
buonaccordo
buona notte
buona sera
buon fresco
buon giórno
buon giorno
Buon Natale
burla
burlesca
burlesco
burletta
burro
busna
cabaletta
cabbaletta
caccia
cacciatore
cadenza
cadenza d'inganno
cadenzato
Caffaggiolo
caffè espresso
calamaro
calando
calata
calcando
calmando
calmato
calore
caloroso
cambiare
camera

camminando
campagna
campana
campane
campanella
campanetta
campanile
cancrizante
cannelloni
canone
cantabile
cantando
cantante, basso
cantare a aria
cantata
cantatore
cantatrice
canti
    carnascialeschi
canti di carnivali
cantilena
cantilenare
cantino
canto
canto armonio
canto fermo
canto primo
canto recitativo
canto ripiendo
canzona
canzone
canzonetta
canzoni
capella
capo
capo d'astro
capodastro
Capo-di-Monte
capo di tutti capi
capotasto
cappella
cappuccino
capriccio
capriccioso
cara sposa
carattere, mezzo

carbonari
carciofi
carezzando
carezzevole
carissima
carità
carmagnole
carne
caro
cartellino
casa
casino
cassa
cassa grande
cassa rullante
cassazione
cassone
cassone
castagnette
castagnettes
Castelli
castrati
castrato
castrato
cattivo tempo
cavata
cavatina
cavetto
cavo rilievo
cavo-rilievo
celere
celeste
cellarino
cembalist
cembalo
cembalo d'amore
centone
cercar la nota
certosa
cetera
cetra
che
che sarà sarà
chianti
chiara
chiarentana

chiarezza
chiarezza, con
chiarina
chiaro
chiaroscuro
chiasso
chiave
chiave maestro
chiavette
chiavi
chiavi trasportate
chiesa
chitarra
chitarra coll' arco
chitarrina
chitarrista
chitarrone
chittarone
chiusa
chiuso
chorale partita
chord a vido
ciaccona
ciao
cicerone
cilindri
cilindro
cima
cinelli
cinque
cinquecento
cinque-passi
cioè
cipollata
cipollino
cistella
cithare
citrioli
città
civetteria
clarabella
claricembalo
clarinetto
clarinetto alto
clarinetto basso

Italian, continued

clarinetto
  contrabasso
clarinetto d'amore
clarino
clarino
  contrabasso
clarone
clavicembalo
cocchina
coda
codetta
cogli
cognoscente
cognoscenti
coi
col
colascione
col basso
col canto
coll
colla
colla destra
colla parte
colla punta d'arco
colla punta dell'
  arco
coll'arco
collarino
colla sinistra
colla voce
colle
col legno
collegno
col legno dell'
  arco
colofonia
coloratura
colpo
come
come prima
come sopra
come stà
commedia dell'
  arte
commodo
comodo

compagnia del
  gonfalone
compiacevole
comprimario
con
con abbandono
con affetto
con amore
con anima
con brio
con calore
concento
concertante
concertata, aria
concertata messa
concertati
  madrigali
concertato
concertina
concertino
concerto
concerto a solo
concerto, di
concerto di chiesa
concerto doppio
concerto grosso
concerto grosso
concerto spirituale
concitato
con diligenza
con dolcezza
con dolore
condottiere
con espressione
con forza
con fuoco
con furia
con grazia
con gusto
con impeto
con molta pas-
  sione
con molto pas-
  sione
con moto
conoscente

con ottava
con permesso
con precipitazione
con prestezza
con semplicità
conservatorio
con sordini
con sordino
con spirito
continuato
continuo
contrabasso
contrabbasso
contrada dei
  nobili
contradanza
contra-fagotto
contrafagotto
contralto
contrapposto
contrappunto alla
  mente
contrappunto
  doppio
contrassoggetto
contrattempo
con variazioni
con velocità
conversazione
coperto
coprifoco
coprifuoco
coranto
corda
cordatura
corde
corista
corista di camera
corista di coro
cornamusa
cornetta
cornetta segnale
cornettino
cornetto
corno
corno alto

corno a macchina
corno a mano
corno a pistoni
corno basso
corno cromatico
corno da caccia
corno di bassetto
corno dolce
corno inglese
cornone
corno torto
corno ventile
coro
coro primo
corrente
corta
corto
cosacca
cosacco
cosa nostra
cosí-cosí
cosí cosí
cosí fan tutte
cosí fan tutte
cosí fan tutti
cravicembalo
credenza
cremona
crescendo
cristallo
croma
cromatica
cromatico
cromatico, corno
cucina
cupo
curioso
cymbasso
da
da ballo
da camera
da capo
da capo al fine
da capo al segno
da capo e poi la
  coda

Italian, continued

da capo sin' al
    segno
da cappello
d'accordo
da chiesa
dal segno
dal segno alla fine
danza
danza tedesca
da prima
debile
debole
deciso
declamando
declamato
decrescendo
decresciuto
delicato
delirio
delizioso
desiderio
desinvolto
desinvoltura
desto
destra
destra mano
destro
determinato
devotissimo suo
devoto
devozione
di
dialogo
di bravura
di buon'ora
dieci
diesis
dietro
di giorno
di leggiero
dilettante
diligente
diluendo
dilungando
diminuendo
di molto

di notte
di nuovo
di più in più
direttore
diritta
discretezza
discreto
discrezione
disinvolto
disperato
distanza
distinto
ditirambo
diva
divertimento
divisi
divotamente
divoto
do
doglia
dolce
dolce far niente
dolcemente
dolce stil nuovo
dolce vita
dolendo
dolente
dolore
doloroso
domino
Donna
dopo
Dopolavoro
doppio
doppio bemolle
doppio diesis
doppio
    movimento
doppio pedale
doppio tempo
dramma giocoso
dramma lirico
dramma per
    musica
drammatico
duce

due
duettino
duetto
due volte
duo
duo concertante
duolo
duomo
duramente
durezza
duro
duttile, trombone
e
eco
ed
eguaglianza
eguale
egualemente
elegantemente
elegia
elegiaco
elevato
elevazione
emozione
energia
energicamente
energico
enfasi
enfaticamente
enfatico
entrata
entusiasmo
epitalamio
equabile
equabilmente
equale
eroica
eroico
erotica
esaltato
esatta
esatto
esecuzione
esercizi
esercizio
esonare

esotica
esotico
espagnola
espagnolo
espagnuola
espagnuola, all'
espagnuolo
espirando
espressione
espressivo
espresso
essodio
estinguendo
estinto
estravaganza
estremamente
esultazione
ettachordo
evirato
fa
facile
facilità
facilmente
fagioli
fagottino
fagotto
fagotto contra
fagottone
falsetto
falsobordone
fantasia
fantastico
far niente
fascie
fastoso
fata Morgana
fedele
felice
fermamente
fermata
fermezza
fermo
feroce
fervente
fervidamente
fervido

Italian, continued

fervore
festa
festa teatrale
festivamente
festivo
festoso
fettucini
fiacco
fiamme
fianchetto
fiata
fiate
fiato
fieramente
fierezza
fiero
figurante
figurato
filar il suono
filar il tuono
filar la voce
fin
finale
fine
fino
fioco
fioreggiante
fiorette
fiorito
fioritura
fioriture
flautando
flautato
flauti
flautina
flauto
flauto a becco
flauto amabile
flauto d'amore
flauto d'echo
flauto d'eco
flauto diritto
flauto dolce
flautone
flauto piccolo
flauto traverso

flebile
flebilmente
flessibile
flessibiltà
flicorni
flicorno
fluido
foco
focosamente
focoso
fondo d'oro
forlana
formaggio
forte
forte forte
forte-piano
forte possible
fortissimo
forza
forzando
fra
franchezza
freddamente
freddo
fregiatura
frenetica
frenetico
frescamente
fresco
fresco secco
fretta
fritto misto
frottola
frottole
fuga
fuga doppia
fugato
fughetta
funebre
fuoco
furia
furibondo
furiosamente
furioso
furlano
furore

fusarole
gagliarda
gaia
gaio
gajamente
gajo
galantemente
gamba
ganascione
garbo
gariglione
gaudioso
gavotta
gelato
gemebondo
gemendo
generalissimo
generoso
gentile
gesso
gesso duro
gesso grosso
gesso sottile
ghiribizzo
ghiribizzoso
ghironda
giallo antico
giga
gigelira
giglio
giochevole
gioco
giocondo
giocondoso
giocoso
gioia
gioiosamente
gioioso
gioja
giojosamente
giojoso
gioviale
giovialità
giù
giubilio
giubilo

giulivo
giumarrite
giuoco
giusta
giustamente
giusto
gli
glissando
glissicare
gnocchi
gondola
gondoliera
gorgheggio
gradatamente
gradevole
gradito
graffiti
graffito
gran
gran cassa
grandezza
grandioso
gran-disegno
grandisonante
grand tamburo
gran gusto
gran tamburo
gran turismo
grappa
grave
gravemente
gravicembalo
gravità
grazia
grazie
graziosamente
grazioso
groppo
grossi
grosso
grottesca
grottesco
grupetto
gruppetto
gruppo
guazzo

Italian, continued

guerriera
guerriero
guglia
guistezza
gula
gusto
gustosamente
gustoso
i
il
Il Duce
illuminato
il penseroso
imboccatura
imbroglio
imitazione, aria d'
impasto
impaziente
impazientemente
imperioso
impeto
impetuosamente
impetuosità
impetuoso
imponente
impresario
imprimatura
improvisatore
improvvisata
improvvisatore
in alt
in altissimo
in alto
in bianco
incalcando
incalzando
inciso
incognito
incominciando
incordamento
indebolendo
indeciso
indicato
infra
in fretta
inganno

inglese
in modo di
innamorato
inno
innocenza
inquieto
insalata
in secco
insensibilmente
insensible
insieme
instante
instrumento da
  fiato
instrumento da
  penna
instrumento da
  percotimento
instrumento da
  tasto
insula
intaglio
intaglio rilevato
intarsia
intavolatura
intermedio
intermezzo
intimo
intonaco
intrada
intrepidezza
intrepido
introduzione
ira
irato
ironicamente
ironico
irresoluto
islancio, con
istesso
istoriato
istrumento
  d'acciaio
l'
la

la commedia è
  finita
lacrimoso
la dolce vita
la donna é mobile
lagnevole
lagnoso
lagrimando
lagrimoso
l'allegro
lamentabile
lamentando
lamentazione
lamentevole
lamento
lamentoso
lancio
languemente
languendo
languente
languidamente
languido
languore
lapis-lazuli
largamente
larghetto
larghezza
larghissimo
largo
la ringrazio
lasagne
lasciare
latte
latticinio
latticino
laudi spirituali
la volta
la volte
lavoro di com-
  messo
legabile
legando
legatissimo
legato
legatura
leggero

leggiadretto
leggiadro
leggieramente
leggiero
leggio
legno
legumi
lene
leno
lentamente
lentando
lento
lento assai
lento molto
lesto
leuto
levare
levezza
liberamente
libertà
libretti
libretto
licenza
lieto
lieve
lingua franca
lingua volgare
lira
lira organizzata
lirico
lirone
lirone perfetto
liscia
liscio
l'istesso
l'istesso tempo
literati
liuto
loco
loggia
lombarda
lontano
luce di sotto
lugubre
lunga
lunga pausa

Italian, continued

lungo
luogo
lusigando
lusingando
lutto
luttuosamente
luttuoso
ma
macchia
macchina
macigno
Madonna
madre
madriale
madrigali
  spirituali
maestà
maestade
maestosamente
maestoso
maestrale
maestro
maestro di cap-
  pella
maffia
mafia
mafioso
maggiolata
maggiore
magna
magno
maiolica
majolica
malinconia
malinconico
malizia
mamma mia
man
mancando
mancante
mancanza
mandorla
mandriale
mangiare
mani
manica

manico
manicotti
manieroso
mano
mano destra
manubrio
maraschino
marcando
marcato
marcia
marcia funebre
Marsala
martellando
martellato
marziale
mascherone
massima
massimo
mattinata
me
medesimo
medesimo tempo
melanzana
membretto
men
meno
meno mosso
messa di voce
messa per i
  defunti
mesto
metà
metro
metronomo
mettere
mezza
mezza-Maiolica
mezza voce
mezzo
mezzo carattere,
  aria di
mezzo forte
mezzo-forte
mezzo piano
mezzo-piano
mezzo-relievo

mezzo rilievo
mezzo-rilievo
mezzo soprano
mezzo termine
mezzo voce
mezzo-voce
mi
mi contra fa
militare
millefiori
minaccevole
minaccevolmente
minacciando
minestrone
minore
minuetto
minuge
misterioso
mistero
mistico
misura
misurato
modello
moderato
moderato
  cantabile
modo
molle
mollemente
molto
molto allegro
monferrina
monocordo
monsignore
morbidezza
morbido
mordente
morendo
Moresco
mormorando
mormorante
mormorevole
mormoroso
morra
mosso
motetto

motivaguida
motivo
moto
moto perpetuo
moto precedente
motteggiando
movente
movimento
mozzetta
murmurando
musetta
musica alla turca
musica colorata
musica di camera
musica falsa
musica figurata
musica mensurata
musica parlante
muta
mutano
nacchera
naccherone
napolitana
narrante
nasetto
naso
naturale
negli
negligente
negligentemente
nei
nel
nenia
nera
nero-antico
netta
netto
niellatori
niello
niente
ninfali
ninna-nanna
ninnarella
nobile
noblezza
nonetto

Italian, continued

non mi ricordo
non tanto allegro
non troppo
non troppo presto
nota
nota buona
nota cattiva
nota sensibile
nota sostenuta
notturnino
notturno
nove
novella
nuncio
nuntio
nuova
nuove musiche
nuovo
nutrendo
nutrito
o
obbligato
obbligato/obligato
oboe d'amore
oboe de caccia
octava alta
octavina
od
oficleide
ogni
ondeggiamento
ondeggiando
ondeggiante
ongarese
opera buffa
opera del duomo
opera seria
operatta
oppure
oratorio
ordinario
organo
organo espressivo
orgia
orido
ornamenti

ornatamente
osservanza
osservato, stile
ossia
ostinato
ottava
ottava alta
ottava rima
ottavina
ottetto
otto
ottone
ovolo
ovvero
pacatamente
pacato
pace in terra
padiglione
padre
padrone
padron mio
paesano
palazzo
palcoscenico
Palestrina, alla
panatella
Pantalone
parlando
parlante
parlato
parmigiana
parmigiano
parte
parti
partimenti
partita
partito
partitura
partizione
passacaglia
passamezzo
passemezzo
passionatemente
passionato
passione
pasta

pasta asciutta
pasticcio
pastorale
pastose
pastoso
pastourelle
patetico
patimento
patina
pausa
paventato
paventoso
pedale
pedaliera
pensieroso
pentimento
per
percossa
perdendo
perdendo le forze
perdendosi
per favore
perito
però
perpetuo
pesante
pesce
petra dura
petto
pezzo
piacere
piacere, a
piacevole
pianamente
piangendo
piangente
piangevole
piangevolmente
pianissimo
piano
pianoforte
piano nobile
pianto
piatti
piazza
picchettato

picchiettando
picchiettato
piccola
piccolo
piena
pieno
Pietà
pietosamente
pietoso
pifferari
piffero
pio
piperno
pistone
pistoni
Pittura Metafisica
più
piu
più allegro
più lento
più mosso
piuttosto
piva
pizzicato
placidezza
placido
placito
pleno
pochettino
pochetto
pochissimo
poco
poco allegro
poco à poco
poco a poco
poco curante
pococurante
poco forte
poco più lento
poema sinfonico
poggiato
polacca
polenta
politico
pollo
pomodoro

Italian, continued

pomposo
ponderoso
pondoroso
ponticello
porcellanite
portamento
portando
portato
portico
posizione
possibile
pranzo
precipitando
precipitandosi
precipitato
precipitosamente
precipitoso
precisione
preciso
pregando
preghiera
prego
preludio
presa
pressando
pressante
prestissimo
presto
prima
prima ballerina
  assoluta
prima buffa
prima donna
prima volta
primo
primo basso
prim'-omo
primo nomo
primo tempo
primo tenore
primo uomo
principale
profondo
progressivamente
progressivo
pronto

proposta
prosciutto
Pulcinella
punta
punto coronato
punto d'organo
putti
putto
quadratista
quanto
quartetto
quart-fagotto
quarto
quasi
quattro
quattrocento
questa
questo
quieto
quinta
quinta falsa
quintetto
quinto
rabbia
raddolcendo
raddolcente
raddoppiamento
raddoppiare
raffrenando
raggioni
rallentando
rallentare
rallentato
rape
rapidamente
rapidità
rapido
rappresentativo,
  stile
rapsodia
rattenendo
rattenere
rattenuto
raviolo
ravvivando
ravvivato

re
recita
recitando
recitante
recitativo
recitativo
  accompagnato
recitativo
  parlando
recitativo secco
recitativo
  stromentato
regale
registro
relievo
religiosamente
religioso
repetitore
replica
replicato
resoluto
resoluzione
retardando
rialto
ribattuta
ricercare
richettato
ricotte
ridotto
riduzione
rifacimento
riffioramenti
rigore
rigoroso
rilasciando
rilasciante
rilievo
rima chiusa
rimettendo
rimettendosi
rinforzando
rinforzato
rinzaffato
rio
ripetizione
ripieno

riposatamente
riposato
riposo
riprendere
ripresa
riscaldano
riso
risolutamente
risoluto
Risorgimento
risotto
rispetto
risposta
ristringendo
risvegliato
ritardando
ritardare
ritardato
ritardo
ritenendo
ritenente
ritenuto
ritmico
ritmo
ritmo di tre
  battute
ritornello
ritorno
riverso, al
rivolgimento
robusto
roco
romanesca
romanza
rombando
rondino
rondo
rondoletto
rontondo
rosalia
rosso antico
rotondo
rotunda
rovescio, al
rubato
ruggiero

Italian, continued

russa
russo
ruvido
sacre
    rappresentazioni
salmo
saltando
saltarello
saltato
salterio
salute
sassofono
sassophone
saxofonia
saxofono
sbalzato
scacciapensieri
scaglia
scagliola
scala
scala enigmatica
scalpellino
scampanata
scampanio
scampi
scannello
scannetto
Scaramouche
scemando
scena
scenario
scherzando
scherzante
scherzare
scherzetto
scherzevole
scherzevolmente
scherzi
scherzino
scherzo
scherzosamente
scherzoso
schiacciato rilievo
schietto
schizzo
scialumo

scintillante
scioltamente
sciolto
sciolto, con sci-
    oltezza
scivolando
scordato
scordatura
scorrendo
scorrevole
scozzese
scrittura
scucito
scusa
scusate
scusatemi
scusi
sdegno
sdegnoso
sdrucciolando
se
secco
seconda
secondando
seconda volta
secondo
segno
segue
seguendo
seguente
sei
seicento
semibiscroma
semicroma
semifusa
semiseria
semolino
semplice
semplicità
sempre
sensibile
sensibilità
sentito
senza
senza

accompagna-
    mento
senza organe
senza organo
senza replica
senza sordini
senza sordino
senza stromenti
senza tempo
seppia
septetto
serena
serenata
serenatella
serenità
sereno
seria
seriamente
serio
seriosa
seriosamente
serioso
serpentone
serrando
serrato
sestetto
sestina
sette
severamente
severo
sfogato
sfoggiando
sforzando
sforzato
sfregazzi
sfumatezza
sfumato
sgambato
sgraffiato
sgraffito
sgraffito
sì
si
siciliana
siciliano
signor

signora
signore
signorina
signorino
silenzio
simile
simili
simpatico
sin'
sinfonia
sinfonia
    concertante
sinfonica
sinfonico
sinfonietta
singhiozzando
sinistra
sino
sino al segno
sinopia
si parla italiano
sirocco
sirocco/scirocco
sistema
sivigliana
sivigliano
slancio
slargando
slargandosi
slegato
slentando
smalto
smania
smaniante
smanicare
smanioso
sminuendo
sminuito
smorendo
smorfioso
smorzando
smorzanto
snellamente
snello
soave
soavemente

Italian, continued

Language Index

soavità	sostenendo	sticcato	subitamente
soffione	sostenente	sticciato	subito
soggetto	sostenuto	stile	sugli
sol	sotto in su	rappresentativo	sui
sola	sotto portico	stinguendo	sul
solenne	sotto voce	stiracchiando	sul G
solennemente	spagnicoletta	stiracchiato	sul IV
solennità	spagniletta	stirando	sull
sol-fa	spagnoletta	stirato	sulla
solfeggio	spagnoletto	stornello	sulla tastiera
soli	spandendo	stracciacalando	sulle
solito	sparta	straccinato	sul ponticello
sollecitando	spartire	strada	sul tasto
sollecito	spartita	straffando	suo
solo	spartito	straffato	suonare
soltanto	sparto	strambotto	suoni
somma	spassapensiere	strascicando	suono
sommesso	spassapensieri	strascinando	superba
sommo	spediendo	strascinando	superbo
sonare	sperdendosi	l'arco	supplicando
sonata	spianato	strascinato	supplichevole
sonata a tre	spiccato	stravagante	supplichevolmente
sonata da camera	spiegando	straziante	susurando
sonata da chiesa	spirante	strepito	susurrando
sonatina	spirito	strepitosamente	susurrante
sonevole	spiritoso	strepitoso	svegliando
sonoro	sprezzatura	stretto	svegliato
sopra	spugna, bacchetta	strimpellata	svelto
sopra bianco	di	stringendo	svolgimento
soprana	spumone	strisciando	tacere
soprano	squillante	strisciato	taci
soprano acuto	squillanti	stromenti	taciasi
soprano leggiero	stabile	stromenti da arco	tagliato
soprano sfogato	staccato	stromenti da fiato	tamburino
sorda	stagione	stromenti da	tamburo
sordamente	stampita	percossa	tamburo basco
sordina	stanghetta	stromenti da tasto	tamburo grande
sordine	stecco	stromenti di corda	tamburo grosso
sordini	stendendo	stromenti di lengo	tamburo militare
sordino	stentare	stromento	tamburone
sordo	stentato	strumenti	tamburo piccolo
sortita	steso	strumento	tamburo rullante
sospirando	stessa	stucco lustro	tanto
sospirante	stesso	su	tarantella
sospirevole	stiacciato	suave	tarda
sospiroso	sticcado	suavità	tardamente

Italian, continued

tardando
tardo
tarsia
tasti
tastiera
tasto
tatto
tazza
teatrino
tedesca
tedesca, alla
tedesco
teimpanetto
tema
tema con varia-
zioni
tema
  fondamentale
tempestosamente
tempestoso
tempo
tempo
tempo alla breve
tempo a piacere
tempo commodo
tempo comodo
tempo di ballo
tempo di cappella
tempo di gavotta
tempo di marcia
tempo di
  menuetto
tempo di
  minuetto
tempo di polacca
tempo di prima
  parte
tempo di valse
tempo frettevole
tempo fretto-losó
tempo giusto
tempo maggiore
tempo minore
tempo ordinario
tempo perduto
tempo primo

tempo reggiato
tempo rubato
tenebrosi
tenebroso
tenendo
tenendo il canto
teneramente
teneramente, con
  tenerezza
tenerezza
tenero
tenete
tenore
tenor ebuffo
tenore buffo
tenore di grazia
tenore leggiero
tenore primo
tenore ripieno
tenore robusto
tenorista
tenuta
tenute, tenuto
tenuto
tepidamente
tepido
ternario tempo
terra cotta
terra-cotta
terracotta
terra irredenta
terra rossa
terra verde
terrazzo
terribilità
terza maggiore
terza minore
terza rima
terzetto
terzina
terzi tuoni
tessitura
testa
testo
thema
timballo

timidezza
timidezza, con
timido
timore
timorosamente
timoroso
timpanetto
timpani
timpani coperti
timpani sordi
timpanista
tintinnare
tinto
tiorba
tirando
tirare
tirato
tira tutto
tirolese
toccata
toccatella
toccatina
togli
tombolo
tonante
tondo
tonica
tonitruone
tono
tornando
tornare
torta
torvo
tostamente
tostissimamente,
  tostissimo
tosto
trabattere
tradolce
tradotto
traduzione
tranquillamente
tranquillezza,
  tranquillità,
  tranquillo
tranquillo

trascinando
trascrizione
trasognata
trattenuto
tratto
trattoria
traversa
traverso
travertine
tre
trecento
tre corde
tremando
tremante
tremendo
tremolando
tremolante
tremolo
trenodia
tresca
trescone
triangolo
trillando
trillare
trilletta
trilletto
trilli
trillo
trilogia
trio
triole
trionfale
trionfante
triplice
tristèzza
tristezza
tristo
tritono
trittico
tromba
tromba a
  macchina
tromba bassa
tromba clarino
tromba cromatica
tromba da tirarsi

Italian, continued

tromba di basso
tromba di tirarsi
tromba marina
tromba sorde
tromba spezzata
tromba ventile
trombetta
tromboni
trombonino
tronco
troppo
tubo di ricambio
tufa
tumultuoso
tuoni ecclesiastici
tuono
tuono mezzo
turca
turca, alla
turca, turchesco,
  turco
turco
tutta
tutta forza
tutta la forza
tutte
tutte le corde
tutti
tutti frutti
tutti-frutti
tutti unisoni
tutto
tutto arco
uguale
uguali
ultima
ultimo
umana
umano
umore
un'
una
una corda
una volta
undulazione
ungherese

unisono, aria all'
uniti
uno
un poco
uomo universale
va
vacillando
vago
valore
variamente
variamento
variante
variata
variato
variazione
variazioni
varsoviana
veduta
veemente
velata
velato
vellutata
vellutato
veloce
velocemente
vendetta
ventile
ventile, corno
ventile, trombone
venusto
vera da pozzo
verde antico
verdura
vergette
verghetta
verismo
vermicelli
vernaccia
vetro di trina
vezzosamente
via
vibrante
vibrato
vicendevole
vicendevolemente
vicino

vigore
vigorosamente
vigoroso
villanella
villota
villotta
vino
viola alta
viola bastarda
viola da braccio
viola da gamba
viola d'amore
viola da spalla
viola di bordone
viola di fagotto
viola paradon
viola pomposa
viol da gamba
viol d'amore
viole
violentamente
violento
violenza
violetta
violetta piccola
violini
violini unisoni
violino
violino piccolo
violino principale
violoncello
violoncello piccolo
violone
violotta
virtù
virtuoso
vitello
viva
vivace
vivace ma non
  troppo
vivacissimo
viva il papa
vivamente
vivezza
vivido

vivo
vocalizzo
voce
voce bianca
voce di gola
voce di petto
voce di testa
voce granita
voce mista
voce pastosa
voce spiccata
voce velata
voci
voci eguali
voci equali
voci pari
voglia
volante
volata
volcanello
volta
volte
volteggiando
volti
volti subito
volubile
volubilmente
vuota
vuoto
zabaglione
zabaione
zampogino
zampogna
zampognare
zecca
zeffiroso
zelo
zelosamente
zeloso
zilafone
zingara
zingaresa
zingaro
zoppa, alla
zufolo

Italian + Latin

con ottava ad
libitum

Japanese

aburagiri	buraku	genro	hichiriki
adsuki (bean)	burakumin	geta	Himeji
adzuki (bean)	bushido	gi	hinin
aikido	Butsu	gingko	hinoki
aikuchi	butsudan	ginkgo	Hirado
Aino	byōbu	ginkgo (nut)	hiragana
Ainu	chadai	giobu	Hiroshima
akamatsu	chanoyu	giri	hitschiriki
akamushi (mite)	chashitshu	go	hitsu-no-koto
akebi	Chiba	gobang	hityokiri
Akebia	cho	gobo	Hizen
akeki	chonin	go-moku	Hizen (porcelain)
Akita	chorogi	gomokuzogan	hokku
ama	Chosenese	goumi	iaido
amado	chu	gumi	I-go
Amagasaki	Daibutsu	gun	ikebana
amanori	daikon	guri bori	Imari
Amaterasu	daimio	habatsu	inlayo
andon	daimyo	habu	inro
ansu	Dai Nippon	habutai	ippon
arigato	dairi	hagi	irofa
Aucuba	dai-sho	haikai	iroha
awabi	dai-sho-no-	haiku	Ishihara (test)
ayu	soroimono	hakama	ishime
bai-u	dan	Hakodate	issei
baka (bomb)	daruma	Hamamatsu	itai-itai
bancha (tea)	do	hanami	Ito sukashi
Banzai	dojo	hanamichi	itzebu
banzai	dotaku	hanashika	jaburan
baren	emakimono	haniwa	janken
basho	Eta	haori	jigotai
beddo	fuchi	happi-coat	jimigaki
bekko	fugu	harai goshi	jingu
betto	fuji	hara-kiri	jinja
biwa	Fukuoka	hashigakari	jinkai senjitsu
Bon	fun	hatamoto	jinrickisha
bonsai	funori	hayashi	jinricksha
bon-seki	furoshiki	hechima	jinrikisha
bonze	fusuma	Heian	jinriksha
bu	futon	heimin	jito
Bugaku	gagaku	hiba (arborvitae)	jiu jitsu
Buké	gaijin	hibachi	jiu-jitsu
Bunraku	geisha	hibakusha	Jodo

Japanese, continued

jomon	Kempeitai	koto	Mikimoto
joro	ken	koza	Minamata
joruri	kendo	kozo	(disease)
judo	kesa-gatame	kozuka	mingei
judoka	keyaki	Kubo	miso
jujitsu	kiaki	kudzu	mitsukurina
junshi	kibei	Kuge	mitsumata
kabane	kiku	kumamoto	Miyagawanella
Kabuki	Kikuchi	kumaso	mochi
kabuto gane	kikumon	kumite	moji
kabuzuchi	kikyo	kura	mokko
kadsura	ki-mon	kure	mokum
kago	kimono	kurikata	momme
kagoshima	kin	kuromaku	mompei
kagura	kiri	Kuroshio	mon
kakemono	kirigami	kuroshio	mondo
kaki	kirimon	(extension)	moose
Kakiemon	kirin	kuroshio (system)	mousmee
kakke	koan	kuroshiwo	moxa
kakko	koban	kuruma	mume
Kamakura	kobang	Kurume	mura
kamashimo zashi	kobe	Kutani	muraji
kambara (earth)	kobu	kuzushi	mushi disease
kami	kochi	kwaiken	Nabeshimayaka
kamikaze	kodogu	kwazoku	nagasaki
kana	kofu	kyogen	Nagoya
kana-majiri	kogai	kyoto	nakodo
kanamono	koi	kyu	namban
kanazawa	koi-cha	kyudo	nanako
kanji	koji	mai	Nandina
kanten	kojiri	maiko	Nanga
karate	ko-katana	makimono	Nara
karateka	kokeshi	mama-san	narikin
kashira	Kokka	mamushi	Nashiji
kata	koku	mana	Nembutsu
katakana	kokura	matsu	netsuké
katana	kokyu	matsuri	netsuke
Katayama	kollo	matsuyama	Nichiren
katsu	komban-wa	mebos	Nihon
katsuo	kombu	medaka	Niigata
katsura	koniak	Meiji	nikko
katsuramono	konjak	menuki	niku-bori
katsura (tree)	konnichi-wa	metake	Nip
kawaguchi	Korin	miai	Nippon
kaya	koro	Mikado	nisei
kegon	kotatsu	mikan	No

Japanese, continued

nogaku
noh
noh/nō
nori
norimon
norito
noshi
notan
nunchakus
oban
obang
obe
obi
o-daiko
odori
ofuro
o-goshi
ohteki
oiran
ojime
Okayama
Okazaki
Okazaki
  (fragment)
okimono
omi
Omuta
on
onnagata
onson
origami
orihon
osaekomi waza
Osaka
oshibori (towel)
O-soto-gari
Otaru
oyama
ozeki
pachinko
raku
randori
randori
red tai
renga
ri

ricksha
rickshaw
rikisha
rikka
rin
riobitsu
rioyo
ritsu
Rōjū
Romaji
Romazi
ronin
Roshi
rumaki
ryo
Ryobu (Shinto)
ryokan
Ryukyu
Ryukyuan
sabi
sakai
sakaki
sake
sakura
sama
samisen
samo
samo-tori
samsien
samurai
san
sanpaku
Sanron
sansei
Sapporo
Sasankwa
sasanqua
Sasebo
sashimi
satori
satsuma
sayonara
sen
sendai
Sendai (virus)
sentoku

seppa
seppa dai
seppuku
sesshin
shaku
shaku bioshi
shakudo
shakuhachi
shiatsu
shibuichi
shibuichi-doshi
Shiga (bacillus)
shikii
Shikimi
shikken
shimonoseki
shimose (powder)
Shin
Shingen tsuba
Shingon
shinkansen
Shin-shu
shintai
Shinto
shippo (ware)
shirakashi
shitogi tsuba
shizoku
Shizuoka
shogaol
shogi
shogun
shoji
shomio
Showa
shoya
shoyu
shubunkin
Shuha
sika
Siomio
skibby
skimmia
soba
sodoku
Soka Gakkai

sugi
suiseki
sukiyaki
sumi
sumi-e
sumo
sumotori
sushi
tabi
tachi
Tago-Sato-Kosaka
tai
taiko
Taisho
taka-makiye
Takamatsu
Takaoka
tamo
tan
tanka
tanto
tatami
temmoku
tempo
tempura
Tendai
tenno
tera
teriyaki
tobira
tofu
tokonoma
Tokushima
tokyo
torii
torü
Toyama
toyo
Toyohashi
tsuba
tsubo
Tsuga
tsugaresinol
tsunami
tsurugi

Japanese, continued

tsutsugamushi
  (disease, mite)
tsutsumu
udo
uji
ukiyo-e
ume
urushi
urushiye
wacadash

waka
Wakayama
wakizashi
warabi
wasabi
yagi
yakitori
yakuza
Yamaguchigumi
yamamai

Yamato-e
yamoto
Yawata
yayoi
yen
yenbond
Yokkaichi
Yokohama
Yokosuka
yokozuna

yusho
zaibatsu
zaikai
zazen
Zen
zendo
ziogoon
zogan
zori

Javanese

angklung
batik

bonang
gambang

gamelan
gender

lahar
souling

Kashmiri   karewa

Korean   kimchi

Late Latin   ens   in posse

Latin

a
ab
ab absurdo
ab actu ad posse
  valet illatio
abaculus
abacus
ab asino lanam
ab extra
abies
abi in malam
  crucem
ab imo pectore
ab inconvenienti
ab incunabulis
ab initio
ab integro
ab intestato
ab intra
ab officio et
  beneficio

ab origine
abortus
ab ovo
ab ovo usque ad
  mala
absente febre
absente reo
absit omen
absque hoc
ab uno disce
  omnes
ab urbe condita
accedas ad curiam
accentus
accentus
  ecclesiasticus
accipe hoc
acer
acetum
acetum Italum
a cruce salus

acta
acta eruditorum
actum est
actus
actus curiae
actus Dei
actus purus
acus
ad
ad absurdum
ad arbitrium
ad astra
ad astra per
  ardua
ad astra per
  aspera
ad baculum
ad canones
ad captandam
  benevolentiam
ad captandum

ad captandum
  vulgus
ad crumenam
addendum
additum
a Deo et rege
adeste fideles
ad eundem
ad extra
ad extremum
ad fidem
ad finem
ad fugam
ad gustum
ad hanc vocem
ad hoc
ad hominem
ad hunc locum
ad idem
a die datus
ad ignorantiam

Latin

Latin456# Latin, continued

ad infinitum
ad initium
ad instar
ad interim
ad judicium
adjuvante Deo
ad Kalendas
  Graecas
ad lib
ad lib(itum)
ad libitum
ad litem
ad literam
ad litteram
ad locum
ad majorem Dei
  gloriam
ad manum
ad misericordiam
ad modum
ad nauseam
ad oculos
ad placitum
ad populum
ad quem
ad quod
ad rem
adsum
ad summam
ad summum
ad unguem
ad unum omnes
ad usum
ad valorem
adversaria
adversus
ad vesperas
ad vitam
ad vivum
advocatus diaboli
advocatus
  juventutis
aequisonae voces
æquo animo
aequo animo
aere perennius

aes alienum
aetate
aetatis
aetatis suae
afflatus
a fortiori
agenda
ager publicus
agnomen
Agnus Dei
ala
alea jacta est
alias
alibi
alieni juris
alimenta
aliquando bonus
  dormitat
  Homerus
aliquot
aliud et idem
aliunde
Allium
alluvio maris
alluvium
alluvium
alma mater
alter ego
alter idem
alter ipse amicus
altiora peto
altus
alumna
alumni
alumnus
alumnus
amantium irae
amanuensis
ambitus
ambo
ambulatio
a mensa et thoro
a mensa et toro
amentia
amicus curiæ
amicus curiae

amicus humani
  generis
amicus usque ad
  aras
amor nummi
amor patriæ
amor patriae
amor vincit omnia
anathema sit!
Angelus
Angelus Domini
angina pectoris
anglicé
anglice
anguis in herba
anima
anima mundi
animus
animus furandi
animus testandi
anno
anno aetatis suae
Anno Christi
anno Domini
Anno Domini (A.
  D.)
anno domini
  (A.D.)
anno humanae
  salutis
Anno Mundi
anno mundi
  (A.M.)
anno regni
Anno Urbis Con-
  ditae
anno urbis con-
  ditae (A.U.C.)
annuit coeptis
annus
annus magnus
Annus Mirabilis
ante
ante bellum
ante Christum
  (A.C.)

ante cibum
ante diem
ante lucem
ante meridiem
  (A.M.)
a posse ad esse
a posteriori
apparatus criticus
applicatio
applicatur
a primo
a principio
a priori
aqua
aqua ardens
aqua benedicta
aqua fortis
aqua pura
aqua regia
Aquarius
aqua vitæ
aqua vitae
a quo
arbiter bibendi
arbiter elegantiae
  (elegantiarum)
arbiter
  elegantiarum
arbiter literarum
arboretum
arbor vitae
arcanum (pl. ar-
  cana)
arcus ecclesiae
argentum
argumenti gratia
argumentum
argumentum ad
  absurdum
argumentum ad
  baculum
argumentum ad
  crumenam
argumentum ad
  hominem

Latin, continued

argumentum ad
ignorantiam
argumentum ad
invidiam
argumentum ad
judicium
argumentum ad
misericordiam
argumentum ad
populum
argumentum ad
rem
argumentum ad
verecundiam
argumentum a
fortiori
argumentum a
silentio
argumentum
baculinum
argumentum ex
concesso
argumentum ex
silentio
aries
arma
arma accipere
arma dare
arma virumque
cano
ars
ars amandi
ars amatoria
ars antiqua
ars est celare
artem
ars gratia artis
ars longa, vita
brevis
ars musica
ars nova
Ars Poetica
articulus
Artium
Baccalaureus
Artium Magister

artium magister
(A.M.)
asinus ad lyram
asperges me
aspergillum
a tergo
audi alteram
partem
aura popularis
aurea aetes
aurea mediocritas
auri sacra fames
aurora australis
Aurora Borealis
aurum
Auspex
aut Cæsar aut
nullus
ave atque vale
Ave Maria
a verbis ad
verbera
a vinculo ma-
trimonii
avis
baccalaureus
legum
baccalaureus
musicae
baccalaureus
pharmaciae
bassus
b cancellatum
beatae memoriae
beati possidentes
bello flagrante
bellum
bellum
internecinum
bene
benedicite
Benedictus
beneficium
clericale
bene merenti
bestiarium

bibliotheca
Biographia
Literaria
bis
bona
bonae fidei
bonae fidei
emptor
bonâ fide
bona fide
bona fides
boni mores
bonis avibus
bonum commune
bonus
brevi manu
bucolicum
buxum
buxus
cacoëthes
cacoëthes
carpendi
cacoethes
carpendi
cacoëthes
loquendi
cacoethes
loquendi
cacoëthes
scribendi
cacoethes
scribendi
cadit quaestio
caduceus
caeca est invidia
caecum
caeteris paribus
calendae
camera lucida
camera obscura
campus
Campus Martius
cancrizans
Cantabrigiensis
cantate Domino
canticum

cantilena
cantillatio
cantiones sacrae
cantoris
cantus
cantus choralis
cantus fictus
cantus figuratus
cantus firmus
cantus fractus
cantus gregorianus
cantus
mensurabilis
cantus mensuratus
cantus planus
capias
caput
caput mortuum
Caput Mundi
cara
caret
caries
caritas
carmen
carpe diem
carta
Carthago delenda
est
carus
casus
casus belli
casus conscientiæ
casus foederis
casus fortuitus
cathedra
cauda
causa
causa causans
causa causata
causa efficiens
causa finalis
causa formalis
causa materialis
causa mortis
causa proxima

Latin, continued

causa sine qua non
causa sui
caveat
caveat actor
caveat emptor
caveat venditor
caveat viator
cave canem
cavendo tutus
cave quid dicis, quando, et cui
cede Deo
censor deputatus
censor morum
centum
cepi corpus
certiorari
ceteris paribus
charta
chorda
cicatrix
circa
circiter
circulus in definiendo
circulus in probando
circulus vitiosus
circum
cis
cis-
civiliter
clarum et venerabile nomen
clausula
clausula falsa
clausula peregrina
clausus
clave
claves curiae
cloaca
cloaca maxima
codex
Codex Justinianeus

cœna Domini
cogito, ergo sum
cognomen
collectanea
collegium
collegium musicum
colossus
comes
comitas inter communitates
comitas inter gentes
comitia
commune bonum
communi consensu
completorium
compos mentis
concentus
conditio sine qua non
condominium
conductus
confer
confessio fidei
confiteor
confutatis
congregatio de propaganda fide
conjugium
consensus facit legem
consensus gentium
consilium abeundi
consistorium
consolatio
conspectus
consummatum est
contra
contra bonos mores
contradictio in adjecto
contra jus commune

contra naturam
contrapunctus
controversiae
conversio
coram judice
coram non judice
coram populo
cornucopia
cornu copiae
corolla
corona
corpus
Corpus Christi
corpus delicti
corpus iuris canonici
corpus iuris civilis
corpus juris
corpus juris canonici
corpus juris civilis
corrigenda
corrigendum
cortex
coryphæus
cothurnus
crede Deo
crede experto
credenda
credo
crembalum
creta
crimen innominatum
crimen laesae majestatis
crotalum
crucifixus
crux
crux ansata
crux criticorum
crux interpretum
crux mathematicorum
cubile ferarum

cui
cui bono
cui malo
culpa
culpae poena par esto
cum
cum grano salis
cum laude
cum notis variorum
cum sancto spiritu
cum tacent, clamant
cura
curia
curia domini
curia regis
currente calamo
curriculum
curriculum vitae
cursus honorum
custodes
custos
custos morum
Custos Rotulorum
Custos Sigilli
cyma recta
cyma reversa
cymbalum orale
da dextram misero
damnum absque injuria
data
de
de ambitu
de bonis propriis
decani
de facto
Defensor Fidei
deficit
de fide
de gustibus (non est disputandum)

Latin, continued

de gustibus non est disputandum
Dei gratia
de integro
de jure
delator temporis acti
dele
delenda est Carthago
delirium tremens
dementia
dementia praecox
dementia senilis
demissus vultum
de mortuis
de mortuis nil nisi bonum
De Natura Rerum
de nihilo nihil
de novo
Deo duce
Deo ducente
Deo favente
Deo gratias
Deo juvante
deo volente
Deo volente (D.V.)
De Profundis
de rebus
De Rerum Natura
desiderata
desideratum
Desideria
designatum
desunt caetera/ desunt cetera
detinet
detritus
deus
deus ex machina
deus misereatur
Deus tecum
Deus vobiscum

diabolus in musica
dictum
dictum sapienti sat est
die
dies
dies a quo
dies ater
dies faustus
dies infaustus
Dies Irae
dies non
differentia
difficilia quae pul- cra
difficilior lectio potior
dii penates
directorium chori
discantus supra librum
discere docendo
disjecta membra
distinctio
divisio
docendo discimus
docendo discitur
Doctor Divinitatis
doctor legum
Domine Deus
Domine Jesu
domino optimo maximo
dominus
Dominus providebit
Dominus vobiscum
domus aurea
domus Dei
Domus Procerum
dona eis
dona nobis
donemus
dorsum

do ut des
do ut facias
dramatis personæ
dramatis personae
duces tecum
dulce domum
dulce quod utile
dum spiro, spero
dum vivimus, vivamus
dura mater
dux
e
ecce
Ecce Homo
ecce signum
ecclesia
e contra
e contrario
e converso
editio princeps
editus
e (ex) re nata
ego
ejusdem generis
elegantia
elegantiae arbiter
elevatio
elixir vitae
emeritus
emplastrum
emptor
ens
eo die
eo nomine
epistola
epithalamium
epitonium
e pluribus unum
eques
ergo
errare est humanum
errare humanum est
errata

erratum
esse
esse est percipi
esse quam videri
est modus in rebus
esto perpetua
et
et aliae
et alii
et caetera
et cetera
et cum spiritu tuo
ethica
et hoc genus omne
et incarnatus
et incarnatus est
et in spiritum sanctum
et in unum dominum
et passim
et resurrexit
et sequens
et sequentes
et sequentia
et similia
et tu, Brute
et uxor
et vir
et vitam
eurus
evolutio
ex
ex abundantia
ex aequo
ex animo
ex auctoritate mihi commissa
ex capite
ex cathedrâ
ex cathedra
excelsior
exceptio probat regulam

Latin, continued

exceptis
  excipiendis
excerpta
ex concessis
ex concesso
ex contractu
ex curiâ
ex curia
excursus
ex delicto
exeat
exegetes
exemplar
exempli gratia
  (e.g. or ex. gr.)
exempli gratiâ
exemplum
ex (e) silentio
exeunt
exeunt omnes
ex facie
ex facto
ex gratia
ex grege
ex hypothesi
exit
exitus acta probat
ex libris
ex more
ex necessitate rei
ex nihilo
ex nihilo nihil fit
ex officio
exordium
ex parte
ex pede herculem
experientia docet
experientia docet
  stultos
experimentum
  crucis
experto crede
expertus
explicit
ex post facto

ex post facto/
  expostfacto
expressis verbis
ex professo
ex propriis
ex quocunque
  capite
ex relatione
ex silentio
ex tempore
extempore
ex tempore/ex-
  tempore
extra muros
ex uno disce
  omnes
ex voluntate
ex voto
faber suæ fortunæ
fabula
fabula palliata
fabula togata
fac
facetiæ
facetiae
facile princeps
facilis descensus
  Averni
facilis est descen-
  sus
facta
fac totum
factotum
factum
faex populi
fa fictum
fama
fama volat
fare
fas
fasces
fascia
fas est ab hoste
  doceri
fasti
fata morgana

fata obstant
fatum
fatuus
fec(it)
fecit
felix
felix culpa
ferrum
festina lente
fetus
fiat
fiat lux
fiat voluntas tua
Fidei Defensor
fidei defensor
  (F.D.)
fideliter
fides
fides Punica
Fidus Achates
fieri facias
figura obliqua
filius nullius
finis
finis coronat opus
fiscus
fistula panis
flagrans
flagrante bello
flagrante delicto
flatus
Flora Danica
florilegium
fl(oruit)
floruit
folio verso
fons et origo
fons et origo
  malorum
forensis
fortuna caeca est
fortuna fortes
  juvat
fortuna sequatur
frustra
fugit hora

fuimus
fuit Ilium
furiosus
furor loquendi
furor poeticus
furor scribendi
Furor Teutonicus
fusa
fusella
Gaudeamus igitur
genius loci
genus
genus homo
gloria
gloria in excelsis
Gloria in Excelsis
  Deo
gloria in excelsis
  (deo)
Gloria Patri
gradatim
graduale
gradus
gradus ad Parnas-
  sum
gratias
gratias agere
gratis
habeas corpus
habeas corpus ad
  prosequendum
habeas corpus ad
  respondendum
habeas corpus ad
  satisfaciendum
habet
habilis
haud ignota lo-
  quor
haud passibus
  æquis
herbarium
heu!
hic et ubique
hic iacet
hic jacet

Latin, continued

hic sepultus
hoc age
hodie, non cras
homo
homo covivens
homo faber
homo ferus
homo ludens
homo sapiens
honorarium
honoris causa
honoris gratia
horresco referens
horribile dictu
horribile visu
hortus conclusus
Humaniora
humanum est errare
iacta alea est
iacta est alea
ibidem
ibidem (ibid.)
id
idem
ideo
id est
id est (i.e.)
id genus omne
Iesus Nazarenus
Rex Iudaeorum
ignis fatuus
ignoramus
ignorantia legis neminem excusat
ignoratio elenchi
Ilium fuit
illuminati
imago
imo pectore
impedimenta
imperator
imperium in imperio

Imperium Romanum
impetus
impos animi
imprimatur
imprimi permittitur
imprimi potest
imprimis
improperia
in absentia
in actu
in aeternum
in altissimo
in articulo mortis
in camera
in capite
incarnatus
incipit
incognita
in concreto
incubus
incunabula
in curiâ
in curia
in custodia legis
Index Expurgatorius
Index Librorum Prohibitorum
index locorum
index nominum
index rerum
index verborum
in dies
in dubiis
in dubio
in eadem conditione
in equilibrio
in esse
in excelsis
in extenso
in extremis
in facie curiae
in facto

in fieri
in flagrante (delicto)
in flagrante delicto
in fore
in foro conscientiæ
in foro conscientiae
in foro externo
in foro interno
infra
infra dig(nitatem)
infra dignitatem
infra dignitatem (infra dig.)
in futuro
in genere
in gremio legis
in hoc signo vinces
in infinito
in infinitum
in initio
initio
in jure
in loco
in loco citato
(in) loco parentis
in loco parentis
in malam partem
in medias res
in médiis rebus
in medio
in memoriam
in nomine
in nomine Domini
in notis
in nubibus
in nuce
innuendo
in ova
in ovo
in pace
in partibus

in partibus infidelium
in perpetuam rei memoriam
in perpetuo
in perpetuum
in persona
in personam
in posse
in potentia
in praesenti
in praesentia
in principio
in propriâ personâ
in propria persona
in puris naturalibus
in re
in rem
in rerum naturâ
in rerum natura
in saecula saeculorum
in se
in secula seculorum
insignia
in situ
in solidum (solido)
insomnia
in specie
instar omnium
in statu quo
integer valor notarum
in tenebris
inter
inter alia
inter alios
interea
inter nos
inter pares
inter pocula

Latin, continued

interregnum
in terrorem
inter se
inter vivos
intestatus
in toto
intra muros
in transitu
introitus
in usu
in utero
in vacuo
in ventre
invictus
in vino veritas
invitatorium
in vitro
in vivo
ipse
ipse dixit
ipsissima verba
ipsissimis verbis
ipso facto
ipso jure
ira furor brevis
  est
ita est
ite, missa est
iter
iterum
ius canonicum
ius civile
ius et norma
  loquendi
ius gentium
ius militare
ius municipale
jacta alea est
jacta est alea
januis clausis
Jesus, hominum
  Salvator (I.H.S.)
Jesus Nazarenus
  Rex Judaeorum
Johannes fac to-
  tum

Jubilate
jubili
Juppiter tonans
jure
jure belli
jure divino
jure humano
jure uxoris
juris
juris peritus
Juris Utriusque
  Doctor
jus
jus ad rem
jus belli
jus canonicum
jus civile
jus civitatis
jus civitatus
jus commercii
jus commune
jus devolutionis
jus divinum
jus et norma
  loquendi
jus gentium
jus gladii
jus hereditatis
jus in re
jus mariti
jus mercatorum
jus naturae
jus necationis
jus pignoris
jus possessionis
jus postliminii
jus primae noctis
jus proprietatis
jus publicum
jus regium
jus relictae
jus sanguinis
jus soli
jus suffragii
jus ubique
  docendi

labor limae
labor omnia vincit
lacrimae rerum
lacrimosa
lacuna
lacunae
laesa majestas
lapis lazuli
lapsus
lapsus calami
lapsus linguæ
lapsus linguae
lapsus memoriæ
lapsus memoriae
lapsus pennae
lar
lares et penates
lar familiaris
latet anguis in
  herba
latine
lato sensu
laudamus te
laudator temporis
  acti
laus Deo
lectio difficilior
lector benevole
legalis homo
legatus a latere
lege, quaeso
legibus solutus
levari facias
lex
lex loci
lex mercatoria
lex mercatorum
lex non scripta
lex scripta
lex talionis
lex terræ
lex terrae
libertas
libido
libitum
libris clausis

licet
lignum vitae
limae labor
lingua Adamica
lingua franca
liquet
lis
lis litem generat
lis pendens
lis sub judice
litem lite resolvere
lite pendente
literae humaniores
literati
literatim
litterae
  humaniores
loca supra citato
loci
loco
loc(o) cit(ato)
loco citato (loc.
  cit.)
loco laudato
loco parentis
loco parentis, in
locum tenens
locus
locus citatus
locus classicus
locus communis
locus criminis
locus delicti
locus in quo
locus poenitentiae
locus sigilli
locus standi
longa
loquitur
lubricum linguae
lucus a non
  lucendo
lues
lues
  commentatoria
lues venerea

Latin, continued

lumen fidei
lumina civitatis
lupus in fabula
lustrum
lusus naturae
lux
lux in tenebris
maculatum
magister
Magister Artium
magister artium
(M.A.)
magister bibendi
magister
ceremoniarum
magister dixit
Magna Carta
Magna Charta
magna cum laude
magna est veritas,
et prevalebit
Magnificat
magnum bonum
magnum in parvo
magnum opus
magnus Apollo
Magus
major domo
major domus
majusculae
mala fide
mala fides
mala praxis
mali exempli
malum
malum in se
malum
prohibitum
mandamus
Manes
manet
manibus
pedibusque
manubrium
manu forti
manu propria

mare clausum
mare liberum
mare magnum
Mare Nostrum
marginalia
mater
mater familias
materfamilias
materia medica
materia prima
maxima
maxima cum
laude
mea culpa
mea maxima
culpa
medium, per
me iudice
me judice
membrum virile
memento mori
memorabilia
mensa et toro
mens legis
mens rea
mens sana in
corpore sano
meo periculo
meo voto
merum sal
meum et tuum
miles gloriosus
minima
minusculae
minutia
minutiae
mirabile dictu
mirabile visu
mirabilia
mirum
miserabile dictu
miserabile vulgus
miserable vulgus
miserere
miserere nobis
Missa

Missa bassa
Missa cantata
Missa
catechume-
norum
Missa fidelium
missa lecta
missa parodia
missa privata
missa pro defunc-
tis
missa quarti toni
missa sine nomine
Missa solemnis
missa solennis
missa supra voces
musicales
mittimus
mobile perpetuum
mobile vulgus
modicum
modus
modus lascivus
modus operandi
modus ponens
modus tollens
modus vivendi
monstrum
mons veneris
monumentum
aere perennius
more
more Anglico
more Hibernico
more maiorum
more majorum
more meo
mores
more Socratico
more solito
more suo
morituri
salutamus
morituri te
salutamus

morituri te
salutant
mos majorum
motu proprio
multum in parvo
muscae volitantes
musica falsa
musica ficta
musica reservata
mutatis mutandis
mutato nomine
naenia
natura abhorret
vacuum
nebulae
nefasti dies
nemine
contradicente
nemine
discrepante
nemine
dissentiente
nenia
ne nimium
neoterici
ne plus ultra
ne quid nimis
neuma
neumae
nihil
nihil ad me
attinet
nihil ad rem
nihil dicit
nihil ex nihilo
nihil obstat
nihil sub sole
novi
nil
nil admirari
nil debet
nil sine Deo
nisi prius
nitor in adversum
nocte (*or* noctu)
nocte silenti

Latin, continued

nolens volens
nolle prosequi
nolo contendere
nomen
nomen atque
  omen
nomina
non assumpsi
non compos
  (mentis)
non compos men-
  tis
non concessit
non constat
non culpabilis
non ens
non esse
non est
non est inventus
non libet
non licet
non liquet
non obstante
non obstante
  veredicto
non olet
non omnia pos-
  sumus omnes
non omnis moriar
non placet
non plus ultra
non possumus
non prosequitur
non sequitur
non sum dignus
non vult con-
  tendere
nosce te ipsum
nosce teipsum
nosce tempus
noscitur a sociis
nota bene (N. B.)
novus homo
novus homo
nuces relinquere
nuda veritas

nudis verbis
nudum pactum
nugae
nugae canorae
nugae literariae
nulla bona
nulli secundus
nullius filius
nullo modo
nunc est
  bibendum
nunc pro tunc
obiit
obiit sine prole
obiter
obiter dicta
obiter dictum
obiter scriptum
obscurum per ob-
  scurius
observanda
observandum
occasionem
  cognosce
oculus
oderint dum
  metuant
odeum
odi et amo
odi profanum vul-
  gus
odium
odium
  aestheticum
odium generis
  humani
odium literarium
odium medicum
odium musicum
odium
  theologicum
odor lucri
offertorium
officium
officium
  vesperarum

olim
olim meminisse
  juvabit
omen faustum
omnes
omne vivum ex
  ovo
omne vivum ex
  vivo
omnia ad Dei
  gloriam
omnia bona bonis
omnia mors ae-
  quat
omnia opera
omnia vincit amor
omnia vincit labor
omnium
onus
onus probandi
opera
opera omnia
op(ere) cit(ato)
opere citato
optimates
opus
opus
  Alexandrinum
opus anglicanum
opusculum
opus incertum
opus isodomum
opus postumum
opus reticulatum
opus spicatum
ora et labora
ora pro nobis
orate fratres
oratio vespertina
orbis terrarum
ordinarium missae
ordo exsequiarum
oremus
organum
os

o tempora! o
  mores!
O tempora   O
  mores
otium cum digni-
  tate
Oxoniensis
pace
pace et bello
Pacem in Maribus
pace tanti
  nominis
pace tanti viri
pace tuâ
pace tua
palaestra
palladium
Pandectae
panem et cir-
  censes
pange, lingua
parendo imperat
pari passu
pars pro toto
pars rationabilis
particeps criminis
partim
parva componere
  magnis
passim
Passionis Domini
  nostri Jesu
  Christi
patera
pater familias
paterfamilias
Pater noster
pater noster/pa-
  ternoster
pater patriae
patrem
  omnipotentem
patres conscripti
patria potestas
patris est filius
paucas pallabris

Latin, continued

pauca verba
paucis verbis
Pax
Pax Britannica
Pax Dei
Pax Ecclesiae
pax in bello
Pax Romana
pax tecum
pax vobiscum
peccavi
pecunia non olet
Penates
pendente lite
penetralia
penetralia mentis
per accidens
per ambages
per angusta ad
   augusta
per annum
per ardua ad
   astra
per aspera ad
   astra
per capita
per cent(um)
per centum
per consequens
per contra
per curiam
per diem
perpetuum mobile
per procurationem
per procuratorem
per saltum
per se
persona
persona ficta
persona grata
persona gratissima
persona ingrata
persona muta
persona non grata
per totam curiam
pes

petitio principii
pia mater
pinxit
placebo
placet
plebs
pleno jure
plenum
plica
pollice presso
pollice verso
pons asinorum
posse comitatus
post
post bellum aux-
   ilium
post cibum
post diem
post facto
post-facto
post hoc, ergo
   propter hoc
post judicium
post litem motam
post meridiem
post meridiem
   (P.M.)
post mortem
post nubila Phoe-
   bus
post obitum
post partum
post scriptum
post scriptum
   (P.S.)
post terminum
postulatum
praeludium
praemissis
   praemittendis
praenomen
praesertim
praeteriti anni
preces
prima facie
prima inter pares

primo
primum mobile
primus inter
   omnes
primus inter pares
primus motor
principia
privato consensu
probatum est
pro bono publico
pro confesso
pro et con
pro et con(tra)
pro et contra (pro
   et con)
profanum vulgus
pro forma
pro hâc vice
pro hac vice
promotor fidei
prooemium
pro patria
proprietas
proprio motu
proprium missae
propter affectum
propter delictum
propter falsos tes-
   tes
propter hoc
pro ratâ
pro rata
pro re nata
prosa
prosit
pro tanto
pro tem
pro tem(pore)
pro tempore
proviso
psalterium
publici juris
publico consilio
pudenda
pugnis et calcibus

punctum
   contrapunctum
punctus
Punica fides
purdonium
purpureus pannus
qua
quadratum, B
quadrivium
quaere
quae vide
quantum
quantum libet
quantum meruit
quantum placet
quantum sufficit
quartus cantus
quasi
quem quaeritis
quid nunc?
qui docet, discit
quid pro quo
quietus
quilisma
quincunx
quinquennium
quintus
quiproquo
qui tollis
quo?
quo animo
quod erat demon-
   strandum
   (Q.E.D.)
quod erat
   faciendum
   (Q.E.F.)
quod est
quodlibet
quod vide (Q.V.)
quo iure
quondam
quoniam
quo pacto?
quot homines, tot
   sententiae

Latin, continued

quotidie
quousque tandem
quo vadis
rara avis
re
recto
rectus in curiâ
reductio ad ab-
 surdum
reductio ad im-
 possibile
regalia
regina
regina coeli
regina scientiarum
Regius Professor
religio loci
rem acu tetigisti
remanet
repente
requiem
requiescant in
 pace
requiescat in pace
requiescat in pace
requiescat in pace
 (R.I.P.)
requiescit in pace
res
res adjudicata
res alienae
res angusta domi
res facta
res gestae
residuum
res integra
res ipsa loquitur
res judicata
res nullius
respice finem
responsorium
res publica
reus
re vera
revera
rex

rex bibendi
rex iudaecorum
 (or Judaeorum)
rigor mortis
risus sardonicus
rostra
rota
rus in urbe
sal
Sal Atticum
salve
salve regina
sanatorium
sanctum
sanctum
 (sanctorum)
sanctum
 sanctorum
sanctus
Sartor Resartus
satis accipere
satis, superque
Saturnalia
Saturno rege
scandalum
 magnatum
schema
schola cantorum
scholium
scil(icet)
scilicet
scintilla
scire facias
scripsit
scriptor classicus
scriptor
 proletarius
sculpsit
secundum artem
secundum legem
secundum
 naturam
secundum usum
se defendendo
sedilia
semiditas

semifusa
semiminima
semper
semper et ubique
semper felix
semper fidelis
semper idem
semper idem (fem.
 eadem)
semper paratus
senatus consultum
sensorium
sensu bono
sensu lato
sensu malo
sensu proprio
separatio a mensa
 et toro
septum
sequentia
sequentiae
sequitur
seriatim
serus in cælum
 redeas
Servus Servorum
 Dei
sesqui
sesquialtera
sesquipedalia
 verba
sesquitone
sesterce
sext
sextus
sic
sic itur ad astra
sic jubeo
sic passim
sic semper tyran-
 nis
sic transit gloria
 mundi
sicut ante
si fortuna iuvat
simplex munditiis

sine
sine anno
sine cura
sine die
sine dubio
sine ira et studio
sine legitima prole
sine loco, anno,
 vel nomine
sine loco et anno
sine mascula prole
sine prole super-
 stite
sine qua non
siste viator
solemnis
solennis
solus
Sortes Vergilianae
sparsim
spero meliora
spes
spicilegium
spiritus
spiritus asper
spiritus frumenti
spiritus lenis
spolia opima
sponte suâ
sponte sua
statu quo
statu quo ante
 bellum
status belli
status in quo
status quaestionis
status quo
status quo ante
status quo ante
 bellum
stet
stet processus
striae
stricto sensu
stupor mundi
sua sponte

Latin, continued

sub anno
sub condicione
sub conditione
sub Iove
subito
sub judice
sub modo
sub plumbo
sub poena
subpoena
sub rosâ
sub rosa
sub sigillo
sub silentio
sub specie
substratum
subsultim
sub verbo
sub vi
sub voce
succentor
succubus
sui compos
sui generis
sui juris
summa cum laude
summum bonum
summum jus,
  summa injuria
suo loco
suo motu
suo nomine
suo periculo
suppressio veri,
  suggestio falsi
supra
sursum corda
suum cuique
suum cuique pul-
  crum
suus cuique mos
symposium
tabula rasa
tacet
tactus
taedium vitae

Tantum Ergo
tantum ergo
  sacramentum
Te Deum
Te Deum
  laudamus
te judice
tempus
tempus edax
  rerum
tempus fugit
tempus omnia
  revelat
tenebrae
terce
terminus
terminus ad quem
terminus ante
  quem
terminus a quo
terra
terra alba
terra es, terram
  ibis
terra firma
terra incognita
terra verte
ter sanctus
tertium quid
tesserae
textus receptus
threnodia
tibia utricularis
tintinnabulum
toga virilis
tonus
tot homines, quot
  sententiae
totidem verbis
toties quoties
toto caelo
toto cœlo
totum
totum in eo est
tractulus
tractus

trias
tricinium
triplum
trisagium
tritonus
trivium
trochaeus chorius
trompa
tropus
tuba mirabilis
tuebor
tu quoque
tu quoque, Brute!
turbae
tuum est
uberrima fides
ubi libertas, ibi
  patria
ubique
ubi sunt
ubi supra
ultima ratio
ultima ratio
  mundi
ultima ratio
  regum
ultima Thule
ultimatum
ultimo (ult.)
ultimus
  Romanorum
ultra
umbilicus
una corda
una voce
unda maris
uno animo
usque ad nauseam
usus loquendi
usus promptum
  reddit
ut
ut infra
ut saepe
ut supra
uxor

vacuo
vacuum
vade mecum
vae victis
vagans
vale
valeas!
valete
valete ac plaudite
variae lectiones
varia lectio
variorum
variorum notae
vas
vas deferens
vates
vates sacer
velis et remis
vena
vena cava
venire (facias)
veni sancte spir-
  itus
veni, vidi, vici
ventis remis
ventis secundis
verbatim et litera-
  tim
Verbi Dei Minis-
  ter
verbum sat
  sapienti
versiculum
verso
verso pollice
versus
verte
verte subito
vesperae
vesperale
vestigia
vestigia nulla re-
  trorsum
vexata quaestio
viâ
via

Latin, continued

via dolorosa
via media
viaticum
vice
vice versa
vide
vide ante
vide et crede
vide infra
videlicet (viz.)
vide post
vide supra
vide ut supra
vi et armis

vincit amor pa-
 triae
vinctus invictus
vinculum
 matrimonii
vino veritas, in
Virgo
virtus
virtute officii
vis
vis comica
vis inertiae
vis major
vis mortua

vis poetica
vis vitae
vis viva
vita brevis, ars
 longa
vivat regina
vivat respublica
vivat rex
vivâ voce
viva voce
vive, vale
voces aequales
vox
vox acuta

vox angelica
vox barbara
vox faucibus
 haesit
vox humana
vox populi
vox populi, vox
 Dei
vulgata editio
vulgo
vulneratus, non
 victus
vuota
zonam solvere

Latin from Arabic

hegira/hejira

Louisiana French

lagnappe

lagniappe

Malay

betel

pantoum

sate

Mandingo

mumbo jumbo

Maori

kai
kauri

mana

pakihi

tangiwai

Marathi

tutenag

Mayan

cenote

Mexican

mariachi

sotol

Mexican Spanish

anaqua
ancón
atole

belduque
borasca
canaigre

chivarras
chivarros
pulque

tamal
tamale

Modern Greek

baripicni
ef haristo

moussaka
ouzo

repi
retsina/retzina

romaika
zampouna

Mongolian   gobi   tala

Navaho   hogan

New Latin

cantus firmus   pithecanthropus scala enigmatica   seriatim
cantus planus   erectus

Norwegian

fjeld   glint   krone   slalom
fjeldbotn   halling   seter   springar
fjeldmark   hardangerfele   skal   springdans
fjord   krageröite   skavl   tele
gangar

Ojibway   totem

Old Flemish polder

Old French

a aver et tener blancmange   escritoire   lai
avoirdupois   cap-a-pié   fabliau   oyez

Panjabi   bel   bhel

Persian

bakhshish   kavir   pilaff   subahdar
baksheesh   khmer   pilau   tangi
imam   khushi   pilaw   teppe
kabab   magi   serai

Persian through Latin   magus

Polish

drabant   kouiaviak   kujawiak   mazurka
duda   krakowiak   kujiaviak   polska
kolomyika

Polynesian   kai   papa

Portuguese

a	bons dias	folia	obrigado
abrolhos	bossa nova	follía	padre
a chula	casa	follia	praya
adeus	cascalho	gargulho	rio
até logo	chapeiro	machete	saudades
auto da fé	choros	manioc	senhor
auto-da-fé	Dona	maxixe	senhora
boa noite	fadinho	meu senhor	senhorita
boa tarde	fado	modinha	varzea
bom dia	folía		

Pseudo-French   nom de plume   objet de vertu

Pseudo-Irish   erin go bragh

Pseudo-Italian   glissando

Pseudo-Latin   omnium gatherum

Quechua   pongo

Rumanian   Buhaiu

Russian

agitprop	borzoi	do'brii ve'tcher	halva
apparat	boyar	dobriy den	hopak
apparatchik	bugor	dobriy vecher	intelligentsia
avlakogene	Burozem	dobroe utro	ispravnik
baba	Chernozem	dobroye utro	Izvestia
babushka	commissar	domra	izvestyia
baklava	commissariat	Dosvidanio	kapusti
balalaika	copeck	do svidaniya	kasha
baliki	czar	do svidanya	kharakteristika
barchan	czarevitch	druzhinnik	khavyar
barkhan	czarina	dumka	khuligan
blagodaryu vas	czarowitz	feldsher	kolkhoz
blat	da	gopak	Komsomol
Blini	dacha	gorilka	kopek
Bolsheviki	dachnik	gulag	krasnaya zvezda
borsch	dasvidanya	guslee	krotovina
borscht	defitsitny	gusli	kulak

Russian, continued

kvass	oblast	shaman	tovarishch
lesginka	Oktyabryata	shashlik	troika
lezginka	pereletok	Sierozem	ukase
luli kebab	pirogen	sovkhoz	uyezd
molotov	pirogi	spasibo	úzhin
mussaca	pogrom	sputnik	valenki
muzh	polynya	stamukha	verst
muzhik	Pravda	steppe	volost
nachalstvo	proshchái	stukach	vospitanie
narod	proshcháite	subbotnik	zavtrak
narodnik	ragoke	taiga	zdrávstvui
nekulturny	ropak	takir	zdrávstvuite
nichevo	rynok	talik	zhená
nilas	samizdat	tolkach	zourna
nyet	samovar	tovarish	

Sanskrit

bhuta	khasi	mahayana	prana
Brahma	Krishna	mandala	sandhi
Brahman	Kshatriya	mantra	Swami
dharma	Mahabharata	maya	Veda
guru	maharaja	nirvana	yoga
karma	Mahatma		

Scottish

ceilidh	ceòl mór	leineag	quaich
ceòl beag	communn	luinig	ributhe
ceòl meadhonach	gàidhealach	port à beul	

Serbo-Croatian

Kostenka	polje	ponor	uvala

Sindhi   bhit   pat

Singhalese   beriberi   padmaragaya

Slavonic   dumka   dumky

Spanish

a	aceite	acequia madre	adios
abajo	aceituna	a dio	a Diós gracias
abanico	acequia	adiós	adobe

Spanish, continued

aficionado	arroba	biznaga	candelia
agostadero	arroyo	boca	cañón
agua	arroz	boceto	cañon
aguada	arroz con pollo	bodega	cañoncito
aguardiente	asequia	bolas	cante flamenco
ahí	así	bolero	cante hondo
ajarcara	asturiana	bolson	cantiga
alalá	asturiano	bonanza	cantilenas
alameda	auto de fe	boquilla	vulgares
alamo	auto-de-fe	borracho	cantina
alberca	auto sacramental	botón	capa
alborada	a vuestra salud	braguero	capitan
alcalde	ayer	brasero	caporal
alcázar	ayudante	bravado	capote
alcazar	azafrán	bravo	cara
alfalfa	azogue	brea	caramba
al fresco	azote	brindis	caramillo
alguacil	azul	bronco	carcelera
Alhambra	baile	buena salud	carisima
alhauna	baile flamenco	buenas noches	carne
allí	bajada	buenas tardes	carne de vaca
almena	bamanos	buena suerte!	carnero
alpaca	bamos	buenos días	casa
altiplano	banco	burro	casa grande
amargoso	banderilla	caballad	cascajo
Americano	banderillero	caballada	castañeta
amigo	bandido	caballero	castillane
Amontillado	bandola	caballo	catalán
amparo	bandolero	cabaña	caudillo
andale	bandoneon	cabestro	cay
andaluza	bandore	cabeza	cayo
Año Nuevo	bandurría	cachuca	cazo
apache	bandurria	cachucha	ceja
aparejador	baquero	cacique	cencerro
aparejo	barra	cajon	cenote
aparigerdor	barracon	cala	centavo
aquardiente	barracuda	calabozo	cequia
aquí	barranca	caleta	cerdana
arada	barranco	caliente	cesta
arado	barrera	camarón	chalchihuitl
aragonesa	barrio	camino real	chamaco
arena	bayle	campo santo	chapa
armadillo	berro	cañada	chaparejos
arrastra	bezugo	canción	chaparral
arrastre	biblioteca	cancion	charco
arriba	bisnaga	candela	charqui

473 Spanish

Spanish, continued

charro	corrida de toros	entremés	grama
chica	corriente	espada	granadina
chicalote	cosa	espadrille	gringo
chicle	coumarin	española	guajira
chico	coyote	esperanza	guano
chicote	crotola	está bien	guaracha
chiffadera	cruz	Estados Unidos	guarracha
chile	cuadrilla	estocada	guero
chile con carne	cuarta	estoque	guerrilla
chili	cuatro	estribillo	guia
chinchilla	cucaracha	estudiantina	guitarra
chiquito	cuchilla	estudiantino	Habanera
chirimia	cuesta	evocación	hacendado
chuco	cuidado	ezcudantza	hacienda
chulo	cuñado	factura	hasta la vista
churrasco	cura	faja	hasta luego
cienaga	danza española	fanático	hasta mañana
cienega	danzon	fandango	havelina
cigarrito	danzonetta	fandanguillo	hervidero
cimbalello	de	farandole	hidalgo
cimbalo	de nada	farruca	hidalguia
cimborio	día	fe	hoi! hoi!
cincha	diablo	fiesta	hombre
cincho	diario	flamenco	honda
cinco	diez	flan	hondo
ciudad	diferencias	florida	hoya
clarinero	dinero	fonda	huerfano
colina	domingo	foso	huero
collado	Don	frijol	incommunicado
colorado	Doña	frijole	intrada
cómo está	dorado	frijoles	ista
cómo le va	dos	fritos	jabo
compadre	dueña	frontón	jacal
compañero	dueño	gaita	jácara
con	dulce	gallegada	jacara
concha	ejido	gambusino	jaleo
conga	el	gancho	jamón
conquistador	El Dorado	garbanzo	jaquima
conquistadores	eldorado	garbanzos	jarabe
copla	El Libertador	garrocha	javalina
cordillera	en	gaucho	jefe
corea	encabritada	gazpacho	jefe politico
cornado	enchilada	ginete	jornada
coronado	ensalada	gitana	jota
corregidor	ensaladas	gitano	junta
corrida	entrada	gracias	junto

Spanish, continued

jusgado
juzgado
la
ladino
ladron
laguna
la plaza de toros
largo
larigo
latigo
laúd
laud
lazo
leche
legua
lidia
llama
llano
Llano Estacado
lobo
loco
loma
lomita
lonja
los
machete
macho
madre
madrileña
madroña
maestro
magnífico
maguey
majordomo
malagueña
malpais
manada
managana
mañana
manchega
mano
mantilla
manzanilla
manzanita
maraca
marajuana

marihuana
marijuana
marimba
masa
mascara
matador
maté
mate
matet
matete
mauresco
maxixe
mayordomo
mazapán
mecate
medano
mesa
mescal
meschal
mescol
meseta
mesilla
mesquit
mesquite
mesquits
mestizo
metate
mezcal
milpa
mimosa
mochila
mocho
moderado
moharrie
mole
mono sabio
montera
moresca
moresco
morisca
morisco
morral
morro
mosquito
mozo
muchacha

muchacho
muiñeira
mujer
mulada
mulatto
muleta
murciana
muscal
musqueto
musquit
musquito
mustizo
muy
nada
navarraise
Navidad
niño
noche
noche triste
noria
norte
novela picaresca
novia
ojo
olé
ole
olio
olla
olla podrida
oloroso
orégano
orejones
oule
padre
padrino
paella
paisano
palabra
palo verde
pampa
pampas
pañuelo
partida
pasear
paseo

paseo de las
    cuadrillas
paso doble
paso fino
passacaglia
patio
patron
pedregal
pedrigal
pelado
pelota
peña
peñasco
penco
peñon
peon
peso
peso duro
petate
petenera
peyote
picador
picaro
pilar
pilon
piloncillo
pimiento
piña
piñata
pinole
piñon
pinto
piote
pisco
pita
placer
plata
playa
playera
plaza
plaza de toros
pobrecito
poco
politico
pollo
polo

Spanish, continued

poncho	río	señorito	toril
por favor	rio	serape	tornada
posada	robezo	sevillana	tornadeo
potro	rodeo	si	toro
pozo	romal	sierra	torreon
Prado	romalis	siesta	torta
presidente	romance	siglo de oro	tortilla
presidio	ronda	simpático	tortillia
pronto	rondalla	soga	tosca
pronunciamiento	rondeña	soleá	toston
pueblo	rondena	solo	trabajo
puerto	rueda	sombrero	tracto
pulque	rurales	sótano	trino
pulqueria	sabe	sotol	tripas
puma	sacate	subida	triste
puntilla	sacaton	sudadero	tulare
pyote	saeta	suerte	vaca
quadroon	saguaro	tajo	vacquero
quebrada	sainete	tamal	valgame dios
que dice	sala	tamale	vámonos
que hubo le	salada	tamaule	vamoos
qué pasa	salar	tango	vamoose
querida	salina	tapadero	vamos
querido	saltarello	tapaojos	vamose
que será será	saltierra	tartilloes	vaquero
qué'tal	salud	tauromaquia	vaya con Dios
que tal	saludos	tegua	venta
quien sabe	salvo conducto	tejano	vicuña
quien savvy	samba	tejon	vihuela
quirt	sanbenito	temblor	villancico
ramada	sandia	tequila	villanesca
ramal	sangría	terceto	viña
raña	sarape	tiempo	vito
rancheria	sardana	tiento	viva
ranchero	sarepe	tierra blanca	volador
rancho	savannah	tinaja	xabo
real	savez	tinajita	xacara
reata	segarrito	tiorba	xaleo
rebosa	seguidilla	tirana	xota
reboso	seguro	tonada	yerba
rebozo	se habla español	tonadilla	yerba (maté)
remonta	sendero	tono	yucca
remuda	señor	tonto	zacate
repartimiento	señora	toreador	zacaton
ria	Señor Don	toreo	zamacuca
rincon	señorita	torero	zambacuca

Spanish, continued

zambra	zanjón	zarape	zequia
zampoña	zapateado	zarzuela	zortziko

Swahili

bwana	simba

Swedish

dy	krona	palsa	smorgasbord
fjäll	lagg	pipkrake	stentorg
fjard	marin gräns	polska	tjaele
fors	mo	skärtrag	trap
gyttja	nyckel harpa	skolien	varve
havsband			

Swiss French

ranz des vaches	sérac

Swiss German

kar	Mondmilch	Putsch

Tatar

aladzha	khan

Thai

krewain

Tibetan

Dalai Lama	lama	Teshu Lama	yeti
glingbu	sherpa		

Turkish

aga	kebab	loukoum	pilav/pilaf
agha	khan	macramé	shish kebab
cinelle	kiosque	molla	yali
fez	kismet	mollah	yardang
janitscharen	kussir	pasha	yashmak

Urdu

bhabar	bhangar	bhur

Vietnamese

nuoc nam

Welsh

| canu penillion | cymanfa ganu | pibcorn | pibgorn |

West African   zombie

Yakutian   boolgoonyakh

Yiddish

Adonai	balmalucha	bubeleh	-chik
Adoshem	Bar Mitzva	bubkes	chillul ha-shem
Agada	Bar Mitzvah	bulba	chillul hashem
alav ha-sholem	baruch ha-Shem	bulbanik	chloppeh
alav ha-sholom	Bas Mitzva	bulbenik	chmallyeh
aleha ha-shalom	Bas Mitzvah	bulvan	choleria
aleha ha-sholem	batlan	bulvon	cholilleh
aleichem sholem	batlanim	burtchen	chometzdik
alevai	behama	cabala	chossen
alevay	behayma	cabbalah	chotchke
aleyhem ha-	behayme	canary	chotchkeleh
sholem	ben	chacham	chozzer
aliyah	bentsh	chachem	chozzerai
alter kocker	berrieh	chachma	chuppa
amain	Bes din	Chaim Yankel	chuppah
am ha-aretz	Bes Midrash	chalileh	chutspa
apikoros	Bet din	challa	chutzpa
aroysgevorfen	Beth din	challeh	chutzpadik
Ashkenazi	Beth Hamidrash	chaloshes	cockamamy
Ashkenazic	Bet Midrash	chalutz	Cohen
Ashkenazim	bialy	chalutzim	colboy
-atsh	blintz	Channukah	darshan
averah	blintzeh	Chanukah	darshanim
aydem	blintzes	charley	daven
Baal Shem	Bnai Brith	Chasid	dayan
badchanim	bobbe-myseh	Chasidim	dayanim
badchen	bobeleh	chassen	dayen
bagel	bobkes	chasseneh	dayyan
balabatish	bonditt	chas vesholem	doppess
balabos	boobe-myseh	chaussen	draykop
balabustah	bopkes	chaver	draykopf
balbatim	bren	chazzen	dreck
balbatish	bris	chazzer	dreml
balebatim	brith	chazzonim	dybbuk
baleboosteh	broche	cheder	dzhlob
balebos	bubbe	Chelm	edel
baleboss	bubbe-mayse	cheppeh	edelkeit
balmalocha	bubee	chevra	einredenish

Yiddish, continued

-el
Elohim
Epicoris
eppes
Eretz Israel
Eretz Yisrael
Eretz Yisroel
farbissen
farbisseneh
farbissener
farblondjet
farchadat
farfufket
farmisht
farpatshket
farpotshket
farshtinkener
fartootst
fartootsteh
fartootster
fartumelt
fartutst
faygele
faygeleh
feh
feygele
fifer
fin
finif
finiff
finnif
flayshedig
flayshig
folks-mensh
fonfer
fress
fresser
frosk
frum
frummeh
frummer
Galitzianer
galus
galut
Gan Eden
ganov

gaon
gebentsht
gebentshteh
gebentshter
gefilte fish
gefulte fish
Gehena
Gehenna
gelt
Gemara
Gematria
geshmat
geshmott
gesundheit
get
gevald
Gevalt
gezunthayt
gilgul
glatt kosher
glitch
glitsh
goldeneh medina
golem
gonef
gonif
goniff
gonov
Gott
Gottenyu
goy
goyim
goyish
gozlen
gozlin
graub
grauber
graubyon
gridzheh
gunsel
Gut Shabbes
Habdala
Habdalah
hachma
Hadassah
Haftarah

Haftorah
Hagadah
Haggadah
haham
haimish
haimisheh
haimisher
hak a chainik
Halakah
Halakha
halava
halavah
halevai
halla
hallelujah
halutz
halva
halvah
hamantash
Hannuka
Hanuka
Hanukkah
Hashem
Hasid
Hasidim
Haskala
Haskalah
hassen
hasseneh
Hassid
Hassidic
Hassidim
has vesholem
Hatikva
Hatikvah
Havdala
hazzan
hazzen
heder
Hillul Hashem
Hillul ha-Shem
hok
hok a tchynik
homentash
hometzdik
hoo-ha

Hotzeplotz
hozzer
huppa
huppe
hutspa
hutzpah
in mitn derinnen
in mitske derin-
  nen
Judesmo
kabala
kabbala
kabbalah
kabtsen
kabtzen
kabtzonim
Kaddish
kalikeh
kalleh
kalyike
kapora
kaporeh
Kapoyr
kasheh
kashrut
kayn ayn hore
kayn aynhoreh
khaloshes
khaluts
khasseneh
khaukhem
khaukhma
khaver
khazen
khazer
kibbitz
kibbitzer
kibbutz
kibbutzim
kibitz
kibitzer
kichel
Kiddush
Kiddush Hashem
Kiddush ha-Shem
kind

Yiddish, continued

kinder	kvetch	matzo	Mishnah
kinderlach	kvetcherkeh	matzoh	mishpocheh
kine-ahora	kvetsh	matzos	mishpokhe
kineahora	kvitch	maven	mitzva
kishka	Ladino	mavin	mitzvah
kishke	lag baomer	mazel	mitzvoth
kishkes	landsman	Mazel tov	mizrach
kittel	latke	mazik	mizrachi
klap	L'chayim	mazuma	moel
klezmer	lendler	mazzel-tov	Mogen David
klop	letz	mechaieh	mohel
klotz	levaya	mechuleh	moichel
klutz	l'havdil	medina	Moishe Kapoyr
k'naker	Litvak	megilla	momzer
knaydl	loch in kop	megillah	motzi
knetcher	loksh	melamed	moyl
knippel	lox	Melech	mutche
knippl	L'shone toyve	Ham'lochim	naar
knish	luftmensh	mench	naarishkeit
knishes	luftmentsh	menorah	naches
k'nocker	lump	mensh	nadan
kobtzen	maarev	mentsh	nafish
koch alayn	maariv	meshiach	nafka
kochalayn	macher	meshpocheh	nakhes
kochleffl	machetayneste	meshuggah	narr
Kohen	machetuneste	meshugge	narrishkeit
kolleh	machetunim	meshumad	nayfish
Kol Nidre	machuten	metsieh	nebbech
kolyika	machutin	mezuzah	nebbish
kopdrayenish	Magen David	mezuze	nebech
koptzen	maggid	mezzuza	nebechel
kosher	mah nishtana	midrash	nebechl
koved	mah nishtannah	miesse meshina	nebish
kovid	mah nishtanu	mikva	nechtiger tog, a
krechtz	mairev	mikvah	nefish
krenk	makhutin	mikveh	neshoma
kreplach	makkes	milchedig	neshuma
kreplakh	malakh	milchik	Neturey Karta
kreplech	mamale	mincha	-nick
krich arein in di	mama-loshen	minhah	-nik
bayner	mama-loshn	minyan	noch
kugel	mamzarim	minyen	nokh
Kuni Lemmel	Marrano	minyon	noo-ooo
Kunye Leml	Mashiach	mishegaas	nosh
kurveh	maskilin	mishegoss	noshen
kvell	matmid	mishling	nosher

Yiddish, continued

nu
nuchshlepper
nudj
nudnick
nudnik
nudzh
nudzhedik
nudzheh
nudzhik
nu-nu?
omeyn
ongepatshket
ongepotchket
opgeflikt
oy
oyoy
oy-oy-oy
oyrech
oys-
oysgematert
oysvorf
oytser
parech
pareve
pareveh
paskudnak
paskudne
paskudneh
paskudnyak
paskustva
patch
patshke
payess
peckel
pekel
pekl
Pesach
peyes
pilpul
pisher
pisherkeh
pishke
pishkeh
pisk
pitsel
pitseleh

platke-macher
platz
pletsl
plosher
plotst
plotz
pogrom
potch
potchkee
potchkeh
prost
pupik
Purim
pushke
putz
rachmones
Reb
rebbe
rebbetsen
rebbitsin
Reb Yankel
Riboyne Shel
   O'lem
Rosh Hashanah
Rosh Hashona
Rosh Hashonah
Rosh Hoshanah
rov
Sabbati Zvi
sachel
sanhedrin
schatchen
schaygetz
schicker
schiksa
schlack
schlag
schlemiehl
schlemiel
schlemiel/
   schlemihl
schlemihl
schlemozzle/
   schemozzle/
   shemozzle
schlep

schlimazel
schlock
schlok
schloomp
schlump
schmaltz
schmalz
schmo
schmuck
schnaps
schneider
schnook
schnorrer
Seder
Sefer Torah
Sefirah
Sefiras Haomer
Sephardi
Sephardic
Sephardim
sh-
Shabbatsi Zvi
Shabbes
Shabbes goy
Shabtsitvainik
Shabtsi Zvi
Shabuot
shachris
shadchen
Shah
Shalom
shammes
shammus
shamus
shaygets
shayner Yid
shaytl
Shechinah
sheeny
Shehecheyanu
sheitel
shekel
Shekhinah
Shema
Shema Yisrael
Shemona Esray

shemozzl
Shevuoth
sheygets
shiddach
shikker
shiksa
shikse
shikseh
shivah
shlemazl
shlemiehl
shlemiel
shlemihl
shlemozzl
shlep
shlepper
shlimazl
shlock
shloomp
shlub
shlump
shm-
Shma
shmaltz
shmatte
Shma Yisrael
shmeck tabac
shmeer
shmegegge
shmei
shmeikel
shmeker
shmendrick
shmendrik
Shmerl Narr
shmo
shmontses
shmoos
shmooz
shmooze
shmotte
shmuck
shmues
shmulky
shnaps
Shnippishok

Yiddish, continued

shnir	singlemon	tsatske	yarmulke
shnook	succah	tsatskeleh	Yekke
shnorer	Succoth	tsedoodelt	yekl
shnorren	tachlis	tsedoodelteh	yenta
shnorrer	talis	tsedoodelter	yente
shnoz	talith	tsedraydelt	yents
shnozzle	tallis	tsedrayt	yentz
shnuk	tallit	tsedrayteh	yentzer
shnur	talmid chachem	tsedrayter	yeshiba
shochet	Talmud	tsedreyt	yeshiva
shofar	Talmud Torah	tsedudlt	yeshiva bokher
sholem	tararam	tsetumlt	yeshiva bucher
Sholem aleichem	tarrarom	tsetummelt	YHVH
sholom	tata	tsetummelteh	yiches
sholom aleichem	tata-mama	tsetummelter	yichus
shool	tateleh	tsimmes	Yid
shpilkes	tcheppeh	tsimmis	yideneh
shtarker	tchotchke	tsitser	yihus
shtchav	tchotchkeleh	tsores	yingatsh
shteiger	tefillin	tsoriss	Yisrael
shtetl	Teitch-Chumesh	tsouris	Yisroel
shtik	Teitsh-Chumash	tsuris	Yizkor
shtikeleh	teivel	tsuriss	yok
shtikl	terrarom	tsutcheppenish	yold
shtiklech	teufel	tuches	Yom Kippur
shtoop	teuvel	tuchis	yom tov
shtreimel	t'fillin	tummel	yontif
shtunk	timtum	tummler	yontifdig
shtup	Tisha B'ab	tush	yontifdik
shtus	Tisha B'av	tushy (tush)	yontiff
shtuss	Tisha Bov	tzaddik	yontik
shul	toches	tzedaka	Yortsayt
shvartz	tochis	tzitzit	Yortzeit
shvartzeh	tokus	Tziyon	zaddik
shvartzer	Torah	ungepotchket	zaftig
shviger	. . . toyten bankes	utz	zaftik
shvitzbad	trayf	vitz	zayde
shvitzbud	treppverter	vuden	zchuss
shvitzer	treyf	yachna	zetz
Siddur	treyfener	yachne	zeyde
simcha	treyfnyak	yahrtzeit	zhlob
Simchath Torah	trombenik	Yahveh	zhlub
simche	trombenyik	Yankel	Zion
Simhat Torah	tsadaka	yarmulkah	Zohar

Zulu assegai

Educational Linguistics/TESOL/ICC
Graduate School of Education
University of Pennsylvania
3700 Walnut Street/Cl
Philadelphia, PA 19104